Uprisings in Eighteenth-Century Britain

Cultures of Early Modern Europe

Series Editors: Beat Kümin, Professor of Early Modern European History, University of Warwick, and Brian Cowan, Associate Professor and Canada Research Chair in Early Modern British History, McGill University

Editorial Board:
Adam Fox, University of Edinburgh, UK
Robert Frost, University of Aberdeen, UK
Molly Greene, University of Princeton, USA
Ben Schmidt, University of Washington, USA
Gerd Schwerhoff, University of Dresden, Germany
Francsesca Trivellato, University of Yale, USA
Francisca Loetz, University of Zurich, Switzerland

The 'cultural turn' in the humanities has generated a wealth of new research topics and approaches. Focusing on the ways in which representations, perceptions and negotiations shaped people's lived experiences, the books in this series provide fascinating insights into the past. The series covers early modern culture in its broadest sense, inclusive of (but not restricted to) themes such as gender, identity, communities, mentalities, emotions, communication, ritual, space, food and drink, and material culture.

Published:
Food and Identity in England, 1540–1640, Paul S. Lloyd (2014)
The Birth of the English Kitchen, 1600–1850, Sara Pennell (2016)
Vagrancy in English Culture and Society, 1650–1750, David Hitchcock (2016)
Angelica's Book and the World of Reading in Late Renaissance Italy, Brendan Dooley (2016)
Gender, Culture and Politics in England, 1560–1640, Susan D. Amussen and David E. Underdown (2017)
Food, Religion, and Communities in Early Modern Europe, Christopher Kissane (2018)
Religion and Society at the Dawn of Modern Europe, Rudolf Schlögl (2020)
Power and Ceremony in European History: Rituals, Practices and Representative Bodies since the Late Middle Ages, Anna Kalinowska and Jonathan Spangler (eds.) with Pawel Tyszka
Private/Public in 18th-Century Scandinavia, Sari Nauman and Helle Vogt (eds.)
Catherine the Great and Celebrity Culture in the Eighteenth Century, Ruth Dawson
The Books that Made the European Enlightenment: A History in 12 Case Studies, Gary Kates

Uprisings in Eighteenth-Century Britain

Mediation and the Transformation of Political Culture

By
Monika Barget

BLOOMSBURY ACADEMIC
LONDON • NEW YORK • OXFORD • NEW DELHI • SYDNEY

BLOOMSBURY ACADEMIC
Bloomsbury Publishing Plc
50 Bedford Square, London, WC1B 3DP, UK
1385 Broadway, New York, NY 10018, USA
29 Earlsfort Terrace, Dublin 2, Ireland

BLOOMSBURY, BLOOMSBURY ACADEMIC and the Diana logo
are trademarks of Bloomsbury Publishing Plc

First published in Great Britain 2024

Copyright © Monika Barget 2024

Monika Barget has asserted her right under the Copyright, Designs and
Patents Act, 1988, to be identified as author of this work.

Cover image: Burning Of Newgate (© Print Collector / Getty images)

Bloomsbury Publishing Plc does not have any control over, or responsibility for, any
third-party websites referred to or in this book. All internet addresses given in this
book were correct at the time of going to press. The author and publisher regret
any inconvenience caused if addresses have changed or sites have ceased
to exist, but can accept no responsibility for any such changes.

Every effort has been made to trace the copyright holders and obtain permission
to reproduce the copyright material. Please do get in touch with any enquiries
or any information relating to such material or the rights holder. We would be
pleased to rectify any omissions in subsequent editions of this publication
should they be drawn to our attention.

A catalogue record for this book is available from the British Library.

A catalog record for this book is available from the Library of Congress.

ISBN:	HB:	978-1-3503-7713-4
	ePDF:	978-1-3503-7715-8
	eBook:	978-1-3503-7716-5

Typeset by Integra Software Services Pvt. Ltd.

To find out more about our authors and books visit www.bloomsbury.com
and sign up for our newsletters.

Contents

List of figures	vi
Acknowledgements	vii
Note on the text	viii
List of abbreviations	ix
Introduction	1
1 Agency through communication: Media genres and terminologies	11
2 Monarchs and aristocrats: The constitutionalization of leadership and the dialogization of political communication	27
3 Parliament, parties and politicians: Conflict negotiation through representation	43
4 Religious communities and religious leaders: Inclusive and divisive potentials of faith after the Glorious Revolution	59
5 Regular troops, militia and armed civilians: Military and paramilitary agency as vehicles of national identity and social integration	79
6 The people and the impact of public opinion	91
Conclusion	105
Notes	113
Bibliography	164
Index	216

Figures

0.1 Screenshot of the zoomable digital map highlighting different types of conflict within the early modern British Empire. With a view to future updates, events of the sixteenth and seventeenth centuries have also been included. The categories on the right can be (de-)selected in the interactive legend. Created by the author and available via GitHub: https://monikabarget.github.io/Revolts/event-map/event-map.html 6

3.1 Map of eighteenth-century riots relating to elections and political rights in the British Isles. Events in North America can be viewed in the digital map on GitHub: https://monikabarget.github.io/Revolts/event-map/event-map.html 46

4.1 Map of places in the British Isles where anti-rebellion sermons were printed between 1684 and 1800: based on metadata extracted from WorldCat, see zoomable map on https://monikabarget.github.io/Revolts/sermons.html 66

4.2 Number of printed anti-rebellion sermons per publication year between 1685 (Monmouth Rebellion) and 1800: metadata automatically extracted from WorldCat, see full metadata in ZOTERO library: https://www.zotero.org/groups/2351893/british_riots_and_revolts_of_the_enlightenment_age 66

5.1 Partial map of unrest related to peacekeeping and military regulations in Britain, based on the digital map created by the author: https://monikabarget.github.io/Revolts/event-map/event-map.html 80

5.2 Timothy Green (ed.), 'To the People of America: Stop Him! Stop Him! Stop Him!' New London, CN, 1775: https://www.loc.gov/item/rbpe.0030310a/ 83

6.1 Partial map of unrest concerning social or economic grievances within the British Isles, including several food riots: based on data collected from Wikidata, the UK National Archives and printed sources. Created by the author 92

Acknowledgements

I would like to thank the many people who have supported me throughout the making of this book financially, academically and emotionally.

I thank my PhD supervisors Malte Griesse and Rudolf Schlögl at Konstanz University, my external reader Daniel Szechi, colleagues who have given me valuable feedback during workshops and conferences, my supportive office mates, the anonymous peer-reviewers, my editor Rhodri Mogford and his team, my copy-editor Simon Fletcher (Bourchier), my family, the Women in Academia Support Network, my friends, the parishes that have offered me a home away from home during research trips abroad, and, last but not least, the taxpayers whose money was spent on my contracts and grants.

Note on the text

Contemporary eighteenth-century punctuation and spelling (including capital letters and italics) have been followed in all quotations, except for the extensive use of capitals in publication titles.

Typographical errors in modern quotations and unusual early modern spelling have been marked with [sic]. Common early modern illegible words in early modern prints and manuscript sources are transcribed in brackets. Square brackets indicate my comments or additions. Deletions not found in the original texts are likewise put in parentheses.

Throughout the text, I have quoted foreign-language sources in English and used my translations unless indicated otherwise. In the case of longer quotations, the texts in the original languages are given in the footnotes. Dates before the British calendar reform of 1750 always follow the sources. Remember that early modern continental-European dating differed from the British calendar. In British–continental correspondence, however, simultaneous Julian and Gregorian dating was common and has been kept wherever possible.

As names of authors and publishers, family names without academic titles or aristocratic titulary have been used in the footnotes. Pseudonyms are marked with [pseud.] or the attributed authors' names in squared brackets. Ruling monarchs are referred to by their Christian names. Honours and titles by which persons are known in addition to their family names are included in the alphabetical bibliography. I have shortened extensive early modern titles whenever the abridgements did not lessen the informational or stylistic value. Following Anglo-American cataloguing rules, I have indicated assumed places or attributed editors and publishers in square brackets.

Abbreviations

BL	British Library
Cal. Br.	Calenberg, Briefschaftsarchiv
Hann.	Hannover (Hanover)
HO	Home Office
NLI	National Library of Ireland
NLS	National Library of Scotland
SP	State Papers
T	Treasury Board Papers
TS	Treasury Solicitor

Introduction

Analysing expressions of violence in different periods is a recurring research objective in historiography as well as the social sciences, and has resulted in explanatory models and semantic categorizations that are often applied across time.[1] In early modern history, researchers try in particular to make sense of the ubiquity of violence[2] in an age of confessionalization, state formation, globalization, imperialism and social innovation.[3] Eighteenth-century elites and intellectuals perceived the time in which they lived as a period 'in which revolutions progressed as quickly as an act of a comedy on stage'.[4] This was not so much because of an actual surge in numbers but rather down to perception at a time when the 'ideological, social, technical and cultural conditions of war' were changing.[5] A transregional trade in weapons and mercenaries was breaking traditional feudal hierarchies and rules of conduct.[6] Most European regions during the Enlightenment experienced armed and unarmed conflicts that affected increasing numbers of people across larger territories,[7] and such disputes followed internationally recognized patterns.[8] Violence and its legitimations or limitations, including forms of asynchronous violence between subjects and rulers or violent conflict between subjects, played an essential part in early modern writing.

Treating the British Empire in the long eighteenth century between the Glorious Revolution and the Napoleonic Wars as a case study in 'management of disagreement',[9] this book aims to shed light on the constitutional effects that different forms of (potentially) violent inner-imperial conflict – ranging from local riots to transregional uprisings – had on political structures and communication infrastructures. Constitutions, in the sense used here, are expressed in established practices as well as in written laws, which conforms with concepts found in the eighteenth-century sources.

Early modern constitutional developments in continental Europe were strongly shaped by the Peace of Westphalia, which was signed in the Westphalian cities of Münster and Osnabrück in 1648 and promoted cross-border recognition of the law and usage of nations.[10] In the Holy Roman Empire in particular, the influence of religion, as well as the agency of the emperor and other princes, became enshrined in a well-documented legal framework (the *'forma Imperii'*).[11] Britain remained a more complex and contradictory case, even more so as its dominions included many overseas colonies. Focusing on five prominent groups of agents in early modern British society (monarchs and aristocrats, Parliament and politicians, religious communities, regular troops and militia and – last but not least – the people), I analyse how the accepted agency of each of these groups was renegotiated in the course of insurrections in different regions and the media strategies that each of these groups could apply to consolidate their positions.[12]

This means that I am interested in overarching developments rather than individual events and their short-term results. An equally broad study of Britain's conflict landscape from the Jacobite rebellions of 1715 and 1745 to the Irish Rebellion of 1798 is Ian Gilmour's *Riots, Risings and Revolutions* of 1995. According to his publishers, 'Britain in the eighteenth century was deeply divided, and riots over politics, food, and religion were endemic.'[13] In his analysis, which has a social and economic focus, Gilmour highlights the aspect of liberty in the British system, which allowed the ruling class to serve their interests and also permitted the rise of an economically agile middle class. About half of the population, however, Gilmour describes as 'dependent'.[14] In his review, Daniel Szechi points out that Gilmour's work draws heavily on the 'Marxist canon' of English history, while also presenting a progress-oriented Whig interpretation of the British eighteenth century.[15] My longue-durée perspective acknowledges the importance of economic, demographic and infrastructural change (as discussed by social historian E. P. Thompson),[16] while it also shifts the focus from social division to procedures and the by no means exclusively class-bound identities that evolved throughout the struggles.

The analysis here applies different zoom levels from the local to the imperial, drawing attention to the numerous minor riots, protest marches or individuals' acts of resistance during and between more notable uprisings. This perspective moves away from the insurgents' momentary motivations and uncovers the overarching conceptions of agency and crisis communication that eventually made formal and accepted opposition possible. This emphasis on communication in politics associates this work with sociological communication theories such as Manuel Castell's much-discussed observation that 'politics is fundamentally media politics'.[17] According to Castell, successful resistance may evolve when oppositional agents adopt an established 'mechanism of power-making', for example 'by engaging in the cultural production of the mass media, and by developing autonomous networks of horizontal communication'.[18] While Castells and other sociologists mainly focus on present-day societies and digital change, a systematic analysis of communication is also at the heart of the so-called new cultural history, which considers communication, not least in the form of ceremonies, as an expression of a fundamental 'human ability to generate symbolic meaning'.[19] New cultural history emerged in American scholarship during the mid-twentieth century as a new dialogue between social history (influenced by Marxist theory and the French Annales school), anthropology and literary studies.[20] Michel Foucault's history of culture exerted a particular influence on analyses of crowds and communities, and on the performative aspects of social order undertaken by new cultural historians in North America as well as in Europe.[21] According to Barbara Stollberg-Rilinger, one of the German proponents of new cultural history, politically relevant rituals range from court ceremonies as 'instruments of power' to deliberate inversions or subversions.[22] Acts of (collective) violence, for their part, may also fulfil 'pacifying' functions in larger communicational frameworks if they serve as temporarily condensing concerns and belonging.[23] In this sense, I understand violent conflict in the evolving nations of eighteenth-century Europe as deeply transactional and as an inherent element of state-building. Although British state formation was already comparatively advanced by the seventeenth century, because the Henrician Reformation (marked by Henry VIII's break with Rome in 1534) had successfully centralized government and crushed baronial as well as ecclesiastical resistance even in the far-off provinces of Gaelic Ireland, not all inhabitants were willing to accept their new roles that had been defined by the London-based administration.[24] People's religion, profession, class, ethnicity and dynastic solidarity accounted for collective identities that often overlapped and expressed themselves in diverse oppositions. Most of the events covered in this book were, in fact, multi-motivational and included agents from different strata of society.

Trying to uncover the constructive effects of destructive acts (including damage to people and property), however, also allows us to transcend the immediate and often negative reactions of early modern observers. A gloomy mid-seventeenth-century text anticipating another civil war was the *Royall Merlin; or, Great Brittains loyal observator*, which was released in late 1654 or early 1655.[25] This royalist pamphlet challenged the Cromwellian Protectorate and described Britain's fate as an ongoing succession of 'changes and revolutions' that were not likely to come to an end.[26] The *Royall merlin* predicted 'the revolt of some eminent officers and commanders', 'the new rising of the Scots',[27] and international warfare. After 1685, contemporaries in Britain were even more convinced that they were living in a time of instability and danger.[28] The Glorious Revolution compounded religious, economic, dynastic and legal challenges of the Restoration period, and made Britain one of the most carefully observed theatres of conflict.[29] The Hanoverian Succession triggered international controversies about whether English politics was superior to the course taken by France or the Holy Roman Empire, and if the British model should prompt reforms across Europe.[30] According to many early modern observers on the continent, the ubiquity of violent antagonism did not recommend the British model at first sight.[31]

Although the lawyer Christian Wildvogel (1644–1728), Privy Councillor to Duke William Henry of Saxony-Eisenach, admitted that tumults and riots would now and again break out in any society, he perceived rebellions and revolts as fundamentally English problems.[32] Recounting a long history of political conflict from the Gunpowder Plot to Jacobite resistance, Wildvogel accused the English political system of 'procreating' rebellion, and derogatorily called England the 'mother of factions'.[33] Rejecting English perceptions that foreign agents caused rebellion, Wildvogel saw internal 'discord' ('*discordiae*') as the major reason, and underscored that 'England [was] an immortal animal as long as she [did] not tear herself apart'.[34]

Indeed, history seemed to be repeating itself when Scottish anti-Unionists, North American colonists and Irish nationalists sought decentralization or even self-government. The war in North America, in particular, disappointed continental European reformers who had praised Britain as 'the powerful champion of liberty'.[35] Even the French Jacobin Society saw the British constitution as especially difficult to judge. In a 1794 tract on the 'vices of the British constitution',[36] Jean-Charles Laveaux commented that England had 'the most bizarre of governments; a government composed of the two forms of tyranny combined, [yet] linked with a glimpse of popular authority'.[37] The two tyrannies that Laveaux was referring to were aristocracy and monarchy, including the belief in the hereditary rights of rulers. Both European monarchists and republicans thus found fault with how the British Empire was governed, but also had to acknowledge that conflicts arising from these weaknesses were more consciously and controversially discussed and remembered than in regions whose rulers implemented a *damnatio memoriae* (*condemnation of memory,* initially a posthumous punishment in ancient Rome) policy.[38] Because of Britain's common law system, past insurrections were regularly evoked in courts of law as well as in the press, and different forms of (violent) resistance mattered not only as actual events but also as powerful topoi.

Nuanced opposition discourses and extensive legal trials of the eighteenth century can often tell conciliatory stories between the lines, and the positive effects of violent conflict on the transparency of political procedures or political participation became more visible. Foreign observers who analysed British laws and judicial procedures noted the many categories of punishments that took the nature of the crime and the conditions of the persons committing them (e.g. pregnancy) into consideration.[39] Comparing the French and English penal codes, criminalist Scipion Jérôme Bexon (1750–1825) remarked that British punishments ranged from physical penalties and transportation to the colonies to removal or exclusion from public office, the confiscation of property and pecuniary punishments.[40] This reflected a plurality of identities and interactions among citizens, or between citizens and the state, which made Britain an interesting topic of debate even for those who rejected monarchical government.

Taking both the eighteenth-century criticism and the eighteenth-century appreciation of British conflict management into account, this book traces cross-medial differentiations of political culture (see Chapter 1) occasioned by local and large-scale insurrections in the British Isles and North America. This analysis assumes physical violence was often coupled with more subtle forms of asserting power or claiming participation. Furthermore, it acknowledges that violence only reached its full potential when its effects were communicated through media. This is highly relevant in today's digital societies, where public unrest are often preceded, accompanied and followed by social media campaigns. Indeed, violent opposition has recently resurfaced in Western democratic societies to a degree that challenges teleological concepts of state development. While we tend to take violent protest for granted in pre-democratic or failing states, present-day escalations of protest in Western democracies have led journalists and politicians to assert that 'this isn't who we are'.[41] Although modern democracies ideally offer forms of participation and negotiation that render violence unnecessary, even established democratic states in Europe and North America are now being forced to manage more radical expressions of discontent and growing social divisions.[42] Preventing such events in the future requires us to consider the underlying societal problems as well as the communication networks that polarize loosely connected (online) communities. Analysing communication within and beyond violent opposition groups of the early modern period, and understanding their strategies of legitimation, can lead to an interesting comparison with modern rhetorics of dissent. Critical voices have discussed a decline in democracy since the 1990s, linking it mainly with a 'destabilisation of political communication systems'.[43] Radical social media communities, in particular, have shaken our belief in the 'communicative interaction among citizens' that theories of democracy had previously situated at the heart of politics.[44] Dahlgren, Davis and others have described these oppositional social media communities as 'counter-public',[45] or 'anti-public',[46] spheres, and stressed their rejection of mainstream values. Violence past and present, however, can also be read as hyper-interaction with political leaders or as an extreme form of identity formation within a movement. The plurality of motivations and addressees often found in public outrages today have a precedent in the complexity of eighteenth-century riots and revolts, which allows this book to make a methodological contribution to conflict studies over time.

In relation to the historiography of early modern Britain, this book continues the ongoing reinterpretation of inner-state conflicts in anglophone historiography, which has moved from the teleological narratives of classical liberalism and the emancipatory agenda of social history to re-evaluations of monarchical government.[47] Gary W. Cox summarized modern debates on the Glorious Revolution as a juxtaposition of 'minimalists',[48] who claimed that there was 'no sharp change at the Revolution',[49] and historians who have tried to stress considerable constitutional progress. Minimalist readings were inspired by Geoffrey Elton and the British revisionists of the 1980s, who interpreted eighteenth-century Britain as an integral part of a pre-democratic Europe and took great interest in the political achievements of foreign government structures such as the German Imperial Diet and the centralized administration in France's *ancien régime*.[50]

Post-revisionist studies by Steven Pincus, Tim Harris and Tony Claydon (among others) have acknowledged the 'revolutionary nature of 1688–1689',[51] but do not necessarily agree on the consequences that the overturn of the Stuart dynasty had for the British Empire at large. Pincus neither follows Whig historiography, which portrayed King James as 'a religious zealot pursuing irrational policies', nor revisionist views that James was 'a political moderate committed to the principle of religious toleration and uninterested in claiming new or unprecedented powers'.[52] Rather, Pincus claims that 'James pursued an aggressive and very modern ideological agenda – modern not because it was particularly tolerant but because it adopted the most up-to-date notions of state-building'.[53] Scott Sowerby, too, sees James VII/II as a thoroughly modern ruler, but challenges Pincus's focus on state-building by highlighting the king's cooperation with a dissenting faction to influence Parliament.[54] Making Parliament permeable to minority opinions was, indeed, an important element of present-day democratic government that the Glorious Revolution did not achieve. This reveals that early modern uprisings were hardly provoked by the misadventures of a single ruler but resulted from broader institutional and procedural antagonisms.

For Eveline Cruickshanks, Daniel Szechi, Murray Pittock, Paul Kléber Monod and other researchers specializing in Toryism or Jacobitism, the British rebellions were processes of political integration and the consolidation of diversity.[55] The Jacobite rebellions of the first half of the eighteenth century were supported by leading Scottish noblemen as well as middle-class city dwellers in Manchester and rural supporters in Catholic Ireland.

Therefore, the effects that rebellions had on the British constitution were not exclusively bottom-up changes implemented under pressure. The uppermost levels of the British administration – the Crown included – were able to anticipate conflicts and implement their own reforms in time.[56] In his book on the English Reformation, Ethan H. Shagan describes the great achievement of British political history ever since the Henrician Reformation as the government's conscious cooperation with its subjects – and as the citizens' more conscious 'co-opting [of] state power'.[57] Similarly, Matthew McCormack has broken with Thompsonian narratives of crowd action,[58] and a glorification of the comparatively urbanized British Isles as epicentres of bottom-up reform, because he views riots and the arming of the people not only as anti-state action.[59] On the contrary, McCormack highlights the co-existence of conservative and reform-oriented outlooks in the British militia system. This confirms the broad consensus in present-day historiography that reforms implemented by rulers and changes demanded by oppositions both contributed to the more efficient administration of public affairs and the rise of 'popular politics'.[60]

In order to give readers unfamiliar with conflicts in the British Empire an overview and suggestions for further reading, I have collected dates, places, agents and outcomes of selected conflicts in a spreadsheet, which I have geocoded to map spatial relations. While some of the information has come directly from sources or secondary works used in this book, other events have been automatically harvested from Wikidata as one of the web's largest and fastest-growing resources of structured information. In addition, I have analysed archival abstracts provided in the National Archives of the United Kingdom catalogue. The Wikidata IDs as well as the archival references are included in a fully searchable data table that I intend to update over time.[61] My data table and the zoomable, interactive map based on it can by no means offer a complete trajectory of

Figure 0.1 Screenshot of the zoomable digital map highlighting different types of conflict within the early modern British Empire. With a view to future updates, events of the sixteenth and seventeenth centuries have also been included. The categories on the right can be (de-)selected in the interactive legend. Created by the author and available via GitHub: https://monikabarget.github.io/Revolts/event-map/event-map.html

insurrections, but indicate patterns of conflict across space and time. Figure 0.1 shows a screenshot of the interactive web map with selectable category filters on the right.[62]

Some related events (e.g. anti-Catholic riots in reaction to the Catholic Relief Act) occurred in several places, and many smaller skirmishes (marked as 'supplementary' in the data table and map) were directly linked with more general crises such as the Glorious Revolution, the Jacobite risings and the American Revolution. My thematic categorization of events is an attempt to underscore the central impact area or motivations behind them, but in many cases, causes are not immediately obvious ('unclear context') or overlapping. One such chain of events was the American Revolution. In 1994, J. C. D. Clark's book *The Language of Liberty* challenged interpretations that the spread of Enlightenment thought, republicanism and liberalism had played a major role.[63] Rather, he pointed out that (less avant-garde) issues of religion and law were at the heart of the debate. Given such uncertainties and changing perceptions in historiography, my own classification can only be a starting point for further research and a way in which general trends in violent opposition can be diachronically identified.[64]

Until the mid-eighteenth century, many local riots were either explicitly linked with controversies over dynastic succession or suspected Jacobite riots. Towards the end of the century, there was much fear of republican movements inspired by the French Revolution, which led to several treason trials against presumed political radicals.[65] In addition, many local uprisings throughout the century either opposed rising prices, taxation, the exportation of food or fundamental changes in Britain's maritime trade or they rejected military regulations and recruitment practices for the regular army as well as the militia. Last but not least, the overall growth of the British Empire accounted for an increasing number of transregional unrest or unrest from an imperial perspective. The Calico Riots in which London weavers protested against the importation of Indian cotton in 1719–20 are one prominent example.[66] Similarly, the Glorious Revolution had repercussions in the North American colonies, and the American War of Independence was linked with James Aitken's arsonist attacks of 1776 and with the 1775 sabotage and prison escapes in Liverpool. Complicating matters further, fights over land and resources in colonial settings often implied that settlers temporarily allied with indigenous groups to gain an advantage over other Europeans. This is why colonial settlements in North America, as well as Asia, were affected by many small-scale raids whose underlying conflicts often dragged on for decades.[67] Events that I have classified as 'privateering/ piracy' show that lines between inner-state violence and conflicts involving foreign troops are equally difficult to draw in the context of Britain's imperial history. Privateering, which meant the approved contribution of private naval entrepreneurs to armed conflict at sea, could become piracy once fighting had officially ended.

While classifying conflicts by insurgents' major motivation or their societal impact areas is best suited to the aims of this book, eighteenth-century unrests might also be categorized by their immediate outcomes. Some local riots were peacefully dissolved by local magistrates willing to enter into dialogue and negotiation; others were violently put down or even resulted in deaths.[68] After people were killed in the riots in St George's Fields (1768), Boston (1770), Bristol (1793), Tranent (1797) and, perhaps most prominently, Peterloo (1819), sympathizers of the rioters labelled the fatal armed interventions 'massacres',[69] and questioned their legitimacy. In most cases, unrest did not simply end with the dispersal of the crowds but triggered public media debates, private correspondence and government investigations either into the people's conduct or into the conduct of the local authorities and troops involved. In particular, the many petitions of men and women who were implicated in riots or were linked to alleged rioters as family members, neighbours or employers tell interesting stories of expected citizen conduct, citizen rights and accepted grounds for pardons. Among the most extensively discussed riots of the eighteenth century were the 1725 Glasgow Malt Tax Riots.[70] According to the surviving archival records dating from both 1725 and the following years, the authorities engaged in a complex analysis of guilt, compensation claims and petitions for pardons. Similarly, the anti-Catholic violence ignited by the Catholic Relief Act in Glasgow (1778), Edinburgh (1779) and London (1780) provides us with ample sources to analyse the agency of crowds and the self-perception of political leaders.[71] Smaller and locally confined events of violence included election riots, and also non-political riots that resulted from popular blood sports such as bull-baiting or exuberant festivities.[72] In some cases, feast-day gatherings that got out of hand were misinterpreted as deliberate disturbances of the peace.[73]

Naturally, only a small proportion of the events mapped for this book can be addressed in the chapters that follow. Instead, the riots, revolts and revolutions that have been selected exemplify overarching developments. Expressions of disagreement ranged from mock processions and the burning of effigies to violence against people, and these were recorded in a broad range of handwritten and printed sources – among which the thriving periodicals of the eighteenth century contributed in particular to extending political discourses to previously excluded strata of society. In an effort to understand the transregional and diachronic development of opposition discourses imparted by the sources, I have collected the metadata of 1,278 sources dated 1688 to 1800 and including genres from poetry and song to petitions and Acts of Parliament.[74] The metadata collection was semi-automated, using Python scripts to systematically harvest digital library catalogues.[75] All metadata are available in a public ZOTERO library, which I have divided into two main folders for manuscripts and prints created before 1900 and secondary works published after 1900. The folder of manuscripts and prints published before 1900 contains several sub-folders for key events sorted by date as well as several folders focussing on concepts and media genres. While this extensive collection of metadata has allowed me to perform high-level, quantitative analyses of keywords and peaks of media engagement, the structure of the metadata library also gives readers a chronological overview of the events and contemporary records central to this book. My analysis focuses on sources that were linked with a particular group of agents and played an especially prominent role in controversies over legitimate political agencies (see Chapter 1). The majority of sources consulted for this book are held at British and American libraries and archives and were written in English, though, additionally, sources in French, German, Latin and Dutch were consulted to cast further light on the European contextualization of British developments. The continental-European manuscripts analysed primarily came from the state archives of Lower Saxony in Hanover.

After general observations on the eighteenth-century media landscape and conflict-relevant means of communication and eighteenth-century terminologies of conflict

(Chapter 1), Chapters 2 to 6 align key groups of agents with their most prominent conflict media to evaluate changing positions between the poles of institutionalized, procedure-oriented politics and bureaucratic administration on the one hand and open-ended, less formalized political activities on the other. Apart from the changing roles of monarchs and aristocrats (Chapter 2), this book analyses the position of parliament, parties and politicians (Chapter 3), religious communities and religious leaders (Chapter 4), military and paramilitary agents (Chapter 5) and a more indistinct public often conceptualized as *the people* (Chapter 6). Whenever possible, I also draw attention to neglected agents who sadly remain absent from my own research as they are absent from the sources that have been consulted. Slave revolts, for instance, only became a prominent matter for debate after the 1790s, when several revolts of (former) slaves occurred in the Caribbean, inspired by the Haiti revolution. Notable slave revolts in independent America included Gabriel Prosser's slave rebellion in Virginia in 1800, the Igbo Landing in Georgia in 1803 and the Chatham Manor rebellion in 1805. For much of the eighteenth century, however, political authors either disregarded slaves' interests or stressed their purported inability to go through with their demands (examples are given in Chapters 2 and 6). On the contrary, actual, alleged or merely anticipated uprisings of disadvantaged groups were often exploited as arguments against their emancipation before gradual public recognition of their visible self-organization allowed for (reluctant) integration into political exchanges. In the course of the eighteenth century, women and religious minorities also experienced exclusion, but examples in Chapters 4 and 6 nevertheless prove that seeds of their political self-assertion were planted.

Many of the case studies assembled in this book show that rather than the actual course of events, it was the debates preceding, accompanying and following them that mattered most to the development of Britain's political culture.[76] As an expansion of public communication can already be dated to the mid-seventeenth century, the 'communication revolution' that earlier historiography has situated in the late seventeenth and early eighteenth centuries was, in fact, owed to a refinement of quality and clarification of communicative norms rather than a rise in quantity.[77] This book tells the history of eighteenth-century riots, revolts and revolutions in the British dominions as an imperfect yet encouraging process of differentiation and professionalization on interlocking levels.

1

Agency through communication: Media genres and terminologies

Before analysing the role of individual groups of agents, it is necessary to clarify how eighteenth-century political agency is manifested in the (mostly textual) sources that have come down to us, and what the media genres and terminologies used tell us about changing perceptions of (violent) opposition beyond 'unnatural rebellion'.[1] As outlined in the Introduction, most crises in early modern Europe coincided with a redefinition of media usage and the 'media topography of space'.[2] Incidents of violence potentially interrupted the dissemination of media, but in many instances 'continuity of communication' could be achieved,[3] setting positive examples for future conflict management. Negotiations on the exchange of prisoners, and the 'will to preserve civil relations throughout Scottish society even in the most extreme circumstances' of the 1715 Jacobite Rebellion,[4] are examples of such productive crisis communication in the eighteenth-century British Empire.

Furthermore, differentiated opposition discourses were rooted in older political theories. While anthropologically pessimistic political philosophers such as Jean Bodin (1530–96) and Thomas Hobbes (1588–1679) had viewed civil war as the sad yet unavoidable state of uncivilized humanity,[5] John Locke (1632–1704), Montesquieu (1689–1755), Rousseau (1712–78) and Scottish Enlightenment authors began to discuss rebellions as a necessary counterpart to power and as potentially progress-inducing events of transition. In a review of the 1745–6 Jacobite rebellion in Scotland, dissenting Whig politician James Burgh (1714–75) stated that times of rebellion were wholesome occasions of learning and debate through which the entire nation could improve and mature. Although Burgh condemned the Jacobites as enemies of the British constitution, he put the act of revolt in a forward-looking, positive context that contrasted with more traditional interpretations of uprisings as God's punishment for the nation's sins. Rebellions were, in his opinion, the 'proper season for suggesting to them [the people] thoughts'.[6] The objective of eighteenth-century authors who wrote about conflict was not so much their extinction or even prevention, but understanding the powers and interests at work. Whereas definitions of either rebellion or revolution had been absent from most seventeenth-century anglophone dictionaries,[7] Edward Phillips's *Nevv Vvorld of Vvords* (*New World of Words* in modern typeface) of 1678 defined rebellion, resistance and revolution both scientifically and politically.[8] Alongside historiographies, dictionaries and lexicons, travel guides, private memoirs and – most importantly – widely circulated periodicals reflected upon resistance movements, oppositions and political agency.[9] In contrast to earlier, much more derogatory accounts of political violence, British media began to tell stories of revolt and violence as more impartial, comparative histories on an international level.[10]

The other side of the coin was the chance that authorities had to prevent conflict through more reliable and engaging communication. Prolonged 'bodily disaggregation' in a globalized world called for the professionalization of political communication.[11] The expansion and refinement of printed distance communication and postal services in the eighteenth century did not curtail oral culture or physical manifestations. In the sense of 'symbolic communication',[12] many media only fulfilled their agitational potential when they were read aloud, read in certain places or passed on from one person to the next. Therefore, refined media usage in the eighteenth century implied the conscious demarcations of political spaces. Only in this way could a culture of collective and synchronous media perception emerge without which the dialogue-oriented public sphere imagined by Jürgen Habermas would have been entirely impossible.[13] While older historiographies stressed newspapers and periodical journals as the key media of the Enlightenment, 'gesture, oral discourse and manuscripts' have since been rediscovered as equally valuable though perhaps less innovative tools.[14] 'Print was never the only available medium of controversy' in early modern England, where 'sermons, plays, public gossip, manuscript libels and popular shaming rituals' remained essential channels of reciprocal exchange.[15] David Hume (1711–76), for example, valued the positive impact that the Wars of the Three Kingdoms had had on the development of parliamentary debating and political speech in his *History of England*:

> Civil wars, especially when founded on principles of liberty, are not commonly unfavourable to the arts of eloquence and composition; or rather, by presenting nobler and more interesting objects, they amply compensate that tranquillity of which they bereave the muses. The speeches of the parliamentary orators during this period are of a strain much superior to what any former age had produced in England; and the force and compass of our tongue were then first put to trial.[16]

Several important media genres were disseminated in more than one form. Proclamations and sermons, for instance, were both delivered orally and in print, whereas petitions and witness statements were handwritten and oral. Cultures of performance were linked with all genres. Engraver George Bickham saw his own media environment as a collage of different forms and contents that could be colourful and exciting as well as confusing. In his print titled *The Champion; or Evening Advertiser by Capt. Hercules Vinegar*, published on 30 September 1740, Bickham presented a satirical 'medley' of mid-eighteenth-century media,[17] ranging from the Bible to newspapers, essays, portraits and songs. The producers behind these media were publicly visible but not yet a distinct political voice in the sense of our modern-day independent press. If the essence of modern political interaction in the public sphere is 'mutual observation',[18] the early modern public could not yet guarantee immediate and conscious options of observation or action. Therefore, eighteenth-century media could not derive legitimation from a pretended outside position.[19]

Although some euphoric British contemporaries saw the emerging press as 'the free will of twelve million of people',[20] it was only in the nineteenth century that stable production conditions and an independent, speedy distribution framed mass media as an autonomous voice.[21] Eighteenth-century printing, publishing and bookselling were paid professions that required specific technical skills and access to necessary government licences, but media production was often a collaboration between full-time and amateur media producers.[22] Above all, many part-time printers and occasional authors could provide the necessary funds and social connections. The expanding world of eighteenth-century media offered more of everything, and with respect to the quickly expanding newspaper market, there was also 'more of the same'.[23] The improvement of European infrastructures, the consolidation of postal services and the success of the overseas colonies since the seventeenth century had established more frequent and structured exchanges between rulers and subjects as well as among citizens.[24] Nevertheless, political interactions mainly took place in ad hoc networks and hardly reached the public as a whole. Therefore, the British public of the eighteenth century did not conform to 'Habermas's idealizing portrayal',[25] of a 'bourgeois',[26] or truly 'participatory' public,[27] but was a predominantly *informational* public in which participation was simulated or imagined rather than practised.[28] Very much in accordance with Ellen R. Welch's analysis of French public opinion as a powerful narrative rather than a real-world space,[29] situational perceptions of the British eighteenth-century public could include or exclude ethnic groups such as the Irish or the Scottish Highlanders as well as urban and semi-urban professional groups (e.g. migrant craftspeople).[30]

On the one hand, the inclusion of the absent into early modern communication was a decisive step towards new 'concepts of dynamic change and self-regulation'.[31] On the other hand, long-distance media were only successful if traditional hierarchies of communication either persisted or could be replaced by new structures and limitations. The American Revolution was one eighteenth-century crisis during which existing communication networks were fundamentally questioned. Governor Francis Bernard of Massachusetts, for instance, lamented that the American colonists did not communicate with him as he had hoped they would, but rather addressed the king, Parliament and other assemblies on the American continent directly.[32] He took even greater offence that council members ordered 'their said answer to be published in one of the news-papers of that day [...] before it was presented to him'.[33] To the British administration, the conflict with the American colonists was only in part a matter of content; it was even more a matter of form. In Bernard's opinion, no grievance however legitimate justified 'addressing the King, remonstrating the Secretary of State, and employing a separate Agent, as if they were the States General of the Province, without a Governor or a King's Council'.[34] Bernard's own communication as a 'professional administrator' was formulaic,[35] and – in his own words – primarily concerned with 'the Ordinary Business of the Government'.[36] This British–American miscommunication was worsened by the inherent time lag in early modern long-distance communication. In the best of circumstances, distance communication could successfully sustain the idea of national unity and relieve early modern agents from the pressures of agreement as complaints could be ignored and decisions delayed.[37] In many cases, however, the time lag proved problematic.[38]

Communication between the colonies and London was often complicated if letters either arrived late or not at all.[39] In his correspondence with the British Ministry, Governor Francis Bernard hinted that some postal packages took thirteen days to reach him from New York. Such timing problems inevitably led to a divergence between actual events and the narratives about them.[40] The recipient cultures created through printed distance media were not simultaneous either, and cannot easily be deducted from the overall media output of the time.[41] Sudden intensifications or spatial extensions of media dissemination could thus turn non-violent disagreement into open rebellion.[42] Many conflicts in the British Empire resulted from the unwillingness or inability of agents in formal politics and popular political agitation to accept each other's media and semantics as valid expressions of their respective roles.[43] As a consequence, the Enlightenment experienced a severe credibility crisis in terms of its media.[44] In the Holy Roman Empire, the comparatively unfettered British printing industry was perceived as the chief cause of uproar and violence.[45] Following the Glorious Revolution, both the embattled Tory faction and Whigs wishing to preserve the new establishment lamented the detrimental effects of untrustworthy newspaper publishing and pamphleteering.[46] In 1713, the Tory newspaper *The Examiner* stated that

> it were better that *Printing* had never been Invented, than that the *Majesty* of *Heaven* and *Earth* should suffer by it; better that Ignorance and Barbarity should prevail, than that those Moral and Sociable Vertues [sic], which even *Pagans* revere and observe, should be lost or impair'd by the Use of *Letters*.[47]

After the accession of King George I, however, Tory writers defended the right to publish books and newspaper articles anonymously as they feared the bias of Whig audiences against their works.[48] In general, anonymity in media could enhance public appeal, and the development of commercial newspapers would not have been possible without it.[49] But while anonymity ensured that readers would not judge arguments by the social status or gender of the author and protect opposition writers from prosecution,[50] many eighteenth-century observers feared a 'war of paper politicks',[51] or 'personal abuse'.[52] Forged proclamations, anonymous newspaper articles, fraudulent petitions and rumours irritated authorities and opposition movements alike.[53] The international dissemination of news and the obscurity of their sources was, for example, criticized by Elizabeth Charlotte, Duchess of Orléans (1652–1722), who concluded that the many newspapers available in major cities such as Paris and London did not contain credible information.[54]

During the Jacobite rebellions, the greatest problem for the British government was not a lack of intelligence but that it was hard to weigh and analyse the torrent of reports from Scotland, France, Italy, Germany and the Low Countries. Over-eager diplomatic correspondence warning London of Jacobite intentions to strike 'a secure blow in England' frequently bordered on scaremongering.[55] The Stuarts' adherents in Scotland, most prominently the Earl of Mar, balanced the Stuart's prolonged absence through steady dissemination – if not unauthorized counterfeiting – of handwritten proclamations that unmistakably updated and revived the Jacobite claim.[56] Affected by the anti-Catholic mob violence in Glasgow, Vicar Apostolic George Hay, serving in the Scottish Lowlands from 1778 to 1805,[57] was enraged that most of the anti-Catholic propaganda in Edinburgh and Glasgow prior to the riots of 1778–9 had been spread anonymously and given readers a false impression of the authors' importance.[58] Hay did not contest the Protestants' right to speak their mind, but was unhappy that readers were led to overestimate the number and rank of Protestant opinion-makers, whom Hay considered 'a set of [...] insignificant People'.[59]

Forgeries also peaked on both sides of the conflict and among foreign observers during the American Revolution.[60] Oxford scholar Edward Bentham (1707–76) lamented that patriot agents multiplied 'false rumours and vain fears',[61] which frightened and enraged the population. Such fears of anonymity and invention often mingled with a fear of foreign correspondence.[62] In the United States, for example, popular protest ran high when secret presidential negotiations with France during John Adams's presidency became known.[63] Last but not least, caution by government and opposition alike was prompted by possible postal interceptions.[64] The London administration successfully intercepted Jacobite letters and American patriot correspondence, but mainly treated them as confidential intelligence.[65] No letters were printed on behalf of the royal administration, which rather wished to 'conceal from the public the extent of the [interception] practice'.[66] Many correspondents of the time nevertheless knew about it, and occasionally demanded the return of their letters.[67]

American patriots, for their part, frequently had intercepted letters published.[68] American agents in England, for example, forwarded 'authenticated copies' of Governor Bernard's correspondence with the ministry to the Sons of Liberty,[69] who had them printed by Edes & Gill in Boston.[70] Soon afterwards, Bernard's letters to the Earl of Hillsborough, which had been part of the Boston edition, were sold in Britain by John Almon.[71] In late 1769 and in September 1775, the Continental Congress ordered two more editions of Bernard's letters with the view to present British policy as biased and uncompromising.[72] Governor Thomas Hutchinson (1711–80) of Massachusetts Bay, whose private letters were intercepted and printed in 1774, replied that '[his letters] are expressly confidential, notwithstanding which, they contain nothing more respecting the Constitution of the Colonies in general than what is contained in my speeches to the Assembly and what I have published in a more extensive manner to the World'.[73]

This betrays the fact that the British authorities were not entirely averse to public communication but lost control of book and newspaper sales.[74] In the eyes of British officials and loyalist citizens, patriot media usage clearly undermined their own attempt to argue out the American conflict among gentlemen. One long-term consequence of media crises in eighteenth-century Britain and the colonies was that traditional censorship declined in favour of more modern and subtle forms of 'cultural control,'[75] and more elaborate governmental counter-propaganda.[76] The fact that newspapers and journals were printed periodically and replaced more topical newsletters made it easier to survey them and to react to individual cases of seditious libel.[77] At the same time, princely courts depended on the very same periodical press to sustain their successful representation. As Andreas Gestrich has pointed out, 'inter-court communication via the press' fostered 'public communication' far beyond the confines of aristocratic circles.[78]

The royal government was therefore a solvent associate for ambitious printers even after print licences and privileges granted by the Crown subsided.[79] The government also profited financially if the press flourished. Taxation on raw materials and trade regulations such as the notorious Stamp Acts became the most common supply-side forms of media constraint.[80]

Moreover, the abolition of formal censorship in the 1690s strengthened the informal media control exerted by lawyers and – last but not least – politically aware citizens.[81] The common law interpretation of the Treason Act of 25 Edward III had made 'the writing, printing or publication of a seditious libel' punishable as high treason,[82] and when preliminary censorship was abolished, the British public was encouraged to make such publications known to the authorities. Eighteenth-century lawyers did not perceive this as a break with the liberty of the press but – as Neil York has shown in the case of jurist William Blackstone (1723–80) – clearly distinguished between 'previous restraints upon publications',[83] and 'censure for criminal matter when published'.[84] Political conflicts were thus frequently acted out in the courtroom, and the possibility to press seditious libel charges against authors, printers and booksellers remained a powerful tool to enforce verbal moderation.[85] In practice, though, the seditious libel charge was seldom equated with treason but more often punished as a misdemeanour, which resulted in 'relatively small fines and brief prison sentences'.[86]

Similar to the worlds of parliamentary debating and street protests, the world of political writing became segregated into decent media producers, who treated the objects of their observations with respect, and 'rascal printers', who were accused of 'cheating' or 'abusing' their enemies at will.[87] C. D. Piguenit, who was himself a London publisher and bookseller active from the 1770s to the 1790s, commented in his *Essay on the Art of Newspaper Defamation* that 'the Liberty of the Press [would] become a dangerous Nuisance' if such methods were tolerated.[88] Yet even in the troublesome year of 1768, British authorities were reluctant to reintroduce *ex-ante* censorship. In a letter to Lord Shelburne, Governor Francis Bernard of Massachusetts explained his reasons for forbearing patriot propaganda:

> The Time is not yet come when the House is to be moved against popular Printers, however profligate and flagitious. But if there was a View of Success, I should by no Means thin it proper to make such An Attempt now when the House shows so good a Disposition to a Reconciliation to Government, of which they have given good Proof, since the Date of my former Letter. They have acted in all Things, even in their Remonstrances (as far as I who have not been allowed a Sight of it can learn) with Temper and Moderation; They have avoided some Subjects of Dispute, and have laid a Foundation for removing some Causes of former Altercations: I speak this only from private Report, nothing of this Kind very material having as yet come up to me.[89]

Other British officials in North America shared his reluctance, and explicitly warned the royal government in London that any attempt of direct 'cultural control' would be counterproductive.[90] William Bollan, who had served as the agent of Massachusetts

Bay in London from 1757 to 1762 and was one of America's most prolific writers, also praised the 'great wisdom' with which British law 'distinguished offences [*sic.*]'.[91]

The most famous eighteenth-century court trials against writers, printers and booksellers also confirmed the criminal liability of all agents involved in the production or dissemination of prints. In John Almon's trial at the King's Bench,[92] which began after the scandalous republication of the oppositional *Junius* letters in the *London Museum* in 1770, it was debated whether publishers and booksellers who were not themselves authors of seditious publications had any moral obligation to hinder the dissemination of such works prior to a government investigation.[93] Lord Mansfield confirmed with the approval of the jury that booksellers could indeed be held accountable for all works sold in their shops.[94] This strict interpretation of the law was facilitated by evidence that piracy printers used respected authors', printers' or publishers' names to enhance sales, thereby undermining the credibility of printed media.[95] Although some defendants tried to play themselves off against each other and understated their own connivance, most media entrepreneurs subsequently cooperated with the authorities in what they perceived to be a win-win situation. Responsibility and self-control permitted writers and editors to secure their sales markets more effectively and to heighten their public reputation as morally upright experts.[96] Oppositional radicalism was more frequently expressed in petitions or physical demonstrations, and legal restraints adapted to this unspoken consensus.[97]

Even as seditious libel trials peaked in the 1780s and 1790s, George III's government could hardly have advanced the persecution of authors, booksellers and printers if there had not been considerable citizen cooperation. In line with the Treason and Misprision of Treason Act passed in 1748, which boosted local law enforcement in Scotland,[98] later Georgian legislation extended civil rights and regional authority to assist with crime prevention.[99] Many investigations were instigated by non-governmental informers. In the case of Anne West, whose newspaper the *Westminster Journal* was under attack in 1796, accusations came from militia officers who felt offended by the 'evil Tendency' of a report on their soldiers' conduct.[100] The *Westminster Journal* had alleged that members of the militia supplied French prisoners of war with white bread in 'direct disobedience of orders'.[101] After a preliminary investigation, the Solicitor General advised the officers to drop their accusations against Anne West because he thought 'it very probable, upon attending to the Matters disclosed in the proofs, that upon the Trial, Evidence may be offered of the Truth of some of the Circumstances stated in the paper, proposed to be prosecuted'.[102] On other occasions, charges against authors, printers and booksellers were instigated by conscientious newspaper readers, lawyers or individual politicians.[103]

Court trials for seditious libel, however, ran aground if the extensive written – and sometimes even ciphered – material produced as evidence confused rather than clarified matters. The London Corresponding Society, a consortium of local reading and debating associations, and other societies campaigning for parliamentary reform raised suspicion of conspiracy at a time when the radicalization of the French Revolution united the monarchies of Europe. In 1794, members of the London Corresponding Society were arrested and tried because of their foreign correspondents. However, the counsel for the defence successfully interposed that the Crown's advocates '[had] produce[d] a mass of papers, letters, addresses, and resolutions without end', and that this 'multitude [...] took thirty hours in reading': '[to] observe upon them was beyond the power of human strength'.[104]

The lawyers further noted that only an overt act of high treason was punishable.[105] Attempts to construct 'such things as an accumulated treason in the English Law',[106] and to deduce it from separate statements in different media, would have to be refuted. Orality saw a considerable revival in the eighteenth-century courtrooms of speeding up trials, and also prevented the use of manufactured evidence.[107] In the course of the investigations into Bishop Francis Atterbury's (1663–1732) participation in the Jacobite plot of 1725, for instance, Philip, Duke of Wharton, had denied that 'producing decypher'd Letters, full of fictitious Names and Cant Words' was sufficient evidence when the court 'had not one living Witness that could charge the Bishop with any thing, not even so much as a Letter under his own Hand'.[108] In 1748, King George II and his Parliament passed 'An Act for the more effectual Trial and Punishment of High Treason and Misprision of High Treason, in the Highlands of Scotland', which stated that the former practice of 'reducing into Writing the Evidence given in Criminal Causes and Prosecutions' had caused 'great Delay, as well as Expence'.[109] The Act inferred that the witnesses' evidence should in the future be 'viva voce'.[110] Oral communication also played a particular part in military contexts. George Washington's farewell address to his soldiers, which was 'issued to the Armies of the United States of America the 2d day of Novr 1783 on Rocky Hill, near Princeton',[111] emphasized orality as the most trustworthy and memorable form of communication. In other words, eighteenth-century communication was not exclusively message-oriented but in itself a process of building societal structures.[112] Political groups tended to be more successful if they used a wider range of media and if physical presence and distance media enforced each other.

Marginalized agents had to make a special effort to construct their own communicational identities and make their distinctive demands generally understood.[113] This resulted in the special role of hybrid media that combined handwriting and print, personal delivery and mass distribution, reading, copying or retelling. Even today, political movements, especially the more radical ones, are especially successful if they resort to hybrid communication and manage to synthesize discourses that were 'formerly siloed across multiple domains'.[114] Papers circulated before, during and after riots have often come down to us as collections of official or private elite correspondence preserved in archives. One example is the 1795 Corn Riot in Birmingham, where – according to the authorities – 'inflammatory and seditious handbills had been distributed about the streets'. In order to discover the authors behind the handbills, a reward was offered, and the magistrates published their own handbills to prevent further disturbance.[115]

Similar to handbills that were passed on in a neighbourhood, petitions directly addressed to the authorities were not just written texts but required formal handing-over. They were often carried to places of power in procession and gave people beyond those who had drafted them an opportunity to participate. American patriots enthusiastically used handwritten or cheaply printed leaflets to evade British surveillance of their postal exchange, periodicals and commercially distributed publications.[116] During the anti-Catholic Scottish riots (1778–9), the Gordon Riots (1780), in English and Scottish radical circles,[117] among Orangemen in Ireland,[118] and in the Priestley Riots (1791), handwritten leaflets played a vital role, and were often perceived as more dangerous than elaborate printed material.[119] Most importantly, oppositional handwriting flourished not only on paper but also on walls. Priestley reported of the Birmingham riots:

> On the walls of houses, &c., and especially where I usually went, were to be seen in large characters, MADAN FOR EVER, DAMN PRIESTLEY, NO PRESBYTERIANS, DAMN THE PRESBYTERIANS, &c. &c. At one time I was followed by a number of boys, who left their play, repeating what they had seen on the walls, and shouting out, *Damn Priestley, damn him, damn him for ever, for ever, for ever*, &c. &. This was, no doubt, a lesson which they had been taught by their parents, and what these, I fear, had learned from their superiors.[120]

This intermediality indicates that there was a high level of unconscious or subconscious politicization in eighteenth-century Britain that the intellectual elites found hard to handle. Moreover, identities of agents could overlap or change in the course of conflicts, inciting revised media policies.[121] Despite the plurality of media genres used in conflict communication, there was also a growing refinement and normalization of conflict terminology, some of which was only used in clearly defined contexts. Articles in newspapers that began to reach wider audiences in the eighteenth century have been digitized for the British Newspaper Archives. For the years 1700 and 1799, these digitized articles contain more than 15,000 entries for 'riot' and 'rebellion' (see graph Github deployment), whereas there are only 7,000 mentions for 'tumult' and 6,000 mentions for 'revolt'. 'Uprising', 'disturbance' and 'insurrection' were even more rarely used in newspapers, but appeared in historical and legal texts of the time. This hints at a highly differentiated, context-aware and at the same time normative vocabulary for various forms of conflict.[122] In the titles of all conflict-related primary sources collected for this book, I have identified 3,600 unique words. Although the initial selection of works was eclectic, it is notable that most content-relevant words fit into one of seven categories. The first group of words describes people and groups, either using their proper names, professions or titles. The second group describes power relations and agency. The third group relates to development and movement. The fourth group describes information and communication. The fifth group evaluates the quality or status of people and objects. The sixth group denotes locations and institutions. The seventh group refers to time (e.g. the order of events). This range of meanings shows that situations of conflict were described in broader societal contexts and that careful reconstructions of motivations, as well as event chronologies, mattered.[123]

The agent-related keywords suggest that princes were still perceived as the major political stakeholders, but religious communities, political parties, societies or associations also claimed to represent the true interest of the nation.[124] Apart from neutral, descriptive terms for professions and official titles clearly defined throughout the period, many agent descriptions bore positive or negative connotations. On the one hand, derogatory labels could cast doubt on agents, especially if the chosen vocabulary deliberately referenced earlier periods of conflict (e.g. 'Leveller'),[125] or religious concepts of evil. On the other hand, differentiations between good and bad proponents of social or religious groups permitted intermediate stances and reconciliation narratives. Referring to those who followed a rebellion leader as 'dupes',[126] for instance, suggested that they were deceived innocents with whom negotiation might still be possible. Similarly, oppositional agents were judged by their (collective) behaviours in specific spatio-temporal settings, on which the circumstances of their birth as well as their education or more general natural and social environments supposedly made an impact. Terms such as 'reason(s)', 'apology', 'justification', 'intention' and 'confession' hint to the importance of providing convincing argumentative patterns and personal aims in eighteenth-century political communication, whereas adjectives such as 'accurate', 'false', 'unmask[e]d', 'discover[e]d', 'fomented', 'original' and 'intercepted' denote a great concern for the quality of information. Across ideological divides, 'untruths', 'threats' or 'frivolous promises' were condemned, whereas 'security', 'freedom', 'preservation', 'welfare', 'dignity' and 'amity' were collective values placed over 'private interest'.[127]

The noun 'politics' and the adjective 'political', too, were widely used, underlining a gradual pluralization of agency concerned with public affairs. In a more traditional sense, 'politics' referred to the 'rights and status' of individual citizens.[128] In a more contemporary eighteenth-century context, however, it described 'the art of government [...] and the day-to-day management of public affairs'.[129] Mid-eighteenth-century radical Whig James Burgh (1714–75), for instance, defined politics as plain sense 'applied to national instead of private concerns', and 'the true principles according to which the British Empire ought to be governed'.[130] However, the term could also be used ironically to denote skilful negotiations behind the scenes, including 'all the reports, lyes, and stories, which were the fore-runners of the Great Revolution in 1688'.[131] The adjective 'political', too, referred not only to the official management of public affairs but could also apply to the entire community as the object of politics or to the welfare of the commonwealth as a goal, and in the later eighteenth century these two points of reference were often inseparable.[132]

Edward Bentham, a loyalist Oxford professor who opposed the American Revolution, used the Latin term *'prudentia politica'* to describe the wise man's ability to apply political reasoning and methods when and where they were necessary.[133] Reform-oriented Unitarian minister Joseph Priestley defended the rights of all social and religious groups in British society to have their say in matters of public relevance. Political reasoning was, in Priestley's opinion, no longer the prerogative of hereditary, privileged leaders, but the duty of every mature citizen.[134] Some commentators even went so far as to claim that all conflicts had political roots but were falsely put down to other motives. One commentator in early eighteenth-century Britain quipped that he perceived thirst for power as the only true motivation of rebellion: 'Ther [*sic*] is no *Rebellion* but for *Power*. Other things, as *Religion, Liberty*, &c. are made the *Pretence*, to stir up the People. But Power is the *Mythologick* Sense!'[135]

Since allegiance to an abstract nation replaced dynastic ties, rulers and oppositions alike welcomed extended popular cooperation as a vital sign of their legitimation. Even though elite discourses did not necessarily trickle down to the lower classes, the elites became more and more concerned about their opinions and demands. The *people* and the *mob* as two antithetical concepts of the faceless mass were re-evaluated when political influence became demographically quantifiable, and *public opinion* constituted a substantial claim of legitimacy.[136] Furthermore, being political became an important aspect of people's individual and collective identities. Frederick Barlow's English Dictionary of 1779, for example, stated that Ambrose Philipps and Alexander Pope were personal enemies because they were 'of different political principles'.[137] At the same time, private and political (in the sense of collective or corporate) roles were more clearly distinguished. In 1792, another law dictionary published by Richard Burn explained that freemen of cities or boroughs had private identities as well as a trans-personal, collectively shared 'political capacity, created by the law, and styled a body politic',[138] which gave them rights as well as obligations.[139] Quoting fifteenth-century lawyer Fortescue, Jacob Giles's New Law Dictionary of 1756 also distinguished the monarch's regal rights from his political duties:

> The Nature of the Government of our King, says Fortescue, is not only Regal, but Political: If it were merely the former, *Regal*, he would have Power to make what Alteration he pleased in our Law, and impose Taxes and other Hardships upon the Subject, whether they would or no; but his Government being *Political*, he cannot change the Laws of the Realm, without the People's consenting thereto, nor Burthen [*sic*] them against their Wills.[140]

'Politicks' and 'political' in eighteenth-century usage thus denoted complex symbioses between the monarchy, a professionalized administration, a self-confident Parliament, a history-conscious legal system and nondescript agents representing different strata of society. Although politics was often connected with the evolving state and its institutions, it was never completely detached from the civic sphere. The degree to which each institution or group of agents maintained or challenged government procedures was contested, but the necessity of some form of politicization was widely accepted. In modern political theory and sociology, too, the question if and when different state bodies or social groups ought to be politicized to revive or reveal disagreement and competition has been repeatedly discussed.

In the 1980s, sociologist Charles S. Maier understood politics as being fixed regulations and procedures aiming at creating binding decisions,[141] whereas he defined a less formal expression of opinions and problem-awareness as 'the political'. The political can be claimed by or attributed to very different social fields ranging from the economy to science or education, and each shift ideally strengthens the ability of politics to find a compromise.[142] German research influenced by Niklas Luhmann's system theory, too, operates with the concept of 'the political' as a necessary antidote to procedurality,[143] placing special emphasis on its communicational aspects. French political theory has operated with a '*le politique*' versus '*la politique*' dichotomy,[144] and distinctions between '*le politique*' in the singular and '*les politiques*' in the plural.[145] As the modern French administration can routinely be politicized through posts that are reassigned whenever a new government is formed, French scholars in particular have considered the advantages of integration between a competitive political dimension and the 'high administration' ('*haute administration*').[146]

Although these levels of theoretical sophistication only evolved with the development of various democratic government systems in the nineteenth and twentieth centuries, the eighteenth century was undoubtedly not only the first 'age of revolution(s)',[147] but an age that carefully theorized political interaction both within and without individual dominions. The political discourse of the eighteenth century was the complex development of reference systems in which power was at least implicitly divided. Uprisings, for their part, functioned as transitions from one organizational regime to another, but did not necessarily question the existing order in general. Thomas Jefferson hinted in his memoir that rebellions could, in fact, replace those in charge without reforming the foundations of government:

> What a stupendous, what an incomprehensible machine is man! Who can endure toil, famine, stripes, imprisonment, and death itself, in vindication of his own liberty, and, the next moment, be deaf to all those motives whose power supported him through his trial, and inflict on his fellow men a bondage, an hour of which is fraught with more misery, than ages of that which he rose in rebellion to oppose![148]

Modern differentiations of political agency as different spheres of participation can help us understand why institutions or groups of agents occupied specific roles and why they cannot be analysed in isolation. Political philosopher Jacques Rancière has pointed out that the study of politics must not be limited to 'the exercise of power and the struggles for obtaining it',[149] but ought to consider the role of agents.[150] In the British eighteenth century, both the *public* and the *nation* emerged as concepts that allowed class-transcending identities and broader political agency, but also required conformity. Although more agents could choose their roles more freely, each role was context-bound and in itself more rigidly defined. In order to claim legitimate agency, oppositions had to pay attention to their scheduling as well as to the clothes they wore or objects that they carried, while previously non-political spaces such as urban streets or open fields could now function as places of lawful opposition.[151] Refined choreographies of power and resistance required careful planning or even rehearsals, and, above all, a general understanding of accepted conduct.

Legitimate political action was often situated at the crossroads of the public and the arcane.[152] Old and new 'social elites increasingly withdrew from coffeehouses into private members' clubs in the later part of the century in order to maintain exclusivity, leaving artisans and tradesmen to their own devices'.[153] In spite of commercial interests and the authors' quest for fame, a considerable number of political writers still intended their publications to be exclusively for the learned.[154] Much more than physical access to media, the ability to process information into knowledge was the main foundation of political participation, and this ability was often impaired by 'the lack of leisure, the cost of candles (or of spectacles), as well as educational deprivation'.[155] Tendencies to attribute almost any written source to some kind of public or semi-public discourse have therefore weakened the analysis of actual empowerment.[156] Even 'popular' uprisings,[157] such as the Monmouth

Rebellion of 1685 and the Glorious Revolution of 1688, were not created exclusively by printed propaganda but drew particular strength from the oral rejection of (mis)information provided by newspapers or government publications. Although Monmouth's elaborate declaration outlining the reasons for his resistance to James VII/II widely circulated among non-involved third parties in continental Europe and pretended to reflect the opinions of his men at arms,[158] this was unknown among his English supporters.[159] Recruitment through personal encounters and oral instruction played a vital role in Monmouth's attempt to prevent James's accession,[160] and there is reason to believe that this communicational traditionalism was more than a pragmatic concession to the peasants and craftsmen fighting for the duke. Court testimonies and what may be called public relations strategies of the various societies and political associations in eighteenth-century Britain reveal that self-imposed limitations of communication to accepted spaces (administrative buildings, law courts) and traditional rules of conduct were embraced to enhance a group's political standing.[161]

The London Corresponding Society, one of the liberal associations suspected of conspiracy in the late eighteenth century, decided prudently when and where to post bills 'in the streets', and when to distribute pamphlets exclusively at society meetings.[162] In his interrogation by the Lord President of the court, a witness, Mr Davis, who was a London printer, stated:

> Thelwall ordered me to print off 2000 copies, and then to stop. 200 of them I soon completed, and carried to the Globe Tavern, a place of meeting for the London Corresponding Society. I met the Prisoner on the stair-case. I had been previous to that time often at the meeting of the Society and knew him as Secretary to it. He ordered me to take the 200 I brought with me back. I did, and returned to dinner at the Globe. After dinner the copies were sent for to the Meeting, and distributed. The copy I had on the 18th, and this delivery took place on the 20th: 300 people were present, and among them the prisoner. Thelwall was in the chair. I afterwards printed 2000 more. Most of these I gave to the Prisoner, the rest I distributed to the members as they came and asked for them. Besides these, 6000 more were published by the Prisoner's order, who told me to go on till I was desired to stop: they are not paid for, but the Society is credited for them. On other occasions I printed for the Society, and the Prisoner, as Treasurer, paid me for it. The last publication was an Address to the People of Great Britain and Ireland.[163]

The long eighteenth century was marked by the sophistication of existing media genres and their distribution rather than by groundbreaking revolutions in communication.[164] Media fulfilled relational and representative functions in specific places and at specific times.[165] Between proceduralized decision-making ('politics'), a more controversial and competitive exchange of ideas ('the political') and an administration that managed day-to-day affairs, a (by no means all-inclusive) 'public' began to play a central part in the sphere of the 'political'. The Anglican Church (or religious communities in general) and military stakeholders also became more involved in political opinion-making beyond institutionalized decision-making, whereas Parliament as the seventeenth-century stronghold of opposition took on greater responsibility in politics. The following chapters will show that any vacuum of opinion-making or interest-representation was immediately filled by one group or the other. With Parliament moving more from grass-roots interest intermediation to decision-making with or even for the Crown, the Crown itself moved from lawmaking to a more administrative role as guardian of the constitution. This opened up new opportunities not only for the Church of England and other religious communities, but also for civic associations and (para-)military organizations.

The three most important ideological shifts behind these structural outcomes are, first, the rise of nationhood that allowed churches, the armed forces and different civic societies to present themselves as legitimate political embodiments of 'Britishness' while traditional elite networking aroused suspicion. Patriotic commitment to the British constitution became a token of good governance and lawful opposition.[166] Biographical, fictional or semi-fictitious stories of reconciled rebels, turncoats, spies and traitors played a considerable role in eighteenth-century political literature, and highlighted individual accountability.[167]

Secondly, aristocratic rebellions were gradually replaced by uprisings in which the insurgents shared an economic status or an ethnic identity. The Jacobite rebellions marked an important transition as local administrators and a provincial aristocracy at odds with the central government played an important part.[168] Political roles were gradually detached from dynastic affiliations and feudal hierarchies, and defined by aptitude, proper conduct and compliant communication. In all eighteenth-century conflicts, the availability and trustworthiness of media were, therefore, vital in the rise and success or extinction of riots, rebellions and revolutions. In general, political negotiations in eighteenth-century Britain built upon a far-reaching parliamentarization in style and rhetoric, as eloquent speeches, open debates, responsive lines of argumentation and direct interaction with audiences were heightened in different social settings.

Thirdly, conflicts about legitimate spatial settings of power, which had dominated the first half of the eighteenth century, were eventually superseded by a focus on procedure that inspired new possession and border debates. While political gatherings that were respected as such could take place in various settings beyond palaces and the Houses of Parliament,[169] the great challenge for the authorities was to balance local, centrifugal interests and the spreading of administration at the national level.[170] Chapter 6 puts these long-term developments in British constitutional history into a European perspective, and discusses how the concept of a mixed constitution and refined perceptions of treason eventually took root. While states in continental Europe mainly 'juridicised',[171] or 'criminalised',[172] uprisings, Britain and the colonies moved towards a system of internal competition – expressed in elections, parliamentary debating, legal bills, petitions or even courtroom pleadings. In eighteenth-century Britain, stability and peace were not self-evident.[173] The British Empire did not always successfully prevent or repress violent opposition, but British political controversies opened up spaces of communication in which political identities and reliable procedures could be reframed.

The Glorious Revolution triggered a lasting transformation of the dynastic composite state into a modern nation in which immediate access to government offices or material power was no longer the central objective of political action.[174] It was not only – as Harris said – 'the great crisis of the English monarchy',[175] but the conjunction of British-post-Reformation history with world history at large, and generated multilateral techniques of constitutional control. The constitutional idealism of the Restoration period was followed by an era of pragmatism, which led to a gradual transformation of contractual theory into representational theory and permitted a constant renewal of mutual responsibilities. However, these control mechanisms must not be romanticized as a highway to legal equality and voting rights for all. In his much-acclaimed analysis of early modern radicalism in Ireland, historian Kevin M. Whelan has opposed the euphemisms connected with politicization in twentieth- and twenty-first-century historiography. Whelan defines politicization as an interest group's 'quest for linear dominance through propaganda and the work of [party] organizers'.[176] In this sense, political action is never completely inclusive but relies on potentially exclusive justifications. The following chapters relate these overarching observations more closely to the agents defined in the Introduction.

2

Monarchs and aristocrats:
The constitutionalization of leadership and the dialogization of political communication

As is outlined in the Introduction, long-term analyses of British political culture should not reduce eighteenth-century conflicts to a simplistic king versus people formula. Although perceptions of the Glorious Revolution in historiography have differed widely,[1] recent research agrees that the changes initiated in 1688–9 were not predominantly a personalized war against one incompetent monarch or a religious struggle, but a trial of strength between professionalized politics and popular political agitation.[2] Sowerby claims that James VII/II never imitated continental styles of government, but rather tried to shape a modern nation with his very own reformatory zeal.[3] What enraged James VII/II's opponents was, according to Tim Harris, not a break with the legal heritage of England and Scotland but his reign of hesitancy and ambiguity.[4] After all, James VII/II also knew how to appeal to '"Whiggish" Jacobites', styling himself as a 'promoter of liberty' in 1693.[5] Putting it differently, we might say that the problematic aspect of late Stuart politics was not the false apprehension of royal power, but the increasingly unpopular pre-eminence that was given to statutory law over case law.[6] Nevertheless, James VII/II's attempts to modernize and centralize his kingdoms and the overseas colonies, exterminating secondary administrative channels and local institutions that competed with the government, were not reversed by the Glorious Revolution but were henceforth managed by different agents.[7]

Differentiating the motivations for physical, verbal or symbolic attacks on kingship in the eighteenth century, this chapter traces how, after the heated dynastic debates of the Glorious Revolution and the Jacobite rebellions, the British monarchy assumed a more generally constitutional function. This revision of the role of British monarchs has to be analysed with regard to the Crown as an institution, but it also concerns the role of royalty in the wider context of aristocratic leadership in Enlightenment Europe. On both levels, traditional patterns of communication and self-representation were challenged, which is why this chapter also analyses media usage and, last but not least, the use of violence as a performative expression of power.

As Frank Prochaska has shown, the present-day British 'welfare monarchy' that ultimately replaced the imperial monarchy of the nineteenth century took root in the eighteenth century and is a complex response to changing constitutional necessities.[8]

Overarching concepts of leadership were at stake and decisively shaped by violent conflicts within the British Isles and British colonies. Uprisings that were clearly monarchy-related ranged from more or less forceful opposition to the reigning dynasty to attempted introductions of a new system of government.[9] Continuing the conspiratorial climate that had given rise to the Popish Plot (1678) and the Meal-Tub Plot (1680), Queen Anne's reign was another heyday for (fictitious) conspiracy. After an alleged Whig conspiracy against the queen and her ministers known as the Screw Plot (1708), a Whig faction supposedly attempted to assassinate the Lord Treasurer in the so-called Bandbox Plot (1712).[10] Attacks on local administrators (e.g. colonial governors) who were perceived as deputies of royal authority could also express disaffection with the monarchy.[11] In many cases, curses and slander were not addressed to any one person or group but jointly to the Crown, the Privy Council, government ministers, Parliament or individual Lords and Commons.[12] These often fluid overlaps show how tight-knit – and, to outside observers, confusing – relations between the Crown and the state's various legislative or administrative assemblies were perceived to be in the eighteenth century (see Chapter 3).

Unsurprisingly, the most overt public statements against an individual eighteenth-century monarch date from the contested beginnings of King George I's reign. In 1716, stocking-maker John Applin of Glastonbury reported disaffection against the king in his hometown. He told the authorities that a local man named Benjamin Taylor had said that 'King George was a usurping King and that in a little time he hoped to see him sent home to his own country to sow turnips'.[13] In addition to oral insults, which had to be proven by witnesses, attacks on British monarchs were also found in handwritten or printed documents, which often circulated during or after public protests. The mocking or execution of members of the royal family in effigy was also reported. One example is a riot at Walsall, Staffordshire, on 29 May 1750, when an effigy of George II was hung on Church Hill.[14] Apart from during the Jacobite era, open anti-royal sentiment briefly peaked in the 1790s when the chant 'No Royalty' was heard in several local riots,[15] but widespread abhorrence for the French Revolution's escalating violence and stricter legislation (the Seditious Meetings Act of 1795) seems to have inspired such rallying cries.

Most protests during the second half of the eighteenth century attacked the monarchy metaphorically or by proxy. The American Revolution and the economically challenging 1790s in particular were occasions when puns and caricatures abounded. In illustrated patriot prints, America was often depicted as a violated virgin, whereas Britain was personified as Britannia, a lion or John Bull. Both the lion and John Bull were often depicted wearing the British crown, and although King George III was not mentioned by name, John Bull was in many cases clearly modelled on his physical appearance. In a 1792 satirical print by James Gillray, for instance, King George, the queen and six princesses were depicted as 'John Bull and his family'.[16] One example of a later American print that featured King George as John Bull is a caricature of England's naval losses in the War of 1812, which was published as 'A boxing match, or another bloody nose for John Bull' in 1813.[17] Such indirect references to the king in combination with John Bull as a personification of England leave ample room for interpretation.

Criticism of royal or aristocratic demeanour was also voiced in relation to foreign princes, which may at times have been a way of avoiding direct criticism of the British monarchy. In 1792, Charles William Ferdinand, Duke of Brunswick and commander of the Prussian army, famously issued a warning to the revolutionaries of Paris. He was burnt in effigy on 5 November by an English crowd expressing support for the French Revolution. A printed paper circulated on the occasion mocked the Duke of Brunswick's proclamation and presented him 'as a victim of his pride, ignorance, ambition and vanity'.[18] The burning of an effigy of the duke coincided with Guy Fawkes Night. This annual commemoration of the 1605 Gunpowder Plot was a general occasion for bonfires and public celebrations that could subtly integrate oppositional aims. In other riots, lawmakers in the House of Commons and individual 'Hell-Born ministers' were unfavourably compared with 'the Empress of Russia, the King of Prussia or the Emperor of Germany'.[19] As such incidents are often only reported in private correspondence and, unless tried in court, are difficult to contextualize, it is impossible to state how far disaffection with either individual British monarchs or the monarchy in general was implied. We can say, however, that later eighteenth-century political controversies generally discussed kingship within larger constitutional contexts and sought reforms on several levels.

Administrative institutionalization in Britain had begun in the twelfth century.[20] Opposition to the monarch, too, had older, often pan-European roots, including classical republicanism.[21] Similar to the Holy Roman Empire, Britain had a strong tradition of dualistic sovereignty, reconciling the sovereignty of power with the sovereignty of the people.[22] Seventeenth-century scholar Johannes Althusius from Emden, for example, based his contractual theory on the 'ethos of the German guild-towns' and promoted 'consociation' and 'communication',[23] in order to integrate families and small communities into larger societies of shared interest and common values. British contractualism disengaged the individual ruler's *potestas regalis* from the nation's *potestas politica*.[24] The collective body of the people could lawfully defend itself against 'the vilest usurpation, and the most infamous tyranny' by individual rulers.[25]

If a king or queen were illegitimate, favoured certain courtiers or ignored baronial privilege, he or she could justly be deposed as a usurper or tyrant.[26] Every king or queen of the Tudor and Stuart dynasties saw a major uprising. When Parliament violently opposed King Charles I and the Cromwellian Commonwealth was created, however, non-monarchical government became a realistic alternative, but the role of religious dissent, for example Puritanism, as a uniquely English source of resistance theory may have been overestimated in the past.[27] The reception of republican theory remained elitist after 1688 but reinvigorated a multilateral ideal of responsible government that had first flourished in the power struggles of the Anglo-Norman period.[28] Although Macpherson quipped that the Glorious Revolution in Scotland had been little more than 'a change of tyrants',[29] the 'Revolution of 1688' began a considerable theoretical clarification of royal duties,[30] and also the duties of those who interacted with British monarchs.[31]

This was expressed, for instance, in the consistent publication of academic and educational works such as legal and political dictionaries. One law dictionary reprinted twice in the early eighteenth century was a once-banned early seventeenth-century publication. Written by John Cowell (1554–1611) in his last years, the dictionary defined common legal terms and described the central competencies of British constitutional institutions such as the king or queen. It was republished in a sixth edition in 1708, and its foreword, provided by the bishop and antiquarian White Kennet (1660–1728), recounted the controversy that the dictionary had created when it was first published in 1607. As Cowell, in the opinion of the Commons, overemphasized royal prerogative, King James VI/I was asked to suppress the book, which he did in a proclamation of 1610.[32] Readers who had already bought the book were ordered to submit their copies to the Lord Mayor of London or to sheriffs in their counties. But in 1640 the book saw an unexpurgated second edition, and several more were issued up until 1727.[33]

Despite its controversial contents, the book must have been successful as a concise and alphabetically ordered work of reference; it offered readers of several generations necessary ammunition in the ontological warfare that surrounded constitutional debates at least since the mid-seventeenth century. The foreword to the 1708 edition justly noted that it was 'infinitely hard to speak of Prerogative, Property, Government, Laws, and mutual Rights, with that caution and regard, as not to make some to murmur, and others to insult'.[34] The evolution of British kingship was never a break with past concepts but rather a cyclic reinterpretation of a broad set of rights and duties in which theoretical consensus was occasionally valued more than the actual business of government.

While James VI/I's proclamation condemning Cowell's book still described the 'deepest mysteries of Monarchy and Politick Government' as 'things above their [men of "civilian professions"] capacity' and announced that books on such subjects should henceforth be 'more narrowly looked into', the Glorious Revolution made constitutional debates a public matter.[35] According to Cowell's dictionary, the king or queen 'hath the highest Power, and absolute rule over the whole Land'.[36] This power was inherently linked to the monarch's being 'a Corporation in himself' and 'not subject to his death'.[37] Cowell's definition was used verbatim in Timothy Cunningham's *New and Complete Law Dictionary* of 1765. But Cunningham went into more detail, explaining royal prerogative and its limits.[38] So by the 1760s, the qualities of kingship depended entirely on the validity of the British constitution at large.[39] In a 1765 session in Parliament, whose proceedings were published in the *Scots Magazine*, a clear distinction between the constitutional identity embodied by the monarch and the ill effects of unjust ministerial decisions was discussed as follows:

> though it be a maxim of our constitution That the King can do wrong, yet if any wrong be done, the King's ministers and advisers may be punished for it: and from parity of reason, though it be a maxim, That the King pays no costs, yet if a groundless and vexatious prosecution be commenced in the King's name, his ministers, who commenced, or advised commencing, that prosecution, ought at least to be obliged to pay the costs which an innocent subject has thereby been put to.[40]

Throughout the eighteenth century, many political debates among the educated did not explicitly mention the ruling monarch but focused on two concepts deeply rooted in Britain's history: *law* and *liberty*. These concepts provided a rhetorical framework in which power relations could be renegotiated in the spirit of constitutional continuity. Following the discursive tradition of the sixteenth and seventeenth centuries, both government supporters and oppositions referred to the two concepts as their guiding arguments, and thus contributed to a process of juridicization essential for the development of early modern European states.[41] In 1683, Tory publicist Edmund Bohun had equated being 'faithful to the Law' with loyalty to the existing royal government.[42] The Revolution settlement fostered a positive evaluation of reform and 'an increasing (if still incomplete) willingness towards a compromise that allowed rival views to coexist',[43] but also led to a renegotiation of the credo 'liberty through law',[44] which had shaped English politics since the later Middle Ages.[45] In the decades after 1688, idealists who wished to settle kingship on the 'best man in the kingdom' competed with pragmatists,[46] who concentrated on an undisputable line of succession.[47] The question was whether good government depended on able rulers alone, or if it depended solely on reliable constitutional regulations.[48] Whigs presumed that a reduction of state interference – above all in religious matters – would best secure it, whereas Tories believed that the abolishment of the penal laws and other regulations would eventually destroy traditional English liberties.[49] In many Jacobite tracts, the central argument for the restoration of the Stuart monarchy was also an unbroken rule of law.[50] In battle and in dealing with civilians during the Jacobite campaigns, Jacobites took care to cautiously and justly apply martial law and prove themselves true adherents to the ancient British constitution. Their opponents, however, denounced their version of liberty as 'slavery'.[51]

Regional pro- and anti-Jacobite riots – often incited by members of the lower classes such as domestic servants – likewise expressed concern for Britain's legal traditions. During the trial at the Old Bailey on 6 September 1716 of John Love, Thomas Bean, George Purchase, Richard Price and William Price, for damage to property, the rioters were accused of rude anti-Hanoverian polemics,[52] but the *Last Speech and Confession of Thomas Bean, one of those Executed for the late Riot in Salisbury-Court at London* mentioned neither the Hanoverians nor the Stuarts. Rather, the printed pamphlet detailed the rioters' alleged zeal for 'the ancient Laws of this Kingdom, and the undoubted Liberties of this once Free People'.[53] The insurgents had stood up to 'certain Diabolical Healths publickly drunk in Defiance of all Law, as well as Religion, and particularly of Confusion to the Church of England'.[54] Although this confession was most likely not written by Thomas Bean but by a High Churchman fearing the growing influence of Protestant dissent, it presents a recurring narrative in post-revolutionary conflicts: Monarchs had become constitutionally non-essential in the face of overarching state formation, whereas the central conflict played out between more generally liberal and etatist concepts of governance.[55] Just as much as the Jacobite rebellions have been termed 'the last aristocratic rebellions' in British history,[56] they also emerged as the first constitutionally motivated uprisings whose reasoning was by no means backward but amplified organizational concerns that had already been voiced during the Glorious Revolution.[57]

In the following decades, the juxtaposition of liberty and slavery, which had dominated the rhetoric of the Jacobite risings, was replaced by an even firmer rhetorical symbiosis of law and liberty when the 'Wilkes and Liberty' debate of the 1760s,[58] and the American patriots' fight against British colonial administration escalated. In 1764, government attempts to publicly burn issue 45 of the *North Briton*, in which oppositional politician John Wilkes had mocked the royal government, were interrupted by rioters.[59] In 1768, another protest in favour of John Wilkes, then imprisoned for seditious libel, was violently quelled at St George's Fields, London, and saw innocent bystander William Allen killed.[60] The great popularity that Wilkes thus gained made his supporters wear pins commemorating issue 45 of the *North Briton*, circulate prints celebrating Wilkes as a champion of liberty and produce items of everyday use, such as mugs and teapots, depicting his portrait.[61] At the outbreak of the American Revolution, conservative observers in Britain felt that the patriots' interpretation of liberty opposed 'the undenied power of the British legislature',[62] and was nothing but 'a cloke [*sic.*] of maliciousness'.[63] The anonymous author who used the pseudonym *Political Looking-Glass* in the *Morning Post* of 22 September 1775 suggested that riots and rebellions were especially numerous 'in this Country [the American colonies] more than any other, where freedom is the wide boundary, and every species of licentiousness reigns unchecked, under the veil of liberty; every settled form of government becomes a load, and variety, as to the prostitute, becomes a charm to every republican and factious Spirit'.[64]

In moderate circles, which feared 'the Gallic principles of sanguinary reform',[65] liberty was contrasted not only with tyrannical perversions of royal power, but also with every attempt to overturn the law. George III 'was not a tyrant', even in the age of 'personal government'.[66] As a consequence, critics no longer feared the once-contested negative veto invested in the monarch but 'the bribes and emoluments now given to the members of Parliament'.[67] Especially after 'the fall of George III's prime minister, Lord North' in 1782,[68] the British monarchy seemed to be firmly embedded in a balanced constitution. Legal constraints on royal and, more generally, aristocratic power were not unique to Britain, but also shaped monarchies on the continent. Similar to Britain's much-praised 'rule of law',[69] even pre-revolutionary France was a 'judicial society', in which the king took pride in following and applying the principles of the law.[70] France, however, was also an 'administrative monarchy', in which law courts were independent enough to openly criticize the government but where a rigid organization of public and courtly life only permitted sporadic interventions.[71] When France saw a clash of 'the divine right of kings, rooted in tradition and most clearly expressed in the ceremony of anointment, and those who advocated a contractual monarchy based on natural law theories',[72] English political theory had moved beyond dichotomies. British concepts of royal rule aligned more with the German model, which could tolerate a higher degree of 'royal incompetence' than France.[73] Britain's highly competitive political culture played out in Parliament as well as in its courts of law, which gave monarchs a more passive yet also less assailable metapolitical position.[74]

The old Roman paradigm 'Salus reip[ublicae] Suprema lex esto',[75] 'the welfare of the republic ought to be the highest law', was cited by authors who wished to balance the pre-revolutionary emphasis on eternally binding laws and inherited power on the one hand and the post-1688 emphasis on more flexible parliamentary legislation on the other.[76] A traditional idea of 'republican liberty',[77] which was closely bound to the fulfilment of public duties, prevailed across the political spectrum and placed the general welfare of the nation above the rights of individual freemen.[78] This eighteenth-century constitutionalism implied that the Crown was the 'Head of the Commonwealth',[79] bound by oath but also an institution beyond faction. The ideal of no-party or neutral kingship was put forth by authors adhering to different political and religious groups.

One prominent proponent was Henry St John, 1st Viscount Bolingbroke. He saw the 'fury of party' of the early Hanoverian period as a relic of peer bonding,[80] which hindered the rise of true patriotism (see Chapter 3). Parties and their 'measures of unexpected violence' Bolingbroke said, were the sole reason for the Jacobite rebellions and the involvement of George I, whom he saw as 'no way sanguinary', in a bloody war.[81] Conservative strands of Enlightenment thought created the image of politically neutral kingship as a strong counterpart to party politics, localism and religious factions.[82] Bolingbroke outlined his concept of monarchical patriotism in his book *The Patriot King*. Originally written in 1738, it was officially published in 1749 and became a guideline of the country party and a standard reference of Britain's conservative Enlightenment.[83] In Bolingbroke's conception of a limited monarchy, patriotism was the most important virtue for king and citizens alike because it would help monarchs choose the right mode of administration and nourish moderate opposition.[84] This thoroughly political concept of royal leadership outshone older ideals of the British monarch such as the Protestant 'miles Christianus' ('Christian soldier').[85] Both Restoration concepts of the monarch's divine right and theories of an original contract dwindled in favour of a pragmatic historicization of government within the confines of a constitution: 'Likewise our King is such by the Fundamental Law of the Land: by which Law the meanest Subject enjoys the Liberty of his Person, and Property in his Estate; and it is every Man's Concern to defend these, as well as the King in his lawful Rights.'[86]

Although the Revolution of 1688 had 'deprived posterity [the Stuarts] of the liberty of exercising the same right',[87] it established a new dynastic succession to which all citizens owed obedience as long as governing monarchs fulfilled their duties.[88] If British kings failed to comply, the people had a right 'to pull down Oppression',[89] but would have to elect a new monarch 'from within the reigning family'.[90] In addition to the control of the monarchy exercised by Parliament and the law courts, the eighteenth century also broadened control vertically.[91] Strengthened by an expanding media market, the monarchy was also observed by a reading public whose educated members actively contributed to the interpretation of the nation's constitution.[92] The spread of bespoke news media from the mid-seventeenth century had made politics accessible to non-elites and often relied on strategies of 'public diplomacy',[93] for example through the dissemination of real and alleged intercepted letters.[94]

In this environment, neutral kingship was a paragon of peace and unity in a divided nation, but it also involved the risk of rendering monarchy replaceable. This risk was inherently linked with an enlightened valorization of acquired skills and financial resources over inherited privileges. In an economy dependent on global trade, people of the highest social rank, traditionally belonging to the landowning class, did not necessarily have access to the greatest sources of income or the expertise to manage market developments, which could threaten their political status. An autonomization of economic policy had already set in when the Crown outsourced its finances to the Exchequer in the early thirteenth century.[95] Now the executive had to conform to new ideals of austerity that gave those controlling trade and finances inherent political power. Temporary army funding was replaced by permanent national debt, cementing this peculiar dependency.[96] Passing new governmental budgets, imposing taxation and collecting revenue became acknowledged political tasks and bureaucratic procedures, while financial success evolved as a major criterion of good governance.[97] As a consequence, political factions began to represent conflicting economic interests, which at least temporarily replaced other divides such as religious convictions. While Whigs were mostly concerned with 'trade and empire',[98] favouring an expansionist foreign policy and free investments, Tories stood up for 'the landed interest',[99] and for Britain's domestic agriculture. The Tory and Jacobite oppositions of the early Hanoverian reign accused George I's Whig ministry of mingling their private interests with the supposed welfare of the nation, and denounced the 'monied interest' as corruption and sedition.[100] In the eyes of Tory observers, an unbalanced public household was the main grievance of the 1720s to 1740s.[101] Government debt and the subsequent inability of the state to equip an army, whenever 'the nation is threaten'd with an invasion [or] a rebellion is suspected or broke out at home',[102] were frequently addressed as the major 'folly of our statesmen'.[103] All factions, however, judged British monarchs and their ministers by their economic foresight.[104] This was in line with an international 'shift from "ceremonial representative" to "economic cameralist" monarchical legitimation',[105] which responded to earlier discourses on luxury and frugality.[106]

Yet in their responses to economic crises, British monarchs either remained deliberately silent or incapacitated while vocal partisan groups addressed fears of rising public expenses and increasing taxes.[107] Among the eighteenth-century texts that openly acknowledged the limited influence of monarchs on adverse climates, crop failures and exploitive business schemes was, ironically, an anti-rebellion poem published in a collection of educational verses in 1795.[108] The only consolation the poem could offer was that the situation in many other parts of Europe was supposedly worse. In the 1760s and 1770s, the taxation crisis in America and the economic decline of the East India Company added to a culture of rationality and competition in which economic reasoning either created new connections between different strata of society or caused new divisions. In many eighteenth-century riots, violence was directed against economically privileged groups such as merchants, and the overall conflict lines seemed to be hard to pinpoint. In March 1769, a riot accompanied the merchants' address to the king at St James, which provoked newspapers, including the *Bath and Bristol Chronicle*, to mention several conflicting motivations. While some reports alleged that the rioters feared that the merchants intended to complain about 'a certain popular gentleman' (i.e. John Wilkes),[109] banners carried suggested that the death of 'young Allen' at the hand of soldiers in the 1768 riot in St George's Fields was behind the uproar.[110] In addition, one article in the *Bath and Bristol Chronicle* even stated that 'the dislike expressed in the city to the Trader's procession yesterday, was not so much from the rabble as from the better sort of people, who were almost unanimously against it, and publicly avowed their disapprobation by hissing and hooting at their own doors'. Nonetheless, rioters apologized to two dukes when they had 'mistaken their Graces for some other persons' and thrown dirt at their carriages.[111] And although the paper also published the merchants' actual address and the king's response, which was more opaque than the rioters may have feared, the newspaper coverage presented George III as a mere bystander in the conflict.[112] The king's *Proclamation for suppressing riots, tumults, and unlawful assemblies* occasioned by the events of 22 March did not address the specific circumstances of the St James's riot but remained highly formulaic, which reflected the general crisis in royal communication.

Proclamations as a central media of exercising royal prerogative and communicating with subjects are described in the previously mentioned law dictionaries of the eighteenth century. While Cowell's dictionary, originally published in 1607, merely stated that a proclamation was 'a Notice publickly given of any thing, whereof the King thinks fit to advertise his Subjects',[113] Cunningham listed several specific occasions on which proclamations could be used. Among the prerogative acts a monarch could issue by proclamation were the calling and dissolution of Parliament, declarations of war and peace, the appointment of fasts and days of thanksgiving, and the legitimation of foreign coins.[114]

A valid proclamation, Cunningham stressed, had to be issued under the great seal. Proclamations had seen a considerable rise in the rule of Queen Anne, where they were mainly used to enforce parliamentary legislation. They were an important tool to expand royal power across space and time, also symbolizing the procedural refinement of eighteenth-century politics. Proclamations were not the law itself but a communicational measure that proved the monarch's vigilance and care for the country. However, such general exhortations eventually led oppositional groups to harshly deconstruct royal communication, even more so as the expanding eighteenth-century newspaper market exposed monarchs and their governments to increasing public scrutiny.[115] Although most proclamations did not necessarily reflect the monarch's personal views, they could be misread as arbitrary and oppressive by subjects who did not have access to the political networks in and around London. Queen Anne's *Proclamation for the due observance of an act made in the last session of Parliament*, for instance, stated:

> We are therefore taking the same into Our serious Consideration, to the end no person may pretend Ignorance of the said Law, and the Penalties, by Virtue thereof, to be Inflicted on such as shall Act contrary thereunto, have thought fit, by the Advice of Our Privy-Council, to Issue this Our Royal Proclamation.[116]

By its nature, a proclamation was a unidirectional affirmation of laws and did not allow for a response.[117] If subjects wanted to address their grievances to the monarch, they needed to petition, but petitioning was a great logistic challenge for inhabitants of the British Empire's more remote regions. As most areas experienced the monarch's permanent absence, the abundance of peacekeeping proclamations issued against riots and revolts exposed a problematic disconnection between the symbolic powers of kingship and a failure to embody this power across distances. Proclamations as the royal medium par excellence were, therefore, exposed to criticism and subversion in several crises of the eighteenth century.

Competing Stuart and Hanoverian media strategies during the Jacobite Rebellions in 1715 and 1745–6 showed how important a careful synthesis of different, textual and performative, communication channels was to monarchical rule. Temporary successes of the Stuarts were owed to the family's skilled use of media in politically and historically significant spaces, supported by sympathizers across Europe.[118] George I's Huguenot secretary Robethon reported to the king's ministers in Hanover in November 1714 that the Pretender had published declarations to assert his rights, and sent them to his followers in Scotland as well as to members of the royal household and the government in London.[119] Although James Francis Stuart (known as 'the Pretender') was not physically present during most of the campaign, and even though his personality was anything but staggering, his royal printing press in France and partisan printers in Britain efficiently arranged for his virtual presence.[120] Robethon related to Hanover that Scottish Jacobites, whom he called 'les chefs des Rebelles', frequently gathered in council meetings ('leur grand conseil') to give their actions and decisions legitimacy.[121] When James Francis finally arrived in Scotland, George I's ministers were far more worried about his attempts to proclaim himself king at the medieval Scottish coronation site of Scone than by his military actions.[122] Likewise, James Francis's son, Charles Edward Stuart, gained substantial ground during the first half of his campaign as he and his supporters combined the publication of proclamations with a visibly staged presence. On the day of his landing, the prince is said to have published two proclamations, which had been prepared and printed in Rome. During his advance south, Charles Edward released further instructions in order to establish a new administration and win over procrastinators. In his autobiography, Jacobite soldier James Johnstone explicitly mentioned that Charles Edward Stuart

> published several edicts [in Edinburgh], one of which prohibited all public rejoicings on account of the victory obtained over General Cope, as it was purchased at the expense of the blood of his subjects. In another, he granted a general amnesty for all treasons, rebellions, or offences whatever, committed against him or his predecessors, since the revolution of 1688, provided the aggressors repaired to the palace of Holyrood-house within the space of four days, and made a declaration in presence of his secretary, that they would live in future under his government as quiet and peaceable subjects. He also sent circular letters to the magistrates of all the towns in Scotland, commanding them to repair immediately to Edinburgh, to pay their proportion of the contributions which he imposed on every town; and he dispatched other letters to all the collectors and controllers of the land-tax and customs, ordering them to bring to his palace their books and the public money in their hands, on pain of high treason.[123]

As soon as the Jacobite troops had crossed the English border, however, and dissension arose about whether they ought to march on London, the Young Pretender's public profiling seems to have ebbed away. The disastrous Battle of Culloden in April 1746 was above all a psychological blow to the Stuart campaign as it gave rise to rampant media speculation.[124] The uncertainty of Charles Edward's fate for most of 1746 concerned and confused his friends as much as his enemies: press reports ranged from the prince's death to adventurous stories of escape.[125] In the aftermath of the rebellion, Jacobite literature of the time appealed to 'personalities and romance',[126] contrasting the Stuarts' merciful commitment to the happiness of their people with the despotic cruelty of King George II and his son, the Duke of Cumberland.[127] Without physical demonstrations of Stuart claims, however, the throne was no longer attainable, and the Hanoverian dynasty had a similar experience when distance communication failed in North America.

Disappointed with British rule in the colonies and recent 'unpopular actions' passed by Parliament,[128] patriot authors and publishers systematically ridiculed hierarchical forms of political communication on the part of the king as well as on the part of London-appointed colonial governors. American patriots even broke the rule that 'no private person can make any proclamation of a publick nature'.[129] When General Thomas Gage made an offer of amnesty and oblivion to the patriot insurgents but excepted Samuel Adams and John Hancock as the principal leaders,[130] his offer was considered supercilious and injurious by the American public.[131] Although most of the governors' briefs and proclamations published in the colonies concerned uncontroversial business such as feasts and fasts, popular complaints or collections for the victims of a great fire in Canada,[132] colonial North Americans opposed the highly formalized genre of official proclamations and the 'bureaucratic concepts of citizenship' behind them.[133] Above all, the patriot movement expressed its unease with 'confusing voices from nowhere', and the 'reproduction of voice detached from the body'.[134] In reaction, proclamations were also parodied in print.[135] In his proclamation of 14 June 1775, Gage raged against 'the infatuated Multitudes, who have long suffered themselves to be conducted by certain well-known Incendiaries and Traitors, in a fatal Progression of Crimes, against the constitutional Authority of the State'.[136] The day after, patriots reprinted his proclamation, calling it 'an infamous Thing handed about here Yesterday [...] replete with consummate Impudence, the most abominable Lies, and stuffed with daring Expressions of Tyranny, as well as Rebellion against the established, constitutional Authority of the AMERICAN STATES'.[137] In the newly added headline, Thomas Gage himself was decried as a 'perfidious, petty Tyrant'.[138] And Jonathan Trumbull's mock proclamation called *A New Proclamation* of the same year went even further.[139] *Notes to the Burlesque* once more attacked Thomas Gage and suggested that he would not be able to exercise the powers that he held according to his proclamation.[140] Trumbull's aim was to 'inspire [...] Contempt of the British Troops, [and to] throw Contempt on the Tories'.[141] When patriots began to issue their own instructions to the American public, layout and style were strikingly different (see Chapter 5). Instead of insignia of power and rank, patriot publications highlighted content and often presented text in simple newspaper-style columns.[142] After the American Revolution, a 'patriotic proclamation' entitled *Caricature Anticipations* appeared in London.[143] It attacked 'the rapid progress of political corruption',[144] as well as the decline of religion and morals.[145] The mock proclamation was one of the most creative oppositional media genres of the century.

Between 1765 and the treason trials of the mid-1790s, unilateral royal and government communication lost ground to more simplified, dialectical and above all dialogue-oriented modes of political communication that were often championed by oppositions.[146] In print publications relating to inner-British political conflicts of the later eighteenth century, the king was often only present by title (*Rex*) as trials against rioters or presumed conspirators were instigated by the Attorney General and tried at the King's Bench. Several of these trials involved members of reform-oriented citizen associations and highlighted an even more challenging form of political imitation: In the high treason trial of Robert Watt and David Downie of 1794, they and other members of the so-called British Convention, a joint body of the corresponding societies in England and the Scottish Friends of the People, were accused of mimicking organizational structures and self-descriptions popularized by the revolutionaries in France.[147]

Simultaneously, British radicals spoke of kingship more with belittling irony than hatred. This attitude can be traced in the printed pamphlets produced on behalf of the men arrested for an alleged attempt to assassinate King George III with a poisoned arrow in 1794 (known as the so-called *Pop-Gun Plot*.[148] While Thomas Upton was suspected of being the mechanic expert behind the construction of the weapon, Robert Thomas Crosfield had allegedly made drawings to guide the production.[149] In the pamphlet *Assassination of the King! The Conspirators exposed*, presented as an impartial 'account of the apprehension, treatment in prison, and repeated examination before the Privy Council of John Smith and George Higgins, on a charge of High Treason' but produced by Smith himself, Crosfield acknowledged that Upton had informed him of making an air-gun, 'but without mentioning whether to kill a king, a thief, or a mad dog'.[150] John Smith brought forth in his defence that the death of a weak, inactive king would make little difference and could not have resulted in the desired change of government.[151] Pamphlets defending the accused also pointed to the king's insignificance to the actual government,[152] and the international press described Britain as a semi-elective oligarchy threatened by 'disloyal, treasonable royal advisors' ('treulose, verrätherische Rathgeber des Königs'),[153] and the 'court faction'.[154] This tied in with biblical condemnations of 'evil counsellors',[155] which were often used by clerical authors defending the British monarchy or merely advocating moderate reform.

The anti-monarchical tendencies of the Civil War era were thus largely eclipsed by anti-ministerialism. Although 'absolutism',[156] as well as 'tyranny',[157] were still frequently voiced battle cries of the opposition, the Crown was by no means the only target of the disaffected.[158] British kingship was, by the end of the eighteenth century, so interpretable that it could be integrated into a wide range of possible constitutional scenarios, which may have prevented more violent republican resistance.

In this context, eighteenth-century reports on slave revolts also betray a rather ambivalent image of kingship. Perceptions of these uprisings equally betray an ambivalent image of monarchs. Instead of anti-monarchical and outright revolutionary aims, insurgents of colour were frequently accused of merely wanting to reproduce existing structures.[159] In the mid-eighteenth-century New York Conspiracy, the stereotype that slaves were not capable of planning anything but mediocre imitations of traditional white society was explicitly voiced in court statements against the convicts:

Gentlemen, no scheme more monstrous could have been invented; nor can any thing be thought of more foolish, than the motives that induced these wretches to enter into it! What more ridiculous than that Hughson [one of the accused], in consequence of this scheme, should become a King! Cæsar [another slave on trial], now in gibbets, a Governor![160]

Purported unrest by people of colour was seen as more ridiculous than threatening, which raises the question if the ironic view of Black monarchs also reflected a growing distance from monarchy as a system of government. Public reactions to slave revolts might, indeed, have been different if the establishment of a Black republic such as the one that Haiti set up after 1791 had been at stake. Furthermore, eighteenth-century kingship was constitutionally tamed, replacing heroic individualism with more generally applicable values. British monarchs accepted these values as members of a European aristocracy that was internationally connected and open to Enlightenment discourse. Especially in England, the aristocracy also had a long oppositional tradition that challenged images of royalty from a constitutionally conservative perspective.

For several centuries, the Lords of the Realm had formed a hereditary body of mutual surveillance that could even oppose the monarch by force.[161] The thirteenth and fourteenth centuries were marked by 'barons' revolts' against English kings,[162] and strengthened the role of the nobility as hereditary counterparts to the monarch.[163] The mid-seventeenth-century crisis weakened noble self-reliance all across Europe and institutionalized control mechanisms in councils and law courts, which did not consist of noblemen alone.[164] Nonetheless, British aristocrats and even members of the royal family remained prominent engineers of opposition, for example by siding with the future heir to the throne.[165] Some eighteenth-century noblemen shifted from outright opposition to strong support for a monarch and vice versa.[166] Philip, Duke of Wharton, for example, seems to have had multiple personal, executive and broadly constitutional reasons when he decided to support Jacobitism in a break with his family's allegiance to the Revolution settlement. Wharton's ambition and constant need for money accompanied his political concerns over 'a wicked ministry, supported by a corrupt Majority in Parliament'.[167] He attacked Walpole's dominance of the government and governmental foreign policy because he was personally affected by the stock market collapse of 1720. Yet he also feared that King George I had betrayed essential promises of the Glorious Revolution.[168]

In this twofold function as members of a traditional elite that relied on blood ties and networks of trust, on the one hand, and as members of strictly procedural institutions such as Parliament, on the other, noblemen could contribute to a circumspect redefinition of kingship. At the same time, their political and legal roles afforded new justifications.[169] When predominantly functional definitions of the nobility supplanted dynastic solidarity and personal obligations towards subjects,[170] being noble was no longer a trait that was passively inherited from one's ancestors.[171] Although exceptional bodily features such as greater height, higher weight or earlier sexual maturity still mattered as outward signs of noble birth in the mid-eighteenth century, they combined with an emphasis on individual achievement.[172] Noblemen's political power was gradually 'demystified',[173] and the physical and emotional particularities of the aristocracy, which allegedly equipped them for leadership, had to be matched with actual commitment and effort.[174]

Moreover, the gentry and nobility had to adapt to new economic limitations. Embracing technical progress and 'a new form of consumer culture',[175] Britain's aristocratic elites defended their social and political position more successfully than their peers in other European regions.[176] On an individual level, British monarchs, too, could benefit from a more modern self-representation in architecture, art or music, although they failed to mitigate the adverse effects of economic change for the lower classes. For example, the Enlightenment introduced new concepts of politeness and honour that replaced presumably affected manners of the courtier for the ideal of the decent citizen ('*redlicher Bürger*').[177] This bourgeois turn in leadership also went along with a renegotiation of gender roles and gendered metaphors of leadership, especially when comparing monarchical and republican governments.

Observing the unfolding revolution in America, continental European observers tried to understand the difference between monarchical and republican leadership.[178] In his 1781 study *On North America and Democracy*, Prussian oppositional writer Johann Christian Schmohl, born as a farmer's son in Anhalt-Zerbst, dealt with royalist accusations that democracy was tyranny under a different name. Schmohl willingly conceded that democracy resulted in the rule of the few over the many just as monarchy did, but he was convinced that time-limited governments and a democratic right of the mighty one ('*Stärkerecht*') would not generate governments 'despotically through riches, honour of birth and therefore factitious attachment, [...] but through innate strength and virtues'.[179] In antagonism to those who had fearfully compared the masterminds of the American Revolution to Lord Protector Oliver Cromwell (1599–1658) and his son Richard (1626–1712), Schmohl said that experiences of usurpation in the past should not blind his contemporaries to examples of human greatness in the present.[180] The prolonged perseverance of the American cause proved to him that those who had incited opposition to the Crown had not been motivated by frail greed or ambition, but by genuine patriotism.[181] Fittingly, the conservative supposition that a respectable leader was a 'father of his country',[182] above all, enraged radical Republicans of the 1770s and 1780s.[183] Schmohl followed the French Enlightenment and opposed family-related metaphors for government because any political system modelled on blood ties, marital love or both would eventually betray the sovereignty of the people.[184] Even in biblical times, he argued, the power of judges and kings had solely fed on 'personal strength and virtues, especially military ones', which secured voluntary obedience ('*freywillige Folger*'),[185] and the easy replacement of men who failed.

When family-related political metaphors declined, gender, sexuality and the political role of women likewise appeared in a different light.[186] The lust and licentiousness of monarchs and their family members had been essential elements of satire and propaganda at least since the Protestant Reformation,[187] but the eighteenth century exploited alleged sexual degradation even more ubiquitously as a metaphor of political intrigue and unmerited leadership in opposition to virtue and 'superior humaneness'.[188] After the death of King George II and Prince Frederick, Dowager Princess Augusta and John Stuart, Earl of Bute, her late husband's friend and her son George's tutor, became the major targets of sexualized public criticism in

England. German-born Princess Augusta was accused of an affair with the Scottish nobleman, and their non-English descent added to their ill repute.[189] However, the traditional fear of female influence on politics was far less prominent in their opponents' publications than the accusation that Lord Bute took advantage of the widow's loneliness and weakness.[190] Male conduct and male role models were clearly at the centre of the debate as political cultures in both Britain and America experienced considerable 'masculinization'.[191]

Nevertheless, women – as wives and female heroines in literature and art – were necessary to highlight the non-military, civic aspects of men's lives. Some women, namely 'patriotic ladies' and female freeholders,[192] supported oppositional politician John Wilkes ideologically and sent him presents, but they were in a danger of being ridiculed if their intellectual independence and modern lifestyles were considered 'disreputable'.[193] Femininity stood for emotional, individual decision-making in an increasingly bureaucratic system of politics. Romantic encounters with women who did not necessarily share men's political opinions or women's bravery as accomplices in escapes were an almost stereotypical ingredient of rebellion narratives.[194] Especially in revolutionary America, patriotic female characters dedicated to their families and local communities were indispensable for the national communication of ideal citizenship.[195] Although leadership in itself was not feminized, a ruling man's relationships with women (and other 'weaker' members of society) revealed his moral character to the world.[196] The assault by mentally ill Margaret Nicholson on King George III in 1786, though unavailing, boosted the king's popularity because of the presumed compassion and forgiveness he showed towards the attacker. In this instant, the king embodied human qualities valued in enlightened English society, and future British monarchs, too, were primarily expected to give their nation's sentiments on moral and social issues a voice. Liberals and conservatives of the 1790s alike promoted a remarkably 'sentimental' image of kingship,[197] which was – according to Linda Colley and John Barrell – increased by George III's illness and the Regency crisis.[198] In the British public, the 'king's paternal "tenderness" for his people',[199] and his own vulnerability, echoed British abhorrence of the imprisonment of the royal family in France.[200]

Last but not the least, several European princes robed care for the nation in the ideal of a rational, unpretentious and hard-working 'soldier king',[201] whose talents were most impressively exemplified by Frederick II of Prussia and to a lesser degree embodied by Frederick II of Hesse-Kassel.[202] On the one hand, military forces quickly professionalized and standing armies became more and more frequent, but, on the other hand, kings tended to refrain from active warfare. King George II was the last British king to take up arms in battle: his professional interest in military affairs was sincere, his armed forces served an important representative purpose.[203] Just as much as the Church of England and the royal army offered noblemen, gentry and bourgeoisie influence and recognition beyond the political sphere, they helped to maintain solidarity within a diverse society at least until the mid-nineteenth century. Consequentially, the universal eighteenth-century abhorrence of 'unkingly cruelty' and excessive state violence did not primarily reflect real atrocities,[204] but constituted a more general narrative of good governance that recontextualized and enforced old theories of humanity and peace.[205]

Although eighteenth-century political culture welcomed purposeful state violence,[206] the actual use of force was limited. Apart from Christian humanism, the centralization of the administration contained older forms of feud, self-defence or local policing and encouraged the appeal to courts rather than armed conflict. The image of the 'real patriot' provided British political debates with a socially inclusive rhetoric,[207] and cemented Britain's middle position between French concepts of royal singularity and German egalitarianism.[208] Although political representation eventually amounted to 'interest intermediation' through delegates,[209] a more traditional top-down communication of power relations and political identity survived.[210] Both the British Empire and the young United States promoted representative rule as an antidote to plebiscitary rule, and the Americans retained monarchical elements in the public representation of presidential power.[211] Regardless of their political systems, early modern societies sought checks and balances (either structural or situational) to ensure the best rule possible. As more diverse groups became visible and audible in the public sphere through their own voices or through influential advocates, the criteria that applied to the legitimate exercise of power also became more complex.

Chapter 3 examines criticism aimed at Parliament and equally highlights how vital a revision of communicational strategies was for public conflict management in the eighteenth century.

3

Parliament, parties and politicians: Conflict negotiation through representation

Eighteenth-century riots and rebellions challenged the role of Parliament as profoundly as that of the Crown. Critics of the period perceived the London Parliament as too permanent and too powerful. The Triennial Act of 1694, which had ensured frequent elections, was superseded by the Septennial Act in 1716, which incited fierce debates on 'the Abuse of Standing Parliaments, and the Great Advantage of Frequent Elections'.[1] Controversies over elections, lawmaking and the men in Parliament led to new oppositional strategies both within and beyond the two Houses. Several riots and rebellions of the eighteenth century were at least partly motivated by opposition to parliamentary politics or by opposition to individual members. Open protest also affected the Irish Parliament in Dublin.

Violent expressions of discontent often blended with non-violent agitation (e.g. through media campaigns) and were carried out by visible, self-conscious interest groups. Throughout the eighteenth century, these groups (often led by skilled communicators and connecting Parliament with local voters or even the non-voting public) were associated with the concept of *party*. As Max Skjönsberg has noted in his study *Persistence of Party*, party or partisanship described a broad range of eighteenth-century movements, ranging from the Whig and Tory parties to religious divisions (also see Chapter 4), juxtapositions of court and country, antagonisms of the Lords and Commons, or a 'political or parliamentary connection, that is, a smaller political group led by an identifiable leader'.[2]

As their organizational levels varied, these parties have to be distinguished from modern political parties with their clear-cut ideological frameworks, membership and legal status. Nevertheless, the eighteenth-century controversies over party were vital to the highly competitive nature of British political culture and informed debates on constitutional reforms, last but not the least in revolutionary America. Tracing the position of Parliament after the Glorious Revolution and three types of Parliament-related resistance, this chapter analyses how the concept of party escalated or de-escalated conflicts, how extra-parliamentary oppositions evolved and how the perception of men active in politics changed.

Whereas a Whig interpretation of parliamentary history suggested that parliaments of the early Stuart period had functioned as England's opposition *per curiam*, recent scholarship analysing early seventeenth-century narratives of parliamentary practices suggests that, even then, parliament was perceived as an 'arena of faction' but – in contrast to the Tudor period – frequently described in distinctly 'politic terms'.[3] This means that histories of Parliament written in the early Stuart period demonstrated a clear sense of 'rule-based processes', 'procedural infractions' and even 'institutional failure'.[4] Parliament was, in this perspective, not treated as exceptional but discussed in a larger context of decision-making assemblies including ecclesiastical assemblies, 'trading companies' or 'borough assemblies'.[5] The 1640s saw a 'vulgarisation of knowledge about how parliament worked'.[6] In King Charles II's and King James VII/II's reigns, Parliament acquired greater influence on lawmaking as well as extensive 'judicial capacities',[7] and moved towards the administrative centre of the state. The considerable participation in government business achieved by Parliament during the Glorious Revolution undermined Parliament's claim to impartially control the monarchy and weakened its intercessional functions.[8] The Whig journal *Pegasus* run by John Dunton even stated in 1696 that there was no need to argue over James VII/II's hereditary rights because 'our Representatives in Parliament, who are certainly the best Judges in the World as to our own Constitution, have determined it otherwise'.[9] Most importantly, though, the Revolution Settlement 'force[d] the Crown to bargain with Parliament over the main revenues of the state',[10] and moved Parliament from topical political action to institutionalized politics. Although early Hanoverian government was still a 'household government […] in the shadow of the throne',[11] the Glorious Revolution supplemented traditional baronial rights to 'veto new taxes', with extensive parliamentary rights to 'veto new debt'.[12]

While English Whigs of the late seventeenth and early eighteenth centuries claimed that the 'wishes of the nation' rested in the 'wisdom' of the Lords and the Commons,[13] the Jacobite Risings betrayed a polymorphic and cross-cultural opposition against the Revolution Settlement.[14] At the same time, parliamentary politics were shaped by an often uncompromising Whig–Tory division. In historiography, the 'age of party rage' has been dated to the last two decades of the seventeenth century and the first two decades of the eighteenth century.[15] Specific historiographic dating, however, differs. While some historians situate the peak of party struggle more narrowly between the Glorious Revolution and the Peace of Utrecht in 1713,[16] others suggest the Hanoverian accession in 1714,[17] the Septennial Act (1716) or the end of the Bangorian controversy in 1721 (see Chapter 4) as the most important markers. The tensions of this era were met with incomprehension abroad and gained Britain the reputation of a troubled and unstable nation.[18] In Queen Anne's reign, Hanoverian intellectuals blamed British controversies over the Treaty of Utrecht,[19] and Protestant division in the north of Europe on the inconsistency and dishonesty of English party politics.[20] And in April 1714, Elisabeth Brandshagen, wife to a Hanoverian minister in London, complained in a letter to her friend Leibniz that England was 'a confuse [*sic.*] nation [which was] very much at varience [*sic.*] with one another', and that 'all the Lords were very hot upon each other'.[21] Steinghens and Leibniz advised that the future King George I should avoid any partiality with either Whigs or Tories.[22] By June 1715, however, George I sided with the Whigs to secure supplies and executive powers in a time of conflict.[23] According to Cruickshanks and Bennet, this alienated 'the vast majority of his new subjects who supported the cause of the Church and the landed interest [from the beginning], which drove many Tories into the more radical Jacobite opposition'.[24] This view has been questioned by Linda Colley and Clyve Jones, who thinks 'that only *some* [of the Tory party] were Jacobites, far fewer than Dr. Cruickshanks believes'.[25] Undoubtedly, though, contested political labels played a vital part in public controversies of the early Hanoverian period, and the fierce factionism percolated into local riots instigated by members of the professional classes, domestic servants or students. In these riots, which were often linked with public celebrations or well-frequented places such as taverns, members of the lower classes often echoed polemics that also circulated in pamphlets and papers (see the trial of John Love, Thomas Bean, George Purchase, Richard Price and William Price that is discussed in Chapter 2 and the birthday and coronation riots discussed in Chapter 6). In the first half of the eighteenth century, British observers thus shared a negative view of faction and feared that party polarity could even drive a wedge between the two Houses of Parliament.[26] Speaking on behalf of rebel bishop Francis Atterbury of Rochester in 1723, Philip, Duke of Wharton, cautioned his fellow peers not to abuse their right to issue parliamentary attainders as this might mean 'That the Lives, Liberties, and Fortunes of every Subject in Britain are in the utmost Danger, and liable to be sacrificed to the Fury of a Party'.[27] When the act to inflict pains and penalties on the bishop was nevertheless passed by a majority in the Commons, the Lords protested for fear of losing their status to the Lower House of Parliament.[28]

In this atmosphere of division, violent protest first of all aimed to influence the selection of parliamentary members in both Britain and Ireland. In an attempt to apply the 'Revolution Maxims' of the late seventeenth century not just to the Crown,[29] conflict over the nation's best possible representatives was taken to the streets (see the limited politicization of the people discussed in Chapter 6). Although only a small minority of Britons were eligible to vote, election riots contesting the selection of members for Parliament and other public offices were inherent in British eighteenth-century culture. They allowed non-voting local populations a public and often highly ritualized participation in an otherwise elitist political process. Unfortunately, rioters' motivations are difficult to trace. Although the more problematic election outrages have been recorded in government as well as private correspondence (see Figure 3.1), relevant newspaper reports are mainly limited to a few lines whose stylized language is hard to contextualize. The earliest digitized newspaper record of an election riot to be found in the British Newspaper Archives (at the time of writing) relates to an incident in Galway, Ireland, in 1732:

> We hear from Galway in Ireland, That the Election for a Member to represent that City in Parliament, which began on Monday the 17th of April last, continued for four Days with great Warmth and Opposition. 'Tis said to have cost Edward Eyre, Esq; one of the Candidates, above a Thousand Pounds in the Entertainment of his Friends; notwithstanding which, and the Great Riots and Disorders of the Mob, it was carry'd by a great Majority, and almost universal Concurrence of all the Voters of Distinction and Gentlemen, by Tho. Slaunton, Esq; Recorder of that City.[30]

Despite their brevity, the ubiquity of such reports indicates that representation in Parliament mattered to the constantly growing number of newspaper readers. The

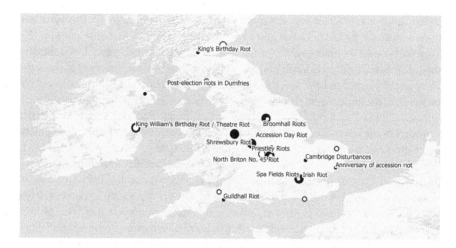

Figure 3.1 Map of eighteenth-century riots relating to elections and political rights in the British Isles. Events in North America can be viewed in the digital map on GitHub: https://monikabarget.github.io/Revolts/event-map/event-map.html

media coverage also matched the time, effort and money that those already sitting in Parliament or running for seats spent negotiating their positions. Especially in the reigns of Anne and George I, contested elections, impeachments, penalties and exclusions occupied much debating time in both houses of Parliament.[31] Private letters exchanged between election candidates testify how carefully election campaigns were crafted, and how important it was to calculate and influence a possible voter turnout in advance. On 21 November 1753, the Rev. William Vyse, canon of Lichfield,[32] wrote from Birmingham to his friend Mr Barker of Lichfield, who hoped to enter the House of Commons for Staffordshire, that he had been active on his behalf: 'Sir, [...] you will let us know when you wou'd have us send our Voters from hence. I wrote such a Letter on Sunday Evening to Southwell of Wellington as I think will at least make him keep his Nephew at Home.'[33]

While most election riots were clashes between indistinct groups of supporters resulting in property damage and minor injuries, the eighteenth century also saw verbal or physical attacks on individual candidates or their more prominent patrons. In 1725, James Scot was attacked by a mob in Dundee on his journey home from an election. He asked that 'punishment be imposed, as further leniency will only mean that no Parliament man' would be safe.[34]

The persistence of election-related outrage throughout the eighteenth century went along with a persistence of party and the importance of publicly visible political allegiance. In older historiography, the concept of party in conjunction with a long-term vision of opposition between parliamentary factions was often associated with Edmund Burke's political writings of the later eighteenth century.[35] Yet initiatives for giving party a more permanent and potentially constructive outlook had already sprung up at the height of the Whig–Tory divide and laid foundations of a 'multi-party structure' that briefly flourished in the later eighteenth century.[36] Max Skjönsberg has analysed more constructive visions of party or faction in the writings of Henry St John, 1st Viscount Bolingbroke (1678–1751).[37] Motivated by his experience as a former Jacobite, Bolingbroke imagined the ideal parliamentary opposition as a reprisal of former country parties that had fought for the preservation of liberty and against the self-enrichment of the court factions.[38] In his opinion, only a permanent opposition that used 'constitutional methods and a legal course of opposition to the excesses of legal and ministerial power' would be able to safeguard the liberties of the nation.[39] Such opposition should be purely functional and focus more on 'things' than on 'people'.[40]

Interestingly, the oppositional Anglican bishop Francis Atterbury,[41] famously involved in a Jacobite plot named after him, also suggested a more callous approach to party when the Tory interest declined after 1714. He suggested that the divided Tories ought to reunite and focus on 'the Church and the landed interests'.[42] Moreover, in order to make their demands heard, they should 'be ready to serve the new King – but as members of a party with definite policies and acknowledged leaders'.[43] Although Atterbury's intentions to collaborate with the Hanoverians were not sincere and he was forced to go into exile in 1723, his pragmatic reflections on party politics tie in with Bolingbroke's.[44] According to both Atterbury and Bolingbroke, party and opposition were not identical yet were necessary for one another. The ultimate defeat of Jacobite attempts to reconquer Britain and Ireland for the Stuart dynasty did not deplete the spirit of opposition, and neither was party a thing of the past.[45] Despite 'the consolidation of the Whig regime in Parliament' in the 1720s, a 'formidable parliamentary opposition' not only persisted but also split into new and powerful factions.[46] And by the second half of the eighteenth century, many political authors accepted party as a natural element of Britain's 'mixed constitution'.[47] The author of the *Politician's Dictionary* found parties in Britain 'almost impossible […] to avoid' because 'the just balance between the republican and monarchical part of our constitution, [was] really in itself so extremely delicate and uncertain, that when joined to men's passions and prejudices, it [was] impossible but different opinions must arise concerning it, even among persons of the best understanding'.[48]

Political goals in the eighteenth-century British Empire were threefold. The first focused on a horizontal balance of power and stressed personal liberties in the tradition of the post-revolutionary Whig faction. The second emphasized a vertical balance of powers and favoured a strong and efficient executive, careful foreign policy and a pronounced imperial identity. This concept was, inter alia, embodied by the Tories, various court factions and loyalists during the American revolution. In between these two, the third consisted of different movements that focused on the development of regional administrations, sought religious emancipation of minorities or condemned ministerial corruption.[49]

As partisan groups, especially those in opposition, became more policy-centred, toned down religious schism,[50] and reconciled with broader concepts of the 'public good',[51] they became 'essential to the practice of politics',[52] and ensured a growing political identity even among the lower classes, building bridges to the purposeful and discernible procedures of organized politics.[53] Charles Watson-Wentworth,

2nd Marquess of Rockingham, was one of the first statesmen who saw a purpose in spending 'most of his career in opposition',[54] and in forming a small but highly motivated opposition party (the so-called Rockingham Whigs, 1766-70). From the 1750s to the end of his political career thirty years later, Lord Rockingham developed an influential concept of party politics and opposition that combined more conservative ideas of elite leadership with a more radical appeal to the public.[55] Rockingham opposed the American Stamp Act,[56] but defended Parliament's rights of general taxation.[57] Much as William Pitt, 1st Earl of Chatham, dreaded moderation as hesitancy,[58] men such as Rockingham championed the figure of the moderate reformer,[59] who would complement the patriot king.[60] Elections in the 1780s showed that political factions on a local level were by then 'socially diverse but ideologically coherent groupings', and attracted the attention of the middle classes.[61]

When Rockingham died in 1782, Charles James Fox, son of successful parliamentarian Henry Fox, took over as the most distinguished oppositional parliamentarian, and perfected the art of resistance on principle.[62] His Whig supporters soon became known as 'Foxites', and even after his death in 1806, he continued to be held up as a champion of liberal reform.[63] With Fox, party politics would become more aggressive and determined, moving on from both traditional Whiggism and 'no party men',[64] such as William Pitt the Younger. While Rockingham had viewed parties as transparent means to formulate minority interests and to legitimately organize opposition,[65] Fox, for his part, perceived parties as more general tools of politics and paved the way for popular political action and an 'extra-parliamentary nation'.[66] In Fox's opinion, opposition was not a task reserved for office holders alone but 'a fundamental attitude of Englishmen both within and outside Parliament'.[67]

In spite of a sense of reform and innovation, however, eighteenth-century political movements also sought deliberate links with the past and continued to apply political terminology of the seventeenth-century Civil War and the Restoration to deliberately claim continuity or denounce opponents. In a 1713 Tory publication, for instance, the Whigs were denounced as 'levellers', 'roundheads', 'calf's heads', 'radicals' and 'republicans',[68] while Tories were known as 'Cavaliers'.[69] Patriots, for their part, were initially identified as those supporting Hanoverian politics before those seeking American independence began using the same label.[70] Criticizing the flaws of such comparisons, the author of the *Politician's Dictionary* assumed that such anachronisms were chosen because his contemporaries were 'at a loss to tell the nature, pretensions and principles of the parties'.[71]

In the second half of the eighteenth century, a more constitutional and pragmatic approach to party also made coalitions of rival factions possible. Although newspapers and low-brow pamphlets often criticized coalitions between factions as dishonest networking and a betrayal of electoral promises,[72] champions of opposition such as Rockingham and Fox were involved in several party alliances in both government and opposition.[73] Trying to reconcile King George III and his court faction with another opposition led by Charles James Fox, Sir John Macpherson urged his moderately liberal friends to promote 'the necessary union on all sides' and to bring the 'greatest talents' together,[74] in defence of the nation.[75] Fox, who was the arch-rival to William Pitt the Younger, had taken a radical turn since the American Revolution, but in his undated draft letter, Sir John Macpherson expressed high confidence that the power of economic interests would eventually bring the opposing factions in Parliament together.⁷⁶ Macpherson was convinced that if Mr Fox 'explain[ed] his last speech more effectually' and proved his intended reform to be 'less alarming' than the government had feared, a 'union of Talents and system to meet the plans of the Enemy' would be possible.⁷⁷ Critical of party struggle for the sake of personal ambitions and sensitivities, he pointed out that England's international affairs made it necessary to keep 'parties from alternately destroying and being destroyed'.⁷⁸ In fact, multifactional ministries led by at least two influential leaders proved more successful than the critics of the mid-1780s anticipated.

The second form of Parliament-related unrest centred on the problem of perceived inefficiency or injustice in lawmaking, including undue (geographic) extensions of parliamentary competencies within the Empire. When a parliamentary union between England and Ireland was for the first time suggested in 1691 to break the Irish support for James VII/II, John Phillips cautioned in his monthly paper *The Present State of Europe* that this might 'provoke the Irish, who tho' allow'd to sit in the Parliament of England, would still believe themselves to be no more than a Province of England'.⁷⁹ He further observed that the

> Parliament which is already so numerous, that it is not altogether free from delays, and inconveniences incident to Multitude, would thereby be much more augmented, and more subject to the same Inconveniences. Moreover, therefore to speak my Sentiments freely, I do not believe this Union will ever come to pass; because it seems to be agreeable with the Disposition of neither of the Three Nations.⁸⁰

Although a parliamentary union between England and the Kingdom of Ireland only became reality in the 1800 Acts of Union, the English–Scottish union had already materialized in the Union with Scotland Act (1706) and the Union with England Act (1707), which met with opposition. Plans to install a remote relative of the Stuart family, the Electress of Hanover, on the thrones of both London and Edinburgh first motivated the union and a joint British parliament in London. Scottish author Patrick Abercromby, a committed Presbyterian and Scottish 'patriot',⁸¹ saw disturbing historical parallels between royal usurpation and parliamentary lust for power, which could only be tamed by strict limitations on general parliamentary duties. In Abercromby's opinion, the one-sided glorification of parliamentary 'authority' and 'wisdom',⁸² which he detected in English Whig pamphlets, was just as dangerous as the Stuarts' inclination to absolutism. Law, Abercromby recollected, was the very basis of the British nation but had frequently been altered in the past:

> We have seen Parliaments comply Backward and Foreward [*sic*] with the Fate, and Fortune of Princes, in Deposing and Re-inthroning [*sic*] them alternately; – We have seen a Parliament Confirm the Usurpation of Richard the Third, the greatest Tyrant that ever England brought forth; – King Henry the Eighth made a Popish Parliament pull down the Supremacy of Rome, and set up the King's; – Queen

Mary Re-established Popery, and unraveled [sic.] the Reformation of King Edward; and still the Parliament consented. – One Parliament voted Queen Mary Legitimate, and Queen Elisabeth a Bastard; – Another Parliament Legitimated Queen Elisabeth, and Repudiated Queen Mary. – Queen Elisabeth undid all her Sister had done, – and all was by Authority of Parliament.[83]

Union act riots in Scottish towns took place in 1706 and 1707. In 1759, renewed rumours of an Irish–British union incited riots outside the Houses of Parliament in Dublin.[84] Likewise, the 1710 trial of Anglican minister Henry Sacheverell (see Chapter 4) 'was very much a parliamentary event'.[85] Sacheverell was accused of libellous sermons and put under a preaching ban, which caused his supporters in London to violently roam the streets.[86] Other protests against parliamentary legislation bearing a strong religious connotation were the Scottish and English riots against Catholic Relief (1778–80). The unpopular decision to improve the legal status of British Catholics was either blamed on Parliament itself or put down to Parliament's failure to exert the necessary government control. Whig lawyer Thomas Erskine, 1st Baron Erskine (1750–1823), for instance, suggested in his defence of Lord George Gordon, who was accused of inciting anti-Catholic riots in 1780, that misinterpretations of the law or unlawful extensions thereof had repeatedly occurred in the reigns of 'bad princes',[87] who were 'assisted by weak submissive parliaments'.[88]

Concerns that proceedings in Parliament were inefficient or not transparent were uttered by ideologically diverse oppositions of the eighteenth century and often fuelled by disagreements between Members of Parliament (MPs), local authorities, local landowners and the regular army. During the 1779 anti-Catholic riots in Edinburgh, 'Lieutenant Ralph Dundass, regulating Officer for the Impress Service at Leith, and his Press-Gang',[89] offered to put the insurrection down with force and enrol all rioters in the colonial army, but according to eyewitness George Hay, Lord Provost Walter Hamilton of Edinburgh decided to expel Lieutenant Dundass from the city. Hamilton, for his part, did not take any further action to restore order, and the city guards left the attacked Catholics to their fate. When demonstrations and stone-throwing continued and two men were severely injured, the captain of the city guards argued that he was not allowed to intervene without an official warrant.[90] This hesitancy incited Charles Montagu-Scott, fourth Duke of Buccleuch (in some sources Buccleugh), to summon his own armed men and march in from his nearby castle.[91] Buccleuch hoped to quickly quell the riot in accordance with the Riot Act, but another intervention by the Lord Provost ended his campaign and forced him to set his eight captives free.[92] The Gordon Riots of 1780, which posed a physical threat to the Houses of Parliament, likewise exposed indecision among political and military leaders.[93] In response to the riotous proceedings in London, Sir (then Colonel) Charles Stuart, son of former British prime minister John Stuart, was stationed in the city and sent his father first-hand accounts in several letters. On 3 June 1780, he expressed his disappointment at the foot-dragging and discord that – in his opinion – let the outrage continue for too long.[94]

While conservatives such as Stuart hoped for a more cooperative spirit and moral improvement among the nation's leaders, more liberal or even republican circles linked political failure more fundamentally with errors in how important figures such as MPs were chosen. While election disputes often focused on the qualities and failures of specific candidates, the representation debate called the legitimation of parliamentary decision-making into question. The *Politician's Dictionary* of 1775 estimated that Britain, at the time of writing, had a population of 8 million people out of whom only 'a thirty-second part, or something more' had votes as freeholders, freemen or through town corporations.[95] According to the author, who professed to have made several calculations, this was 'a very imperfect representation'.[96]

In America, a re-evaluation of representation and elected majorities was closely linked with scepticism about party. Although the independent United States also developed its first party system,[97] the American revolutionaries had been as cautious to embrace party as Britons of the eighteenth century had been. In line with continental republicanism advanced by French Enlightenment theorists, American patriots initially feared that interest-driven factions would result in 'egoism and lack of civil solidarity'.[98] Moreover, there was a strong incentive to limit plebiscitary influence.[99] John Adams and other political thinkers, therefore, debated a systematic power limitation through improved representational structures.[100] Learning from mistakes that Britain had made in governing the distant North American colonies, regular changes of government, as well as the accountability of office holders, were meant to mitigate the disadvantages of territorial disparity and prevent a single faction from becoming all-powerful.[101] The American revolutionaries also questioned the validity of majority decisions in a national assembly and aimed for representational structures balancing statutory acts, common law and – last but not least – 'the law of common sense'.[102] According to John Adams, a representative assembly 'should be in miniature an exact portrait of the people at large. It should think, feel, reason and act like them'.[103] This issue had also been raised by critics of the London Parliament in England, including the London paper *The Observator*, which looked to the development of national councils abroad and warned that England might one day become a tyranny like France if majorities in Parliament consisted of the wrong men and voted for oppressive legislation.[104]

In a retrenchment of earlier contractual theory, 'Neo-Calvinists and freethinkers' began to concur that the individual was 'incapable of withstanding on his own the temptations of power' while minorities had to be protected.[105] Although David Hume had criticized Thomas Hobbes's pragmatic and even pessimistic view of society, which was 'fitted only to promote tyranny, and [...] to encourage licentiousness',[106] the newly founded United States adopted much of Hobbes's anthropological pessimism.[107] Already the first version of the United States Constitution, the *Articles of Confederation*, published on 1 March 1781, rested upon multiple interlaced and pyramidal degrees of representation to resolve the many 'disputes and differences' that would naturally result from human nature.[108] American Founding Father James Madison (1751–1836) summarized:

> that, however small the republic may be, the representatives must be raised to a certain number, in order to guard against the cabals of a few; and that, however large it may be, they must be limited to a certain number, in order to guard against the confusion of a multitude.[109]

However, the proposed national constitution met with fierce opposition in several states, and George Washington, in a gloomy letter of 1786, already saw the infant nation 'fast verging to anarchy and confusion'.[110] On 31 March 1787, Washington added in another letter to Madison: 'I confess however that my opinion of public virtue is so far changed that I have my doubts whether any system without the means of coercion in the sovereign, will enforce obedience to the ordinances of a general government; without which, everything else fails.'[111]

As the debates wore on, the fear of civil war in America rose. The Pennsylvania and Massachusetts rebellions of 1787 incited Commonwealth officials to indict several hundred citizens for high treason. They also disquieted local farmers, whose lives and properties had not been sufficiently protected.[112] Newspapers such as the *Independent Gazetteer*, published in Philadelphia, promoted rejection of the new federal constitution at all costs.[113] James Madison and Benjamin Franklin (1706–90), however, pointed out that the union was important to contain discord among the people: 'If men were angels, no government would be necessary. [...] It is of great importance in a republic not only to guard the society against the oppression of its rulers, but to guard one part of the society against the injustice of the other part.'[114]

In the same spirit, Alexander Hamilton (1755–1804), New York delegate to the Constitutional Convention, wrote in a newspaper article for *The Federalist* on 28 May 1788 that

> the additional securities to republican government, to liberty and to property, to be derived from the adoption of the plan under consideration, consist chiefly in the restraints which the preservation of the Union will impose on local factions and insurrections, and on the ambition of powerful individuals in single states, who may acquire credit and influence enough, from leaders and favorites, to become the despots of the people.[115]

After the constitution was passed in June 1788, unionist majoritarianism and anti-centralist republicanism accounted for the development of America's first party system.[116] 'Responsible constitutional opposition' in the young United States could especially be credited to Thomas Jefferson.[117]

Whereas representational reform in Britain was only gradually introduced in the nineteenth century, eighteenth-century Britons resorted to oppositional action outside Parliament. Extra-parliamentary oppositions were, in part, popular branches of parliamentary factions or autonomous citizen associations. One example of a hybrid organization was the Protestant Association opposing Catholic Relief (see details on the so-called Gordon riots in Chapters 4 and 6). According to Eugene Charlton Black, the Protestant Association was 'an ill-defined amalgam of extra-religious and extra-parliamentary organizations', which was created in London but most effectively developed in Scotland.[118] Deliberately moving outside church hierarchies and including only one clerical member, the Protestant Association defended the socio-economic status of the Protestant population that was challenged by the advance of toleration.[119] Other extra-parliamentary movements also primarily responded to economic grievances and Parliament's extended financial responsibilities. In a society that had become an economy, individual citizens' contribution to the welfare of the nation was revalued, and this led to a growing self-esteem of the professional classes.[120] Scottish economist Adam Smith (1723–1790), for example, proposed a liberal society in which the common good came as a natural by-product of economic growth and in which 'the individual is both the main actor in the market and the entity to which civil rights are given'.[121] The educated classes took a keen interest in the state's expenditure and often criticized Parliament for the high level of national debt.[122] Lower-class objections to economic policy were mainly linked to rising prices and global competition. The Calico Riots in 1719–20, for instance, expressed popular protests against the importation of calico cotton from India. The first anti-calico 'mass rally' had been held at Parliament in 1697,[123] and included men as well as women and children. In general, eighteenth-century artisans and professionals expected Parliament not only to protect the nation from excessive taxation but also to regulate imperial trade.

Several taxation-related riots of the eighteenth century concerned the production of alcohol and the paper trade. *An address to such of the electors*, which explained the stance of the cider-producing counties on taxation in 1763, mentioned that protection of the people's interest did not come from parliamentary legislation but from trial by juries, expressing hopes that legal institutions would restore a balance between government interests and opposition.[124] Paper taxation was prominently at the heart of the American stamp tax controversy. The stamps imposed by the far-away London Parliament were denounced as the result of a dangerous 'power congestion',[125] and 'virtual representation',[126] which derived legitimation from an abstract commonwealth concept rather than the people concerned. In a patriot handbill printed in May 1775, the committee of the provincial government in Massachusetts Bay declared that Americans would never 'become abject Slaves, to the mercenary, tyrannical Parliament of Great-Britain'.[127] Even British colonial governor Francis Bernard (1712–79) was convinced that the Lords and Commons were more opposed to tax relief for America than the king himself.[128] Resistance to the 'uncontrouled [sic] power' of the British Parliament,[129] which was propagated in colonial America after the Seven Years War, aligned with broader economic grievances and found sympathizers within the British Isles.

The last major eighteenth-century unrests directly linked with parliamentary affairs were the Opening of Parliament Riots of October 1795. These riots in London were incited by the war against revolutionary France, which weighed heavily on the British economy and became increasingly unpopular. When a new session of Parliament was to begin, an enraged crowd attacked the coach of George III and shouted 'down with George, No King, No Pitt, No war'.[130] In addition, the coach windows were broken, and the king was threatened with a gun. Public outrage, however, was not restricted to the capital city or to criticism of the king and government ministers. Robert Fellowes of 'Shotisham' wrote on 19 October 1795 in anticipation of local food riots that 'a man wearing a hat with a ribband or cockade made a speech and gave away leaflets' to protest against high price of corn and other necessities. Fellowes also enclosed a manuscript copy of a paper dated 16 October 1795 and signed 'A friend to reform' that demanded the 'abolition of sinecures and adequate representation to control expenditure'.[131] The same manuscript scorned the House of Commons as an assembly of 'land-monopolists, commissaries, contractors and pensioners'.[132] In reaction to the events of October 1795, further legislation to restrict reform-oriented and anti-war activities passed.[133] This legislation was most prominently directly against the London Corresponding Society, founded in 1792.

The London Corresponding Society and the local clubs it represented mark an important professionalization of oppositional agitation in extra-parliamentary spaces.[134] This development was possible because party was no longer linked with national and deeply ideological concerns but could rest on different levels of interest intermediation. Skjönsberg has found that 'one underlying dimension of the debate about parties in the eighteenth century was the belief that partisanship was a key component of man's social nature'.[135] This view is reflected in the distinction between 'personal' and 'real' parties proposed in an anonymously published *Politician's Dictionary* of 1775: 'Factions or parties may be divided into personal and real; that is, into factions founded on personal friendship, or animosity amongst those who compose the factions, and into those founded on some real difference of sentiment or interest.'[136] This definition takes individual human motivations for party formation into account and goes beyond the bipolar party allegiance that had dominated 'voting behaviour from the end of William's reign to 1714'.[137] As the concept of party become more pluralistic, members of the public could also be included in political opinion-making and the creation of political identities.

Faced with accusations of complacency and seclusion that were voiced in many uprisings of the eighteenth century, Parliament, parties and individual MPs also had to work on their public communication. Kyle and Peacey have shown that the rise of committees in the seventeenth century contributed to increasing seclusion of the 'private male world of Parliament' to public (and female) lobbying. This meant that 'Parliament sought increasingly to control access to its meeting places, [...] turning Parliament from a rather accessible public arena into a public arena to which access was highly controlled, in other words, into a private space to which the public had some (approved and appropriately managed) access.'[138]

Parliament only reluctantly 'relaxed the secrecy formerly surrounding decision-making',[139] and this took place when debates and committee reports first appeared in print.[140] Publications of parliamentary speeches could still not be taken for granted in the eighteenth century as politicians still believed that the quality of politics depended upon its relative exclusivity.[141] Nevertheless, printed 'parliamentary journals' recounting debates,[142] bills for proposed legislation or individual petitions excited great interest among eighteenth-century readers.[143] Where the actual information was not available, fictitious reports met the demand, which was also true of judicial proceedings disseminated in print.[144]

This also put pressure on men in political office or those leading partisan groups to actively shape their public image. They could not exclusively legitimize their roles through hereditary status but had to stress personal achievements. There was consensus that the nation's leaders were 'not born with [civil authority]', but that such authority had been 'delegated to certain individuals for the advancement of the common benefit'.[145] This need for a convincing self-representation was fostered by the evolution of the *politician*. In contrast to our more narrow usage today, a politician of the eighteenth century was not necessarily a person actively shaping politics but first and foremost a person studying politics as a 'science'.[146] The handbook *The Politician's Creed* of 1799, for instance, set out to refute the common misconception that everyone knew 'medicine, politics, and the art of mending a dull fire'.[147] Thus, promoting the politician as a man of serious learning and a builder of new governments,[148] those practising politics could not fall behind. Although politicians in our modern sense still came from a limited set of influential families and acquired privileges through blood ties and patronage,[149] most eighteenth-century ministers and masterminds of parliamentary opposition shared a certain experience of the fleeting nature of power and felt the need to publicly legitimize their actions.[150] From 1721 until the end of the Pitt–Newcastle era in 1761–2, the circle of men who held government positions remained small, but their responsibilities frequently alternated or overlapped.[151] John Stuart, Lord Bute, for example, first entered politics as an ally to the Prince of Wales in opposition to King George II before he briefly served as prime minister to King George III from 1761 to 1763. Throughout his opposition years, he pursued conservative policies such as the establishment of a strong monarchy and placid relations with Britain's continental neighbours, but also placed his long-term vision of the British Empire above allegiance to the king.[152] In defiance of public allegations that he was in truth a Jacobite and a secret ally to the king of France, Lord Bute called himself a loyal Briton and a patriot.[153]

In fact, prominent statesmen such as Bute were carefully monitored by a privately owned press. British media entrepreneurs remained sceptical of charismatic opinion-makers and frequently accused them of manipulating Parliament to facilitate their careers.[154] Even more than hereditary office holders, those who voluntarily took up politics as a profession were often seen as antagonists to decent and hard-working citizens.[155] Many charismatic leaders and their adherents were mocked as criminal gangs or cultish clubs.[156] In 1765, the party in support of John Russell, 4th Duke of Bedford, was sarcastically referred to as the 'Bloomsbury Gang',[157] named after a district of central London now in the London Borough of Camden, whereas supporters of John Stuart, Earl of Bute, were denounced as his 'praetorian band'.[158] Secret influence on the ministry was often referred to as 'the Butean system',[159] and politicians who changed their party allegiance or sought cooperation with former enemies were also regarded with suspicion.[160] In general, aspiring MPs had to distance themselves from a corrupted court culture as well as uneducated 'coffee-house politicians',[161] who were not suited to guide the nation. Even in the late 1780s, the supposition that leading politicians habitually manipulated elections reverberated in serious political pamphlets as well as caricatures.[162] Such manoeuvres, of course, gave 'politicks' a lingering aftertaste,[163] and anonymous addresses to the electorates of individual boroughs or counties openly expressed dissatisfaction.[164]

Politicians, above all non-noblemen, had to ensure that they were not taken for fortune-hunters.[165] Almost all factions in British politics detested 'obscurity of birth' and 'meanness of capacity',[166] because men 'whose fortune hung upon [the king's] favour' were considered to be impressionable and might not possess 'sufficient influence to resist [the king's] wishes, when they were to [his] dishonour'.[167] The aspired counter-image was that of the disinterested 'statesman'.[168] An honourable (country) MP was expected to prove himself 'a conscientious member of parliament, whose chief business, independent of all party, is [...] to guard the public purse against plunder, and the constitution of Great Britain from innovation'.[169]

However, the 1760s also saw the rise of media campaigns staged in close collaboration between individual political figures and commercial printers.[170] John Almon's polemic publishing on behalf of John Wilkes (1725–95) is one example of joint activism.[171] John Wilkes, who proudly called himself the 'Freeman',[172] was the most notorious MP and magistrate of the 1760s and 1770s. Apart from considerable financial investments including bribes, Wilkes built his career on a skilful use of a wide variety of print media. In his fictitious dialogue with an English courtier, who proclaims the superiority of the English constitution over purported French absolutism, Wilkes ironically cited Alexander Pope's famous claim that the form of government mattered little if bribery and manipulation prevailed among those selected for administrative offices.[173]

Promoting himself as a champion of liberty, John Wilkes capitalized on personal eccentricity and scandal as proof of his independence and artlessness.[174] His ruthless use of foul language made him one of the more extreme agitators of his time, but he was not the only politician building his public image on calculated breaks with convention.[175] In the 1780s, Charles James Fox's charismatic style of leadership and his talents to gather fervent adherents nourished a romanticized idea of the 'full-time politician solely dedicated to his MP seat'.[176] In reality, Fox had many engagements outside politics, and although he took a keen interest in literature and the study of (ancient) history, he hardly ever dealt with contemporary political or economic theory.[177] Other MPs saw their role in supporting native Indians in the corruption trials against the East India Company or showing solidarity with Catholics affected by the Relief Act Riots.[178]

While eighteenth-century British political culture thus valued a certain degree of social maladjustment, individuality and innovation among its celebrated political leaders, it also pushed for a clear distinction between the 'civilised' and the 'uncivilised',[179] when it came to the public behaviour of those who rallied behind the influential figures. As Chapter 6 covers in more detail, the 1770s to 1790s were the period in which different strands of street agitation and popular petitioning were disciplined and standardized not only through legislation or 'breeding' and 'cultivation',[180] by the nation's 'eminent men',[181] but also by competing groups of citizens who rivalled for legitimation. To ensure efficient public action, opposition organizers needed to communicate through handwritten letters and printed media. While printed pamphlets often created a more abstract sense of identity and addressed specific political issues,[182] handbills whose dissemination often required personal contact between people were especially important in stirring individuals to action or in managing crowds. In addition, local newspapers provided up-to-date information on planned meetings or election candidates.[183]

In an attempt to suppress 'urban radicalism',[184] the constitutionally conservative mainstream in the anglophone world embraced limited popular agency.[185] Political balls, dinners and other private entertainments with a potentially seditious purpose had acquired a negative reputation at the time of the Jacobite risings when both Stuart supporters and those loyal to the House of Hanover staged such celebrations for their inner circles.[186] The Birmingham Riots in 1791 were caused by rumours that a group of dissenting gentlemen had not only organized a festive dinner in celebration of the French Revolution but also given the treasonous 'toasts, *No church, no king,* and *The King's head in a charger*'.[187] During the high treason trial of Thomas Hardy in

1794, the conservative London paper *True Briton* reported that the Attorney General was greatly concerned about 'the evil machinations of designing individuals', but even more alarmed 'that Clubs and affiliation of Clubs were daily increasing'.[188]

In order to sort the wheat from the chaff, religious processions and popular celebrations were thus more clearly differentiated from politically defined demonstrations. And associations lobbying for parliamentary reform, such as the London Corresponding Society, aimed to legitimize their activities through an orderly meeting culture that included open discussions, minute-taking and transparent finances.[189] Announcing 'that the number of our members be unlimited',[190] and attracting new members of the professional classes with low weekly subscription fees, the London Corresponding Society stretched political self-organization beyond elite circles. Their internal proceedings against disloyal members such as Upton, who had been censored by fellow members 'for seeking to destroy the confidence of the society in their Executive Committee',[191] mirrored the example of parliamentary impeachments. Most importantly, privacy or even secrecy were reduced in favour of more predictable assemblies that not only followed accepted rules of conduct but were also ideally announced in advance. Other eighteenth-century citizen associations, too, announced schedules for political action in the newspapers, and ensured that all of their meetings were 'quite open'.[192]

In public assemblies, the wearing of cockades and the carrying of flags as clear symbols of identification also became important public displays of political identities.[193] The local museum of Loughgall in Armagh, Northern Ireland, where the Orange Order was founded and the Constitution of the Loyal Orange Society was written in 1795, has preserved a wide range of 'Orange paraphernalia',[194] including sashes, flags and banners.[195] In the case of the United Irishmen, public ceremonies such as triumphant marches 'with green flags, green boughs and ornaments of different descriptions',[196] or festive funeral processions for deceased members, ensured the attention or even participation of 'vast crowds',[197] and made sure that the organization was not mistaken for a secret group of plotters. Before tensions escalated and resulted in the failed rebellion of 1798,[198] the rhetoric of soldierly virtue and military discipline in Ireland had done much to achieve political self-awareness and a sense of belonging that was harder to create in this socially and religiously bipolar country than in the comparatively prosperous American colonies.[199]

Nonetheless, the militarization of citizen associations in the British Empire had to stop where subversive violence began (see Chapter 5).[200] During the legal investigations into the convention summoned by the London Corresponding Society in 1794, the jury found that the promotion of parliamentary reform was only lawful as long as it did not cover up 'the purpose of destroying the King'.[201] The accused society members Adams, Sharp, Widdison, Broomhead and Davidson 'all accorded they had no design to destroy the Government, nor did they believe that any such design ever existed'.[202] Another member, Mr Tooke, even confirmed that 'if a revolution was to take place, he expected to be the first victim'.[203] However, the discovery of weapons and evidence that the London Corresponding Society and the Society for Constitutional Information at Sheffield intended to order a considerable number of steel pikes had cast doubt on their peaceful self-representation and led to extensive court examinations.[204] William Carnage, former

Secretary of the Society for Constitutional Information at Sheffield, found it hard to prove 'that the Society should be armed to protect itself' against the Sheffield people.[205]

The 1796 pamphlet *On The Sacred Duty of Insurrection*, which was published in the name of the then-deceased 'Rockingham',[206] tried to strike a balance between radical reformers and moderates who distanced themselves from republican tendencies.[207] The pamphlet appealed to the prudence and responsibility of British parliamentarians, and defined those as the country's best statesmen who were 'most fervently devoted to the Constitution'.[208] According to the author, this implied constant moderation and the earnest attempt to seek remedies '*within* the pale of the Constitution',[209] rather than 'open rebellion'.[210] Violent resistance – which equalled the dissolution of society and the reversion of power to the individual – was seen as justified only when the evil was 'not [...] of a light nature, but of the very first magnitude'.[211] The very fact that philosophers such as John Locke (1632–1704) and David Hume (1711–76) had never explicitly '[drawn] the line when obedience ought to end and when resistance must begin' proved to the author that the threat of rebellion was above all a bargaining counter in the hands of the opposition.[212] In the long run, protest either conformed to elaborate standards of peaceful performance or was otherwise delegitimized. In a series of engravings of Birmingham houses published after the local riots of 1791, descriptions below the illustrations compared the rioting to attacks of 'Goths and Vandals'.[213]

On the one hand, violence as an end in itself became politically unacceptable and a counter-image to lawful party formation and opposition.[214] On the other hand, political associations of both liberal and conservative orientations respecting a certain conduct became forerunners of modern 'people's parties'.[215] Their sense of cooperative antagonism, similar to the 'harmonious discord' that Skjönsberg has described for parliamentary parties of the later eighteenth century,[216] paved the way for future efforts such as the Chartist movement's fight for workers' rights and suffrage reform in the nineteenth century. But the election reform of 1832 was far from a constitutional watershed. It changed numbers, but not the underlying concepts of participation.[217]

Trends towards a more general politicization of eighteenth-century society as described in this chapter can also be traced in the development of Britain's religious communities, as party formation and political self-organization often overlapped with denominational affiliation. This aspect of what Britons termed their 'happy Constitution' is the focus of the following chapter.[218]

4

Religious communities and religious leaders: Inclusive and divisive potentials of faith after the Glorious Revolution

As Chapter 3 outlines, religious affiliation played an important part in eighteenth-century political identities and was, in the first half of the century, inseparable from the concept of party. Religiously influenced unrest, however, was often dismissed as backward or ineffective in 1990s historiography.[1] Daniel Szechi, by contrast, has acknowledged religious rioting as 'very effective' because 'the moral economy was not just about the price of bread [... but] encompassed all kinds of customary values – including keeping papist and dissenters in their place'.[2] J. C. D. Clark even proposed that eighteenth-century Britain was still a 'confessional state',[3] in which popular protest and violent uprisings were, inter alia, triggered by Protestant and Catholic opposition to an Anglican hegemony.[4] Taking the self-perception of eighteenth-century Britons seriously, accepting that 'religion [was] so connected with the state in England [that] it [was] impossible to reform one without the other',[5] this chapter traces the involvement of religious communities or individual religious leaders in British conflicts from the Glorious Revolution to denominational tensions in the Irish Rebellion of 1798. It shows that religious argumentation remained a vital source of political legitimation, although both the Church of England and less privileged religious communities assumed new roles in public life.[6] This came with communicational challenges on a local and an imperial scale, advancing the adaptation of traditional religious communication channels such as sermons to an increasingly pluralistic media landscape.[7]

The examples presented on the following pages especially question a simplistic view of religious politics in Britain that opposes Anglicanism to all other denominations.[8] Although the Jacobite rebellions were undoubtedly perceived and denounced as Catholic uprisings in their own time, they were socially as well as religiously much more diverse.[9] Anglicans, too, contributed to oppositional thought or even violent resistance. While some considered it 'monstrous to see an established episcopal clergy in declared opposition to the court, and a nonconformist presbyterian clergy in conjunction with it',[10] the author of the *Politician's Dictionary* regarded this inversion of alliances as the result of two extremes. On the one hand, High Churchmen had 'espoused monarchical principles too high for the present settlement, which is founded on principles of liberty'; but, on the other hand, Nonconformists made compromises with the government merely for fear of the High Church party.[11] While religion was thus perceived as inherently political, primarily religiously motivated protest is hard to define and distinguish because early modern religious identities blended with more general categories of cultural and social belonging. In creating my digital map of events, I have therefore applied a joint religious and cultural category to events ranging from the escalated preaching controversy known as the Sacheverell Riots of 1710 to incidents of violence against dissenters (e.g. in Norwich and Yarmouth in 1752 and 1752) or Catholics (e.g. the Gordon Riots of 1780), to riots against the redesign of local church buildings (Lincoln, 1726). Furthermore, several events I have classified as predominantly social and economic were influenced by denominational tensions. Religious groups and their leaders undoubtedly played important parts not only in the Jacobite rebellions but also in the American Revolution and the Irish Rebellion.

Secularizing tendencies of the period were not a unidirectional attempt to limit church interference with the state either;[12] they were often an attempt by church leaders to assert distinctly ecclesiastical authority and defend religious matters against instrumentalization. Fighting injustice and self-serving 'under a cloak of religion', some ecumenically minded Christians stressed the overall societal 'usefulness' of religion and the community services of moderate religious ministers, who ought to 'tolerate each other, though they cannot follow Jesus in the same way'.[13] In truth, religious argumentations invoking patriotism, citizen rights and the law often allowed generalizations of interests or neutralizations of conflicts that complemented political debates or made room for previously excluded agents.[14]

This was a subtle break with Britain's period of state-driven confessionalization of the sixteenth to seventeenth centuries, in which the Church of England had been reputed for close ties to king and government, claiming to have delivered the nation from 'popery', 'arbitrary power' and 'slavery'.[15] From the Henrician Reformation to the Stuart Restoration, established religion and the Crown legitimized each other.[16] Acts of resistance against the union of Church and Crown were denounced as both heresy and disloyalty, which gave the government a double legitimation.[17] The Church encouraged obedience to God and King and the 'dignity of a King',[18] criticizing rebellions as 'wylfull'.[19] The process of confessionalization all over Europe initially 'politicised politics',[20] and increased public interest in governmental decision-making as well as an active commitment to a new denominationally defined commonwealth. Politics and religion fostered each other's growth and autonomy and often engendered parallel institutions (e.g. ecclesiastical courts in Britain). In England, Henry VIII did not need to invent a political Church, but could easily refine a medieval tradition of episcopal administrators in state service.[21] Although some historians claimed that the English Reformation was a forward-looking liberation of national interests from ecclesiastical ideology,[22] Henry VIII implemented an even stronger collaboration between loyalist clerics and state in the sixteenth century. The credo of the age was that 'he can never be called a good Subject who reviles *Men* in *Authority*, and *speaks Evil* of *Dignities*; so neither can he be reputed a *good Christian*, who indulges himself in the open Practice of Calumny and Defamation, against the *Ministers* of that Religion, and the *Stewards* of its *Mysteries*'.[23] Yet while religion could legitimize power change, it was also subjected to political concepts of lawful organization and media usage. Protestant princes acted as bishops, but wherever the confessional landscape remained split between two or more denominations, religion could also align with political opposition. Nigel Yates states that the Established Churches, that is Anglicanism in England, Wales and Ireland alongside Presbyterianism in Scotland, were an 'integral part of the British constitution', while there was 'limited recognition of other religions'.[24]

After the Thirty Years War, Britain had to navigate a more clearly defined secular political culture on the European stage.[25] Religious disagreement no longer hindered international military collaboration, and England's conflicts with France were predominantly described in secular terms. Nevertheless, the secularization of political language that had taken place in the mid-sixteenth- to mid-seventeenth-century German principalities could not gather momentum within Britain as religion was still permitted to 'nationalize monarchical ritual',[26] and to broaden the popular support enjoyed by a dynasty.[27]

The doctrine of obedience to civil authority promoted by the Anglican hierarchy had made Church and State indispensable allies, even for Catholic King James VII/II.[28] During the reign of William III, the author of the *Athenian Gazette* reminded his readers that the Anglican morning prayers included an intercession that God should defend Church and King against all those 'whose Religion is Rebellion, and whose Faith is Faction'.[29] This close link between religion and nationhood, however, was challenged when the deposition of the Catholic Stuarts made the accession of continental European rulers from other non-Anglican traditions necessary.[30] Although the government change pleased many Anglicans who had feared the growing influence of Catholicism, the Whig decision to invite William of Orange to rule over England weakened their position and caused internal division.[31] Tory attempts to sustain the Restoration narrative that religious dissenters were 'Propagating Heresie [sic] in the Church, and Confusion in the State',[32] were no longer assertive. Even the strictly monarchist *Boston News-Letter* mocked the High Church faction's 'idle Clamours of the CHURCH's DANGER',[33] claiming that 'the Church they mean [was] not the Church of England, but that of Rome'.[34] Anglicanism's aim to provide cultural identities for all inhabitants of the Empire thus conflicted with often dissatisfying Church–state relations,[35] and many Anglicans became active members of the political opposition.[36] They deliberately revived the pugnacious tradition of the Henrician Reformation when Queen Anne's Tory ministry failed and Elector George Louis of Hanover claimed the throne of Britain.[37] Many clergymen openly acted as publishers or diplomats in defiance of King George;[38] some of them even hoped for a Stuart restoration controlled by Parliament and the Anglican episcopacy.[39] Those Anglicans who had refused to swear allegiance to King George I had – contrary to their ideology – proved themselves as a dynamic community whose members frequently drifted towards active Jacobitism, setting an involuntary example for future generations of clergy in opposition.[40]

To the majority of Tories and Whigs who defended the new religious establishment,[41] religion mattered as an organizational principle. Confessional uniformity – or at least a submission of minority religion to the rules of the Established Churches – was deemed necessary for successful state formation.[42] Political writers such as the Scottish physician and antiquarian Patrick Abercromby freely admitted that the

Catholic majority in France had the same right to defend 'Uniformity in Matters of Religion amongst themselves' as the British nation,[43] and accepted that religious cohesion could only be demanded in a limited geographical space. When it came to national security, British contemporaries held a pessimistic view of religious diversity as a source of violence and disintegration for much longer than intellectuals within the Holy Roman Empire.[44] Above all, they feared the seditious potential of religious groups who did not make their intentions known. Most prominently, 'disguised Jesuits' were criticized for wearing civilian dress and working in a worldly trade.[45]

Although the aggressive religious iconography of the Williamite era, which depicted the king as a valiant defender of Protestantism,[46] was not revived in the Hanoverian period, George I's attempts to dissipate religious tensions in Britain were overturned by his heir. George II and especially his staunchly Protestant wife Caroline of Brandenburg-Ansbach aimed to meet British expectations of a Protestant royal couple to the fullest possible extent.[47] During the Jacobite rebellions, strong Protestant kingship was successfully extolled as a necessary bulwark against the continental European powers of 'Priestcraft and Tyranny'.[48] When George II's son-in-law, Frederick II of Hesse-Kassel, converted to Catholicism in 1749, his daughter Mary was expected to abandon her husband; she took with her their three sons, whom Frederick did not meet again until 1782.[49] This model of Protestant kingship even survived the first republican revolutions in America and France.[50]

On the one hand, the demonization of allegedly despotic Catholic politics made the Anglican establishment more likely to accept opposition in an expanding and diverse Empire;[51] on the other hand, religious prejudices prevented more effective political cooperation or fostered political radicalism.[52] Protestant opponents of a British–Irish union, for instance, rejected cooperation with Catholics.[53] In between, Protestant denominations offered multiple opportunities to experiment with governance and concepts of participation. Although 'Old Dissent', Quakers, Baptists, Congregationalists and Presbyterians, was declining in numbers by the 1730s, 'New Dissent', the evangelical revival driven especially by different strands of Methodism,[54] added novel force.[55] The 1851 census revealed that the Church of England had only slightly more church attendees than Protestant Nonconformity, which shows that smaller communities could rely on particularly committed members.[56] Moreover, foreign Protestant communities such as expelled Huguenots also shaped the religio-political landscape of the British eighteenth century.[57] Challenged by this inner-Protestant heterogeneity, arguments about religion concerned organizational alternatives in government and society as much as doctrine.

As 'the early modern theology of power' decreased,[58] non-governmental groups in Parliament as well as extra-parliamentary agents gained opportunities to employ religious rhetoric for oppositional causes.[59] British political history of the eighteenth century owed much to civic self-organization both within and outside the Anglican Church. Ecclesiastical conciliarism was an important source for organizational structures of both politics and the political in early modern Europe.[60] Clergymen of every rank and every political persuasion would not let themselves be confined to the pulpits but ostentatiously engaged in public discourse.[61] The tradition of forming clubs, societies and associations, seen among Anglican students of divinity at Oxford and

Cambridge as well as Jacobites and Freemasons, became the most important way to exert civil opposition in late eighteenth-century Britain.[62] In general, behaviours and attitudes of churchgoers became less predictable, and greater overlaps and changes of faction were possible after the repeal of the Test and Corporation Acts as well as the introduction of the Catholic Relief Act.[63] Wesleyan electors and Irish Catholics, for instance, emancipated themselves from the views of their respective church leaders and supported various political parties.[64] As a consequence, 'non-sectarian politics',[65] as well as 'personal religion',[66] evolved as a central goal of liberalism. 'Practical religious toleration' and moderate oppositions finally emerged as a necessary,[67] but to no degree deliberate, outcome of a changing constitutional and territorial framework. In theory and on the level of familial relations and private acquaintances, the eighteenth century underlined the inclusive, conversational aspects of the Christian tradition over the confrontational potential it entailed, but the public nature of religion was a very different story. Denominations in Britain took up a wide variety of discourses ranging from science to economics, but they also attempted to give non-religious fields a 'theological dimension'.[68] Even though Anglicanism was inclined to defend 'the "natural" hierarchy of mutual obligations that were thought to provide social cohesion',[69] church historian E. R. Norman has also justly noted that the later eighteenth century was a period of 'laicisation',[70] in which non-clerical believers influenced Church and State as self-confident disciples of Christ.[71] Over the course of the century, religious communities discovered the advantages of grass-roots campaigning, and no longer depended on the ruler's willingness to engage clergymen as political advisors. From the old Anglican doctrine of passive obedience, which had sprung from fear of anarchy and social break-up after the execution of Charles I and the terrors of the Cromwell Protectorate,[72] the British view of religious agitation gradually developed into well-organized interest groups on a par with political parties during the French and American Revolutions.[73]

Dissenting clubs and societies, too, transformed British sociability and were particularly keen to draw up petitions and addresses.[74] In many urban communities, different dissenting factions were associated with craftsmanship and wealth.[75] James E. Bradley believes that what unified dissent in the eighteenth century were not primarily specific political issues but a sense of national rights and class identity.[76]

Last but not least, religious communities played a vital role in bringing political awareness to remote or rural areas of the British Isles and the colonies. Thompson has confirmed that dissenting religion was an eminently important factor in the politicization of rural communities. Where dissenting meeting houses offered alternatives to the Anglican establishment, religious assemblies such as Bible societies and Sunday schools could serve important political functions and provide the necessary terminology and symbols for self-representation.[77] Dissenters, in particular, remarked that 'the savage reprisals' that had followed the defeat of the Jacobite army at Culloden might eventually endanger British political culture at large.[78] The voices of clergymen resounded in the various media that covered the bloody Hexham riots of 1769.[79] These riots in west of Newcastle were brought about by widespread resistance to new balloting regulations that were introduced to recruit militiamen, and a violent confrontation between professional soldiers and an enraged crowd was set off.[80]

Anglican priests William Totton, Peter Rumney and John Brown as Vicar of Newcastle condemned the riots and recounted the people's 'natural Duty of a Personal Service, in Defence of Ourselves and Our Country'.[81] The Independent Church at Hexham, led by the Rev. John Scott, however, sympathized with the protestors;[82] and the Rev. William Cooper eternalized the militiamen's inability to peacefully disperse the protestors in his satirical poem *Will of a Certain Northern Vicar*.[83] Church structures were imagined as an essential basis for reform when conventionist Joseph Gerrald proposed in the 1790s that 'a stratum of parochial, primary assemblies should choose ten electors each to attend a regional assembly which would finally elect deputies to a national convention for constitutional reform'.[84] Parish structures were thus envisaged as the basis of neighbourhood democracy and traditional religious infrastructures linked to institutionalized politics and the people.[85] Religion was valued as the active citizen's innermost compass, above all in the decades of modern conservatism after the American and French Revolutions.[86] At the same time, dissenters in North America advocated a formal separation of Church and State, which also influenced the British Isles.[87]

These trends coexisted thanks to a diverse media production that – often in concentric circles– linked the local and the national, and potentially addressed all strata of society. Whatever communication opportunities arose from in-person religious worship, printed media enabled clergy to reach audiences beyond their parishes.[88] English-speaking religious periodicals in the eighteenth century were dominated by Anglican publications as the mid-seventeenth-century crisis had already made the Anglican Church a substantive media enterprise. The early religious newspapers and journals were highly topical, running only for a few months or years. According to *The New Cambridge Bibliography of English Literature*, the earliest periodical that clearly represented political Protestantism was *A Pacquet of Advice from Rome*, which first appeared on 3 December 1678.[89] Similar publications peaked in the 1680s but declined after the Glorious Revolution. In the eighteenth century, news-oriented religious periodicals became culturally more inclusive and included historiographical pieces.[90] In the 1790s, several new publications with a Christian outlook were founded in response to the French Revolution, some of which advocated moderate constitutional reforms. *The Patriot, or Political, moral, and philosophical repository*, for instance, appeared from October 1792 to March 1793 with contributions from lay authors as well as clergy. Under the slogan 'Populus, Libertas, Lex, et Rex' ('People, Liberty, Law, and King') displayed on the cover page, the journal assembled articles on parliamentary reforms (e.g. the full disclosure of the pension list) and religious toleration in the service of the general advancement of British society.[91] The nineteenth century then saw dissenting Protestant journals, as well as Catholic and Eastern-rite Christian publishing, overshadow Anglican or Episcopal periodicals in the US and British colonies.[92]

A trans-denominational ideal of the clergy as patriotic citizens can also be traced in eighteenth-century newspapers, many of which accepted advertisements and letters to the editors. Apart from the many reports that addressed foreign religious conflict (e.g. in Rome and France) rather than events at home,[93] some newspapers published contributions praising clergy of different denominations, including Catholics, for preventing violent escalations of regional conflicts.[94] *Saunders's News-Letter*, one of Dublin's most important papers of the mid-seventeenth to late eighteenth centuries, reported on 13 September 1786 in the context of the agrarian White Boy disturbances in Munster, Ireland, that potential rioters had deliberately attended Church of Ireland parishes to use pretended religious conformity as a disguise during riots and disorder. The same article stated that a Roman Catholic clergyman had then collaborated with the Anglican parishes 'in the preservation of good order' by speaking in the Anglican church, and Protestant magistrates had addressed Catholic communities. These unanimous actions, the article noted, were 'the death warrant of bigotry and fanaticism in this kingdom'.[95] Such evidence, though anecdotal, hints at a gradual pluralization of Britain's religious landscape and a pan-Christian redefinition of political identities, differentiating more between communication among the faithful and between religious leaders and the nation at large. These developments can best be analysed through sermons as persistent and widely used Church media which often bridged oral preaching and print publishing.

Sermons written on political occasions integrated changing ideas of the political rights and duties of monarchs, ministers, MPs and the 'everyday people'.[96] Although sermons responding to political unrest mainly represented the voice of pro-government clergy, many of whom were deans and bishops, they were also tools of nuanced communication between the clergy and a wider circle of clerical and lay readers, several of whom published critical responses. Furthermore, political sermons were preached not only by Anglican clergymen, but also by loyal Protestants of other denominations, and even by Protestants in opposition to the government. Warren Johnston's book on thanksgiving sermons analyses 587 sermons that were published between 1689 and 1816, and finds that their writers' 'predominant impulse was Britain's involvement in war'.[97]

From the WorldCat online catalogue, I have extracted 690 metadata of riot- and rebellion-related sermons, mock sermons and responses to sermons published between 1688 and 1800. Because of the different cataloguing conventions applied in different libraries and archives, sermon titles and authors are not recorded uniformly, which leads to a high number of potential duplicates in the data. At the same time, many sermons were printed in more than one place or reprinted in several editions.[98] Like the thanksgiving sermons analysed by Johnston, the majority of the sermons addressing riots and rebellions were supportive of the government and condemning violent opposition. The map in Figure 4.1 shows the places within the British Isles where rebellion sermons were (supposedly) published between 1684 and 1800. Although London is over-represented, publishers in Scotland, Ireland and North America were also involved, and sermons were most likely circulated beyond the immediate places of publication.[99] In addition, the place of publication must not be confused with the places where sermons were initially delivered. Hints to the places of preaching or the preachers' places of residence indicate that clergy from many more towns composed anti-rebellion sermons.

The timeline in Figure 4.2 shows that the vast majority of the (mock) sermons and responses were published in connection with the Jacobite risings. These numbers were not reached again in the second half of the eighteenth century.[100] Sermons approved and printed by order of Parliament held their ground well until the 1770s, but court sermons rapidly declined in influence.[101] In general, political sermons became less topical and more consensual.[102] Preaching on the occasion of political assemblies and elections continued but was more closely monitored.[103] National days of fasting,

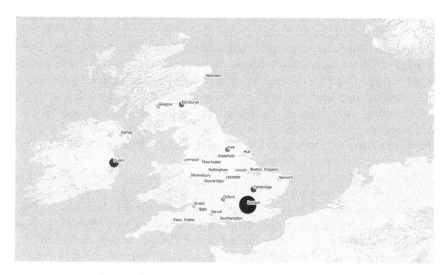

Figure 4.1 Map of places in the British Isles where anti-rebellion sermons were printed between 1684 and 1800: based on metadata extracted from WorldCat, see zoomable map on https://monikabarget.github.io/Revolts/sermons.html

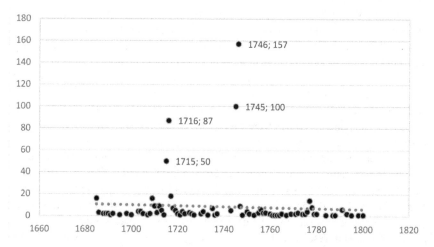

Figure 4.2 Number of printed anti-rebellion sermons per publication year between 1685 (Monmouth Rebellion) and 1800: metadata automatically extracted from WorldCat, see full metadata in ZOTERO library: https://www.zotero.org/groups/2351893/british_riots_and_revolts_of_the_enlightenment_age

mourning or celebration that had often given less-restrained preachers an occasion to indulge in religious controversialism and political opinion-making were eventually toned down.[104]

While printed riot and rebellion sermons in Britain initially propagated a close alliance of Church and State, those published in the second half of the eighteenth century allow for more varied interpretation. A word tree of the sermon metadata for the years 1684 to 1750 collected from WorldCat shows the predominant structures of rebellion-related sermon titles.[105] While thanksgiving sermons in support of the government position stand out as a popular preaching occasion,[106] the word tree also highlights the various spatial settings of political sermons, which ranged from cathedrals to parish churches or private chapels and reached audiences from aristocrats to university scholars and ordinary people. Moreover, the titles as well as the overall literary form of these sermons were consistent even across confessional divides. Despite Anglican calumny that Protestant dissenters were 'an [sic] usurping faction',[107] who hypocritically practised 'occasional conformity',[108] and aspired to 'new forms of government, all of them oppressive to the subject and destructive of religious and civil liberty',[109] most Presbyterian preachers of the Jacobite era carefully avoided references to the death of Charles I. On the contrary, they successfully evoked a common Protestant interest and formed unexpected coalitions.[110] Trans-denominational Protestant collaboration, for example, was vividly reflected in the countless anti-Jacobite sermons delivered even in small rural parishes.[111] The unusual number of sermons that were printed in London, Edinburgh, Belfast and North America illustrates the political relevance of preaching and the temporary willingness to put aside doctrinal disagreement.[112] In style and content, these sermons mimicked secular speeches and ancient rhetoric.[113] First, the printed sermons were clearly structured and followed logical argumentative structures. Second, the Biblical quotes and metaphors employed primarily adapted Old Testament stories of kingship and nationhood, whereas New Testament exegesis or explicitly denominational doctrines were hardly ever mentioned.[114]

These sermons were delivered on various occasions from imminent conflict to the anniversaries of past conflicts. Similar to historiography, these sermons kept the memory of political conflict alive and integrated more recent uprisings into a complex and often teleological narrative of British history.[115] Generally speaking, Hanoverian anti-rebellion sermons praised Britain's constitutional progress from the 'times of darkness and confusion before the Reformation',[116] to the 'old parliamentary constitution in a limited monarchy'.[117] Anglican and Presbyterian preachers alike agreed that the initial spirit of freedom had originated in the Roman Empire and endured through the dark reign of Mary I to the era of Queen Elizabeth I, and her 'happy union of church and state in a national parliamentary establishment of a truly Christian free government both in church and state'.[118] Protestant preachers were eager to focus on Catholicism as the common enemy, and devoted lengthy analyses to the political failures of the Roman Church and Catholic princes.

Whereas Jacobites were either denounced as 'slaves to lust'[119] or as adherents of 'unwilling, forced obedience to God',[120] Britons loyal to the Protestant Succession were described as partakers in 'salvation',[121] and 'heaven'.[122] Salvation and heaven, however, were not merely spiritual categories; they also represented the restitution of temporal law and society's ability to comply with it. In his sermons of 1746, the Anglican priest the Rev. Mr Dobbs from Belfast even described heaven as 'the divine-life seat of law-making',[123] thereby drawing a parallel between Britain's earthly constitution and the kingdom of God. Some sermons also popularized contractual theory. Dobbs, for example, described the Christian covenant freely formed with Jesus Christ as a model of the mutual love and trust between princes and their subjects.[124] However, factions critical of government policy also made use of sermons or at least carefully imitated and subverted them in print publications such as the ironic 'layman's sermon'.[125]

Preaching controversies thus played an important part in the early modern shaping of public opinion and allowed even low-ranking and lesser-known clergymen a say in ongoing debates.[126] Many eighteenth-century clergymen proved their talents as media entrepreneurs who wittily combined preaching, printing, advertising, newspaper publishing and, above all, a definite profit orientation.[127] In the decades after the Glorious Revolution, radical High Church men, in particular, gathered large crowds.[128] Although these men meant to speak on behalf of the true royal faction, their opinions displeased the government and forced them to attach themselves to political oppositions. The Sacheverell Riots of 1710 and the Bangorian Controversy (mostly dated to the years between 1716 and 1721) revealed how eagerly clergymen contributed to early eighteenth-century debates on reform and resistance. Henry Sacheverell, a fervent defender of High Church and Tory interests, condemned Presbyterian theology,[129] and attacked Whiggism.[130] Some of his printed sermons sold more than 40,000 copies before Sacheverell was tried for seditious libel in 1710.[131] Some sales estimates even suggest that he sold as many as 100,000 copies.[132] Two of his printed sermons were 'ordered to be burnt by the common hangman'.[133] In his self-defence, Sacheverell cited the duty of preachers to defend morals and orthodoxy beyond the law.[134] He thus invoked a constitutional concept in which truth and justice were not debatable but transcendental and firm. What he considered a defence of politics against undue politicization of dissenting religion, however, was perceived as revolt and illegitimate political action from below by most government members and parliamentarians of his time.[135]

Nevertheless, Sacheverell's supporters rioted in the streets of London and Oxford, causing 'the most serious disorder on London's streets since the revolution'.[136] Although Sacheverell was banned from preaching for three years, he remained an almost iconic figure.[137] His down-to-earth and entertainingly offensive manner of preaching was often criticized by well-educated contemporaries but earned him success with women and the lower classes.[138] The unpopular proceedings against him eventually provoked the shift of power from Whigs to Tories in the late reign of Queen Anne.[139] As such, the Sacheverell riots of the early eighteenth century manifested a new role of religious leaders.[140] Although actively promoting political change from below was the domain of dissenters, Church of England clergy such as Sacheverell also understood and exploited the power of popular support. Britain's parish system with its strong administrative communalism and the assertive, independent theological colleges at Oxford were vibrant fountains of oppositional agitation.[141] Stuart sympathizers strove to present their cause as trans-confessional, occasionally mocking pro-government sermons in printed preaching parodies.[142] In fact, the Crown and Parliament could not exploit anti-rebellion preaching during the Jacobite uprisings without denying Stuart Prince Charles Edward's semi-Protestant upbringing and his conversion to Anglicanism in London.[143] Following the arrests of radical High Church men during the reign of George I, the 1740s and 1750s saw the arrests of liberal preachers who, it was alleged, 'tend[ed] to alienate his Majesty's Subjects from their Duty and Allegiance'.[144] Political sermons thus fuelled the competitiveness of British politics and raised fundamental questions on the relationship between spiritual authority and temporal power.[145]

According to Andrew Starkie, the 'most bitterly fought ideological battle of eighteenth-century England' was the so-called Bangorian Controversy led by Thomas Sherlock and William Law as representatives of High Church Toryism against Low Church Bishop Benjamin Hoadly (appointed to the bishopric of Bangor in 1715).[146] The actual debate was started by Hoadly's controversial sermon *The nature of the Kingdom, or church, or Christ* held before the king in 1717 and argued out in pointed political treatises as well as periodicals.[147] In his sermon, Hoadly denied that the Church had doctrinal or disciplinary authority and disputed that allegiance to the Church of England should condition admission to public office.[148] This question concerned Protestant dissenters as much as Anglican non-jurors, and the fierce pamphlet war that followed reflected the diversity of the theological as well as the political spectrum.[149] Over two hundred pamphlets linked to the controversy were published by fifty-three writers in less than six months.[150] An Anglican with Puritan roots, Benjamin Hoadly was better known for his texts on the British constitution, civil government and resistance than for spiritual works.[151] His main opponent Thomas Sherlock also became an active pamphletist and controversialist. Although Sherlock was a Tory, he was no Jacobite, but was initially favoured by George, Prince of Wales, and his wife Caroline during George I's reign.[152] From 1737 onwards, Sherlock expressed his opposition to several law bills and even publicly entered the debate on the treatment of the Highlands in 1745.[153] As one of the 'best-selling religious writers' of his century,[154] Thomas Sherlock pioneered a 'loyal opposition' that became the standard modus operandi among Anglican bishops.[155]

Therefore, the Bangorian debate must be viewed in the wider context of the transformation of the British party system in King George I's reign. As Chapter 2 details, the early days of Hanoverian rule did not so much tighten the triumph of Whiggism over Toryism but reflected 'fierce divisions amongst the Whigs'.[156] When party allegiance diversified and downplayed 'religious truth' in favour of more fluid representations of 'interest',[157] the Tories, in particular, faced the problem of 'party continuity'.[158] Apart from High Church Anglicanism, which tended to be 'ultra-monarchist' in terms of government,[159] there were Low Church Anglicans and even High Church Calvinists, who rejected the influence of bishops but staunchly supported the king as the supreme head of Church and State. In general, boundaries between pro-government and oppositional clergymen were no longer clear-cut, and Anglicanism sided more frequently with non-governmental agents. This increased the political opportunities of all Protestant denominations to play the nationalist card, presenting their actions as legitimate expressions of the public interest.[160] Religious argumentation became one possible justification among others and lost its exclusive appeal.[161]

Whenever one faction heavily relied on religion as a justification, the opposing party would try to expose its hypocrisy. Clergymen still sat in Parliament and continued to hold political office,[162] but attempts were made to circumscribe the role of clergymen in politics more clearly.

William Wake, Archbishop of Canterbury between 1716 and 1737 and known as 'one of the most important and committed ecumenists' of his time,[163] debated in 1703 whether church conventions called by the Crown and parliamentary attendance were historically 'a Burden and a Grievance' or a privilege.[164] Medieval absence from Parliament was, according to him, based on an agreement that the clergy already 'did his [the king's] business elsewhere'.[165] Following the 'limitation of the Clergy's Power',[166] and legal restraints imposed since the reign of Henry VIII, however, the clergy of his own time ought to regard parliamentary duty not only as 'service to the King' but also as a contribution to 'the Affairs of the Kingdom' in collaboration with 'other great Men, and Nobles of the Kingdom'.[167] Wake thought that an assembly composed of 'ecclesiastical persons' could be a convention of a 'civil nature'.[168]

Such debates also referenced French Jansenism, a theologically pessimistic movement accused of Calvinist tendencies, which was linked with Gallicanism and advocated conciliar autonomy from Rome.[169] On the one hand, seventeenth- and early eighteenth-century Jansenism spoke to British hopes for a more rational Catholicism and their own idea of a state-oriented national Church at home. It also seemed to permit Irish Catholics to 'ease political and confessional tensions'.[170] On the other hand, Britons feared that the moral rigour inherent in Jansenist thought would lead to a potentially revolutionary detachment of believers from temporal authorities.[171] Britain's own religious mainstream settled somewhere in between. This included the attempts by Catholic lawyer Francis Plowden to redefine the Church–State relationship in a way that would permit a multi-confessional British Empire in which temporal and spiritual authority were separated yet supported each other.[172]

Plowden promoted a 'submission to both these [the spiritual and temporal] powers or authorities',[173] as 'Man's conscience [was] bounden by his Creator to obey the laws',[174] which would eventually contribute to peace between different denominations:

> It must be the general wish of all peaceable Subjects and good Christians, not to widen, but to close, if possible, the breach that exists between different societies of Christians. [...] In searching into the nature of temporal and spiritual, I do not mean to weaken either, but to inculcate and enforce submission to both.[175]

Although Plowden's hopes for a reconciliation between Catholics and Protestants in the British Empire were not fulfilled in his own lifetime, a multifaceted Protestant engagement in public discourse at least permitted Anglicans and dissenters to move more freely between the different political factions and to respond more spontaneously to concerns within their local communities.[176] E. P. Thompson stresses that certain Nonconformist groups even de-politicized themselves and hoped to retreat into private self-exclusion, while others displayed 'submission and zeal in combating the enemies of established order'.[177]

In the decades between the last Jacobite Rebellion and the brutal climax of the French Revolution, some clergymen even emerged as 'apostles of modernity',[178] advocates of 'freethinking',[179] and pioneers of 'free-speaking'.[180] A dissenting minister, John Henley, who described himself as a 'Rationalist',[181] explicitly defended the 'liberty of preaching'.[182] He claimed that critical preachers like himself did not 'intend to sow Sedition in the Minds of his Majesty's Subjects, to alienate them from their Duties and Allegiance, and to stir up Rebellion'.[183] Rather than condemning oppositional preachers for their 'seditious words',[184] 'Princes of superior Spirit [ought to] like Preachers and Writers against them, as their best Friends, an Antidote to the Fatality of Flatterers, Knaves and Fools'.[185] In his opinion, preaching was superior to political pamphleteering because it had the longest tradition of reaching the simple folk, and because preachers had the least interest in working to their own advantage.[186] The religious sphere of eighteenth-century Britain was reconstructed as a reliable arena of debate and inseparable from the freedom of the press.[187] Biblical justifications for specific policies were given up in favour of a more general Christian call to contribute to society with wisdom and honesty.

Except for the revival of inherently theological argumentation within the abolitionist movement, most clergymen who acted as political speakers and authors in the later eighteenth century adopted a more worldly style, and even the most loyalist clerical publications were now perceived as personal contributions to an open-ended debate rather than official statements.[188] Preachers directly employed by the British government or colonial officials in New England professed neutrality in party politics, focusing instead on general aspects of good governance.[189] On the eve of the American Revolution, in 1774, American preacher the Rev. Gad Hitchcock summarized the eighteenth-century controversy over the boundaries of opposition in a sermon:

> If it be true that no rulers can be safe, where the doctrine of resistance is taught; it must be true that no nation can be safe where the contrary is taught: If it be true that this disposeth men of turbulent spirits to oppose the best rulers; it is as true that the other disposeth princes of evil minds, to enslave and ruin the best and most submissive subjects. [...] And which of the two shall we chuse [sic], for the sake of the happy effects and consequences of it?[190]

Hitchcock advised the Massachusetts governor and council to act likewise, while the function he attributed to the churches was to encourage 'the religion of rulers',[191] so that 'good disposition' would always inspire their public conduct.[192] The compromise suggested by Hitchcock was to define legitimate government in Britain and the colonies not as instituted 'by God', but as government 'from God'.[193]

Conversely, political sermons or prayers were composed or commented upon by non-clergymen.[194] On a more general level, religious politics on a national or imperial scale made way for more diverse and often regional church lobbying on behalf of certain segments of society. Christian agents contributed to the development of 'pro-Americanism', as well as a more general 'political radicalism',[195] which arose in Britain.[196] After the foundation of the Society of Constitutional Information and other more radical associations in the 1780s, loyalist sermons 'became noticeably more conservative',[197] and supported government authority more than ever since the heyday of High Church Toryism, but this could not retract the constitutional compromise formed between religious communities and public opinion in the two previous decades.[198] Some preachers saw their role between religion and politics with self-irony, for example when authors jokingly referred to 'theologico-political Sermons' that would see 'rapid circulation' in print.[199]

The demagogic potential of preaching and religious publishing, however, was real. From 1779 to the turn of the century, conspicuously conservative and socially stratified '"Church and King" disturbances' forced the ruling government to ensure that religiously motivated acts of popular violence would no longer be tolerated.[200] This referred to the Anglican relationship with Protestant dissent, but also to Anglican relations with Catholics.[201] Although the Roman Catholic population in the early modern British Isles is difficult to estimate because it did not have a 'Nonconformist concept of membership',[202] Irish (labour) migration to England meant that Ireland's purported 'monastic piety',[203] as it has been called, was now a national concern.[204] In Ireland itself, aggressive religious publishing had devastating effects.[205]

When the trans-confessional United Irishmen movement was violently defeated at its last stand in County Wexford, religious sectarianism triumphed.[206] The County Armagh clashes between the Protestant Peep o' Day Boys and Catholic Defenders of the 1780s had already foreshadowed the propensity of volunteer groups in Ulster to commit religiously biased atrocities, and as the proportions of Catholics and Protestants in Northern Irish communities evened out, rioting increased in frequency.[207] The churches began to serve as unrivalled opinion-makers, educators and political motivators.[208] Although the 1798 Rising pursued many non-religious goals, and the United Irishmen affirmed that 'nothing was farther from their view than a religious war',[209] the active engagement of Catholic priests such as the Rev. James Coigly from County Armagh and Father John Murphy from County Wexford revived Protestant fears of Popish plotters.[210] After the deadly Dublin riot of 23 July 1803, Catholic Archbishop Dr John Thomas Troy felt obliged to speak out against 'the rebellious outrages in this city',[211] and to affirm Catholic opposition to revolutionary endeavours in contrast to Robert Emmet's attacks on the government.[212] Irish Catholics were said to be 'ready for any Change because no Change [could] make them worse'.[213] Nevertheless, serious research into the Catholic history of the British Isles increased in the late eighteenth century, and Scottish antiquarians, among others, paved the way for gradual integration of Catholicism into their country's national heritage.[214]

The fact that Catholics in England and Scotland advocated neutrality of the state towards religious communities was often not interpreted in their favour. Although the reputation of the Catholic minority in Britain had been tainted ever since the Gunpowder Plot of 1605,[215] the Holy See had generally opposed armed rebellion in official writings but encouraged Catholic subjects to engage in 'passive resistance'.[216] As a consequence, British Protestants alternately described Catholics as rebellious or enslaved and immature.[217] In a sermon preached in York on 29 September 1745, the Rev. Zachary Suger called the Stuart family and their supporters 'the idolatrous Assyrians',[218] denigrating their faith and foreign relations. However, while Jacobitism was predominantly equated with Francophile, Scottish or Catholic in English propaganda, elite solidarity was not completely superseded by religious factionalism or political allegiance during the Jacobite rebellions.[219] In his book on the 1715 Jacobite rebellion, Daniel Szechi has uncovered negotiations and reconciliations between Hanoverians and Jacobites in Scotland, which either recalled past alliances or build strategic relationships among neighbours.[220] In the later eighteenth century, when republicanism emerged as the most dangerous oppositional force, the Catholic clergy and laity managed to present themselves as loyal subjects and trade opposition to American patriots for religious liberty. 'Moderate Catholicks' were encouraged to accept the Protestant crown and Protestant supremacy for the sake of prosperity and peace.[221] The Rev. John Arbuthnot tried to convince them that the kings and queens of England had always treated them with the 'utmost Lenity'.[222]

When violence erupted in Glasgow on 18 October 1778, Catholics praying in a private home were attacked 'without the smallest interposition of the Civil Magistrate at the time, or the least notice being taken of it since'.[223] Similar events followed in Edinburgh in 1779. This prompted George Hay, the apostolic vicar in the Scottish Lowlands, to compose *A memorial to the public, in behalf of the Roman Catholics of Edinburgh and Glasgow*, denouncing the riots as unconstitutional.[224] His line of argumentation went against the existing penal laws but sketched out the conformity of the Catholic community with more general perceptions of Britishness and good citizenship.[225] Hay asserted that religious prosecution must not be camouflaged as a fight against 'enemies to government and society' as long as Catholics proved to be loyal subjects to the king and supporters of the 'happy Constitution'.[226] In his view, his Catholic community at Edinburgh could neither be called 'bad subjects' to the Crown[227] nor 'bad citizens' with respect to society as a whole. After all, the Catholics of Edinburgh had willingly answered the king's call (in 1778) for military assistance in America, and this show of loyalty should elicit equal rights.[228] His perception of citizenship and pleas for governmental neutrality catered to both the liberal conviction that religion was essentially a private matter and to more traditional takes on the collective relevance of the faith.[229] Repudiating uncompromising majority rule, Hay imagined the British constitution as an institution that rose above the fickle whims of the populace and seditious tendencies even among presumably loyal Protestants.[230] In Hay's opinion, the Nonconformists' claim that religion was the basis of free-floating, unregulated popular political participation was the greatest danger to the British constitution, and he criticized publications of the Society for Propagating Christian Knowledge as insolent attacks upon the king in Parliament.[231] Hay's approach, which reinforced the supremacy of institutionalized and representative politics, may be termed 'civic Catholicism' or 'high constitutionalism', in contrast to more radical strands of Catholicism in Ireland and among exiles in continental Europe and America.

In the course of Lord Gordon's trial, Lord Mansfield and other government members paraphrased anti-Catholic treason laws as conditional and temporal restrictions, which could be relieved if necessary.[232] Supporters of Gordon's Protestant Association, by contrast, held fast to the belief that all seventeenth-century laws against potential Catholic conspirators ought to be preserved as 'salutary regulations to which this country owes its freedom and his majesty his crown'.[233] Allan Ramsay wrote in response to the Gordon Riots that English laws should not seem to 'imply a power permitted by statute to the rabble to pull down places of religious worship of a certain description; a permission inconsistent with every principle of civil government; and which discovers, as much as any part of this statute, the narrow and temporary views of those who had the framing of it'.[234]

In 1791, the authorities were eager not to intensify religious fervour when crowds in towns such as Manchester and Birmingham rioted against liberals and dissenters who were celebrating the fall of the Bastille.[235] In Birmingham, enraged Anglicans attacked the dissenting meeting house and the private home of the Unitarian minister Joseph Priestley, who was said to admire the French Revolution and to 'scruple no means to overturn not the church only, but also the state'.[236] In his defence of English Unitarians written after the Birmingham Riots, Joseph Priestley underscored that his denomination bore 'no relation to any system of politics',[237] and that 'there are Unitarians among the friends, as well as the enemies, of what is called government'.[238] In general, Priestley and other eighteenth-century dissenters did their best to present themselves as 'the best friends to the present government',[239] and the monarch's 'faithful subjects'.[240] While the government in London took a thoroughly rational approach, avoiding the question of denominational conflict in all public statements, the *Boston Gazette* reprinted a detailed account written by an Englishman on the conservative, religious background of the riots in its issue of 19 July 1791.[241]

In the same year, the Rev. James Wilkinson, a reform-oriented Anglican vicar in the Broomhall district of Sheffield, became the victim of mob violence when an enraged crowd attempted to set fire to his house. The mob succeeded in burning his dinner table and several books before dragoons were able to quash the riot.[242] Although Wilkinson had been an advocate of parliamentary reform and a man of social commitment, public opinion turned against him when he agreed that a part of the parish graveyard be demolished to widen Church Street.[243] His decision was taken for haughtiness, and the people's violent reaction deeply unsettled Wilkinson, who refrained from further political action.[244] In this case, too, the potential religious motivations of the rioters were not publicly discussed. But as a clearer separation of Church and Crown made divisions within British Protestantism more visible in the streets, some political authors feared that radical or violent groups would entirely monopolize religious rhetoric.[245] Mirroring attacks on seventeenth-century Puritan regicide and Catholic conspiracies, accusations of unduly mingling political and religious zeal were especially directed against democratically minded clergymen.[246] Statesman Edmund Burke (1729–97) criticized Richard Price, Joseph Priestley, Thomas Paine and other opposition writers as 'political theologians' and 'theological politicians'.[247] And as the fear of republican conspiracies peaked in the 1790s, so did British debates on the compatibility of ordination and public office. Eventually, clergymen were (temporarily) excluded from the House of Commons. The year 1801 saw the Clergy Disqualification Act (popularly known as the Horne Tooke Act) in reaction to the radical political agitations of English clergymen John Horne Tooke, who had been tried for treason in 1794.[248]

In America both before and after independence, similar conflicts divided patriot Protestantism into 'rationalists' and 'revelationists'.[249] Thomas Jefferson addressed religion as a predominantly private matter that should not influence political action, but although Adams and other founding fathers agreed with him that America ought to guarantee religious freedom, they were less 'secretive about [their] religion'.[250] John Adams, for his part, perceived religion as both public and political, although the different Churches had to be clearly separated from state politics. In the early days of the American Revolution, Christian meeting houses hosted many of the public steps towards independence, in which fiery preachers such as the Rev. William Emerson from Concord figured prominently.[251] Appealing to traditional religious community values and the equality of all Christians before God provided them with a powerful alternative to the remarkably functional but at the same time hierarchical British administration. They consciously rejected concepts of citizenship that the colonial governors tried to impose on them and aimed to construct their very own social roles.[252] Politicizing American citizens in 1774 meant activating their religious sense of duty. Secularization was certainly not 'the foundation of the founders' republican ideas'.[253]

On the contrary, the Bible was a vital source of legal argumentation, if not among all 'A-list founders', so among a considerable number of Calvinists on what Rick Kennedy calls the 'B-list'.[254] W. A. Speck's biography of Thomas Paine confirms this view and stresses that there was a strong religious imperative in *Common Sense*, 'which was littered with Biblical references showing that God had specifically denounced monarchy'.[255] Officers of the British Grenadiers stationed in New England loathed the religious fervour at work among the patriots before French (Catholic) engagement on the side of the Continental Army seems to have taken the wind out of their sails.[256] British soldier Sir (at the time: Captain) Charles Stuart, who was stationed in Boston shortly after the Battle of Bunker Hill, complained about the American recruiting system. He noted that American patriots went to the churches right after Sunday services to try and win over the congregations. Because some rebel leaders were even allowed to speak from the pulpit, the people were – in Stuart's view – deceived, foolishly mistaking opposition propaganda for a calling from God.[257] Charles Stuart even went so far as to accuse the Americans of fanaticism and 'enthusiastic frenzy', which he considered to be worse than any 'Roman (Catholic) bigotry' in history.[258] In his anti-American pamphlet of 1776, the Anglican Professor Bentham from Oxford grumbled that the Patriots were proud enough to believe 'that they alone practiced true Protestantism' ('eos solos vero Protestantismo studere').[259]

German lawyer and writer Christoph Heinrich Korn (1726–83) disdained that several Protestant preachers in America had left traditional parish positions to become members of the armed forces, where they not only admonished soldiers but 'climbed from the pulpit unto the horse, and from the skirmish onto the pulpit' ('von der Kanzel aufs Pferd, und vom Scharmützel auf die Kanzel zu steigen').[260] He clearly anticipated the danger of letting radicalized religion undermine political structures. Christian minorities had always exerted significant influence on American politics,[261] but the religious rhetoric was bolstered when patriot propaganda directly related England's political arrogance to the 'hypocrisy' and oppressive nature of the Anglican Church.[262] The accusation that 'all that infers infallibility and implicite [sic] Faith in Government is as much Popery, as the like in Religion' was popularized by the patriot polemicist Thomas Paine,[263] and remained an important justification for dissenting opposition to the king until the end of the eighteenth century. Although the exercise of violence in the name of hereditary, divinely instituted powers had been rejected, violence could nevertheless be spiritually sanctioned.[264] Religious lines of argumentation were now revived to juxtapose men's individual freedoms and an abstract machinery of power.[265]

Even half a century later, confessional frictions and conflicting perceptions of the constitutional role of religions threatened to tear the United States apart.[266] This was, however, not merely an inter-Christian conflict but involved other religious minorities who were considered foreign to the predominant Anglo-American culture, including Freemasons, some of whom acted as radical advocates of resistance theory or even republicanism.[267] Whereas Freemasons in Scotland were strongly linked to the Stuart dynasty and retained Jacobite sympathies,[268] the Grand Lodge of London and Westminster (often referred to as the Premier Grand Lodge of England in historiography) made sure to distance itself from conspiracies and Catholicism in its 1717 constitution.[269] The most political grouping through the century was perhaps Irish Freemasonry alongside oppositional Freemasons in the overseas colonies.[270] Their republican leanings and internationalism reflected popular stereotypes.[271]

Moreover, anti-Jewish stereotypes shaped political thinking in the United States as well as in Britain.[272] Jews had been banned in the reign of Edward I and were only readmitted in 1656.[273] From the reign of Queen Anne to the so-called Jew Bill of 1753,[274] derogatory references to the 'Unbelieving Jews',[275] and a deep-seated fear that Jews were foreign spies and enemies to Christian society, pervaded party propaganda as well as the gossip of the lower classes.[276] Some uprisings in the eighteenth century were marked by a peculiarly rationalized form of anti-Judaism, which foreshadowed the political anti-Semitism of the centuries to come.[277] In fact, fears of the mobile and well-connected Jewish minority were bound to replace fears of a French-Catholic invasion.[278]

On the global level, the necessity to rule a vast colonial empire at the smallest financial cost possible and with a minimum of military deployment gave an incentive for religious pluralism.[279] Native religions in America and India as well as Catholics in Canada received toleration. The fact that 'the English had made no attempt to convert the heathens',[280] although they seemed to be good-natured and naturally disposed to monotheistic religion, surprised Hessian theologian and poet Johann Gottfried Seume during his involuntary service in King George's Canadian army. Imperial religious diversity contributed to the decline of censorship and the consolidation of a free press,[281] which, in turn, guaranteed that religious communities could subsist as important para-political entities.[282] Overseas engagement also forced the Church of England to collaborate extensively with Church of Ireland clergy and other Protestant denominations such as Lutherans.[283] Although the overseas British Empire was to a large degree an 'empire of dissent',[284] and the Church of England was slow in setting up overseas bishoprics,[285] Anglicanism provided a cultural bond until the American crisis and again in the nineteenth century.[286] National or ethnic identities provided by the Anglican Church as a 'constitutionally incorporated entity',[287] for instance, found their expression in colonial architecture. In the 1840s, Anglicanism developed 'a new response to its metropolitan political situation, which initiated a revival in its colonial engagement'.[288] Most importantly, however, Britain's colonial expansion offered lay people opportunities to shape societal developments through religious organizations. In the nineteenth century, laymen of all the key denominations ran charitable organizations as well as missionary societies, which often amended social policies and Britain's expanding imperial administration.[289]

Social engagement could thus become an implicit form of political participation. The rise of 'Christian social teaching' transformed Anglicanism earlier than continental Catholicism,[290] and brought about 'a new critical spirit' within the episcopal hierarchy.[291] Anglicanism propagated moderate social but radical moral reform, and voiced such calls for change 'quite independently of the example of the Revolution in France'.[292] The anti-revolutionary concord in British society even permitted the Church of England to take a more progressive stand on educational reform.[293]

Religion was a field in which opinions could be formed and expressed in an institutionalized, collective manner, anticipating some of the functions that would later be fulfilled by explicitly political associations. A similar source of identity and interest mediation was the regular troops, militia and paramilitary organizations of the eighteenth century. Chapter 5 discusses how Britain's men in arms contributed to the development of national identity, influenced leadership concepts and challenged political procedures.

5

Regular troops, militia and armed civilians: Military and paramilitary agency as vehicles of national identity and social integration

The previous chapters have outlined that a more differentiated perception of society in eighteenth-century Britain influenced political roles outside governmental circles. To draw an analogy with religious communities, the regular army, militia and paramilitary groups emerged as important settings of opinion-making and collective identities. On the one hand, army and militia service had the potential to bridge class boundaries, at least rhetorically. On the other hand, the army and militia made important contributions to the eighteenth-century performance culture. Sociability was an important factor in the evolution of the eighteenth-century nation, and sociability among men in service proved a powerful blueprint for a controlled top-down politicization of society as well as for popular opposition.[1] Men in arms were both involved in the successful suppression of unrest and in unrest itself. One reason why British military service was a constant source of discontent and disagreement throughout the eighteenth century was that British society was averse to 'military government',[2] and thus relied on the temporary engagement of considerable numbers, especially in domestic peacekeeping.[3] Volunteer corps, for example, acted as local police forces and regularly put down riots.[4] In ideal circumstances, they gave citizens a chance to participate in the enforcement of law and order and to develop an active relationship with the body politic – a 'sense of belonging'.[5] Reforms of the militia service were especially encouraged by the Seven Years War and included a balloting system to choose servicemen from among the able-bodied men in each parish.

Local populations feared, however, that militia service at home would also oblige them to fight abroad. Eighteenth-century protests against militia and army regulations included the 1747 Knowles Riot against navy impressment in Boston, Massachusetts, the 1757 Militia Act Riot in the parish of Sibsey near Boston (England),[6] the 1761 Durham Riot opposing the new balloting system, the 1761 Hexham Riot[7] and the 1797 Massacre of Tranent, resulting from objections to the conscription of Scots into the British militia. Another category of military-related uprisings were those instigated by men in arms themselves and could come in the form of mutiny, the unwarranted removal of ammunition or the unjustified arming of civilians.[8]

The 1721 Bridgwater Army Riots, for instance, involved men of Brigadier Honeywood's Regiment.[9] In December 1745, a crowd in Manchester gathered and declared their willingness to fight the Jacobites. This led to a disagreement between principal inhabitants of the town who wished to supply the men with weapons and Robert Booth, Justice of the Peace, who felt that the Riot Act should be read to the crowd. In the end, Booth managed to disperse the crowd 'by other means'.[10] The 1775 Gunpowder Incident in Williamsburg, Virginia, was a conflict between the royal governor, Lord Dunmore, and militia led by Patrick Henry who had removed military supplies without permission.[11] In the same year, the American Revolution began with the Battle of Lexington and Concord, which resulted from a British search for hidden Patriot military supplies.[12]

My digital map of eighteenth-century uprisings deployed via GitHub displays these events as related to peacekeeping and military regulations (Figure 5.1). Though by no means exhaustive, the map highlights that many such events occurred in seaports and economically important towns such as Hexham, which was an eighteenth-century centre for the leather trade. The eighteenth-century militarization of British political culture played out in connection and often in competition with the economization mentioned in Chapters 2 and 3 and had constructive as well as divisive effects.

Despite the negative experience of the mid-seventeenth-century Civil War, Oliver Cromwell's New Model Army had revolutionized military leadership and fostered an ambiguous adulation of Britain's armed forces.[13] Cromwell was not egalitarian in a political sense, but was very much aware that his men in arms welcomed spiritual equality and a sense of brotherhood.[14] Even after the Restoration, Cromwell's social climbing brought about by personal effort and individual qualities was positively

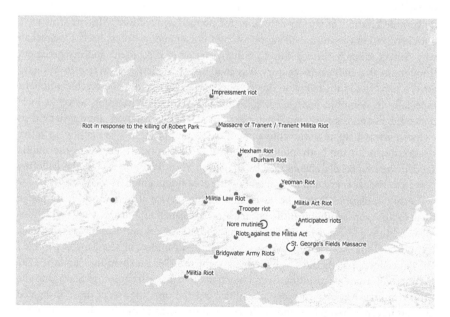

Figure 5.1 Partial map of unrest related to peacekeeping and military regulations in Britain, based on the digital map created by the author: https://monikabarget.github.io/Revolts/event-map/event-map.html

contrasted with the hereditary position of his noble opponent, Prince Rupert.[15] In that sense, the Civil War put the aloof and solitary heroism of traditional leaders into perspective and obliged future kings of England to choose a more cooperative mode of representation.[16] The lower classes and the nobility were thus encouraged to identify with new concepts of citizenship and nationhood that would outlast dynastic change. Throughout the later Stuart period, there was enthusiastic support for the British navy,[17] and even the popular discontent with 'James's standing army' during the Glorious Revolution could not completely turn the tide.[18] When the Revolution Settlement 'transformed an ascriptive aristocracy into an oligarchy of achievement',[19] the army played a major role in bringing old and new elites together. The very first addresses delivered to George I by the Commons recalled the country's successes in the glorious war ('une guerre si glorieuse') for maritime domination.[20] Although George I's administration was initially inclined to negotiate with France and Spain and strengthen diplomatic ties with the Holy Roman Emperor,[21] the newly elected magistrate of the City of London demanded that George I commit himself to further military action abroad.[22] In contrast to the rather negative perceptions of arming citizens that had dominated the influential political philosophy of Jean Bodin,[23] the British moved during the eighteenth century towards integrationist concepts of the military, as a means of controlling and educating the potentially violent masses from within.[24]

The concept of a ruler in arms and the brave citizen fighting by his side gained a powerful symbiosis. Reviving the strong link between soldierly commitment and political identity that the Wars of the Three Kingdoms had first brought about, eighteenth-century royal leadership was moderately militarized. Whenever William III, George I or George II publicly displayed themselves as 'soldier kings',[25] this implied active cooperation with their noble officers and common recruits, who in turn were obliged to show their colours. The appeal to soldierly virtues offered possibilities to combine old traditions of patronage and heroism with a new national and rational outlook.

Both in monarchical and republican world views, the civic soldier symbolized a common identity and national spirit that had formerly been represented by the aristocracy alone.[26] This is also evident in the militarization of French society in Louis XIV's age, which temporarily strengthened the Crown and yet provided the centralized, nationalist infrastructure that late eighteenth-century revolutionaries needed to implement a change of government.[27] The self-image of Britain as a 'warlike nation' proved outstandingly powerful in the fight against Jacobitism and in the struggle for colonial expansion.[28] A telling anti-Jacobite propaganda poster kept at the National Library of Scotland shows loyal soldiers marching in formation to defend 'King and Country',[29] while a cartouche at the top shows two hands joined in a circle of light. Many such prints circulated during the 1745 Rebellion, heralding the engagement of 'middling Englishmen, armed and ready to fight, who fearlessly proclaim for "King, Country, Shop and Family"'.[30] Former Jacobite Henry St John, 1st Viscount Bolingbroke, outlined the skills necessary to good governors and successful opposition leaders in the metaphor of two armies preparing for battle:

> When two armies take the field, the generals on both sides have their different plans for the campaign, either of defence or of offence; and as the former does not suspend his measures till he is attacked, but takes them beforehand on every

probable contingency, so the latter does not suspend his, till the opportunity of attacking presents itself, but is alert and constantly ready to seize it whenever it happens; and in the mean time is busy to improve all the advantages of skill, of force, or any other kind that he has, or that he can acquire, independently of the plan and of the motions of his enemy.[31]

The qualities of military generals that political leaders were encouraged to adapt to their everyday business were careful strategical planning, temperance and commitment to their cause. As men in arms were esteemed as exemplary servants of the public good,[32] radical politicians such a John Wilkes even demanded that 'those who serve deserve the vote'.[33] The British government did not make this concession, but military recruitment betrayed an emancipatory approach towards the lower classes. Especially during the American War of Independence, both the British and patriot forces entered into an active dialogue with the population and presented military service as a way to improve oneself financially and, above all, morally and intellectually. A British recruitment call stressed that men could acquire the 'polite accomplishments of a soldier',[34] and presented army service as a collective cultural achievement. Stressing a sense of community beyond rank and ethnic background was especially necessary with a view to the diversity of Britain's troops fighting in North America. Wilhelmy has consciously portrayed the British army of the American revolutionary war as an 'Anglo-German army' because many Germans joined as 'soldiers for sale' and often stayed when their service ended.[35] The American Continental Army, for their part, appealed to the colonists' individual ambitions.[36]

Patriot recruiting and more general calls to support their cause even conveyed an anonymous intimacy as they addressed readers collectively yet charged their statements with strong emotion. A telling example of this is a public address to the inhabitants of Rhode Island that was written in 1767, inciting citizens to enter the local customs house and violently withdraw tax money.[37] The authors of the pamphlet could never be traced, but it is an important document in content and style. Despite its anonymity and generality, it suggested great closeness – with the citizens being addressed as 'dear children'.[38] The text evoked a sense of familiarity and 'friendship',[39] but also conveyed unscrupulous intimidation of those who opposed the patriot cause. Whoever dared to remove the pamphlet from their doorstep was warned: 'Take this down and you die before morning!'[40] Another patriot handbill, addressed 'to the people of America',[41] was published in New London on 4 May 1775 with the intention of tracking down Isaac Wilkins, a loyalist who was known to be an 'obnoxious Tory scribbler'.[42] It was addressed 'to the people of America' and offered a reward for his apprehension, using repetitions and exclamation marks (Figure 5.2).[43]

Handbills forced the unsuspecting readers to take a political decision, and openly threatened those who opposed patriot actions or wished to remain neutral with physical intimidation. A single-sheet bill, published by the 'true Sons of Liberty',[44] stated that all supporters of the *Non-Importation Agreement* were:

> determined to resent any the least Insult or Menace offer'd to any one or more of the several Committees designated by the Body at Faneuil-Hall, and chastise any

> ## TO THE
> # PEOPLE OF AMERICA.
> ### Stop him! Stop him! Stop him!
> #### One Hundred Pounds Lawful Money Reward!
> #### A Wolf in Sheep's Clothing!
> # A TRAITOR!
>
> WHEREAS Isaac Wilkins, of the Province of New-York, has made his escape from the place of his former residence, after having betrayed the confidence of his conftituents, and villanoufly confented, that they, and their pofterity, fhould become abject Slaves, to the mercenary, and tyrannical Parliament of Great-Britain; and hath, in divers other inftances, endeavoured to deftroy the Liberties of America, in which *only* Freedom will reign amidft the moft fanguinary machinations of her inveterate enemies.——Therefore, whoever apprehends the faid Ifaac Wilkins, and fecures him, that he may be fent to the Provincial Camp, in Maffachufetts-Bay, fhall receive the above reward, of the Commanding Officer of the faid camp.
>
> By order of the committee.
>
> NEW-LONDON, May 4, 1775.

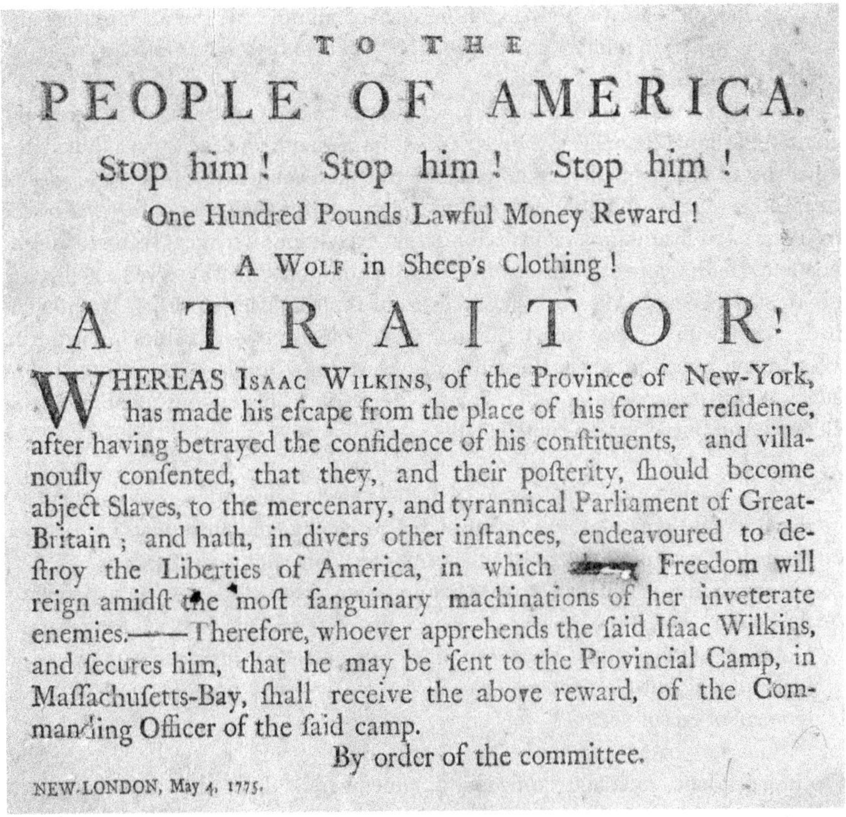

Figure 5.2 Timothy Green (ed.), 'To the People of America: Stop Him! Stop Him! Stop Him!' New London, CN, 1775: https://www.loc.gov/item/rbpe.0030310a/

one or more of them as they deserve: and will also support the Printers in any Thing the Committees shall desire them to print. AS [sic] a Warning to any one that shall affront as aforesaid, upon sure Information given, one of these Advertisements will be posted up at the Door or Dwelling-House of the Offender.[45]

Such distance media transgressed printing conventions, as short handwritten leaflets were copied and further distributed by receivers. Patriot media often imitated direct speech to expose the emptiness of royal distance communication, and their eminently interactive approach often surpassed British propaganda in threat and resolution.[46] Although historians agree that modern militarism only took centre stage during the French Revolution and that the 'nationalization of war and bellicism' dates to the 1860s,[47] the eighteenth century was nevertheless a period in which military conflicts were interpreted as the 'people's wars',[48] rather than the cabinets' policy strokes. The 'patriotic conduct' of regular soldiers and above all militiamen in the Gordon Riots of 1780 was praised in public and still remembered ten years later.[49] For a moment in time, the army successfully anticipated more egalitarian and multi-denominational party formation. This was reflected in military communication between officers and soldiers as well as in military communication with enemy troops. Violence was never a replacement for verbal exchange.[50]

However, military communication always had to consider the enemies' communicational channels. Generals of the Continental Army knew that although the open spread of information could generate trust and solidarity, it might also inspire treason. George Washington was very much aware of the dangers of betrayal by his own men, and made sure that plans for daring expeditions were kept secret as long as possible. He developed a conservative information policy that reserved intelligence for trusted insiders. After British successes in the south in late 1778, Washington had to cope with General Henry Clinton's strategy to avoid open battles in the north. Washington hoped to attack isolated British posts, and in July 1779, he intended to attack a British garrison at Stony Point, New York. In his famous admonitions to General Anthony Wayne, he noted that

> secrecy [was] so much more essential to these kind of enterprises than numbers, that I should not think it adviseable [sic] to employ any other than the light troops – If a surprise takes place they are fully competent to the business – if it does not numbers will avail little. As it is in the power of a single deserter to betray the design – defeat the project – & involve the party in difficulies [sic] & danger, too much caution cannot be used to conceal the intended enterprise to the latest hour from all but the principal officers of your Corps and from the men till the moment of execution.[51]

Pro-independence media recorded and remembered – yet they also concealed and forgot.[52] Glorification of revolutionary heroes such as George Washington, for example, eventually drowned out the more ambivalent American voices.[53] Simultaneously, narratives of spies, saboteurs and mutineers flourished as a deterrent, and also to make sense of the grey areas in human behaviour.[54] As mutiny had been severely punished and reported in public papers, sixteenth- and seventeenth-century accounts frequently shifted between the danger that mutiny posed to the security of the nation and outspoken solidarity with the rioting soldiers.[55] During the English Civil War, mutiny within the parliamentary army was predominantly spread by the royalist press in favour of the revolting soldiers. A pamphlet printed for Richard Balden in London stated that Captain Wiles had 'tyrannize[d] over his souldiers [sic]', and 'revolt[ed] to His Majestie [sic]', which is why 'his souldiers [sic] gave him his due reward in slaying him for his treacherous heart'.[56] But in the eighteenth century, mutineers and deserters were more likely to be described as extraordinarily cowardly and unmanly, whereas loyal individuals who had withstood them were praised for their soldierly discipline and patriotism.[57] Parallel to the growing public regard for military service, acts of resistance among soldiers were covered in a wide range of media.[58] Ship mutiny was often reported in port cities and offered the opportunity to discuss political developments and social hierarchies. Similar to more extensive rebel biographies circulated in the eighteenth-century, newspaper reports on ship mutiny also contained narratives of reconciliation or even reintegration.[59] One concise example is a report on pardoned mutineers from Gosport in September 1748:

Wednesday last being the Day appointed for the Executing of seven Men who mutined [sic] on board the Old Noll Privateer, and who were tried and condemned some Time ago, the Boats belonging to each Ship in Commission in the Harbour, went out to Spithead early in the Morning, with a Lieutenant and File of Musqueteers in each, and about Ten o'Clock the Prisoners were brought upon the Deck of the Prince Henry, to have their Sentence executed; the Blocks were reev'd, the Halters about their Necks, the Death Flag let fly, and the Signal Gun fired for their being drawn up, when to their un-speakable Surprize, their Caps were pulled from over their Eyes, and they informed, that they were reprieved.[60]

In the American Continental Army more than anywhere else, accounts of failed mutiny were disseminated to keep ranks closed in times of hardship.[61] In the troublesome years from 1779 to 1781, when American motivation was low and the British had a real chance to win the War of Independence, the Continental Army was rocked by the ship mutiny of 1779 and the Pennsylvania winter mutiny of 1781.[62] In 1779, John Paul Jones shot a sailor who had attempted to strike his colours and reconcile with the British, and a print celebrating Jones as a hero of liberty was immediately published by printer Carrington Bowles.[63] In 1781, General Anthony Wayne, who was famous for his fearlessness in battle, tried to single-handedly quell a mutiny of Pennsylvania troops who rejected federal orders on the grounds that they felt 'only responsible to state law'.[64] Updating the religious concept that one should act according to one's conscience either in defending or defying state power,[65] the old narrative of the pious rebel martyr was replaced by the more secular transconfessional narrative of the brave soldier who remained true to his cause. This valorization of military virtue also compensated potentially seditious decisions of conscience with a strong sense of overall accountability. Yet even though the collective was paramount in military rhetoric, there was room for individual opinions and personal decisions of conscience. On several occasions, the authorities' communication deliberately addressed soldiers as mature citizens able to make their own choices, especially if they intended to sow discord among armed oppositions. In response to several British and Hessian mutinies, for example, Sir Henry Clinton offered 'free pardons to those who would return to the royal standard',[66] although the mutineers as a group were condemned and stigmatized. Decisions of conscience and personal accountability could be positively contrasted with the negative towering figure of the deceitful, self-motivated subversive who eluded description and categorization and whose deeds abnegated society in its entirety. Stories of proto-'terrorism' obsessed British and American media throughout the American Revolution,[67] but even more so during the Irish Rebellion of 1798 and the war with revolutionary France.[68] Although this term was not used in contemporary sources, the 'vagrant arsonist' and the fanatic saboteur,[69] who were feared in the eighteenth century, were both successors of the seventeenth-century 'papist conspirator' and predecessors of the nineteenth-century anarchist terrorist.[70]

All of these groups constitute an abstract yet universal menace that affects not just the ruling classes but each and every citizen. When open war broke out between Britain and America, a series of incendiary attacks upon the seaports of Portsmouth and Bristol, which held military supplies for royal navy expeditions to the colonies, frightened the government and many loyal purveyors of news.[71] Many observers suspected that these attacks had been organized by a well-connected band of American patriots, and the public was greatly surprised when it turned out that a single person, James Aitken, had been responsible.[72] Most official accounts stated that James Aitken had sided with the American cause because he was personally disappointed in King George III's reign, and as the court trial proved, Aitken's attempts to establish closer links with the American patriots during a trip abroad failed. He had not received order from the colonies but acted on his own behalf, which was unusual and excited public interest even after his execution.[73] Whether texts defied or supported Aitken, they all stressed his deeply personal motivations and his wish to 'do some notable action, that would shew how much I loved my country'.[74] In this way, the last dying speeches or life stories of famous rebels could indeed advance the necessity for every man to contribute to the welfare of his home country either as a soldier 'in the field' or as a loyal civilian who 'light[s] a torch'.[75] Needless to say, accounts of sabotage and attempted assassination could generally be used to justify 'organized fire-fighting, policing, and measures against the homeless poor'.[76]

Yet in contrast to the earlier 'fear of witches, poisoners or Jewish plotters',[77] which had primarily strengthened the authorities' monopoly on violence, eighteenth-century scenarios of terror also served to award the broader population an active role within the political body and to channel bourgeois activism into pro-government engagement. The fight against organized crime forced rulers and subjects as well as law courts and armed forces to cooperate, and even people who were normally excluded from formal political participation could contribute to the perpetuation of constitutional values. Whenever citizens helped to track potential offenders down and showed support for the state apparatus, they benefited from political self-assurance.[78] This move towards general but hierarchical politicization is also reflected in the trials of those justly or unjustly convicted of organized arson, as their acts were punished as thoroughly political crimes rather than attacks upon private property.[79] To some degree, Dillinger even sees a rise in alleged political crimes as the natural consequence of state formation and expanding administrations.[80]

When faceless subversives became major public enemies on both sides of the Atlantic,[81] this did not indicate a state's decline or inability to modernize, but signified that power was newly distributed or that monopolies of authority had dissolved once and for all.[82] Daniel Brion Davis and Richard Hofstadter even go as far as to claim that the 'paranoid style' of early American governmentality enhanced the politicization of society as a whole,[83] because it linked 'private and collective fantasies' of danger.[84] In contrast with earlier no-popery hysteria yet similar to the eighteenth-century mutiny tales, American republican conspiracy theories switched public attention from the identity of the enemy to the identity of those resisting him for the sake of the nation. While most real plotters were rather unsuccessful, public belief in the strength of almost interchangeable conspirators from royal ministers to anti-abolitionists hints at the self-referential importance of 'countersubversion' in 'a nation born in revolution and based on the sovereignty of the people'.[85] Last but not least, this differentiation was a potential tool of reconciliation. The ideal of the 'common soldier' was eventually translated to civic life,[86] and made the heroic fulfilment of one's duty a metaconstitutional narrative nourished by the 'example of the greatest men in history'.[87] Above all, the concept of military virtue was internationally connectable, and stabilized international relations in the face of fierce competition between the European colonial powers. The modernization of the French army in Louis XIV's reign and similar reforms in Prussia set examples for their European neighbours, who successfully integrated the nobility in centralized, rationalized states by offering them careers as officers.[88] German media were not surprised when Frederick William of Prussia 'gave high-ranking military officers precedence over ministers and other state officials and courtiers'.[89]

Whereas the appointment of governors with military backgrounds had undoubtedly created tensions in colonial North America,[90] military concepts of leadership, which were also disseminated in popular printed portraits of rulers and rebels, eventually bridged representational divides between monarchist traditions and republicanism in the late eighteenth century.[91] At the same time, the use of physical force by governments required careful legitimation. Already in the course of the Jacobite rebellions, allegations of brutality shattered people's attachment to their leaders. This discourse resurged in the course of the American Revolution, which was not only characterized by incidents of actual fighting but even more so by extensive media debates on moral justifications.[92] In a response to the occupation of Boston, the town's board regretted in an address to General Gage 'that any occasion had been given for riots and disorders', but advised the governor to resort to purely legal rather than military measures.[93] The board rejected any notion of stationing troops in Boston because 'the civil power does not need the support of troops; and that it is not for his Majesty's service nor the peace of this province that any troops be required, or that any come into the province'.[94] Observers in New England tolerated violence exclusively in the form of lawful punishments against convicted individuals whereas military interventions in the political sphere would be 'as if in an enemy's country'.[95] At least temporarily, the actual outbreak of violence between the British troops and patriots cost the London government much of its esteem and made an agreement with the colonists less likely.[96]

At the turn of the 1780s, British troops and the American Continental Army had agreed upon a general 'sympathy towards a soldier' in the mutual treatment of their prisoners of war.[97] Respectful military correspondence allowed for humanitarian discourse and courtesy between enemies who did not consider each other as social equals.[98] American historiography would venerate British spy John André as an archetype of patriotic self-sacrifice for one's country,[99] while British historiography conciliatorily styled Irish rebel general Joseph Holt as 'a rebel against his inclination'.[100] An unsolvable political conflict could thus be reframed as a military combat among men of honour. Monarchical and republican ideals of leadership overlapped in the concept of the soldierly hero, which became especially apparent in the many portraits of American revolutionary leaders circulated not only in North America but also across Europe.[101] The life of a soldier, which implied the possibility of one's own death at the enemy's hands, had a levelling function in a continuously fragmented and hierarchical society.[102] Eventually, the cross-border value system of the military also bridged gaps between the United States and the old monarchies of Europe.[103] During the international crisis of the 1790s and the broad European alliance against revolutionary

France, even former revolutionary George Washington became an acceptable role model in British eyes. In 1799, the loyalist London magazine *True Briton* stated in an article on recent artistic production in England:

> Heath proceeds vigorously with his large Print of Washington, from the excellent Portrait by American Stewart. Now that all political animosities between this Country and the American State have happily subsided into alliance and attachment, every man who reveres the merit of consistent patriotism, and admires great talents, will be glad to have a Portrait of Washington, a zealous friend to the Liberties of his Country, but a decided enemy to the innovating doctrines of France, which, under a vain pretence of impracticable Freedom, tend to the subversion of all civilized Society.[104]

Furthermore, the London government realized that it could only limit the use of force if it developed alternative ways of exercising authority. The stationing of regular troops in front of the London Parliament in 1780 to keep rioters from entering was contested even by those who were meant to profit from it.[105] Parliamentarians such as Mr Fox 'lamented the necessity of calling in the assistance of the military, which he attributed solely to the weak administration of public affairs' because he felt that such measures would damage Britain's foreign reputation and make other countries 'see that those men who were at the head of Administration were incapable of governing the affairs of a state'.[106] Means of coercion were thus limited to more clearly defined cases.[107] Potential scenarios of intimidation often mattered more than the actual use of force.[108] The ability to use violence was important bargaining material.[109] In the late eighteenth century, the British state clearly attempted to limit government-enacted violence and reduce its more theatrical elements.[110] After 1780, the British army was subject to statute law and parliamentary supervision.[111] The meaning of public executions in early modern England also shifted from an ostentatious re-establishment of public order to personal contrition.[112] When British legislators granted prisoners and those condemned to death more humane treatment in the 1780s and 1790s,[113] torture in court trials had already fallen out of use.[114] In 1782, Scottish traitor David Tyrie, who had treacherously corresponded with the French, was the last man in British history to be hanged, drawn and quartered alive.[115] In independent America, too, attempts were made to cautiously demilitarize society without sacrificing the all-important appeal to the common people that military rhetoric had permitted.[116]

The downsides of British-imperial militarism and paramilitary organizations were escalations. Below government level, incidents of militia violence committed either in loyalty to the authorities or in order to make up for the authorities' neglect put public expectations to the test. In 1768, 1793, 1806 and 1819, four famous 'massacres',[117] in which British militiamen shot protesting and predominantly unarmed citizens, kicked off an intense public debate.[118] The shootings of Peterloo (Manchester) in 1819, which killed men, women and children rallying for social reform, were a perversion of volunteering.[119] In 1775, the American Provincial Congress, too, had to tackle issues of discipline and passed the 'Rules and regulations for the Massachusetts Army',[120] which united all patriot soldiers in a single army.[121] The potential danger of over-militarizing the state was thus closely linked with a danger of over-militarizing the public and placing too much power in the hands of recruited men. British officer Colonel Charles Stuart, who came to Boston in 1775, reported to his father that he and his fellow royalists dreaded a 'mobbish war' and much unnecessary bloodshed.[122]

Negative outcomes of army and militia service were even more controversially discussed when it came to non-white or even enslaved men. In 1788, James Ramsay suggested in his defence of abolitionism that former slaves might also be trusted with arms as they had already 'formed a part of the militia in Barbadoes [sic], and have been found faithful. This would universally be the case, were they advanced in society'.[123] Non-regular violence, however, turned out to be most destructive in Ireland, which was officially a separate kingdom of the Crown but treated 'as a British dependency'.[124] In the late 1770s, when Britain was fighting the war in North America and regular troops were withdrawn from Ireland, the Irish Volunteers formed as local Anglican and Presbyterian militia to keep the peace. Soon they acted as a political organization and lobbied for parliamentary reform.[125] When the Irish Volunteers movement was flourishing in the 1780s, armed parades became an influential form of political self-expression. Anticipating modern party formation, the Irish Volunteers used traditional occasions of military deployment such as the commemoration of William III's Irish battles in order to oppose the Navigation Act, demand free trade or even support religious toleration. They acted as an unofficial popular wing to Henry Grattan's Irish Patriot Party and advanced a moderately nationalist agenda that still respected Ireland's social and religious stratification. When, however, the parliamentary reform movement failed in 1784 and more radical reformers renounced Grattan's conservatism, Irish citizen engagement moved towards violence and, driven by a duplicitous government at Dublin Castle, a revival of confessional sectarianism.[126] Volunteering was suppressed in favour of government-paid militia and – after 1794 – the formation of radically loyalist yeomanry corps.[127] When the Peep o' Day Boys (an agrarian society of Protestant Irishmen) and Catholic Defenders intended to stage a major battle near Loughgall in 1795, the Dublin government failed to intervene while local merchants, magistrates and priests attempted to prevent bloodshed in vain. As only individual groups of fighters could be withheld, the so-called Battle of the Diamond took place, costing the lives of thirty Defenders.[128] Irish historian Thomas Bartlett has conceded that 'it was the Volunteers of 1782 who launched a paramilitary tradition in Irish politics, a tradition which, whether nationalist or unionist, has continued to shape Irish political activity'.[129] Therefore, the long-term consensus between governments and moderate reformers was that the use of force on either side could cause a devastating state of war and ought to be avoided. When the United Irishmen still styled themselves a thoroughly political movement in the early 1790s, however, they explicitly conformed to British laws and strict moral guidelines to prove that they intended 'nothing [...] treasonable or dishonourable'.[130] Inter alia, they fought drunkenness and bad conduct within their own ranks.[131]

Although military comradeship and soldierly discipline continued to influence popular politics, the public display, distribution or private possession of weaponry became incriminating evidence in high treason trials. During Lord Gordon's trial in London, the court tried to evaluate whether the initial procession staged by the Protestant petitioners had been a violent deployment.[132] One of Gordon's lawyers, Lloyd Kenyon, based his entire defensive strategy on the verification that his client had not been an unlawful, armed insurrectionist but opposed government peacefully.[133] Kenyon claimed that 'the multitude collected together' had not gone 'arrayed in military form', and that those men and women who had committed acts of felony 'had nothing to do with Lord George Gordon'.[134] In the case of David Downie and Robert Watt, members of the British Convention who were tried before the Court of Oyer and Terminer at Edinburgh in August and September 1794, the discovery of several pikes in the convicts' private homes spoke against them.[135] Lawyer Mr Hamilton interposed in his plea for the defendants that the 'smallness of the number (of weapons) was sufficient to prove they could not be intended to be used in any serious attack against the country'.[136] But as further evidence suggested that Watt and Downie had intended to set a fire near the Excise Office of Edinburgh and to seize the judges and magistrates,[137] both men were found guilty.[138] By contrast, Paul Thomas LeMaitre, John Smith, George Higgins and Robert Thomas Crosfield, who were arrested for the alleged *Pop-Gun Plot* (cf. Chapter 2) intended to assassinate King George III, were more successful in proving their radical yet deceitless intentions. A pamphlet printed for LeMaitre and sold by John Smith in 1795 while trials for high treason were pending outlined the London Corresponding Society's commitment to transparency: 'What can spies possibly discover in the Corresponding Societies? We have announced to the world the whole object and design of our meetings. The end which we wish to obtain is Universal Suffrage and Annual Parliaments'.[139] Of all members of the Society arrested, only Crosfield eventually stood trial for high treason but was acquitted.[140] And 'only Higgins did not continue with a rebellious attitude towards the government'.[141] The fear of Jacobin plotting and the French Revolutionary Wars (1792–1802) nevertheless put an end to all notions of republican militarism among reformers.

The nineteenth-century British army impelled top-down obedience rather than bottom-up participation,[142] and all across the Western hemisphere, the glorification of the nation-state and the prioritization of foreign politics undermined the emancipatory qualities entailed by 'civic-military discourses',[143] in the second half of the eighteenth century.[144] Equating liberty with national unity was most drastically pushed in Germany,[145] but there was an unprecedented 'nationalisation of warfare',[146] which affected their European neighbours.[147] Nevertheless, the Enlightenment shifted an earlier focus on peer solidarity and hierarchy by birth at least theoretically towards more inclusive agency. A containment of violence was inherently linked with transparent communication in politically valid media.[148] Moreover, maintaining the fragile equilibrium between the empowerment of citizens and the prerogatives of the institutionalized state entailed the careful management of early modern crowds. Chapter 6 is thus dedicated to the people and the impact of public opinion.

6

The people and the impact of public opinion

The last group of potential agents to consider is undoubtedly the largest and also the most obscure. It is the *people* whose presence in public life can be especially traced in the many media controversies and legal procedures concerning local riots, including riots linked with assault on individuals and trespassing on private property. The people in terms of larger crowds assembled in their own name and addressing more general societal concerns are especially prominent in insurgences related to political freedoms, religious or cultural identities, as well as in unrest driven by social or economic grievances (Fig. 6.1). The latter category comprises a wide range of events, from urban food riots and protest against imperial trade policies to different forms of agrarian riots. Agrarian unrest escalated especially in Ireland, where social conflict often overlapped with religious divisions between Catholics and Protestants or Presbyterians and the Church of Ireland (see sectarian violence covered in Chapter 4). In addition, the people also mattered as an abstract concept and an instrument of power that individual leaders could direct.

Therefore, this chapter traces active, explicit crowd action as well as implicit considerations of 'collective opinion' in the diverse opposition discourses that shaped the eighteenth-century British Empire.[1] Here I am especially interested in strategies of self-representation in textual media and performance through which crowds could, over time, claim lawful agency in public spaces. Since E. P. Thompson's studies on the moral economies of early modern English crowds and the social turn in British 1980s historiography,[2] it has been commonplace in modern research that there is 'power in numbers',[3] but it remains a matter of debate who exactly could participate in early modern crowd action, and how these crowds were evaluated by contemporaries. German philosopher and sociologist Jürgen Habermas popularized the concept of the emergence of a public sphere in the eighteenth century.[4] This rests on an open exchange between reasoning citizens and is connected with the communicational setting of the English coffee house.[5] Indeed, liberal theorists of the Enlightenment such as Benjamin Franklin saw an increase in population numbers as an increase in power and freedom for the entire nation, and encouraged natural population growth as well as the naturalization of foreigners.[6] The citizens whose opinions were heard, however, were still a considerably small group of propertied white men of the Protestant faith, and as politics became more institutionalized, there were new social and economic hindrances to staging effective oppositions.[7]

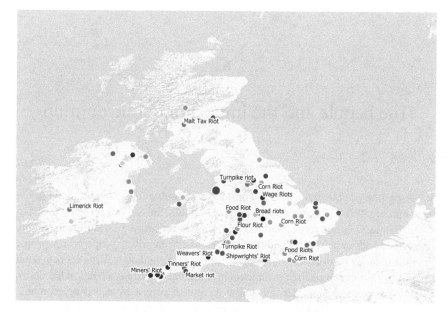

Figure 6.1 Partial map of unrest concerning social or economic grievances within the British Isles, including several food riots: based on data collected from Wikidata, the UK National Archives and printed sources. Created by the author.

Some historians have thus argued that resistance, at least on a large scale, became more elitist in the eighteenth century. Robin Clifton, for instance, has described the Monmouth Rebellion of 1685 as the 'last popular rebellion',[8] owing to its socially diverse recruitment of men who were most likely inspired by speeches they had heard in local taverns. Yet fundamental opposition to the system of government was just one way of expressing discontent. Among the more local, more mundane protests in which otherwise anonymous individuals of the lower classes mattered were food riots, local election riots and local riots against law enforcements, or local riots against military conscriptions (some of which are discussed in Chapter 5). Such riots could indirectly be related with more strictly political controversies or conscious local contributions to an ongoing rebellion elsewhere (see events marked as 'supplementary' on the interactive map presented in Figure 0.1). Eighteenth-century riot and rebellion publications were therefore concerned with a wide range of agents from rural populations to urban professionals.[9] In line with the multiple causes and motivations, agents mentioned in riots and their aftermaths range from post boys and innkeepers to ropemakers, tinworkers, canal construction workers or shipwrights, showing that people's occupations were an important aspect of their public identity and interests. As this chapter explores further, the main opponents in local riots can often be situated in a transition area between politically defined interest groups or parties in a modern sense, and more circumstantial affiliations based on religious and social backgrounds. Above all, eighteenth-century conflicts were often nourished by people finding themselves on different sides of an economic divide. Consumers, producers (especially food producers such as farmers) and traders (often involved in overseas markets) formed three strata of society that pursued different aims and frequently clashed in the public sphere.[10] Such conflicts, however, may be hard to distinguish from personal disputes, and many riots were linked with trespassing on private property or assault on individuals. As such, general measures for riot prevention also protected citizens from each other and could thus increase the negotiation power and acceptance of government officials. In this context, the Riot Tax levied locally in areas whose members took part in riots is important as it served to cover the costs of compensations to shop-owners and others whose property was damaged in times of unrest.[11]

Moreover, the Crown and Parliament relied on a broad range of media channels, including privately run commercial media, to legitimize their decisions. Throughout history, the people as spectators, or spectators representing the people, were inseparable from rituals of power as coronations, processions and executions all came in the form of public spectacles rooted in symbolism.[12] Early modern observers who did not perceive government as being derived directly from the people at least accepted the necessity of the people's acclamation to successful rule, or acknowledged their *sensus politicus*.[13] In Italian diplomat Niccolò Machiavelli's (1469–1527) much-discussed writing on princely leadership, public opinion featured as a prince's 'reputation'.[14] Conversely, protesting crowds of the fifteenth to seventeenth centuries demanded the publication of law texts, and paved the way for 'government control through publicity' (German: 'Herrschaftskontrolle durch Öffentlichkeit'),[15] which was well established in the Enlightenment Age. As governments found it impossible to inhibit public discourse, they actively channelled debates and directed the graduated politicization of the entire population.[16] Supported by the expansion of media in the eighteenth century, an actual dialogue between rivalling members of society and – more importantly – between subjects and their rulers ensued.[17]

The Exclusion Crisis of the 1670s and the Glorious Revolution of 1688 and 1689 were heydays of an elite exploitation of the people as a political catchphrase.[18] John Miller claimed that 'both Whigs and Tories, for different reasons, exaggerated the extent of popular involvement in the campaign to exclude James from the succession'.[19] After the Glorious Revolution, publications relating to the (presumed) voice of the people increased and peaked in the last three decades of the eighteenth century, when liberal revolutions had an impact on British political thinking. The short-lived mid-eighteenth-century revolution in Corsica, which first saw the island transformed into a constitutional monarchy under King Theodor I and shortly after into a republic, triggered many English publications.[20] While Britons sympathized with the Corsican fight against Genovan and French hegemony, they were critical of the Catholic culture of the independent regime and feared the economic consequences of instability. In the 1790s, Britain and the independent United States hoped to prevent that the underprivileged classes would follow a French revolutionary example.[21] And even those who doubted that the uneducated and poor could rise up on their own account still suspected that impressionable crowds could be hired or orchestrated.[22] In fact, a considerable number of local riots linked with the Jacobite rebellions had been 'pitched battles between mobs of Jacobite sympathizers and friends of the new government'.[23] More or less concerted election riots, which could easily get out of hand, were a long-standing element of British political culture and were encouraged by election candidates and partisan clergymen alike.[24] Crowds orchestrated by Whig parliamentarian Thomas Pelham-Holles, 1st Duke of Newcastle upon Tyne and 1st Duke of Newcastle-under-Lyne, fell into disrepute because of the disorders they caused on election days and other politically relevant occasions.[25] Newspaper reports regularly covered such events, but also mentioned attempts to include citizens in the prevention of unrest:

> Our Recorder Sir William Thompson, in his Speech last Thursday at Guildhall, antecedent to the Election of a Sheriff, put the Citizens in Mind of the Importance of that Office, particularly, that it was incumbent on them to suppress all Tumults and Riots in the City, and to preserve the Peace and Tranquillity thereof; and excited them to make Choice of such as are well affected to the present Establishment.[26]

Such communicational empowerment of the masses clearly preceded constitutionally guaranteed active participation.[27] The key concept accepted by all factions from Whig to Jacobite and from High Church Anglican to Protestant dissent was that bearers of valid opinion would need to be specified groups who acknowledged existing etiquettes and proper communicational channels.[28] This consensus encouraged popular self-organization in cooperation with oppositional social elites whose reading clubs, dinner parties and learned societies facilitated an institutionalization of functional roles in an analogy to politics. Most Tories and Whigs agreed that good leaders should take the people's concerns seriously and beware a 'fatal Consequence to the Publick',[29] which ill-considered decisions might have.[30] The conservative Enlightenment represented by Bolingbroke hoped to make clear that the king and the people were not necessarily rival powers but allies.[31] This implied a careful distinction between allegedly more civilized and constructive public controversies in the British Empire and destructive public controversies elsewhere. An anonymous pro-government author writing for the loyalist *Morning Post* in London claimed that, 'when prejudices subside',[32] 'no People under heaven, have a clearer view, or a more forcible understanding than Britons'.[33]

In reference to the famous dictum 'vox populi, vox Dei', which was taken up in many eighteenth-century pamphlets, English intellectuals debated whether the voice of the people heard in the streets could justly be acknowledged as the voice of truth.[34] On the one hand, Daniel Defoe and the anonymous author of the Jacobite tract *Ex ore tuo te judico, vox populi vox Dei*, which led to the execution of its printer John Matthews in 1719, stressed that certain 'tumults of the people' aimed at a just cause,[35] or that political leaders should want to have public opinion on their sides.[36] But on the other hand, 'sceptical Whig' David Hume,[37] and even liberally minded Lord Rockingham, were sceptical of the 'base disposition of the multitude',[38] 'the madness of the people',[39] or the judgement of 'an illiterate mob'.[40] Although 'popular favour' seemed worthwhile,[41] it was certainly not the 'voice of God'.[42] Throughout the early modern period, positive references to the people were countered by negative images of the rabble and the mob.[43]

Such imagery often mingled with biological (e.g. 'the roaring of hungry vultures'),[44] meteorological ('violent torrents',[45] 'tempests',[46] 'a tumultuous Tide')[47] or medical metaphors. While most of these descriptions could also be found in continental Europe, however, Paracelsian metaphors in England attributed rebellions to external contagion.[48] 'True Natural British Mobs',[49] and 'accidental Mobs',[50] were carefully differentiated from cunningly contrived plots and frightful foreign anarchy. The perceived dangers of 'foreign invasion' were linked with a spatial hierarchization in Britain's colonial Empire,[51] and affected many regions on the perceived peripheries, including smaller islands. Political Paracelsianism first and foremost expounded rebellion as a disease and infectious vice among certain minorities or borderland inhabitants that would have to be countered by disarmament and resettlement.[52] Stereotypical rebel biographies published after the Battle of Culloden, for instance, vindicated the gruesome subjugation of the Scottish Highlands and depicted Jacobites as cultural aliens to the British nation.[53] Whereas previous rebellion narratives had often paved the way for the social rehabilitation of repenting rebels and their relatives, post-1746 accounts pathogenized revolt as an inbred aberration in members of certain ethnic groups.[54] John Home's *History of the Rebellion in the Year 1745* and Samuel Johnson's report of his travels through Scotland enforced a widespread ethnic bias of Catholic Highlanders, whom they described as 'different by nature',[55] and unacquainted with the law.

Approaches to native Irishness were equally biased.[56] Anglo-Irish statesman William Temple made the native Irish population's inability to capitalize on 'the largeness and plenty of the soil, and scarcity of people' an argument for the political suppression of the entire country.[57] Contrasting the county of Armagh, which profited from linen trade but was one of Ireland's most conflict-ridden regions,[58] unfavourably with the Low Countries, he reckoned that the Irish were gratuitously prepared to 'indulge themselves in idleness and riot'.[59] Demographic policies were introduced to prevent revolt among the 'naturally wild and untameable' Gaelic-Catholics.[60] At the same time, peacekeeping in geographically remote areas forced the London government to engage more actively with populations who had previously withdrawn from conflict. During the Jacobite Rebellion of 1745, peasants in Northern England were reluctant to participate in fighting across the Scottish border, perceiving warfare as the business of noblemen and professional soldiers.[61] The English campaign in Scotland therefore pushed a nationalist politicization of rural societies that made it impossible to claim impartiality.[62]

Yet statesmen and philosophers also questioned how far legitimate political power could expand territorially. English philosopher Anthony Ashley Cooper, 3rd Earl of Shaftesbury (1671-1713), positively emphasized men's 'herding Principle, and associating Inclination', but claimed that these social abilities would best flourish in smaller communities based on personal relations.[63] In order to bridge larger distances, political philosophers developed the idea of representational government.[64] The famous frontispiece to Hobbes's *Leviathan* conveyed such a composite vision of unity in which humanity's desire for individual freedom was reconciled with collective freedom rooted in natural law.[65] As discussed in Chapter 3, representational government was also controversially debated en route to the American Constitution.[66] But American independence was only achieved because American patriots had first taken a more radical step of governmental decentralization. In their confrontation 'between the metropolis and the peripheries',[67] or between 'island' and 'continent',[68] the North American opposition to London-imposed taxation succeeded where regionalist strands of Jacobitism had failed.[69] The American patriots harked back to the traditional rights and charters of the colonial settlements and rejected a one-sided interpretation of their cultural and religious ties with the mother country.[70] Fearing 'arbitrary Parliamentary supremacy' situated in London,[71] regionalist rhetoric also ran through publications from England.[72] With a view to suffering peasants in scarcely urbanized parts of England, the anonymous author of *Cries of the Public* stated in 1758 that the dominance of London caused economic manipulation and monopolies.[73] In accord with the country party of earlier decades, he demanded that trade ought to be state-supervised and checked by a strong opposition.[74]

In order to construct lawful opposition, political movements needed to perfect their public appearance, or establish private spheres of debate to which the authorities had no immediate access. As for the management of crowds in public demonstrations, opposition leaders had to counter the accusation that they were intending to overthrow officially enacted legislation with the help of unlawful multitudes in the streets.[75] In the particularly heated atmosphere of the 1790s, one author employed the metaphor of a 'ball sleeping in a cannon', in order to express the ambiguous potential of the 'public force' to have either good or bad effects.[76] Similarly, Edmund Burke coined the derogatory metaphor of 'the Swinish multitude'.[77] In a critical response, an anonymous author (most likely Parkinson) thanked Burke for his 'epithet' to the people, and tried to give several reasons for their 'poor and oppressed' nature.[78] He returned Burke's attack, and exposed the animal-like character of tax-squandering politicians, calling them 'ye Swine of quality' in return.[79] However, this criticism of luxury and Britain's financial situation did not directly address political rights and left further demands to the more radical reformers. The eighteenth-century 'cult of commerce' also came with the danger of subversion.[80] A multi-confessional, transcontinental 'commercial civilization'[81] or 'economic nation'[82] could threaten the legitimation of monarchical rule as well as the supremacy of the Anglican Church. Among the government and moderate oppositions, the French Revolution spread the fear that the people could directly interfere in jurisdiction and legislation. The execution of Louis XVI of France in 1793, which Sir Hercules Langrishe, speaking on parliamentary reform in the Irish House of Commons, rejected as a 'cruel and unjust [...] popular domination',[83] went too far for the politically vocal majority in Britain and cemented the status quo. Therefore, many wealthy citizens supported the rulers' 'evolutionary move towards reaction',[84] and castigated the people's 'prevailing disposition to riot'.[85]

Nevertheless, the derogatory topos of the 'hired mob' or 'hired rabble',[86] who blindly followed those who paid them, insinuated that certain forms of self-reliant, heartfelt popular protest could be acceptable after all. In 1707, German lawyer Christian Wildvogel suggested a legal distinction between '*tumultum necessarium*' and '*tumultum voluntarium*'[87] – the former being a legitimate response to obvious dangers to the rights and lives of the people, the latter being 'machinated' by 'seditious and evil men',[88] without respecting law and order. Similarly, Scottish advocate and historian John Dalrymple pointed out that the mob and the people were hardly synonymous. Dalrymple was a supporter of King George III's government, and scorned oppositional attempts to incite and abuse hired crowds as an 'unconstitutional engine'.[89] At the same time, he valued the 'reason of the People of England',[90] and encouraged every citizen not to let the behaviour of mobs spoil the respect that the monarch had for his people.[91] This differentiation referred back to distinctions made 'between the good popolo and the evil plebe' in Italian treatises of the sixteenth and seventeenth centuries;[92] but in contrast to earlier descriptions of the mob as a transitory condition of the anonymous, often innumerable population in rage, the eighteenth century was increasingly concerned with the personal traits of character, attitudes and attire of those who got actively involved in political opinion-making.[93]

One form of protest that was widely tolerated as long as it remained temporary and territorially confined was social unrest aiming at the improvement of living conditions. The rapid economic transformation of society gave political conservatives – and above all aristocratic landowners – a chance to form alliances with the peasantry against salesmen, manufacturers and speculators.[94] Establishing acclaimed 'politics of provision',[95] British elites were able to stabilize existing class relations.[96] Provision shortages, bad housing conditions and high prices were blamed on greedy shop-owners and mismanagement in the private sector,[97] which permitted the authorities to resolve most local food riots without force.[98] The South Sea Bubble crisis of 1720 was the first major incident that 'generated the rhetoric of public spirit as an antidote to party spirit, forming the basis of the nebulous entity called *public opinion* that increasingly took hold in political argument'.[99] Whenever the quality of flour deteriorated or prices of corn and bread skyrocketed, physicians, lawyers or clergymen also took sides with the poorer population and proposed legal and technical amendments,[100] 'to the consideration of the publick'.[101]

In the seaports of Northern England and Ireland, however, public discontent with imperial policy frequently overwhelmed city magistrates.[102] The Liverpool Seamen's Revolt of 1775, for instance, was triggered by a sudden decline in slave trading during the American Revolution, which left many local families without income. Similarly, a mutiny of sailors in Newcastle on May 1785 was said to have arisen from severe living conditions and great sufferings for their families.[103] The American press, which gleefully observed crises in Britain, condemned the failures of economic policy and also highlighted the adverse effects of colonial imports (e.g. Indian corn) on English farmers.[104] Such American solidarity with the British lower classes, however, furthered fears that a republican change of government could be plotted in the social hot spots of the British Isles. The London government took harsh measures against late eighteenth-century 'food riots'.[105] The Revolution in France and its repercussions throughout Europe diminished toleration of social unrest,[106] accompanied by attempts to prevent any generalization or nationalization of local grievances. The political poem *The Riot* (subtitled: 'half a bread is better than no bread'), which was published in a small collection of educational poetry, for instance, aimed to prevent a nationalization of food riots and praised the still fortunate agricultural condition of England as opposed to the Papal States, Spain and even Holland.[107] Food riots in the late eighteenth century only had a chance of succeeding if a high level of discipline was kept, inter alia by involving women and children.

Gender mattered in the evaluation of a person's role in loyal or oppositional politics, and gendered metaphors played an important part in political communication (see Chapters 2 and 3).[108] Most of the rebels mentioned in official documents and commercial media were men, but court records point to an involvement of women in rioting and political action.[109] At the same time, women were active in the production and dissemination of media.[110] While most women in Europe could act as printers or publishers in succession to a deceased husband, women in the colonies had wider opportunities to act as authors and media entrepreneurs.[111] Women are, in fact, found as newspaper editors on both sides of the loyalist–patriot divide in revolutionary North America.[112] However, women also appear as victims of politically charged violence. During the Calico Riot of 1719–20, lower-class women, especially female servants, were attacked for wearing the cotton gowns that weavers blamed for the 'precipitant decline in demand for English wool and silk products'.[113] These attacks built 'upon popular notions of female pride and moral corruptibility', including 'witchcraft imagery'.[114] In the case of the Tring witchcraft hunt in Hertfordshire in 1751, a woman, Ruth Osborne, was accused of witchcraft as well as Jacobite sympathies and murdered.[115] In both cases, the overlap of several attributed identities is notable, as topical argumentations supersede a much older religious conception of defending the common good. The 1795 food riot, known as the 'revolt of the housewives', is one of the riots during which female participation led to 'discipline and good order'.[116]

Instrumental to crowd control was a political culture in which printed and handwritten media did not replace but complemented oral communication. Physical gatherings and visibility remained important tools of representation and could not be entirely replaced by long-distance media.[117] Public days of fasting or thanksgiving, royal birthdays, days of commemoration or elections continued to bring church congregations or the inhabitants of an entire town out onto the streets.[118] Such events often permitted the situational class-transcending engagement even of the non-electoral populace with political issues,[119] but elaborate rules of how public spaces ought to be used evolved. Tim Harris and his co-authors have shown that a growing institutionalization of protest, which conformed to certain expectations, had already made popular opposition more acceptable to the authorities in Restoration England.[120] Moderate opposition movements promoted petitions and remonstrances that were handed over in a civilized manner as just expressions of popular grievance.[121] The people who signed petitions seldom represented the 'voting public',[122] and especially in regions with disproportionately low parliamentary representation, petitioning was a substitute for elections.[123]

In the seventeenth century, both the British Isles and North America had developed a strong tradition of petitioning as parties involved in the Civil Wars,[124] and in the 1676–7 rebellion of Virginia settlers (led by Nathaniel Bacon), forwarded written appeals to the royal government. Complaining about rising levies, the insurgents in Virginia wanted to 'hear and see every particular for what it is raised'.[125] Printed petitions subsequently symbolized a general demand for government transparency and unfolded great 'propaganda value'.[126] Riots could be justified 'as the actions of frustrated petitioners',[127] and in 1698, the Petition of the African Company in Edinburgh featured in newspapers of the day alongside verified government decisions.[128] In this way, petitions gave non-voters a sense of political participation and ensured an emotional link between British monarchs and their subjects.[129] In his history of the American Revolution, which openly took sides with the Patriots, Edward Barnard, headmaster of Eton College, equally confirmed that petitioning was 'an undoubted right of the subject to be heard, and not a matter of favour and grace',[130] and that it was unlawful to limit petitioning to specific times and places or even to groups of certain rank. Most importantly, petitions took hold as prolific media of public interaction among citizens. Officially addressed to rulers and humble in style, their dissemination in print clearly reached out to the petitioners' fellow countrymen and rallied public support.[131] The collections of the Massachusetts Archives in Boston prove that patriots in the Massachusetts House of Representatives and the special Council elected in 1773 and 1774 had to respond to many inner-institutional petitions drawn up by fellow council members.[132] This peer-to-peer communication generally resulted in the creation of committees to 'recommend a course of action'.[133]

The symbolic constitutional value that petitioning had achieved by the end of the American Revolutionary War was, for example, illustrated by a 1787 caricature of Pitt the Younger and Charles James Fox that depicted their quarrel over Fox's 'Petition for redress'.[134] Those who initiated them, however, had to make sure that they would not be turned into 'abusive and illegal coercive behavior'.[135] While 'the poor man's plea against his landlord' was never called into question,[136] collectively written and signed petitions to the government remained heavily contested.[137] Firstly, the question arose in what tone a lawful petition ought to be written. Decency of language, for instance, was discussed in regard to the petition of the Crown by the Council of the Province of Massachusetts-Bay in July 1768.[138] Governor Francis Bernard complained that the American petitions sent to London contained 'many offensive Passages' and 'several bold Expressions'.[139] Reform societies within the British Isles were likewise accused of having replaced a traditional 'humble address' for a 'command'.[140] Secondly, petitions virtualized communication to a degree that many contemporaries deemed unreliable. In the course of anti-Catholic riots in Scotland (1778-9), the Gordon Riots in London (1780) and the Priestley Riots in Birmingham (1791), the credibility of signatures on petitions, public letters or other political statements were doubted by lawyers, clergymen and leading politicians alike.[141] When the Attorney General at the King's Bench asked witnesses in Lord Gordon's trial why a larger assembly of people had seemed necessary for the handing over of the petition in the first place, the answer was:

> that it had been hinted, that it was a very easy matter for a person to sit down and write four or five hundred names to a petition, and therefore it would be necessary that they should appear to their subscriptions, and convince the world that they were not fictitious.[142]

The protocols of the ensuing trial against George Gordon and his Protestant Association thus focused on the behavioural context of public petitions, and private correspondents equally discussed conditions of legitimate petitioning and protest marches.[143] At the time, a lawful petition could not be signed by more than twenty people and could only be handed over by a group of up to ten men.[144] Therefore, witnesses pleading Lord Gordon's cause in court tried to classify the violent protestors as non-political 'banditti of boys',[145] who ought to be distinguished from the small group of peaceful petitioners. Yet matters were complicated by the fact that a considerable part of the mob had put blue cockades in their hats, carried black-and-white flags and voiced religious rallying cries that seemed in line with the aims of the Association.[146] This attire led the soldiers on duty – and many frightened parliamentarians – to suppose that the whole riot had been a well-planned political rising. Members of the House of Commons, among them Colonel Luttrell, were also seen with a blue cockade that very day, which made the distinction of groups even more confusing.[147] At last, the rejection of subversive violence became the decisive criterion that distinguished lawful protestors from the amateurishly armed offenders who had stopped and overturned carriages in the city.[148] At the bar, Mr Spinnage, a supporter of the Protestant Petition, was asked by Mr Erskine, the lawyer who defended Gordon, whether 'the people in the fields [had carried] any weapons or any sticks', and whether 'they [were] well dressed, decent in their apparel'.[149] Mr Spinnage's response was that they were – as Mr Erskine paraphrased it – 'far from being the rabble'.[150] Furthermore, witness Mr Alexander Johnston declared the entire event a formal procession of the Protestant Association, and when Mr Erskine asked him, too, if the 'set of people [he] saw making that riot, were quite a different set of people from the Protestant Association',[151], he confirmed that the rioters had been 'quite a set of pickpockets'.[152] Witness Alexander Frazer further added to this negative evaluation of the rioters that 'many of them were in liquor'.[153] The blame for the acts of destruction and mischief was thus consensually shifted to 'an unconnected mob',[154] or 'men of another description',[155] thereby distinguishing between a constructive body corporate and a destructive entity of innominate non-persons.[156] Gordon's Protestant petition was postponed until the end of the riots. This consensus was later confirmed in an illustrated historiographical report on the Gordon Riots published by Barnard in 1783.[157] Barnard supported the American cause and legitimized both verbal and physical attacks upon Britain's colonial administration, but in the case of the Gordon Riots, he was more reluctant to take sides with the angry crowd.[158] The simple engraving that accompanied Barnard's report showed the crowd burning pro-Catholic declarations by night – a scene that exposed the conspiratorial and chaotic nature of this action.[159]

At the height of the Jacobin menace in 1795, William Burgh of York wrote a letter to the royal government, 'dissociating [himself] and a majority of the householders of York from a petition to the House of Commons purporting to represent the view of the Corporation of York and praying for a speedy peace'.[160] Mr Burgh's reason for denying acceptance of the petition to the Commons was that two opposing factions in his hometown were 'now obtaining signatures to rival addresses to the king' and that some citizens were 'enticing children and paupers to sign with the contents concealed'.[161] Many politicians and political writers suspected long lists of supporters to be fraud.[162] Moreover, most MPs agreed that legislative decisions 'under pressure' would not be valid,[163] and that office-holders should never give in to spontaneous public demands.

From the 1780s onwards, British law courts distinguished more clearly between unlawful unrest and legitimate opposition than ever before, and the violent results of protest – such as the destruction of churches and private property – were no longer blamed on supposed ringleaders if they could give evidence for their own peaceful intentions. Educated leaders were more likely to go free than followers who had thrown stones or set fires. This differentiation between legitimate demands for reform and illegitimate 'mob violence' was made to prevent another revolution like the one Britain had had to yield to in New England,[164] while it connected British citizen rights more tightly with moral superiority, education and civility. In visual representations of Lord George Gordon and the handing-over of his petition, it became apparent that political actors no longer needed to stage elaborate processions. Simplicity and decency in conduct and appearance were sufficient to be heard, and influenced later working-class action.[165]

The second strategy of popular opposition was to situate controversial debates in a deliberately pre-political space. Englishmen concerned for their freedoms advocated the defence of the private, non-public sphere as the last residue of unspoilt, uncorrupted citizenship.[166] The civilian sphere could then function as a temporary exile and incubator in which contested ideas could be carefully reframed and matured before the next officially political exchange. This mitigated the negative image that 'private interest' had had throughout the seventeenth century,[167] and gave 'the Peace of Private Families', as well as 'the Tranquility of inoffending, and worthy Individuals',[168] a positive connotation. When his house was invaded by an anti-French, anti-revolutionary mob in 1791 and private papers of his were stolen or destroyed, Unitarian minister Joseph Priestley wrote to the populace of Birmingham that his 'numerous correspondents in different countries of *Europe*, but more especially those who wrote to me in confidence in this country' were 'much affected by this catastrophe', and that he would have 'destroyed those letters and other private papers' himself if he could have foreseen that some citizens of his home town 'would act the part of brutes, without the least regard to law, to common equity, humanity, or decency'.[169] Priestley and his correspondents were convinced that 'a man's private concerns, in which the state had no interest',[170] ought to be protected even if they displeased the government or the majority of the British population. Similarly, Irish rebel Robert Emmet, who faced public execution after his failed Dublin rebellion of 1803, tellingly asked the crowds who had gathered to witness his death for 'the charity of silence'.[171] Although we do not know for certain if these were Emmet's original words, his demand witnesses how highly critics of the imperial government esteemed privateness and self-determination. Townhouses, coffee houses and lobbies as semi-public spaces of agenda-setting seem to have offered a compromise between the potentially seditious seclusion of private homes and the complete lack of boundaries within the open space. A semi-private politicization of British society was also at the heart of the so-called corresponding societies in London, Sheffield, Birmingham and Edinburgh,[172] as well as the establishment of the Scottish Friends of the People, who promoted parliamentary reform yet distanced themselves from 'unprincipled designs'.[173] It was, however, difficult to maintain the middle ground between transparency and secrecy. The danger of 'underground radicalism' became especially virulent in Ireland,[174] where the branches of the United Irishmen moved into different directions.[175]

Most eighteenth-century crowds in Britain were 'informed, disciplined and in possession of broad notions of the necessity and legitimacy of their actions'.[176] Although

Abigail Adams complains about a competitive and even violent working-class culture in England,[177] British crowds of the 1780s and 1790s mainly targeted property of well-chosen symbolic value and hardly ever used weapons against people. The open field or the city roads were accessible spaces of agitation that nevertheless demanded specific behavioural and communicational patterns.[178] Even if some protestors wished to unleash the masses' destructive potential, such rioters were often discredited by the moderates within their own ranks.[179] Despite occasional warnings that the monarch might not be safe if he ignored the people's complaints,[180] and reformers promoting 'Free-speaking [as] a principal Sign of a Free Government',[181] most political factions in Britain agreed that the government's responsibility to all the people did not mean that public opinion should directly influence legislation.[182]

Local officials, for their part, occasionally accommodated oppositional crowds and personally confronted protestors before the Riot Act was read. In these circumstances, the provisions of the Riot Act were not only measures of top-down violence prevention but also unintentionally led to de-escalating communication. When popular disturbances both in favour and against the Protestant Succession continued, a new Riot Act took effect in 1715.[183] On the one hand, this permitted military interventions and penalized popular outrages in an unprecedented manner,[184] which made critics fear 'that an over-zealous Justice of the Peace might [...] think himself called upon to read the proclamation to the spectators of a horse-race, or a cricket-match'.[185] Allan Ramsay called the riot act 'arbitrary', and claimed it founded 'criminality in a combination of circumstanced, each of them, singly, as innocent as the crime itself in completion',[186] unjustly preventing many lawful assemblies. On the other hand, the Riot Act also required the authorities to communicate prior to intervention and implied that cases of political violence might pass unpunished if local authorities made formal mistakes or could not be present at the scene of events.[187] As one late eighteenth-century critic sarcastically implied, 'twelve thousand idle people might remain together for twelve months, concerting every species of mischief, without there being any legal means of obliging them to go about their business', if the riot act was not read in time or proclaimed 'in a certain form of words'.[188] Authorities could even delay or avoid reading the riot act and resolve conflicts through negotiation, especially if they dreaded casualties following military interventions. As the legal handbook *The Country Justice* stated, not reading the Riot Act and thus not declaring an assembly as a whole unlawful also had consequences if crimes (e.g. damages of property) were committed while the assembly lasted. Suggesting that an assembly was lawful would mean that crimes could only be blamed on the individuals responsible, whereas an unlawful assembly would implicate 'all who were present'.[189]

Moreover, the Riot Act attributed a state-related role to citizens as it explicitly encouraged them to participate in the quelling of tumults.[190] A similar course was taken in the matter of seditious libel. With preliminary censorship having been abolished by the end of the seventeenth century, the persecution of oppositional printers or booksellers could only prove successful if fellow citizens detected, reported and destroyed seditious publications.[191] In 1795, English pamphleteer Smith noted that the government was eager to engage 'the clergy, the army, the navy, lords of the bedchamber, officers of the excise, [and] country squires' in their campaign against republican conspirators.[192] How strongly the eighteenth-century state encouraged Britons to 'co-opt [its] power' becomes obvious in government warrants incited citizens to pass on valuable information to their local authorities and actively contribute to arrests.[193] During the revolutionary 1790s, this government policy was an effective measure to exploit and control popular agitation. Local magistrates willingly responded by having hundreds of local inhabitants sign pro-government resolutions,[194] and the deliberate involvement of loyal citizens was unusually explicit in George III's unpopular Treason and Sedition Bills of 1793.[195] Several citizen associations even pursued their own pro-government agendas. In 1792, John Reeves established the loyalist 'Association for Preserving Liberty and Property' at the Crown and Anchor Tavern in London,[196] to encourage popular solidarity with the king and defy revolutionary tendencies in Britain. Following organizational patterns and media strategies similar to those of liberal and radical societies, his association attracted more than 2,000 local branches and successfully campaigned against oppositional meetings, radical printers and immorality among the lower classes.[197] Moderately reform-oriented groups also participated in a joint monitoring of public space and public communication alongside the authorities.

A possible downside was distrust among citizens fearing the denunciatory zeal of their own neighbours. From the trials against members of the corresponding societies in England to the rebellion of 1798 in Ireland, anti-revolutionary peer-control provoked public criticism.[198] The Pop-Gun Plot of 1795, an alleged conspiracy to murder King George III, was widely perceived as the result of over-eager citizen support for the royal government.[199] In his personal narrative of the Irish Rebellion of 1798, Irish patriot Charles Hamilton Teeling also stated that the 'spy and informer [had] always found encouragement in the bloody annals of Ireland's distress', but that 'in the present period there was a systematic arrangement of villainy and fraud'.[200] A second risk linked with eighteenth-century collaborative riot policy was a simple de-politicization of oppositions, especially those led by minorities. While major enemy images such as Jacobites and Jacobins dominated public discourse and led to conspiracy theories, this narrow political incentive implied that other opposition narratives were devalued or excluded. Public incidents that were not connected with the presumably most dangerous opposition movements of their time could be attributed to 'drinking free beer' or even be labelled 'fun'.[201]

Public disturbance could thus be politically neutralized. In the best of circumstances, this protected participants from severe legal consequences and increased lesser offenders' solidarity with the system. In the worst case, de-politicization subdued all societal concerns that rioters may have intended to communicate in the first place. In the eighteenth century, de-politicization especially affected non-male or non-white agents. Even those in favour of the abolition of slavery played down to ability or even willingness of slaves to assume public agency (see Chapter 2). One of the authors who doubted that abolition would lead to a rebellion among the slaves was James Ramsay, who claimed that 'their spirits are too much broken down to think of rebellion'.[202] Beyond their class-consciousness and ethnic biases, however, the British and American cultures of popular protest shaped 'several decades of sustained political participation',[203] and paved the way for constitutionally guaranteed voting rights.

When the British electorate was raised to 'approximately 20 per cent of the adult male population [in 1832], Parliament created a voting public corresponding reasonably well, proportionately, to that segment of the population apparently meriting inclusion among the electorate',[204] because of its persistent extra-parliamentary engagements.

Conclusion

Summarizing the previous chapters, we find that the eighteenth century in Britain did not bring forth groundbreaking legal and social reform, but a new perception of opposition among practitioners of politics as well as observers of political culture. The Glorious Revolution was not a constitutional landslide, but the first constitutionally consenting political conflict and a model of institutionalized political pluralism.[1] The events of 1688 and 1689 commenced a professional administration of conflict and agreement. Government control and dynastic succession were fixed in statute law for the first time in British history. Although the riots and revolts that affected the British Empire throughout the eighteenth century caused bloodshed and destruction, they also raised public awareness of constitutional questions and the necessity of continued political negotiation in times of conflict.[2] 'Unlawful' opposition was now often referred to as 'unconstitutional', but political theorists also understood that 'constitutional government' required a critical reflection on fundamental laws.[3]

Parliament participated more actively in the government whereas the British people in general did not immediately profit from the changes of 1688. Parliamentary reform and new voting legislation were only introduced in the nineteenth century, whereas the heated political atmosphere of the Jacobite rebellions fostered a political centralization of the British Isles and weakened local economies and political participation in many parts of the Empire. Scotland, which had retained a unique and more mixed legal system since the Middle Ages, adapted more to English standards between 1707 and 1900. It lost its self-government in the Act of Union of 1707, and Acts of Parliament passed in reaction to the risings of 1715 and 1745 curbed the position of the Scottish nobility even further.[4] By contrast, conflicts also encouraged devolution in the fields of law enforcement and national defence. One example was the Riot Act of 1714/15,[5] which clarified the conditions of popular political action and strengthened the legal position of the local authorities in the prevention and suppression of insurrections. Similarly, the Act for the more effectual trial and punishment of high treason in the Highlands of Scotland passed in 1748 extended the responsibilities of regional law courts and prisons in Scotland as well as the scope of the militia in the counties, boroughs, shires or stewartries.[6]

The Church of England moved from strong participation in the executive and judiciary to a no less influential position in public political agitation. The exclusion of non-propertied and non-Anglican Britons from public office and direct political participation was to some degree countered by higher levels of engagement in military service, riot control and the media. Economic change alongside territorial expansion contributed to a shift from court-centred politics of the Restoration to new forms of political participation and a communicational integration of opposition. Eighteenth-century crises were not only destructive to material culture or traumatizing for those directly affected, but also constructive in regard to non-violent conflict culture and consensual identity. This was a decisive turn from the territorialization of power in the seventeenth century to a self-reflective clarification of the state's inner structures.[7]

Perhaps most importantly, historical developments and contemporary political events were carefully monitored and compared from a global perspective. Authors across Europe took an interest in the historical genesis and contractual legitimation, the 'historische Entstehung und kontraktuelle Legitimation',[8] of governments past and present.[9]

In 1769, Unitarian minister, scientist and political reformer Dr Joseph Priestley drew a 'New Chart of History',[10] which was first published in 1770 and reprinted in several editions throughout the century. This historical timeline presented the rise and fall of different sovereignties and ethnic groups in world history and encouraged an empirical, comparative study of past events.[11] Abstracting from the 'odious qualities in the human species',[12] the Enlightenment imagined world history as an open-ended sequence of events, in which different argumentative patterns could be activated. An extract of the map reprinted in the second edition of Charles Allen's English history of 1798 focused on the British Isles from 200 BC to the mid-eighteenth century. In this condensed form, history appeared as a speedy succession of dynasties or individual rulers.[13] Yet although Priestley carefully 'distinguished conquests, and forcible changes of empire from peaceable revolutions, as those occasioned by marriages, voluntary cession, &c.',[14] and admitted that the many broken and irregular lines of his chart illustrated the 'discontent of powerful individuals' and the 'depravity of human passions',[15] he encouraged his readers to consider the overall perspective:

> If we take a more attentive view of wars, and the devastations which have been made by them, we may probably find, that war has not borne a greater proportion to peace, than sickness bears to health in the usual course of human life; which, yet, we think very comfortable upon the whole; and which (like the earth, that abounds with marshes and desarts [sic], and is subject to dreadful storms and tempests) is, notwithstanding, full of the riches of divine goodness.[16]

His aim was to impartially portray the changeful course of history and an obviousness of crisis, which left many contemporaries bewildered yet wielded an increasing scientific fascination.[17] Only a few years later, Thomas Jefferson likewise observed that popular uprisings could not be prevented by 'any degree of power in the hands of government',[18] because even 'in Turkey, where the sole nod of the despot is death, insurrections are the events of every day'.[19] He even went as far as to claim that no country could ever 'preserve its liberties, if its rulers are not warned from time to time':[20] When the Massachusetts Rebellion terrified the US government in 1787, Jefferson wrote to Colonel Smith: 'God forbid, we should ever be twenty years without such a rebellion. [...] Let them take arms. [...] The tree of liberty must be refreshed from time to time with the blood of patriots and tyrants. It is its natural manure.'[21]

In the course of time, revolt became an integral subject of historiography and philosophical reflection.[22] Despite the declamatory style in radical literature of the 1770s and 1780s, the gap between conservatives and reformers narrowed. During the American Revolution, numerous 'friends of both countries' hoped to 'establish a permanent and solid foundation for a just constitutional union between Great Britain and her colonies'.[23] After the American Independence, self-confident citizens across the political spectrum shared a new sense of transition and recognized a culture of 'free discussion',[24] in which different opinions were accepted, as the basis for sound policy decisions. As much as America could claim to be born in a revolution, Britain could claim to be living by its past rebellions.

Fundamental laws as the framework of productive confrontation balanced agents and ideas and made them correctives to each other.[25] In this sense, constitutionalism means that laws are not absolute but politically adaptable.[26] There is often more than a single expression of justice, and the different government branches as well as judiciary and public opinion have their share in the process of interpreting, criticizing and implementing the nation's principles.[27]

An appeal to the constitution as the fundament of justice could accordingly result in the revocation of certain laws passed by either monarchical governments or elected councils. Although written constitutions were mainly introduced in the course of the nineteenth century, their inherent politicization of legal norms was a groundbreaking result of the eighteenth-century struggles and called for sufficient pluralism in making or interpreting law as well as for a new sense of juridical 'solidarity',[28] with minorities whose rights are easily curtailed by majorities.[29] This pluralism guarantees oppositional structures within society and does not limit control mechanism to a single institution such as Parliament.[30] In a state where the constitution stabilizes society, opposition is both permanent and predictable, ensuring a productive balance of unquestioned procedures and controversial debate.[31]

That such concepts of the constitution eventually took root in British political thinking can be summarized in the early modern development of treason charges. In his analysis of the semantics of rebellion, Reinhard Koselleck mentions that the phrase 'high treason' first developed in the Anglo-French conflicts of the mid-fourteenth century.[32] This English term broadly corresponds to *Landfriedensbruch* in German law, a term that also developed in the late Middle Ages.[33] During the German Reformation, *Landfriedensbruch* was a popular justification for counter-reformatory action, particularly because other Protestant powers could be kept out of the conflict if it was not referred to as a religious war.[34] In England, however, the equivalent distinction between heresy and treason developed much later. Many post-Reformation trials for high treason were fraught with strong religious interests, and are difficult to distinguish from convictions for heresy alone.[35] Religious sedition was ascribed to most oppositions in sixteenth- and seventeenth-century England. Ever since the Gunpowder Plot of 1605, the high treason charge, which involved culprits' enmity to the monarch,[36] had connected this with seditious collaboration with foreign, non-Anglican agents.[37]

Nourished by the experience of the Civil Wars, later seventeenth-century legal restrictions on gatherings especially targeted dissenting religious conventicles. In 1681 – shortly after the alleged Popish Plot invented by Titus Oates and amidst controversies over the possible succession of the Catholic Crown Prince James, Duke of York, to the throne of England – an unknown lawyer wrote *Vestigia veritatis, or, The controversy relating to the act of the thirty fifth of Elizabeth, (entituled [sic], An act to retain the Queens Majesties subjects in their due obedience,) truly stated*, which was printed by Richard Janeway in London. This book reproduced an original act signed by Queen Elizabeth I in 1581 in order to 'try and counter the missionary activities of Catholic priests in England',[38] as well as its unchanged confirmations by James VI/I and Charles I and two edited versions enacted by Charles II. Today, the revised acts are known as the Conventicle Act of 1664 and the Conventicles Act of 1670, respectively. Although the unknown commentator's main objective was to prove that neither of Charles II's acts was a novelty (since Elizabeth's regulations had never been suspended), the book also recorded the minor but significant modifications of legal terminology in late seventeenth-century Britain.

The original act that had been passed in the thirty-fifth parliamentary session of Queen Elizabeth's reign placed great emphasis on religious vocabulary, describing attendance at Anglican services as public proof of loyalty towards the monarchy and state government, since 'her Majesties Power and Authority in Causes Ecclesiastical [were] united and annexed to the Imperial Crown of this Realm'.[39] No distinction was made between 'seditious sectaries' and 'disloyal persons',[40] as the act put the Crown on equal footing with the Church and God's law.[41] Consequently, reconciliation was only possible if convicts made a 'Publick and open Submission and Declaration of their Conformity to her Majesties Laws and Statutes'.[42]

In contrast to the Act of 1581, the law signed by Charles II in 1664 spoke of 'the growing and dangerous practices of seditious Sectaries and other disloyal persons, who under pretence of Tender Consciences do at their Meetings contrive Insurrections, as late Experience hath shewed'.[43] This act was part of the so-called Clarendon Code, a set of Restoration laws intended to maintain public order, which also included the Quaker Act of 1662, the Act of Uniformity of 1662 and the Five Mile Act of 1665. The enforcement of all these laws was weakened by Charles II's Royal Declaration of Indulgence of 1672, and regulations concerning Protestant Nonconformists were repealed in 1689.

However, the underlying language regime affected future legislation. First of all, the phrasing 'Tender Consciences' highlighted that the religious minorities of the 1670s were well aware that their practices and beliefs deviated from the Church of England, and that they consciously claimed a right to be different. Secondly, 'seditious Sectaries' were defined as a possible subgroup of disloyal persons, and their disloyalty was no longer exclusively subsumed in their religious dissent. This shifted the focus to the political 'mischiefs' that might follow if dissenters were free to meet and even establish settlements of their own.[44] The public acts of reconciliation in church that repenting convicts had to perform during Elizabeth's reign were no longer explicitly mentioned; fines and simple revocations before the king's secular courts replaced acts of religious atonement.[45]

Conclusion

Although the Act to Prevent and Suppress Seditious Conventicles did not secularize society, the role of religion and above all the Church of England was more sustainably integrated into overarching constitutional and legal concepts. The state's enemy was not the one who worshipped God differently, but the one who strove for counter-structures in opposition to the existing communalism.[46] In this sense, attending, hosting or even presiding over illegal religious meetings was considered not so much a violation of the individual's relationship with God and the monarch, but a potential danger to the lives and property of all citizens.[47] In general, the revised Act of 1681 more carefully distinguished between office holders, corporation members and individuals.[48] It also broadened the jurisdiction of English law to all other royal dominions.[49]

Late Stuart and Hanoverian acts for the safety and preservation of the Crown further stressed 'what is in the Power of several Ranks of People and every Individual in Britain, to do toward securing the State from all its Enemies'.[50] An increasing distinction between riots or legitimate armed resistance and malevolent rebellion eventually broadened the scope of valid political expressions and gave well-argued oppositions an increasing chance to go unpunished. The term 'revolution' mainly implied unforeseeable, fundamental change and social innovation such as those exemplified by the French Revolution.[51] Prior to the Reign of Terror in France, the word revolution was rather used as the positive counter-part to revolt and rebellion, denoting anything but violent or contentious change.[52]

This idea of 'revolutionary sustainability' derived from the term's early modern usage in natural sciences,[53] and gave gentle evolution precedence over rapid change.[54] After the Glorious Revolution of 1688 in England, even the adverb 'revolutionary' became an affirmative political paragon.[55] But further differentiations of opposition became necessary because Whigs, who had been inspired by 'Resisting Principles' in the reigns of Charles II and James VII/II,[56] denounced Tory and Jacobite resistance. The terms 'rebellion' and 'revolt' therefore denoted the renunciation of the existing order.[57] 'Riots' or 'tumults', which addressed the grievances of farmers after a crop failure or opposed special taxes, passed as public acts of violence that only marginally invaded the political sphere. Territorially confined uprisings initiated by a clear-cut group of protestors for the implementation of clear-cut aims were not so much interruptions and hindrances of early modern political life but catalysts of conflict that brought about temporary agreement.[58]

In his academic thesis *De Tumultibus* of 1714, Christian Wildvogel vindicated simple *tumults* or *riots* (in Latin: '*tumultus*'),[59] but condemned well-planned and at the same time more obscure forms of resistance, namely 'factions' ('*factionibus*'),[60] conspiracies ('*coniurationes*'), seditions ('*seditiones*') and rebellions ('*rebelliones*').[61] In Britain, rebellion and revolt were equally linked with cold-blooded conspiracy and distinguished from spontaneous, undisguised rioting.[62] Tracts written by Anglican churchmen sketched the flexible and influential image of the 'fanatic', or 'phanatick',[63] as the nation's number one enemy in a religious and political sense. This invective could label republicans as well as ultra-monarchist polemicists.[64] Accusations of fanaticism were still common in the 1770s,[65] but treason was no longer defined as opposition to a single law or institution but described as an attack upon society at large.[66] Eighteenth-century British lawyers agreed that the basic definition of high treason, 'the ancient law of treason',[67] was derived from a statute of King Edward III, which had not been introduced to increase cases of treason and bring suspects down more easily, but rather to prevent an unjust inflation of criminal convictions:

> What would be the feelings of our venerable ancestors, who framed the statute of treasons to prevent their children being drawn into the snares of death, unless proveably [sic] convicted by overt acts, if they could hear us disputing whether it was treason to desire harmless unarmed men to be firm and of good heart, and to trust to the graciousness of their king.[68]

On these grounds, the legal concept of 'constructive treason',[69] which resembled modern regulations on 'preventive security',[70] was controversially debated. At last, the independent United States had to make up its own mind about these fundamental problems. The first treason legislation issued by the Americans was the 'Act against treason' of 1777, which had been drawn up by the 'Honorable Council of the state of Massachusetts-Bay'. In 1778, a comparable resolution was passed by the United States Continental Congress. The American Constitution tried to limit the range of treason to very specific cases in order to prevent British abuses and wilful prosecution of enemies of the government.[71]

The way in which early modern governments handled political crimes thus had a decisive impact on citizens' readiness to engage in clubs, societies and oppositional action. Arrests, trials, sentences and above all acquittals were carefully monitored by the press and directly corresponded to declining or rising numbers in citizen engagement.[72] Discussing the 'nature of treason',[73] both in court and in the streets, was thus an important aspect of state formation and the differentiation of roles. Although John Barrell has claimed that the late eighteenth-century British government tried 'to shift the goalposts of what counted as treason',[74] the introduction of special rather than general warrants demanded more thorough groundwork from the government attorneys before any formal charge could be made.[75] The fact that many treason trials ended in a vindication of the accused clearly paved the way for the people's more immediate and formal access to political discourse, for example in the nineteenth-century expansion of suffrage and legally protected political lobbying. Contemporaries did not consider the British constitution flawless, but appreciated it as a 'constitution in progress to perfection'.[76]

As this book has explored, eighteenth-century Britain permitted overlapping responsibilities and plural agency, which resulted in a comparatively smooth transition from an early modern segmented society to a modern state.[77] This was, however, never a foregone conclusion and did not apply to all regions of the Empire. Although the people's possible roles were no longer exclusively defined by birth, new hierarchies and exclusion were created by economic conditions, access to education and ethnic biases.[78] As a side effect of a uniform concept of nationhood, British politics was vulnerable to real or imagined foreign conspiracies that fostered isolationist tendencies.[79] The fear of alien infiltration had already pervaded the seventeenth-century commemoration of the Gunpowder Plot, but intensified when early eighteenth-century rebellions seemed to be concocted by multinational agents.[80] This apprehension of dissent goes beyond the conspiratorial governmentality detected by André Krischer.[81] Britain's fear of foreign invasion was not a calculated propagandistic narrative but a far less controllable consequence of claiming supremacy in a globalizing world.

Another perpetual challenge of British state formation and society building was that the local executive on the peripheries of the empire was insufficiently developed by comparison with the national administration, and that regions such as the Scottish Highlands, Ireland and overseas colonies were marginalized. Although historians have often described the colonies as 'England's political laboratories',[82] attempts to rule vast territories with the smallest financial expenses and lowest numbers of administrative staff possible led to asymmetrical deregulations. In the best of circumstances, rule by proxy reduced tensions between a foreign elite and the colonized populations. The willingness to permit 'the coexistence of multiple legal jurisdictions – including those of African polities and American maroon communities of former slaves – which were accepted by English traders, settlers and imperial administrators' also had its downsides.[83] In the West Indies, Ireland, India and – later on – colonial Africa, the British government created a parallelism of structures and institutions that cemented inequality. To give a negative example, the institution of 'separate courts for the free and the unfree',[84] in the colonial Caribbean, hindered a pan-imperial coherence of public roles and government functions. As education and personal compliance became an ever more indispensable foundation of political emancipation, and post-eighteenth-century societies experienced unprecedented vulnerability because a considerable percentage of their members were not permitted or able to keep abreast.

Interestingly, America as Britain's first independent colony experienced similar struggles, although its constitution had deliberately left the British model behind. When several American states rejected the new Continental Constitution, the country drifted towards civil war because popular politicization was connected with 'a distinct frontier ideology',[85] which fed into local self-government.[86] During John Adams's presidency, too, the newly founded nation was politically divided when official American relations with France deteriorated. Notwithstanding the alliance between the Americans and the French during the American War of Independence, the French Revolution and the beheading of the royal family fuelled fears of a second, far more radical and socially aware change of government.[87] The Adams administration subsequently introduced restrictive alien and treason laws that were by no means less discriminating than former British legislation in times of crisis.[88] The young American nation, too, was forced to strike a balance between the principle of stability and the principles of competition. Simultaneously, England and Scotland – not unlike the United States – faced larger waves of immigration, most notably by Irish workers.[89] Riots involving immigrants thus increased from the later eighteenth century and replaced former political divisions with even more violent ethnic conflicts.[90]

This implies that there cannot be a single universal solution for the challenges of government formation.[91] The development of integrated oppositions is possible in monarchies as well as republics, but always depends on a reliable constitution.[92] Successful government systems are never exclusively conflict- or debate-oriented, but combine decision-driven functions (such as regular taxation and long-term budgeting) with debate-oriented functions (such as providing information to the public).[93] Learning from the many extremes and failures of the eighteenth century, the moderate constitutionalists of the early nineteenth century respected the different modes of operation of decision-focused politics and the more representational, competitive aspects of the political. The stability of the state as a constructed community rests on its ability to review and revise itself through the constant re-politicization of its acknowledged political agents and the recognition of new ones.[94] Liberty cannot be passively preserved, but needs to be continuously regained while a stable system of politics constantly requires 're-politicization',[95] in order to serve 'the prior interest of humanity'.[96] In other words, the modern state cultivates the political under the protection of institutionalized politics.[97] Therefore, issues of good governance must always be addressed in relation to the overarching functionality of the society in question.[98] Concepts that abstract and theorize human communities beyond their own limited experiences are one of the most precious and enduring legacies of the Enlightenment.

Notes

Introduction

1. Rose, *A Renaissance of Violence*.
2. Burkhardt, *Die Friedlosigkeit der frühen Neuzeit*; Asche, 'Bellizität, Staat und Migration im Alten Reich'.
3. Johannes Burkhard has attributed this ubiquity of violence to the fact that instruments of peacekeeping and international diplomacy were only about to develop: Siebenhüner and Greyerz, 'Einleitung', 19.
4. 'Ich finde – daß die revolutionen so geschwindt fort [schreiten] – alß wie ein acte von einer commedie. Ich habe von vielen gelehrten gehört – daß woll allezeit große revolutionen in weldt geweßen, seindt aber nie so geschwindt von statten gangen – alß seyder 60 oder 70 jahren, undt noch insonderheit seyder 40 jahren.' Elizabeth Charlotte, Duchess of Orléans, to Mr Harling, Paris, 26 December 1715, letter no. 221, in: Orléans, *Sämtliche Briefe*, 372. Translated by the author. All following translations are also the author's if not indicated otherwise.
5. Föcking and Schindler, *Der Krieg hat kein Loch*.
6. Ibid.
7. Reinhard, *Geschichte der Staatsgewalt*, 354.
8. Ibid., 351.
9. Wefer, *Kontingenz und Dissens*, 97.
10. Concerning differences between England and Western Europe see Voigt, 'Abschied vom Staat', 9. Grimm, 'Abschied vom Staat', 33–4.
11. Lyncker et al., *De Forma Sive Statu S.R. Imperii*; Habermann, *Iurisprudentiae Publicae Romano-Germanicae Dissertatio II de Origine, Finibus, Divisione, Denominatione, Unitate et Forma Imperii Romano-Germanici*.
12. Agency is understood as the possibility to exert influence beyond formal power. The 'agency of the ordinary people' in early modern England has, for instance, been studied in Walter, *Understanding Popular Violence*; Braddick and Withington, *Popular Culture and Political Agency*.
13. Gilmour, *Riot, Risings and Revolution*, publisher's abstract.
14. Ibid., 7–8.
15. Szechi, 'Review of Riot, Risings, and Revolution', 704.
16. Thompson, *Making of the English Working Class*, 451. Some British researchers have defined the period between 1660 and 1730 as an 'urban renaissance': Wood, *Riot*, 118.
17. Castells, *Communication Power*, 8.
18. Pickard, 'Book Review', 55.
19. Barbara Stollberg-Rilinger quoted according to Schwerhoff, 'Review'.
20. For a comprehensive introduction to the basic concepts see the 1989 collective volume edited by Hunt, *New Cultural History*. The role of the literary turn in the development of new cultural history (or: histories) and examples of new cultural history in educational history more specifically are discussed in Gordon, 'Introduction'.

21 Hunt, *New Cultural History*, 7–9.
22 Stollberg-Rilinger, *Rituale*, 52.
23 Ibid., 83.
24 How politically contested Henry's Reformation was has been covered by Ryrie, 'Tudor Brexit', 426.
25 Anon., *Royall Merlin*, title page.
26 Ibid.
27 Ibid.
28 Anon., *Compendious View*.
29 See Hanoverian diplomatic correspondence analysed in Barget, 'The Hatred Which They Bear', 118–137.
30 Lottes, 'Das englische Vorbild', 239.
31 Ward, *Electress Sophia*, 212–13.
32 Wildvogel, *Dissertationem Politico-Iuridicam De Tumultibus*, 9.
33 'Aspice Angliam, felicem tumultum procreatricem, & (vt Cuspinianus in vita Friedr. II Italiam appellat) factionum matrem, vbi proinde novi propullulant motus.' Ibid., 4.
34 'Inde Rex Angliae, nescio quis, dicere solebat: Angliam animal esse immortale, nisi se ipsum trucidaret.' Ibid.
35 Baer, 'Christian Friedrich Daniel Schubart's Deutsche Chronik', 448.
36 Laveaux, *Discours sur les vices*.
37 Ibid., 3.
38 See essays published in Griesse, *Early Modern Revolts*.
39 Bexon, *Parallèle*, 1:14, 23.
40 Ibid., 1:14–15.
41 Lauritsen, '"This Isn't Who We Are"'. While the storming of the US Capitol by supporters of Donald Trump is certainly the most extreme break with democratic traditions which a Western country has experienced in recent years, 'undemocratic climate protests' which 'seek to shape official decisions by using coercion, not just persuasion' and violent demonstrations against COVID-19 measures have also challenged political procedures and institutions often taken for granted. Garcia-Gibson, 'Undemocratic Climate Protests', 39.
42 Rozdilsky, 'Thought the U.S. Capitol Attack Couldn't Happen?'
43 Dahlgren, 'The Internet', 147.
44 Ibid., 155–6.
45 Ibid., 160.
46 Davis, 'The Online Anti-Public Sphere'.
47 Smuts, 'Introduction', 333–4. A prominent example of classical social history and its approaches to power and class is Zagorin, *Rebels and Rulers*, I:87. For a detailed analysis of historiographical trends since the 1970s see Steinmetz and Haupt, 'The Political', 11–14.
48 Cox, 'Glorious Revolution', 571.
49 Ibid., 567.
50 Iggers, *Geschichtswissenschaft*, 118. Flinders, *Defending Politics*, 23.
51 Claydon, 'Revolution in Foreign Policy', 219. See also Dickinson, 'How Revolutionary'. Dillon, *The Last Revolution*.
52 Pincus, *1688*, 120.
53 Ibid.
54 Sowerby, *Making Toleration*.

55 Pittock, *Religious Politics*; Szechi, *Jacobites*; Pittock, 'Jacobite Prisoners'; Erskine-Hill, 'Preface: Eveline Cruickshanks, an Appreciation'; Kléber Monod, Pittock, and Szechi, 'Introduction: Loyalty and Identity'.
56 Voigt, 'Abschied vom Staat', 9.
57 Shagan, *Popular Politics*, 14.
58 E. P. Thompson's influential analysis of the political rise of the English working class was based on the assumption that class-specific protests flourished in the condensed working and living conditions of British industrial towns that grew earlier and faster than their continental counterparts. Thompson, *Making of the English Working Class*, 419.
59 McCormack, 'Supporting the Civil Power'; McCormack, *Embodying the Militia*.
60 Quinault and Stevenson, *Popular Protest*; Caple, 'Popular Protest'; Rogers, 'Popular Protest'; Bawn, *Social Protest*; Archer, *Social Unrest*; Garnham, 'Riot Acts'; Ashworth, 'Riotous Assemblies'; Randall, *Riotous Assemblies*. Phillips, 'Popular Politics'; Wood, *Riot*; Shagan, *Popular Politics*; Haywood, *The Revolution in Popular Literature*; Pickering and Davis, *Unrespectable Radicals?*
61 Barget, 'Chronological Table'.
62 Barget, 'Interactive Map of Uprisings'. Dates of Irish history have mainly been taken from *The Course of Irish History*, 8th ed., Mercier Press, Dublin 1994. The major uprisings have also been extensively covered in historiographical monographs, some of which are listed in the bibliography.
63 See Clark, *The Language of Liberty*.
64 All events are shown as point geometries, some of them representing larger territories, which is why the pop-up map labels should be consulted for further information.
65 Barbara Falk has described treason trials as a 'domestication of an international conflict'. Falk, 'Political Trials'. In her research, Falk has been able to show that political trials are often pushing the limits of the legal system and can be considered 'rule-based eliminations of political foes'. Ibid.; Falk, 'Making Sense of Political Trials'.
66 Harris, 'Moral Economy'.
67 See events marked 'colonial expansion/consolidation' in the interactive map as well as in the data table on GitHub: https://monikabarget.github.io/Revolts/event-table.html.
68 See the Bristol Bridge and Boston Massacres.
69 Revere, *Four Coffins*.
70 Black, *Glasgow Malt Tax Riots*.
71 See Chapter 4 for details.
72 The category 'drunkenness' relates to events in my collection that were most likely not linked with any other intentions, but this tagging is preliminary.
73 '[…] on the previous Shrove Tuesday when about 40 or 50 villagers gathered in the Park "to throw at Cocks" and had dressed up a boy and girl 25 Holly Boy and Ivy Girl according to custom, the Earl had accused them of riot and had had them forcibly dispersed.' [Multiple witnesses], 'U908/L19/6', quoted according to archival description.
74 ZOTERO library: https://www.zotero.org/groups/2351893/british_riots_and_revolts_of_the_enlightenment_age.
75 Scripts for web-scraping as well as scripts for cleaning metadata in Zotero with the PyZotero package are available for reuse in my Digital History repository: Barget, 'Digital History Repository'. A screen capture that I recorded in December 2020 shows the performance of a sample Python script that automatically downloads

RIS files of search results in WorldCat: Barget, 'Automatically Downloading Bibliographic Information'.
76 See research on correlations between political revolutions and media revolutions, also in the digital age: Kovarik, *Revolutions in Communication*.
77 Raymond, 'Newspaper', 113.

Chapter 1

1 This term was already in use in the seventeenth century, but it was especially applied to the Jacobite Rebellion of 1715, which came as a surprise and was led not by a rival to the reigning monarch himself but by local sympathizers of a dynasty in exile: Szechi, *1715*, 2–3.
2 Schlögl, 'Revolutionsmedien', 24.
3 Wefer, *Kontingenz und Dissens*, 43.
4 Szechi, *1715*, 198; Szechi, 'Professor Daniel Szechi (Subject Areas)'.
5 Koselleck, 'Revolution: Rebellion, Aufruhr, Bürgerkrieg', 718.
6 'When publick Calamities have been striking Terror into a People, and the Dread of a general Ruin hastening upon them has forced them on thinking, then seems to be a proper Season for suggesting to them Thoughts of a kind too serious and important to be listened to in Times of Peace and Tranquillity, or in the giddy Hours of Mirth and Wantonness.' Burgh, *Britain's Remembrancer*, 1.
7 Blount, *Nomo-Lexicon*; Skinner, *New English Dictionary*; Coles, *An English Dictionary*; Moréri et al., *Great Historical, Geographical, Genealogical and Poetical Dictionary*.
8 Philipps defined rebellion as 'any *tumultuous* opposing or rising against the authority of the Prince or Supreme Power, established in a Nation'. Resistance was a technical term in political philosophy as well as physics, but revolution was initially an exclusively scientific term: '(Lat.) a rowling back, the turning back of celestial bodies to their first point, and finishing their circular course.' Phillips, *Nevv Vvorld of Vvords*, sec. 'RE', no pages.
9 'In all Plots and Conspiracies ther [sic.] are the Upper and the Under-Spur-Leathers, ther [sic.] are the Managers and the Managed, ther [sic.] are those who Act upon the Stage, and the Prompters who stand behind the Curtain.' Philalethes [pseud.], '[Untitled]'.
10 Parker, *Manifold Miseries*; Griesse, 'Aufstandsprävention', 193.
11 Schnapp and Tiews, 'Introduction: A Book of Crowds', xi.
12 Stollberg-Rilinger, 'Symbolische Kommunikation'.
13 One of Habermas's works translated into English is Habermas, *Communication*. Habermas's public sphere was a free yet well-mannered exchange between reasoning citizens in a setting that was neither private nor defined by bureaucracy, economy (capitalism) or instrumental rationality. These conditions for open debate, however, have been challenged. The diversity of public spheres and the idea of a 'plebeian public sphere' put forth in the 1980s and 1990s is discussed by Würgler, *Unruhen*, 1:36; Schaich, 'Public Sphere', 131.
14 Randall, 'Epistolary Rhetoric', 30.
15 Smuts, 'Introduction', 335.
16 Edited by Hale, *Evolution of British Historiography*, 152. In many cases, conflicts also propelled parliamentary proceedings: Graves, *Parliaments*.

17 Bickham the Younger, *The [Cha]Mpion*.
18 Schlögl, 'Politik beobachten', 614.
19 Ibid., 607.
20 Anon., *Letter*, 1771, 61. 'Entsprechend pries man die Presse als Artikulation des Volkswillens.' Schlögl, 'Politik beobachten', 616.
21 Würgler, 'Rezension von: Das Mediensystem'.
22 Fischer, 'Buchmarkt'; Barget, 'Zwischen Ökonomie und Ideologie'.
23 Black, *English Press*, 163.
24 Kungl. Vitterhetsakademien, 'Media and Political Culture'; Schaich, 'Public Sphere', 136; Schlögl, 'Politik beobachten', 594.
25 Gestrich, 'Early-Modern State', 36–7.
26 Waldstreicher, 'Nationalization', 37.
27 Schlögl, 'Politik beobachten', 581–2.
28 'Medienöffentlichkeit' Rudolf Schlögl according to Würgler, *Medien*, 132.
29 Welch, 'State Truths', 1–2.
30 Barget, 'Stadt, Land und suburbaner Raum', 47.
31 Schlögl, *Anwesende und Abwesende*, 3.
32 Bernard, Gage, and Hood, *Letters to the Ministry*, 7.
33 Gage and Bernard, *Letters*, 46–7.
34 Bernard, Gage, and Hood, *Letters to the Ministry*, 5.
35 Bernard, *Papers of Francis Bernard*, 2012, 2:2.
36 Letter to the Earl of Shelburne, dated Boston, 19 March 1768, Bernard, Gage, and Hood, *Letters to the Ministry*, 15.
37 Schlögl, 'Politik beobachten', 592.
38 Griesse, *Frühneuzeitliche Revolten*, 1.
39 Bernard, Gage, and Hood, *Letters to the Ministry*, 6.
40 Bernard, *Papers of Francis Bernard*, 2012, 2:12.
41 Harris, 'Governed by Opinion', 494.
42 Steinmetz and Haupt, 'The Political', 21. Steinmetz, 'Neue Wege', 32–3. Griesse, *Frühneuzeitliche Revolten*, 1.
43 The idea that waves of media outrage not only followed revolt but also often inspired it is backed by seventeenth-century reflections on the power of 'fama', as discussed by Bacon, Hobbes and others: Würgler, 'Fama und Rumor'; Neubauer, *Fama*.
44 Barker, 'England', 94.
45 Anon., 'Aufruhr in Birmingham', 152.
46 Examples of Whig media criticism are given in Cowan, 'Mr. Spectator'. Moreover, Daniel Defoe's opinions on the press are discussed by Novak, 'From Pilloried Libeller to Government Propagandist'.
47 Anon., 'Nube Cavâ', 2. Pettegree, *The Invention of News*, 315.
48 Dalrymple, *Appeal of Reason*, iii–iv.
49 Randall, 'Epistolary Rhetoric', 198. Dalrymple, *Appeal of Reason*, iii–iv.
50 Piguenet [Piguenit], *Essay*, i–ii.
51 Ibid.
52 Ibid., 2–3.
53 Stanwood, 'Rumours and Rebellions', 191.
54 Orléans, *Sämtliche Briefe*, 370; 374–5; 377–85; 380–3.
55 List and Index Society and Public Record Office London, *State Papers Domestic*, 178. In early June, however, Schaub had to admit that the Jacobites 'though they do not give over their enterprise have resolved to defer it till another opportunity'. Ibid., 179.

56 Mar, 'SP 54/10/32B'.
57 Halloran, 'Hay, George'; Cheney, 'Bishop George Hay'.
58 Hay, *Memorial to the Public*, 8; 15.
59 Ibid., 10.
60 Christian Friedrich Daniel Schubart, a German journalist and avid supporter of the American Revolution, refers to an 'invented letter from Massachusetts': Baer, 'Christian Friedrich Daniel Schubart's Deutsche Chronik', 446.
61 'In Polybio itaque jam nunc cernimus Americano Senatui praesidentes Spendium et Mathonem, ex humilibus initiis ad summa Consiliorum moderamina evocatos, viamque per mille fraudes sibi munientes. Recognoscimus falsos rumores vanosque timores inter Plebeculam disseminator, Tabellariorumque supposititiorum advocationem, ut fides mendaciis malevolis adhibeatur, veritati Tenebrae objiciantur.' Bentham, *De Tumultibus Americanis*, 11.
62 Stanwood, 'Rumours and Rebellions', 198.
63 Copeland, 'America', 151.
64 Flavell, 'Government Interception of Letters', 407.
65 During and after the Jacobite rising of 1715, letters from the Earl of Mar and George Mackenzie as well as declarations by James Francis Stuart were intercepted: List and Index Society and Public Record Office London, *State Papers Domestic*, 177; 185. 'Trusty smugglers' were also sent to the north of Scotland during the 1745 rebellion in order to acquire 'more authentick informations': Stanhope and Pelham-Holles, *Private Correspondence*, 62. Examples of intercepted American letters are to be found in [American colonists], 'CO 5/40'.
66 Flavell, 'Government Interception of Letters', 406.
67 Ibid., 421.
68 Uncommented copies of American letters were published in several newspapers: Anon. [attributed to George Washington], 'Copy of a Letter', 4.
69 Gage and Bernard, *Letters*, 44.
70 Bernard, Gage, and Hood, *Letters to the Ministry*.
71 Gage and Bernard, *Letters*.
72 Ibid., 44; Bernard, Gage, and Hood, *Letters to the Ministry*.
73 Hutchinson, 'Hutchinson's Response', 462.
74 G. Kearly, who had been in conflict with the Crown for publishing John Wilkes's *North Briton*, also published additional letters pertaining to the American crisis in 1770 and named them *American Gazette*. Almon, 'This Day Are Published'.
75 Monod, 'Jacobite Press', 127.
76 Nevertheless, Würgler notes that the final battle against censorship in Europe was only fought in the nineteenth century: Würgler, *Medien*, 127.
77 Gestrich, 'Early-Modern State', 40.
78 Ibid.
79 For the history of licensing and censorship in Britain, see Duff, *English Book Trade*, 124. Kemp, 'End of Censorship', 47. Ibid.
80 Black, *English Press*, 144.
81 Monod, 'Jacobite Press', 128.
82 Ibid., 138.
83 York, 'George III, Tyrant', 436.
84 Ibid.
85 Barker, 'England', 97.
86 York, 'George III, Tyrant', 438.

87 Piguenet [Piguenit], *Essay*, 27.
88 Ibid.
89 Bernard, Gage, and Hood, *Letters to the Ministry*, 5.
90 'In such cases the People would have Reason to triumph over the Impotency of Government, & the Cause of the Mother Country, Instead of being served, would be injured in the worst.' Robinson, 'T 1/463', 463. Thomas Bradshaw (1733–4) himself was Secretary of the Treasury but in secret contact with Benjamin Franklin.
91 Bollan, *Petition of Mr. Bollan*. See also Bollan, *Freedom of Speech*.
92 The King's Bench (Bancus Regius) was the court where the king went to sit in his own person. It dealt with criminal matters. Cowell, *Law Dictionary*, sec. KI, not paged.
93 Minutes dated 30 June 1770, No. 765, Court of King's Bench, 'TS 11/177/765', fol. 8r.
94 Ibid., fol. 3r.
95 Ibid., fol. 6r.
96 Piguenet [Piguenit], *Essay*, 21–2.
97 Thompson, *Making of the English Working Class*, 452; Barker, 'England', 99.
98 Parliament of Great Britain, *Act*, 1748, 5.
99 Ogborn, 'Power of Speech', 116.
100 Referring to Issue No. 2825 of 12 December 1795: Court of King's Bench, 'TS 11/660'.
101 Ibid., fol. 5r.
102 'If it is opposed, the Impression upon the public Mind may be unfavourable: if it is not opposed, it is difficult to say what Evidence may be offered, and therefore very difficult.' Ibid., fol. 6r. Hans Sloane and his officers followed this advised and notified the Attorney General on 19 April 1796 that they wished to 'prevent his further trouble in this business'. Ibid., fol. 5r.
103 In 1817, William Hone was tried for blasphemy after having published 'parodies upon the Catechism, Litany and Creed'. Thompson believes that the real reason for the trial was Hone's criticism of government members and the nicknames he had given to Cabinet members. Hone was sentenced to eight months in prison. Thompson, *Making of the English Working Class*, 721.
104 Anon., 'High Treason', 22 November 1794.
105 Ibid.
106 Ibid.
107 Ogborn, 'Power of Speech', 109–10.
108 Wharton, *Select and Authentick Pieces*, 6.
109 Parliament of Great Britain, *Act*, 1748.
110 Ibid.
111 Lengel, *This Glorious Struggle*, 284.
112 Schlögl, 'Politik beobachten', 591.
113 Hellmann and Fischer, 'Einleitung', 13–14.
114 Davis, 'The Online Anti-Public Sphere', 155.
115 Spencer, Hicks, and Villers, 'HO 32/35/36: Letter'.
116 The People [pseud.], *Whereas It Has Been Reported*, fol. 1r.
117 Society of the Friends of the People, *Minutes of the Proceedings*, 8–9.
118 An Orangeman [pseud.], *Orange Vindicated*, 15–16.
119 Hay, *Memorial to the Public*.
120 Priestley, 'Appeal', 371.
121 Würgler, *Medien*, 68.
122 The importance of widely accepted language regimes in political overturns has been analysed by William Sewell and Lynn Hunt: Iggers, *Geschichtswissenschaft*, 107.

123 See vocabulary tables: Barget, 'British and Colonial Media Production'.
124 Ibid.
125 Cruikshank, *Sedition, Levelling and Plundering*; Association for Preserving Liberty and Property against Republicans and Levellers, *Proceedings*.
126 Arnold, *By Brigadier-General Arnold, a Proclamation*.
127 'Private interest' had already been scorned as a cause of civil war in the seventeenth century: Burke, 'Some Seventeenth-Century Anatomists of Revolution', 31; Koselleck, 'Revolution: Rebellion, Aufruhr, Bürgerkrieg', 705. The eighteenth-century reinterpretation of private interest is described by Steinmetz and Haupt, 'The Political', 21; 32–3.
128 Morris and Morris, *Dictionary*, 455.
129 Ibid.
130 Kramnick, *Republicanism*, 200–60.
131 Anon., *Revolution Politicks*.
132 See definition of the term *commonwealth* in Bohun, *Address to the Freemen*, 110.
133 Bentham, *De Tumultibus Americanis*, 5.
134 'Supposing, however, that I had written much more largely on politics, particular as well as general, is this a subject that *Dissenters* must not touch? As equal citizens, have we not an equal interest in the concerns of the state; and does it not behove us to watch over that interest, as much as others whose stake in it is not greater than ours? When the government was friendly to the Dissenters, our rulers were glad enough to avail themselves both of our pens and our swords. Our *right* to give our opinion in affairs of the state were not then questioned; and what has happened to affect that right since?' Priestley, 'Appeal'. 389.
135 Philalethes [pseud.], '[Untitled]'.
136 See considerations on masses, leadership and motivation by Szechi, *1715*, 3–4.
137 Barlow, *The Complete English Dictionary*, vol. 2, vol. II, sec. PHI [not paged].
138 Burn and Burn, *A New Law Dictionary*, 2:284.
139 Richard Burn, Law Dictionary, 226.
140 In this section, the author of the dictionary quotes Sir John Fortescue (*c.* 1394–*c.* 1476): Jacob, *New Law-Dictionary*, sec. KI [not paged].
141 Maier, 'Introduction'; Offe, 'Challenging the Boundaries'.
142 See anti-science arguments in opposition to Covid-19 measures: Davis, 'The Online Anti-Public Sphere', 149.
143 Steinmetz and Haupt, 'The Political'.
144 Étienne, 'Fin du politique ou fin de la politique?'
145 Palier and Surel, 'Le politique dans les politiques'; Étienne, 'Fin du politique ou fin de la politique ?'; Wolff, 'La politique divise, le politique rassemble'.
146 Visscher, 'Autorités politiques et haute administration'.
147 Jordanova, *Look of the Past*, 111.
148 Jefferson, *Memoir*, 1:428.
149 Rancière, 'Onze Thèses Sur La Politique', 91.
150 'Le propre de la politique est ainsi perdu d'emblée si on la pense comme un monde vécu spécifique. La politique ne peut se définir par aucun sujet qui lui préexisterait.' Ibid., 92.
151 Barget, 'Power and Identity'. Barget, 'Stadt, Land und suburbaner Raum', 49.
152 Griesse, *Frühneuzeitliche Revolten*, 3.
153 Schaich, 'Public Sphere', 128.
154 Bentham, *De Tumultibus Americanis* foreword.

155 Thompson, *Making of the English Working Class*, 713; also p. 704. Also see Rospocher, 'Beyond the Public Sphere', 18–24; Cowan, 'Mr. Spectator', 345–6; 361.
156 Schlögl, 'Politik beobachten', 583.
157 Clifton, *The Last Popular Rebellion*; Pincus, *1688*.
158 Pincus, *1688*, 107.
159 Earle, *Monmouth's Rebels*; Pincus, *1688*.
160 Clifton, *The Last Popular Rebellion*.
161 Some mechanisms of integration through communicational acculturation have been described by Riotte, 'Vom "Staatsfeind" zum "Oppositionsführer"', 32–3.
162 Anon., 'High Treason', 29 October 1794, 2.
163 Anon., 'Trials for High Treason (The Third Day)', 1.
164 Steinmetz and Haupt, 'The Political', 23.
165 Steinmetz, Kröger, and Moltmann, *Abschlussbericht*, 22; Steinmetz and Haupt, 'The Political', 18.
166 Smith is convinced that even the French Revolution was not only a political or social revolution but also and above all an expression of patriotic sentiments that flourished all across Europe: Smith, *Nobility Reimagined*, 268.
167 Claydon, 'Revolution in Foreign Policy', 219–21. The early modern fear of spies and traitors in times of economic growth and territorial expansion is exemplified by Franklin, 'Plain Truth', 154.
168 Brown, 'Scottish Nobility', 378–84. A tendency to stress personal commitment can already be witnessed in the Jacobite rebellions, which had to be organized through small and physically remote Jacobite communities: Szechi, *1715*, 3.
169 Barget, 'Stadt, Land und suburbaner Raum', 49.
170 Steinmetz and Haupt, 'The Political', 14–15.
171 Synchronic and physical confrontations transformed into diachronically mediated confrontations (e.g. court trials and negotiations at the Imperial Diet) and non-violent conflict resolution. See Würgler, 'Modernisierungspotential'; Burkhardt, *Deutsche Geschichte*.
172 Blickle, 'Criminalization of Peasant Resistance'; Blauert and Schwerhoff, *Kriminalitätsgeschichte*; Schmitt, *Kriminalität und Gesellschaft*; Härter and de Graaf, *Vom Majestätsverbrechen zum Terrorismus*, 2012.
173 Steinmetz, 'Neue Wege', 14.
174 Thompson, 'George I and George II'.
175 Harris, *Revolution*.
176 Kevin Whelan, quoted and discussed in Miller, 'Origins of the Orange Order', 585.

Chapter 2

1 T. K. Rabb's position was that the mid-seventeenth-century Civil War had resulted from a conflict over 'how far [...] central power [ought to] extend' and what 'share in central authority' men of property should possess: Rabb, *Struggle for Stability*, 66–7; Clark, *Revolution and Rebellion*, 68. In the nineteenth century, historians began to focus on the Glorious Revolution as putting a halt to monarchical dominance. A pronounced Whig view is most prominently linked with Macaulay. Adamson, 'Eminent Victorians', 641. S. R. Gardiner presented a more objective and comparative view of seventeenth-century political struggles and also 'provided the

impressive scholarly foundations for the belief, which was to inspire a succession of monographs over the next century, that the house of commons was the cockpit of political events.' Ibid., 642. A focus on parliamentary politics was, in turn, criticized by revisionists of the later twentieth century who described the reigns of William, Mary, Anne and George I as a time of counter-productive party thrive, growing class conflict and administrative inefficiency: Clark, *Revolution and Rebellion*, 43; 74–80; Cox, 'Glorious Revolution', 571. In his 1986 summary of earlier British historiography, J. C. D. Clark adopted an intermediate stance and stressed 'relative positions': Clark, *Revolution and Rebellion*, 43; 70; 78.

2 The idea of a Catholic monarchy revolted both the Anglican majority in England and the large number of Presbyterians in Scotland, but religious division was just one difficulty that James II had to face. For recent interpretations of the Glorious Revolution in a broader constitutional perspective see Thompson, 'Hanoverian Succession'; Harris, *Revolution*, 40; Cox, 'Glorious Revolution', 567–9.

3 Sowerby, 'James II's Revolution'.

4 Harris, *Revolution*, 480. This view is confirmed by an article on King James VII/II's reign that appeared in the *Daily Courant* in 1734: Tenax [pseud.], 'To the Author', 1.

5 Monod, 'Jacobite Press', 136–7.

6 Catholic and continental views of restored Stuart kingship certainly did not envisage 'Jacobite tyranny' and a violent conversion of Englishmen to Catholicism, but might have led to 'a more centralized, militaristic and probably increasingly Catholic polity (as evangelism and self-interest drew in new converts)': Szechi, 'A Blueprint for Tyranny?', 365–6.

7 Cox, 'Glorious Revolution', 591.

8 Prochaska, *Royal Bounty*.

9 Riots and rebellions aiming at the overturn of government included the Monmouth Rebellion, the Glorious Revolution, the Jacobite Rebellions and smaller anti-Hanoverian incidents, the Irish Rebellion of 1798, struggles over colonial governance in North America (e.g. Cary's rebellion in North Carolina in 1711) and eventually the different phases of the American Revolution.

10 Accounts of both incidents can be found in Bennet, *Memorial of the Reformation*, 474; Swift, *The Works of Jonathan Swift*, 3:70–1. Bennet even mentions a third plot that allegedly aimed to kill Queen Anne. Both the Screw Plot and the Bandbox Plot, however, were most likely fabrications by Tories to denigrate the Whigs. See the discussion of contemporary newspaper reports in Claffey, 'Thanksgiving in the Reign of Queen Anne', 186.

11 An example of local opposition to law enforcement were the Porteous Riots (sparked by the hanging of a smuggler in Edinburgh in 1736).

12 Franklin, 'On Government. No. II', 15. Satires mocked the king's confidence in his ministers: Williams, *New Minister*.

13 Applin, 'SP 41/5/44'.

14 [Multiple witnesses], 'MS 3069/Acc1926-021/328833'.

15 A 1795 document in the Lancashire Archives reports consecutive nightly riots by a crowd aiming to get to Mr Pitt's house and threatening the Duchess of Gloucester on her way home. According to the report, a crowd followed her carriage with the cry 'no Royalty, no Pitt'. Kenyon, 'DDKE/Acc. 7840 HMC/1393A: Mary, Lady Kenyon, to Lord Kenyon'.

16 Gillray, *Anti-Saccharites*.

17 Charles, *Boxing Match*.

18 [Committee], 'HO 42/22/113'.
19 Robert, 'HO 42/36/85'.
20 Luhmann, *Politik der Gesellschaft*, 73–4.
21 In contrast to Pocock's attempt to detach the post-1640 republican debate from earlier humanist tendencies, Skinner has proven the influence of Italian Catholic authors on English theories of resistance: Peltonen, *Classical Humanism and Republicanism*, 13–20.
22 Machiavelli (1469–1527), Bodin (1529–96) and Hobbes (1588–1679) are three of the most influential early modern authors in terms of power and sovereignty. Machiavelli did not explicitly discuss sovereignty but promoted princely authority, which later interpreters linked with the sovereignty concept. Jean Bodin, for his part, suggested sovereignty as the necessary basis for efficient lawmaking and peacekeeping, and situated it in a more abstract body politic represented by the individual ruler. Hobbes developed an even clearer theory of the state as the creator and preserver of the law.
23 Black, 'Althusius', 8.
24 See the differentiation between the regal and political rights of kings discussed by Jacob Giles, New Lac Dictionary, KI. Debates in modern political theory: Voigt, 'Abschied vom Staat', 16.
25 Bolingbroke, *Letters*, 96.
26 The most important revolts against Tudor rule in England were the rebellions led by Lambert Simnel and Robert Perkin Warbeck in 1487 to 1497, the Pilgrimage of Grace of 1536, Bigod's Rebellion in 1537, the Prayer Book Rebellion of 1549, Kett's Rebellion, Wyatt's Rebellion in 1554, the Northern Rebellion of 1570, Norfolk's conspiracy in favour of Mary Queen of Scots in 1571, the Throckmorton Plot of 1583 and the Babington Plot of 1586, which led to the execution of Mary Queen of Scots: Beer, *Rebellion and Riot*, 1–10.
27 See summary of Anglophone historiography by Peltonen, *Classical Humanism and Republicanism*, 8–17.
28 Martin, 'Normans'.
29 Kidd, 'Rehabilitation', 70.
30 Johnstone, *Memoirs*, 113.
31 Modern concepts of power premise the post-eighteenth-century constitutional state. Early modern European society, by contrast, was marked by a complex overlap of public and private spheres. Power was exerted by multiple agents on different levels: ibid., 69.
32 Chrimes, 'The Constitutional Ideas of Dr John Cowell', 474.
33 Ibid., 475.
34 Cowell, *Law Dictionary* preface, not paged.
35 Original proclamation of 1710 reproduced in ibid. preface, not paged.
36 Ibid., sec. KI, not paged.
37 Ibid.
38 Cunningham, *A New and Complete Law-Dictionary*, II:63.
39 Ryan, 'Freedom', 164. For combinations of contractual theory and divine law theories of power in eighteenth-century German theory see Rolin, *Ursprung des Staates*, 55.
40 Anon., 'Extract from Addresses to the King', 429.
41 See Würgler, *Unruhen*, 1:74–6. From the mid-seventeenth century onwards, European noblemen also employed legal procedures to promote self-discipline: Asch, 'Staatsbildung', 378.

42 'When the word 'Loyal' (which is faithful to the Law) shall be restored to its own meaning, and no longer signifie [sic.] one who is for subverting the Laws.' Bohun, *Address to the Freemen*, 120.
43 Hoppit, *Land of Liberty?*, 9.
44 Gregory and Stevenson, *Routledge Companion*, 210. Also mentioned by Greene, 'Empire'.
45 Smith, *Nobility Reimagined*, 268.
46 Clifton, *The Last Popular Rebellion*.
47 Anon., *Prerogative*.
48 'Can we expect that a government will be well modeled by a people, who know not how to make a spinning wheel, or to employ a loom to advantage?' Hume, *Essays and Treatises*, IV:30.
49 Roberts, 'Politics of Religion', 548.
50 The importance of regaining lost liberty by the law was stressed in the Jacobite propaganda: Anon., *Conquérant d'Écosse*, 10. Jacobites were also hesitant in the implementation of martial law and hoped to prove themselves true to the ancient constitution: Johnstone, *Memoirs*, 61.
51 Piers, *Religion and Liberty Rescued*.
52 Court of the Old Bailey, 'John Love, Thomas Bean, George Purchase, Richard Price, William Price'.
53 Bean, *Last Speech and Confession*, fol. 1.
54 Ibid.
55 Major shifts in political theory were much more a long-term eighteenth-century phenomenon than a speedy seventeenth-century revolution: Peltonen, *Classical Humanism and Republicanism*, 9–10.
56 Krischer, 'Noble Honour', 86.
57 Kléber Monod, Pittock, and Szechi, 'Introduction: Loyalty and Identity', 1.
58 Owen Ruffhead (1723–69), a miscellaneous writer and political editor, saw the public excitement over Wilkes as a London phenomenon and hoped it would not reach the northern parts of the country: Ruffhead, 'MS Hyde 77 (8.196.2)', fol. 2.
59 The event was even discussed in correspondence between Britons abroad: Whitehead, 'SP 89/59/12: Consul J. Whitehead to [E. Weston ?]', 12.
60 Harris, 'The Massacre of St George's Fields'.
61 Anon., *English Liberty Established*.
62 Political Looking-Glass [pseud.], 'For the Morning Post'.
63 Gerard, *Liberty the Cloke of Maliciousness*.
64 Political Looking-Glass [pseud.], 'For the Morning Post'.
65 'It pleases me to hear, that Affairs settle in England London, and the mob are likely to be no longer predominant. I wish, that People do not take a Disgust at Liberty; a word, that has been so much profan'd by these polluted Mouths, that men of Sense are sick at the very mention of it. I hope a new term will be invented to express so valuable and good a thing. It is some time I dreaded the Issue of this Plan of Supervisorship for our Friends. I fear that the Disappointment will be more severe on Ferguson than on Andrew Stuart. But the Moment that delays were interpos'd, it was to be apprehended that Factions wou'd creep in, and disappoint the Proper. I am Dear Strahan Yours Sincerely David Hume.' Houghton Library, 'MS Hyde 77 (5. 418. 1)', fol. 1. Also see Miller, 'Freethinking', 614–16.
66 Buckley, *The Once and Future King*, 4.
67 Blaisdell, *United States Constitution*, 48.

Notes

68 Buckley, *The Once and Future King*, 5.
69 Marshall, 'Rule of Law', 458.
70 Department of Justice Canada, 'French Revolution'.
71 Ibid.
72 Schaich, 'Monarchy and Religion (Introduction)', 1.
73 Henshall, 'Power and Politics'.
74 Stollberg-Rilinger, *Europa*, 71. Also see Luhmann, *Politik der Gesellschaft*, 428. The early modern kingship also reinterpreted medieval royal fields of actions, which had formerly been described as 'competences': Luhmann, *Politische Soziologie*, 382.
75 Anon., *Salus Populi Suprema Lex*.
76 A Native, and Member of the House of Burgesses [Thomas Jefferson], *Summary View*, 42–3.
77 Quentin Skinner has proposed to distinguish the different meanings that 'liberty' could have in early modern England more carefully and call 'republican liberties' of the Civil War tradition 'neo-Roman liberty' instead. Skinner, *Hobbes and Republican Liberty*, ix. ix.
78 Ibid., 176.
79 Jacob, *New Law-Dictionary*, sec. KI [not paged].
80 Bolingbroke, *Letters*, 247.
81 Ibid., 249.
82 Ibid., 148–9.
83 Bolingbroke, *Bolingbroke's Political Writings*.
84 Bolingbroke, *Letters*.
85 Smith, 'Idea of a Protestant Monarchy', 118.
86 Jacob Giles, New Law Dictionary, sec. KI.
87 Anon., 'High Treason', 29 October 1794, 1.
88 Mary II, *Recht des Congressus zur Wahl*.
89 Anon., 'Miscellanea', fol. 2.
90 Meiners and Spittler, 'II. Summarische Entwicklung', 648–9.
91 'Liberty is to the collective body, what health is to every individual body. Without health no pleasure can be tasted by man: without liberty no happiness can be enjoyed by society.' Bolingbroke, *Letters*, 119.
92 Blount, *Nomo-Lexicon*; Coles, *An English Dictionary*; Jacob, *New Law-Dictionary*; Burn and Burn, *A New Law Dictionary*.
93 Helmers, 'Public Diplomacy in Early Modern Europe: Towards a New History of News'.
94 N. D., *Letter Intercepted*.
95 The institution of the Court of the Exchequer in the twelfth century, which was sometimes referred to as 'the wonder and envy of Europe', was perhaps the most outstanding example of the strong revenue orientation in the royal government. It also called for a high level of 'routine procedures' and a gradual reduction of 'traditional local custom'. This system was organized in concentric circles, encouraging clerics and other local authorities to cooperate with the royal administration: Hindley, *Magna Carta*, 47.
96 Luhmann, *Politik der Gesellschaft*, 384–5.
97 Ibid., 386–7.
98 Wilson, *Sense of the People*, 155.
99 Borus, 'Political Parties', 127.
100 Wilson, *Sense of the People*, 119.

101 The economization of politics started with the establishment of state-run banks: Stollberg-Rilinger, *Europa*, 58.
102 Hume, *Essays and Treatises*, IV:136.
103 Ibid., IV:137.
104 Bolingbroke, *Letters*, 190–1.
105 Marschke, 'Princes' Power', 53.
106 Anon., *Letter*, 1771, 31. German novelist and chronicler Korn likewise detected luxury and greed as the causes of political decline: Korn, *Geschichte der Kriege*, vol. IX, 41.
107 Claydon, *Europe*, 272.
108 More et al., *The Carpenter*.
109 Anon., 'London, March 23', 1. Thomas Hughes and Thomas Rose were among those accused as riot leaders. Anon., 'St. James's, March 22', 22.
110 Anon., 'London, March 23', 23; Harris, 'The Massacre of St George's Fields'.
111 Anon., 'London, March 23', 1.
112 Anon., 'St. James's, March 22', 1.
113 Cowell, *Law Dictionary*, sec. PR, not paged.
114 Cunningham, *A New and Complete Law-Dictionary*, II:63.
115 In the independent United States, newspapers played a vital role in the course of the anti-taxation Whiskey Rebellion, which began in 1791 and climaxed in the summer of 1794: Slaughter, *Whiskey Rebellion*, 225.
116 Anne, *By the Queen*.
117 According to Cunningham, a proclamation affirming an existing law aggravated a possible offence: Cunningham, *A New and Complete Law-Dictionary*, II:63.
118 Even though most princes diplomatically referred to 'James III' as 'Chevalier de St. George' and did not openly question George I's reign, they provided passports, financial support and shelter for King James II's family: [Ernest Augustus, Duke of Brunswick-Calenberg and Elector of Hanover], 'Cal. Br. 24, 1700', fols. 27–30.
119 See report from St. James's, 27/16 November 1714: Robethon and Kreienberg, 'Cal. Br. 24', fols. 14–15.
120 Monod, 'Jacobite Press', 125.
121 Robethon and Kreienberg, 'Cal. Br. 24', fols. 14–15; 283r.
122 Robethon informed Hanover in another letter, dated 28/17 January 1716: 'On publioit qu'il [le Pretendant] viendroit à Perth, où M.d Mar estoit attendu à toute heure. On parloit de le couronner à Scoon [Scone] proche de Perth, qui est l'endroit où on a autrefois couronné les Roys d'Ecosse, et qu'il viendroit ensuite tenir un Parlement à Perth. Mais M.d Cadogan espere mettre ordre à cela en marchant pour l'attaque de Perth le 20.e de ce moir, c'est-à-dire vendredy prochain.' Ibid., 303.
123 Johnstone, *Memoirs*, 33.
124 Ibid., 59.
125 Ibid., 155.
126 Smith, 'Idea of a Protestant Monarchy', 93.
127 Anon., *Conquérant d'Écosse*, 12–13; Anon., *Letter*, 1748; Anon., *The Agreable [sic] Contrast*; Anon., *Agreable [sic] Contrast*; Anon., *Agreeable Contrast*; Johnstone, *Memoirs*, 157.
128 Anon., *Satirical Print*.
129 Cunningham, *A New and Complete Law-Dictionary*, II:63.
130 Gage, *By His Excellency*, 1775, fol. 1.
131 Davis and Mintz, *The Boisterous Sea of Liberty*.

132 An evaluation of the British proclamation policy under Generals Gage and Howe is given by Barnard and Millar, *Complete History*, 689. Bernard, Gage, and Hood, *Letters to the Ministry*, 4. In the following proclamation, the governor addresses complaints by the country people that they had been denied due payment: Gage, *By His Excellency*, 1769.
133 Cotti-Lowell, 'Fatal Mark'.
134 Ibid.
135 Gould, *Writing the Rebellion*, 85.
136 Gage, *By His Excellency*, 1775, fol. 1.
137 Anon., *The Following Is a Copy*, fol. 1r.
138 Ibid.
139 Trumbull, *A New Proclamation!*
140 Richardson, *Historical Magazine*, III, 2:8. See also Blakemore, *Literature*; Gould, *Writing the Rebellion*.
141 Blakemore, *Literature*, 44.
142 Bailyn, *Pamphlets*; Davies, *Documents*; Dickinson, *British Pamphlets*; Downes, *Democracy*; Hume, *Popular Media*.
143 Anon., *Caricature Anticipations*, 2.
144 Ibid., 1.
145 Ibid., 6.
146 Bruce, *Reflections*.
147 Anon., *Trials of Robert Watt and David Downie*, 27–8.
148 'The so-called Pop-Gun Plot involved five members of the London Corresponding Society: John Smith, a bookseller, of Portsmouth Street, Lincoln's Inn Fields; George Higgins, a chemist's shopman, of Fleet Market, nowadays Fleet Street; Paul Thomas Le Maitre, a watchmaker, of Denmark Street, Soho; Thomas Upton, also a watchmaker, of Bell Yard, Temple Bar; and Robert Thomas Crosfield (1768–1802), of no fixed abode. Although all were arrested after an investigation by the Privy Council, Crosfield alone faced the ordeal of a trial for high treason. Parkinson appeared for the defence both before the Privy Council and at the trial.' Morris, 'The Pop-Gun Plot', 38.
149 Ibid., 40.
150 Smith, *Assassination*, 27. See also Lemaitre, *High Treason!!*, 57.
151 Smith, *Assassination*, 69.
152 Ibid., 18.
153 Meiners and Spittler, 'II. Summarische Entwicklung', 652.
154 Ibid., 647.
155 This narrative is, inter alia, prominent in the biblical Book of Esther. See Burn and Burn, *A New Law Dictionary*, vol. 2, vol. II, 52 (KIN).
156 Asch and Duchhardt, *Absolutismus*; Baumgart, 'Absolutismus ein Mythos?'
157 Flümann, *Freiheit*.
158 Anon., *Letter*, 1795, 1. Anon., *Grand Coalition Medal*; Anon., *New Coalition*; Humphrey, *Coalition*.
159 The 'black king' trope, which also influenced white perceptions of the Haitian revolution, has been discussed in Fechner, 'Satirical Rebels?'
160 Horsmanden, *The New-York Conspiracy, or, A History of the Negro Plot*, 91.
161 Peltonen, *Classical Humanism and Republicanism*, 20.
162 Riotte, 'Vom "Staatsfeind" zum "Oppositionsführer"'.

163 Hindley, *Magna Carta*, 6–7; 97–108. *Magna Carta* served a justification of noble rights and as a limitation of oppositional actions conducted by non-noblemen. Anon., *Magna Charta*.
164 Ronald G. Asch and Michael Sikora have seen the seventeenth-century and eighteenth-century nobility in crisis because they had to share military and administrative tasks with non-noblemen and were attacked because of inefficient, exuberant lifestyles: Sikora, *Adel*, 29–32; 125–8; Asch, 'Staatsbildung', 381–5. Peter-Michael Hahn, however, says that the seventeenth-century English opposition of court and country was less severe and that the nobility exhibited a more general anti-centralist solidarity: Hahn, 'Besprechungen'.
165 For the troubled relationships between the Hanoverian kings and their eldest sons see McKelvey, *George III and Lord Bute*, ix–x; Schweizer, 'Stuart', 174.
166 Asch and Birke, *Princes, Patronage, and the Nobility*; Wellenreuther, 'Political Role of the Nobility'; Romaniello and Lipp, 'Spaces of Nobility'.
167 Wharton, *Select and Authentick Pieces*, 92.
168 Ibid., 87–8.
169 Griesse, 'Aufstandsprävention', 173. Asch, 'Staatsbildung', 375.
170 Differences between the considerably strong political position of the Austrian nobility and the much weaker, more contested status of noblemen in France are recounted by Asch, 'Staatsbildung', 388. In spite of these divergent developments, there was a general tendency in Europe to consistently and functionally redefine nobility and subject it to the general legalization and bureaucratization of the nation state. Ibid., 391.
171 Asch, 'Staatsbildung', 377–9.
172 Mc Inerney, 'The Better Sort', 51.
173 Harris, 'Governed by Opinion', 495.
174 Mc Inerney, 'The Better Sort', 51.
175 Asch, 'Staatsbildung', 375.
176 Romaniello and Lipp, 'Spaces of Nobility', 1.
177 Stollberg-Rilinger, *Rituale*, 55.
178 Black, 'The Eagle and the Crown'.
179 Schmohl, *Nordamerika*, 64.
180 Ibid., 48.
181 Ibid., 35.
182 Dalrymple, *Appeal of Reason*, 9.
183 The equation of state government with paternal authority was also criticized by Montesquieu, 'Montesquieu: L'Esprit des Lois. Livre I', 19–20.
184 Schmohl, *Nordamerika*, 56.
185 Ibid., 58.
186 The neglect of the role of women in Habermas's theories of eighteenth-century public spheres and the feminist response are summarized in Schaich, 'Public Sphere', 132.
187 Pierce, *Unseemly Pictures*, 15; 50.
188 Anon., *Letter*, 1771, 6; Wilson, *Sense of the People*, 187. These concepts contrasted with the alleged backwardness and inferiority of overseas colonies: Gregory and Stevenson, *Routledge Companion*, 217–19.
189 Anon., *Letter*, 1771, 6.
190 For the early modern gender bias and 'the subordinate status of women' see Ruff, *Violence*, 35; Thyrêt, *Between God and Tsar*.

191 Wilson, *Sense of the People*, 221. The masculinization of politics was a side-effect of a revised noble status and the devaluation of dynastic succession in favour of state service: Godsey, *Nobles and Nation*, 59.
192 Wilson, *Sense of the People*, 225.
193 Ibid., 226.
194 Johnstone, *Memoirs*, 175. Narratives of rebels who escaped from battle or prison in female attire can be found in Fraser, *Genuine Narrative*.
195 American educational historiography was influenced by Scottish Enlightenment thought and the conviction that knowledge is first of all transported by experience and deepened by emotion. Harris, *Public Lives*, 75.
196 Ibid., 86–7.
197 Barrell, *Imagining the King's Death*, 54.
198 Ibid.
199 Ibid., 55.
200 Ibid., 84–5.
201 Smith, *Georgian Monarchy*, 21.
202 Ibid., 107.
203 Ibid., 109.
204 Burgh, *Britain's Remembrancer*, 9.
205 One example is a portrait of the Prince of Wales on horseback by Copley. This painting was publicly exhibited at the 1810 Academy Annual in England but never sold. It was heavily criticized for aesthetic and political reasons. Its depiction of heroic leadership was considered out of date as it was said to make 'the Prince look like a Brobdingnag general at a Lilliputian review'. Hartley, 'John Singleton Copley'.
206 Thompson, *Making of the English Working Class*, 429.
207 Anon., *Letter to His Grace the Duke of N*********, 28–9.
208 Mc Inerney, 'The Better Sort', 52.
209 Maier, 'Introduction', 1. Stollberg-Rilinger, *Europa*, 41–4.
210 Habermas, *Communication*.
211 Barget, 'Concepts of Leadership'.

Chapter 3

1 Anon., *Proposal*; Anon. [attributed to Charles Lucas], *Abuse*, 1.
2 Skjönsberg, *The Persistence of Party*, 16.
3 Millstone, 'Politic History', 173–5, 189.
4 Ibid., 173–5.
5 Ibid., 189.
6 Noahl Millstone's following Jason Peacey's argumentation in ibid.
7 Wharton, *Select and Authentick Pieces*, 3.
8 Claydon, *Europe*, 224–5.
9 Dunton, 'Observator', 1. Whig author Daniel Defoe also stated that oppositional action should be strictly confined to Parliament because he, too, feared uncontrolled, free-floating political agency as expressed in popular pro-Jacobite riots across Britain: Defoe, *Account of the Riots*, 21.
10 Cox, 'Glorious Revolution', 595.
11 Clark, *Revolution and Rebellion*, 70.

12 Cox, 'Glorious Revolution', 581.
13 Defoe, *Advantages*.
14 Szechi, *1715*, 37.
15 The term 'party rage' was already used by eighteenth-century observers. Cruickshanks, *Religion*.
16 Melleuish, 'Of "Rage of Party" and the Coming of Civility'.
17 'The Tories won resounding victories in the general elections of 1710 and 1713, which in many towns were conducted with considerable violence. At the same time, civic celebrations became occasions for partisan rancour and, most often, Tory triumphalism.' Miller, '12 The Rage of Party, 1700–1714'.
18 Borus, 'Political Parties', 128.
19 This peace treaty of 1713 ended the War of the Spanish Succession, brought Queen Anne formal French recognition, and curbed French support for the Jacobites. However, the treaty was contested within Britain, which even incited Jonathan Smith to offer writing a more positive account for posterity: Jackson, 'Jonathan Swift's Peace of Utrecht'.
20 Berlin-Brandenburgische Akademie der Wissenschaften and Akademie der Wissenschaften zu Göttingen, 'Leibniz: Sämtliche Schriften', 17.
21 Ibid., 209.
22 'Au reste je repete et recommande qu'on doit avoir grand besoin d'eviter et (s'il est possible) de détruire la distinction entre les Whigs et les Tories, et n'en taire qu'entre le Jacobites et les bien intentionnés. La declaration nouvelle du Comte d'Anglesea contre le Ministere donne occasion à notre ami d'insister sur ce conseil.' Leibniz to Luise von Hohenzollern, Vienna, 9 May 1714, ibid., 249–52.
23 Thompson, 'George I and George II', 55.
24 Bennett, *Tory Crisis*, 193.
25 Jones, '1720–23 and All That', 41.
26 Tutchin, '[Country-m. Master, Here's a Letter]', 1.
27 Wharton, *Select and Authentick Pieces*, 3–4.
28 See 'The Lords' Protest on Passing the Bill to inflict Pains and Penalties on Francis Lord Bishop of Rochester. To which is added, The Duke of Wharton's Single Protest on that Occasion, referring to the former. Die Mercurii, 15 Maij 1723', reprinted in: ibid., 63–4.
29 Defoe, *Advantages*. Hitchcock, *Sermon*, 22.
30 Anon., 'London', 3.
31 Robethon and Kreienberg, 'Cal. Br. 24, 1713', fol. 115; Bennett, *Tory Crisis*, 186. Ibid., 186. The 'omnipotence of parliament' was also critically discussed by Brandes, 'Ueber die Justiz- und Gerichtsverfassung Englands', col. 1470.
32 Fisher, 'Vyse'.
33 Vyse, 'MS Hyde 77 (8.196.2)'; Elliot, 'MS Hyde 77 (8.196.2)'.
34 Scot, 'SP 54/15/59: James Scot, Reporting the Attack on Him by a Mob in Dundee during His Journey Home'.
35 Skjönsberg, *The Persistence of Party*, 5.
36 Borus, 'Political Parties', 121.
37 'This chapter demonstrates that Bolingbroke was in fact the promoter of a very specific party: a systematic parliamentary opposition party under the banner of the Country party in resistance to what he perceived as the Court Whig faction in power.' Skjönsberg, *The Persistence of Party*, 78.
38 Bolingbroke, *Letters*.

39   Ibid., 117. A permanent, well-conducted opposition as envisaged by Bolingbroke should earn politicians respect and help them address grievances on a par with government members: ibid., 59–61.
40   Bolingbroke, *Letters*, 43–4.
41   Bennett, *Tory Crisis*, 186.
42   Ibid.
43   Ibid.
44   Ibid., 186–91.
45   The History of Parliament Trust, 'Parliaments 1715–1754'.
46   Ibid.
47   Anon., *The Politician's Dictionary*, 2:107.
48   Ibid.
49   See the political agendas linked with the various 'country factions': Bragge, '[Country-m.]'.
50   Ihalainen, *Discourse on Political Pluralism*, 36:187. At the beginning of the English Civil War, William Prynne's view that opposition was only temporarily admissible and potentially destructive was shared by other seventeenth-century theorists: Milbourne, *Originals of Rebellion*. Milbourne, *Sedition and Rebellion*. Even in eighteenth-century political theory, rebellions and revolutions were often discussed as extraordinary events, not as inherent political concepts. Small, *Political Thought*, 45. Speck, 'Current State', 18.
51   Franklin, 'On Government. No. I', 14.
52   Morris, *Sex*, 24.
53   'collectiviser le plan' Thévenot, *L'action au pluriel*, 123. 'la pluralité des régimes' Ibid., 131.
54   Thompson, 'Rockingham'.
55   Aston and Campbell Orr, *Enlightenment Statesman*, 131.
56   Korn, *Geschichte der Kriege*, vol. VI, 93.
57   Thompson, 'Rockingham'.
58   Winstanley, *Lord Chatham*. Moderation was equated with lenity and inefficiency by Oldmixon, *False Steps of the Ministry*.
59   Maseres, *Moderate Reformer*. Moderation also played an important part in Anglican religious identity.
60   Shagan, *Rule of Moderation*, 330.
61   Wilson, *Sense of the People*, 425.
62   Thorne, 'Fox, Hon. Charles James'.
63   Mitchell, 'Fox', 620.
64   In July 1779, Pitt had defined himself as an 'Independent Whig': Evans, *William Pitt*, 34–5.
65   Thompson, 'Rockingham'.
66   Wilson, *Sense of the People*, 123. See also Rockingham [pseud.], *A Few Words*, 17.
67   Similar demands had been voiced by Tories critical of competing Whig factions: Dalrymple, *Appeal of Reason*, 31.
68   Ward and Dunton, *The Whigs Unmask'd*.
69   Anon., *The Politician's Dictionary*, 2:109.
70   Borus, 'Political Parties', 121.
71   Anon., *The Politician's Dictionary*, 2:109.
72   Phillips, 'Popular Politics', 609–10.
73   Political caricatures of 1784 mocked the 'new' or 'grand coalition' of Lord Chancellor Thurlow, John Wilkes and the king, but also ridiculed inner-parliamentary

harmonization: Anon., *Coalition*; Anon., *Grand Coalition Medal*; Anon., *New Coalition*; Humphrey, *Coalition*; Taylor, 'Coalition Dances'.
74 Macpherson, 'MS Hyde 77 (8.170.3)', fol. 2.
75 Sir John Macpherson, a Scottish minister's son, had been involved with the East India Company and served as governor-general of India from 1785 to 1786. He joined the Whig opposition led by Charles James Fox and was a friend to the Prince of Wales till 1802. In 1789, he left Parliament. Macpherson, 'MS Hyde 77 (8.170.3)'.
76 Macpherson, 'MS Hyde 77 (8.170.2)', fol. 1.
77 Macpherson, 'MS Hyde 77 (8.170.3)', fol. 2.
78 Ibid.
79 Philipps, 'Reflections', fol. 3. The principal author and editor John Philips (or Phillips) was John Milton's nephew and both an enemy to strict Puritanism and a supporter of Titus Oates. His newspaper articles were mainly based on French publications from Den Haag and often direct translations: Winkler, *Handwerk und Markt*, 324–5.
80 Philipps, 'Reflections', fol. 3.
81 Abercromby, *Advantages*, 23.
82 Defoe, *Advantages*.
83 Abercromby, *Advantages*, 14.
84 Pitt, 'SP 63/416/3317'.
85 Knights, 'Introduction', 2.
86 Ibid.
87 Gurney, *Trial of George Gordon*, 32.
88 Ibid. Erskine referred to 'the wretched reign of Richard the Second', Mary I and Charles II: ibid., 33; 36.
89 Hay, *Memorial to the Public*, 19.
90 Ibid., 20.
91 Ibid., 22.
92 Miller, 'SP 54/47/217', 217 v.
93 Blanchard, *Proceedings at Large*; Gurney, *Trial of George Gordon*.
94 Bute and Stuart, *A Prime Minister and His Son*, 182–4.
95 Anon., *The Politician's Dictionary*, 2:99.
96 Ibid.
97 Greenstein, 'Presidential Difference', 377.
98 Lamont and Thévenot, 'Conclusion', 310–11.
99 In the 1790s, the execution of the French king Louis XVI was widely perceived as the epitome of an inhumane 'massacre': Anon., *Massacre of the French King*; Gillray, *Tree of Liberty*.
100 Adams, 'Thoughts on Government', 198.
101 On limitations of government in time: Franklin, 'On Government. No. I', 11.
102 A dilettante in law and politics [pseud., attributed to Allan Ramsay], *Observations*, 8.
103 Adams, 'Thoughts on Government', 197.
104 Tutchin, '[Country-m. Master, Here's a Letter]', 2. and could 'equally make it felony to eat buttered peas, or to wear leather breeches'. A dilettante in law and politics [pseud., attributed to Allan Ramsay], *Observations*, 8.
105 Schwartz, 'George Washington', 26.
106 Hale, *Evolution of British Historiography*, 154.
107 Morris, *Sex*, 31.
108 Blaisdell, *United States Constitution*, 5.
109 Ibid., 101.

110 Ibid., 17.
111 Ibid., 19.
112 Speech by Mr Jonathan B. Smith, farmer of Lanesboro, Berkshire Country, in the Massachusetts Ratifying Convention on 25 January 1788, quoted in: ibid., 111.
113 Greene, *Constitutional Origins*.
114 Blaisdell, *United States Constitution*, 118–20.
115 Ibid., 133.
116 The original draft of the Kentucky Resolutions stated that 'the several states composing the United States of America are not united on the principle of unlimited submission to their general government' but that all members of the union reserved 'the residuary mass of right to their own self-government': Jefferson, 'Kentucky Resolutions', sec. 1.
117 Hofstadter, 'Chapter One: Party and Opposition in the Eighteenth Century', 1.
118 Black, 'The Tumultuous Petitioners', 183.
119 Ibid., 188.
120 For example: Massie, *No Ruinous and Riot-Breeding Taxes*.
121 Lamont and Thévenot, 'Conclusion', 310–11.
122 Anon., *The Politician's Dictionary*, 2:101.
123 Harris, 'Moral Economy', 12.
124 Representative of a cyder-county [pseud.], *An Address to Such of the Electors*, 25.
125 Adams, 'Thoughts on Government', 197.
126 Anonymous, *Virtual Representation*.
127 Green, *To the People of America*, fol. 1.
128 Bernard, *Papers of Francis Bernard*, 2012.
129 A Native, and Member of the House of Burgesses [Thomas Jefferson], *Summary View*, 13.
130 British Library, 'Truth and Treason!'
131 Robert, 'HO 42/36/85'.
132 Ibid.
133 British Library, 'Truth and Treason!'
134 Sack, *From Jacobite to Conservative*, 30.
135 Skjönsberg, *The Persistence of Party*, 37.
136 Anon., *The Politician's Dictionary*, 2:104.
137 Borus, 'Political Parties', 128.
138 Dean, 'Public Space', 170; 175.
139 Schaich, 'Public Sphere', 135.
140 Kyle and Peacey, 'Under Cover of so Much Coming and Going', 19–20.
141 Ibid., 15.
142 Almon, 'This Day Are Published'.
143 Christie, 'Crosby'.
144 Popular crime-related publications (including information on court trails and executions) ranged from individual reports on the lives 'from birth to death' of prominent rebels or highwaymen to more general overviews such as the *Newgate Calendars*: Anon., *Complete History*; Anon., *Newgate Calendar*, 1773; Anon., *Newgate Calendar*, 1774; Hogg, *Malefactor's Register*.
145 Hitchcock, *Sermon*, 21.
146 Anon., *The Politician's Dictionary* frontispiece.
147 A lover of social order [attr. to Robert John Thornton], *The Politician's Creed*.
148 Massachusetts Historical Society, *Collections*, 202.

149 Charles James Fox, who later became a supporter of democracy and parliamentary reform, had first been elected to Parliament because his father, Henry Fox, bought a seat for him. Thorne, 'Fox, Hon. Charles James'.
150 Clark, *Revolution and Rebellion*, 73.
151 Morris, *Sex*, 37.
152 Schweizer, 'Stuart', 175. Lord Bute's attitudes to foreign affairs and domestic peace were summarized and praised by Scottish compatriot Dalrymple, *Appeal of Reason*, 17.
153 Dalrymple, *Appeal of Reason*, 8.
154 For the negative reputation of politicians ever since the early modern period see Steinmetz, 'Neue Wege', 13.
155 Anon., *Letter*, 1771, 23.
156 Winkler, *Wörterkrieg*, 722. Mitchell, 'Fox', 621.
157 Anon., *Letter*, 1771, 14.
158 Ibid., 17.
159 Ibid., 27.
160 Ibid., 18–19; 49–50.
161 Fielding, *Coffee-House Politician*, 30.
162 The print *A Sacrifice to Slavery* of 1787 mocked Pitt the Younger's supposed steps to hinder opposition: Humphrey, *Sacrifice to Slavery*.
163 'You say You are starved for want of Politicks. But I am under no Fear on that Intend: For modern Politicks is by no Means a nourishing Diet.' Ruffhead, 'MS Hyde 77 (8.196.2)', fol. 34.
164 Anon., *Address to the Freeholders*, 15–16.
165 Combe, *Royal Interview*, 12. Donald, *Age of Caricature*, 115.
166 Anon., *Letter*, 1771, 15.
167 Combe, *Royal Interview*, 11.
168 Morris and Morris, *Dictionary*, 456.
169 Anon., *Letter*, 1795, 2.
170 Wilson, *Sense of the People*, 165.
171 Barget, 'Zwischen Ökonomie und Ideologie'.
172 Wilkes, *Letters*.
173 Wilkes, *Voluntary Exile*, 7. Also Anon., *Letter*, 1771, 44–5. John Adams rejected Pope's idea because it 'flattered tyrants too much': Adams, 'Thoughts on Government', 196.
174 Dalrymple derived the modern duties of 'public service' from Roman models, distinguishing them from a man's 'private station': Dalrymple, *Appeal of Reason*, 23–4. The importance of decent 'parliamentary conduct' is, for example, outlined by Anon., *Letter*, 1795.
175 Some enlightened monarchs, too, cultivated 'overeager informality'. Marschke, 'Princes' Power', 59; Marschke, 'Von dem am Königl. Preußischen Hofe abgeschafften Ceremoniel', 227; 245; Sikora, *Adel*, 100.
176 Mitchell, 'Fox', 621.
177 Ibid.
178 Hay, *Memorial to the Public*, 36.
179 Mc Inerney, 'The Better Sort', 60.
180 Ibid., 56.
181 'Perhaps there never was a period of time in our history when a larger body of eminent men could be found than at this moment, whose rare attainments and

powers of intellect better intitled [*sic.*] them to so important a trust as the direction of the public mind.' Rockingham [pseud.], *A Few Words*, 5–6.
182 Anon., *Address to the Freeholders*, 7.
183 For example, the election report for Weymouth and Melcomb-Regis in the *Flying Post* of 1698: Snowden, 'By the Dutch Mails', 2.
184 The History of Parliament Trust, 'Parliaments 1754–1790'.
185 Sack, *From Jacobite to Conservative*.
186 Hawkins, 'Imperial '45', 34–5. After the failed Jacobite rebellion of 1745–6, loyalists as far from London as Virginia also organized a ball and evening reception in honour of King George II and his victorious troops: ibid., 37.
187 Priestley, 'Appeal', 357.
188 Anon., 'High Treason', 29 October 1794, fol. 1.
189 The rules of procedure passed by the General Convention of the delegates from the Societies of the Friends of the People throughout Scotland, for example, detailed the mode of discussion and the voting process: Society of the Friends of the People, *Minutes of the Proceedings*, 6–7.
190 Pickering and Davis, *Unrespectable Radicals?*, 26.
191 Lemaitre, *High Treason!!*, 56.
192 Gurney, *Trial of George Gordon*, 14–15. 'The proceedings of the Convention was no secret, for they had been regularly published in the Gazette.' Anon., *Trials of Robert Watt and David Downie*, 51.
193 See Morris, *Sex*, 24. Also see Chapter 5.
194 Maxwell, *Armagh*, 69.
195 One of the most prominent collection item is the Orange banner used in the Dolly Brae conflict, a contested procession by Orangemen in July 1849.
196 Byrne, *Memoires*, 45.
197 Ibid., 14–15.
198 Simes, 'Ireland'.
199 Welsh, *Four Nations*, 230.
200 Anon., 'High Treason', 29 October 1794, fol. 2.
201 Anon., 'High Treason', 22 November 1794.
202 Ibid.
203 Ibid.
204 Anon., 'Trials for High Treason (The Fourth Day)', fol. 1; Anon., 'High Treason', 29 October 1794, fol. 2.
205 Anon., 'Trials for High Treason (The Fourth Day)', fol. 1.
206 Rockingham [pseud.], *A Few Words*, 23.
207 Thorne, 'Fox, Hon. Charles James'.
208 Rockingham [pseud.], *A Few Words*, 9.
209 Ibid., 14.
210 Ibid., 11.
211 Ibid., 12.
212 Ibid. Commenting on the 1745 rebellion, Hume adopted a pragmatic approach to the Glorious Revolution and warned England of a declining reputation if 'disgusted with a settlement so deliberately made, and whose conditions have been so religiously observed, we should throw everything again into confusion.' Avoiding another civil war or revolution was his primary concern. The successful day-to-day administration of public affairs took precedence over matters of legitimation: Hume, *Essays and Treatises*, IV:278–9.

213 Anon., *Views of the Ruins*, fig. 1 (not paged). Also see reception of the 1791 Birmingham Riots in the British press: Gillray, *Birmingham Toast*; Dent, *Revolution Anniversary*.
214 Barrell, *Imagining the King's Death*, 62–74.
215 Formisano, 'State Development', 23.
216 Skjönsberg, 'Party', 7.
217 Kluxen, 'Voters', 465–6.
218 A dilettante in law and politics [pseud., attributed to Allan Ramsay], *Observations*, 20.

Chapter 4

1 See Ian Gilmour's negative assessment of religious eighteenth-century riots: Gilmour, *Riot, Risings and Revolution*, 341.
2 Szechi, 'Review of Riot, Risings, and Revolution', 704.
3 Clark, 'England's Ancient Regime', 450.
4 '[The] Revolution of 1688 did not lead Britain toward a general commitment to religious liberty or political secularization. […] All early modern states, to varying extents, imposed religious monopolies and restricted minorities (see Johnson and Koyama 2019). Rather, we are arguing against the North and Weingast thesis that makes England exceptional.' Kulkarni and Pfaff, 'The "Glorious" Revolution's Inglorious Religious Commitment', 3.
5 A society of gentlemen [pseud.], *The Patriot*, 2:37.
6 See Kulkarni and Pfaff, 'The "Glorious" Revolution's Inglorious Religious Commitment', 2.
7 Preaching as a popular medium was vital in early modern Britain: Taylor, 'Clergy', 130.
8 Roots of apocalyptic anti-etatism in the sixteenth- and seventeenth centuries: Walzer, *Revolution of the Saints*; Zagorin, *Rebels and Rulers*, I:140; Loewenstein, *Representing Revolution*; Villani, 'Seventeenth Century'; Hessayon and Finnegan, *Varieties*.
9 An eighteenth-century source hinting at this diversity is Defoe, *Account of the Riots*, 2.
10 Anon., *The Politician's Dictionary*, 2:109.
11 Ibid.
12 See *Politica sacra et Civilis*, which stated that there was 'no iure divino form' of government but that society was nevertheless 'indirectly' governed by God and 'a divinely sanctioned order worthy of consent'. Lawson, *Politica Sacra & Civilis*.
13 A society of gentlemen [pseud.], *The Patriot*, 2:42.
14 Armstrong, *Fields of Blood*, 281.
15 Bennet, *Memorial of the Reformation*.
16 See metadata of political sermons published prior to 1641: https://www.zotero.org/groups/2351893/british_riots_and_revolts_of_the_enlightenment_age
17 A central document of Tudor thought on rebellion was written by Thomas Bilson, Bishop of Winchester. It was first published in 1585 for Queen Elizabeth I and frequently reprinted: Bilson, *Trve Difference*; Bilson, *Discourse*; Bilson, *Certain Observations*, 1750; Bilson, *Certain Observations*, 1642. Bilson's major argument for strong royal government was that 'the decaied [sic] and accursed kingdom of

Antichrist' would have to be overcome by Christian loyalty to the true monarch: Bilson, *Trve Difference*, fol. 3 v.
18 Mossom, *King on His Throne*.
19 See the editions of 1570 and 1573: Church of England, *Homelie against Disobedience*; Church of England, *Homilie against Disobedience*.
20 Busshoff, *Das Politische der Politik*.
21 The relationship of Church and Crown had already been a matter of concern in the Magna Carta, which was still venerated as the basis of ecclesiastical politics in the early modern period: Hindley, *Magna Carta*, 64–7.
22 Shagan, *Popular Politics*.
23 Anon., 'Ego Primum', fol. 2.
24 Yates, *Eighteenth Century Britain*.
25 Gotthard, *Das Alte Reich*.
26 Schaich, 'Monarchy and Religion (Introduction)', 37.
27 Campbell Orr, 'The Late Hanoverian Court and the Christian Enlightenment', 317; Claydon, *Europe*, 4. For developments in continental Europe see Griesse, 'Frühneuzeitliche Revolten', 13.
28 In contrast to Pincus, who stressed the ubiquity of Catholic missionary zeal and 'Gallican beliefs' at James's court [Pincus, *1688*, 131–5], Harris is more restrained in his analysis of James's religious policy, stating that the king was initially cautious about granting complete freedom to his fellow believers [Harris, *Revolution*, 46.]
29 Dunton, 'Quest', fol. 2.
30 Clark, *Revolution and Rebellion*, 80. Bennett, *Tory Crisis*, vii. Especially among Scottish Episcopalians, King 'Willie' (William III) and German King 'Geordie' (George I) were anything but popular. See the High Church poem *The Curses* in Macquoid, *Jacobite Songs and Ballads*, 43.
31 How Tory Anglicanism was torn between 'indefeasible hereditary right' and opposition to James VII/II's 'Catholicizing tendencies' has been discussed by Szechi, 'A Blueprint for Tyranny?', 348–9. In his well-known letters on the spirit of patriotism, Henry St. John Viscount Bolingbroke carefully mitigated the Tory idea of 'divine government' and criticized that 'the characters of king and priest have been sometimes blended together': Bolingbroke, *Letters*, 78.
32 Anon., 'Nube Cavâ', fol. 1.
33 Green, 'London', fol. 1.
34 Ibid.
35 Strong, *Anglicanism*, 41.
36 Gilbert Burnet was perhaps the last classical example of the Anglican clerical politician who combined an official position at court with an impressive career as a writer. Burnet's intellectual openness towards Catholic theology and a strong sense of common Christian traditions conflicted with his narrow interpretation of the political functions of the Church of England: Burnet, *Engelland*. Greig, 'Burnet', 914.
37 Rogers, 'Popular Protest', 90.
38 Bennett, *Tory Crisis*, vii–ix. See also Strong, *Anglicanism*.
39 For the specific aims of English Protestant Jacobitism see Szechi, 'A Blueprint for Tyranny?', 349.
40 Thomas Deacon and Francis Atterbury, Bishop of Rochester, were two of the most prominent figures of ecclesiastical opposition to the Hanoverian government: Broxap, *Biography*. Bennett, *Tory Crisis*, 295.

41 'Even official Walpolean Whiggery accepted the majority opinion [and refused to] tamper with the Test and Corporation Acts'. Davis, 'English Society', 412. Also see Claydon, *Europe*, 233.
42 Bryan, 'From Jacobite to Conservative', 42. Despite some necessary qualifications, many historians agree that 'the dominant ideology of the period, [...] can be summed up in the slogan "Church and King," in which "Church" meant the religion of the social and political elite and provided the theoretical and moral justification for their privileged position'. Davis, 'English Society', 412.
43 Abercromby, *Advantages*, 33.
44 After the Peace of Westphalia, German authorities and printers abstained from printed sermons as a medium of crisis communication and played down or denounced religious aspects of tumults. Ernest Augustus, father of King George I of Britain, subjected religion to an international balance of powers, closely cooperating with Catholic ambassadors: Guidi, 'Hann. 92, 2221'. He also granted Huguenots a safe exile: German Chancellery in London, 'Hann. 92, 59'.
45 Bilson, *Trve Difference*, fol. 12.
46 Beckett, *King William III*. See also considerations on a 'Georgian Church' by Smith, *Georgian Monarchy*, 163.
47 Smith, 'Idea of a Protestant Monarchy', 92.
48 Green, '[There Having Lately Been Great Endeavours]', fol. 1.
49 Thompson, 'George I and George II'.
50 Campbell Orr, 'The Late Hanoverian Court and the Christian Enlightenment', 317.
51 Claydon shows that 'the cosmopolitanism of late Stuart and Georgian England' was also encouraged by religious debates: Claydon, *Europe*, 5. For the topos of the 'dark forces of popery' in British political theory see Stanwood, 'Rumours and Rebellions', 190–1.
52 Since the nineteenth century, many studies on the impact of religion on political change have either stressed the agitating power of religious practices or singled out the counter-revolutionary, decorous doctrines of obedience and self-abandonment: Schaich, 'Monarchy and Religion (Introduction)', 4.
53 The History of Parliament Trust, 'Parliaments 1754–1790'.
54 Field, 'Counting Religion in England and Wales', 704.
55 'Twenty years later, in the 1790s, the trend had generally been reversed, partly under the impact of the Evangelical revival and partly as a consequence of demographic growth. One dissenting minister claimed in 1790 that the Three Denominations alone were "considerably above a twentieth part of the inhabitants of this country", while a foreign visitor was inclined to estimate all English Nonconformists in 1791 at about 100,000 families, perhaps implying 500,000 souls. This figure broadly combined Baptist, Congregational und Methodist adherence in England (excluding Wales) rising from 320,000 in 1790 to 500,000 in 1800, to reach 8.7 per cent of the adult population.' Ibid., 698.
56 Ibid., 700.
57 Ibid., 709.
58 Shuger, 'Absolutist Theology', 115.
59 Attempts to reform Church and State were seen as an attack upon the English Constitution. The Holy Roman Empire, by contrast, had achieved legalized bi-confessionality in 1555 (Peace of Augsburg), which is why 'even the war 1618–1648 differed fundamentally from Western European religious civil wars': Koselleck, 'Revolution: Rebellion, Aufruhr, Bürgerkrieg', 699.

60 Oakley, *Conciliarist Tradition*, 217; Valliere, *Conciliarism*. Oakley, *Conciliarist Tradition*, 223.
61 One example of clerical radicalism is the Rev. William Jackson's support for revolutionary France: Anon., *Full Report*.
62 It is important to note, however, that groups like the Jacobites and the Freemasons were by no means identical. Whereas the British government certainly suspected freemasonry of Jacobite sympathies, English freemasons were 'determined to "give a public assurance that they were not a political body."' Jones, '1720–23 and All That', 52. For the actual Stuart Masonic networks see Oates, *Jacobitism*, 9; Schuchard, *Emanuel Swedenborg*, 3–7.
63 Brent, *Liberal Anglican Politics*, 25.
64 Ibid., 252–4.
65 Ibid., 300.
66 Ibid., 104.
67 Ibid., 299.
68 Clark, 'The Re-Enchantment of the World?'
69 Norman, *Church and Society*, 15.
70 Ibid., 15–16.
71 Within the Anglican Church, these developments prompted extensive debates on the validity of lay-preaching and 'the necessity of a regular ministry': Anon., *Two Essays*.
72 Ingoldsby, *Doctrine*.
73 On the influence of religion on party formation in the seventeenth century, David remarked that the Puritans had been the first to be identified as a religio-political faction: Hale, *Evolution of British Historiography*, 143–5. Parties in Britain were only gradually secularized: Hatton, *George I*, 290.
74 Bradley, *Religion*, 348–9.
75 Ibid., 205.
76 Ibid., 31.
77 Thompson, *Making of the English Working Class*, 397–9; 715.
78 Anon., *Seasonable Memorial*; Midgley, 'Henley', 357.
79 Smith, 'Hexham Riot'. A general account of the Militia Act riots in Yorkshire is given by Stevenson, *Popular Disturbances*, 36–40.
80 Ridley, *Hexham Chronicle*, 17.
81 Ibid., 24.
82 Ibid., 31.
83 Cooper [purporting to be the will of Reverend John Ellison], *Will of a Certain Northern Vicar*; Smith, 'Hexham Riot'.
84 Barrell, *Imagining the King's Death*, 145.
85 Caudle, 'Preaching in Parliament', 237; McCormack, 'Supporting the Civil Power', 37.
86 In Burke's 1790 *Reflections on the Revolution* in France, we find the following enlightening passage: 'We know, and what is better, we feel inwardly, that religion is the basis of civil society'.
87 Neill, 'The Disestablishment of Religion in Virginia'.
88 Field, 'Counting Religion in England and Wales', 706.
89 Watson, *The New Cambridge Bibliography of English Literature*.
90 See table of religious periodical on GitHub: https://github.com/MonikaBarget/Revolts/blob/master/TABLE_religious-periodicals.csv
91 *Extract from Major Cartwright's Letter to the Duke of Newcastle* and *On Religious Liberty* by an unnamed scholar of divinity in A society of gentlemen [pseud.], *The Patriot*.

92 List of religious periodicals launched before and after 1800: Barget, 'Sermons and Religious Periodicals'. The data are based on Wikidata and quantitative work done by Samuel J. Rogan: Rogal, 'Religious Periodicals in England during the Restoration and Eighteenth Century'. For the history of religious publishing in Britain also see Lake, 'To Lye upon a Stationers Stall', 188–91.
93 These findings are based on full-text searches in the digital British Newspaper Archives and only provide qualitative insights. For quantitative evidence, better OCR of all available newspapers would be needed.
94 A joint Protestant-Catholic prevention of unrest is reported in the *Kentish Weekly Post or Canterbury Journal* of Saturday 27 March 1731 and in *Saunders's News Letter* of Wednesday 13 September 1786: Anon., 'Dublin, March 14', 2; Anon., 'Dublin', 2.
95 Anon., 'Dublin', 2.
96 Caudle, 'Preaching in Parliament', 135.
97 Johnston, *National Thanksgivings*, 2.
98 In my statistics, different editions have been counted separately. Although I have attempted to remove actual duplicates, the metadata certainly require further cleaning.
99 Barget, 'Conflicts'.
100 Taylor, 'Clergy', 151.
101 Schaich, 'Monarchy and Religion (Introduction)', 16.
102 Caudle, 'Nowell', 239; Caudle, 'Preaching in Parliament', 253.
103 Astell, *Impartial Enquiry*, 1704.
104 The controversial culture of political preaching is outlined in ibid. Astell, *Impartial Enquiry*, 1703. The turning point was the parliamentary sermon of 30 January 1772 delivered by the fervent High Church theologian Thomas Nowell. This staunchly monarchist sermon on the anniversary of the execution of Charles I scandalized the nation: Towers, *Letter to the Rev. Dr. Nowell*; Anon., *Critical Remarks*; Caudle, 'Nowell', 240.
105 See charts in Barget, 'Sermons and Religious Periodicals'.
106 Johnston, *National Thanksgivings*.
107 Dobbs, *Thanksgiving-Sermon*, 20.
108 Borus, 'Political Parties', 125.
109 Dobbs, *Thanksgiving-Sermon*, 20.
110 Warren Johnston's book on thanksgiving sermons has analysed 587 sermons between 1689 and 1816 of which 22.8 per cent were 'by Protestant dissenters'. Johnston, *National Thanksgivings*, 3.
111 Abbott, 'Clerical Responses', 332. See also Claydon, 'Sermon Culture'.
112 Abbott, 'Clerical Responses'.
113 Philocles [pseudonym], *Letter*. Thompson has noted that the intense pressure placed on religious groups to be politically correct motivated them to model their sermons on parliamentary speeches: Thompson, *The Making of the English Working Class*, 350. See the development in homiletic literature from political zeal to general morality: Fordyce and Dodsley, *Theodorus*; Marshall, *The Use and Importance of a Preaching Ministry*; Dodsley, *Art of Preaching*; Fordyce and Mitchell, *Preacher's Manual*; Sturtevant and Henderson, *Preacher's Manual*.
114 Dobbs's anti-Jacobite sermon published in Belfast in 1746 was based on Psalm 47, verse 6 and referred not only to the Messiah's heavenly kingdom but also to the worldly kingdom of Britain. Both kingdoms, Dobbs claimed, demanded zeal and eagerness: Dobbs, *Thanksgiving-Sermon*, 19. In the British Library Catalogue and

related search engines, this sermon is wrongly attributed to Arthur Dobbs, but it was in fact written by his brother, the Rev. Richard Dobbs.
115 Astell, *Impartial Enquiry*, 1704; Bean, *Folly and Wickedness*; Suger, *Preservation of Judah*; Dobbs, *Thanksgiving-Sermon*; Dupont, *Peculiar Happiness and Excellency*.
116 Dobbs, *Thanksgiving-Sermon*, 20.
117 Ibid., 21.
118 Ibid., 20. See also Lambe, *When God Is on Our Side*; Lambert, *Sermon*; Abbot, *Duty*.
119 Dobbs, *Thanksgiving-Sermon*, 19.
120 Ibid.
121 Ibid., 17.
122 Ibid., 18.
123 Ibid.
124 Ibid., 7–8.
125 Layman [pseud], *Layman's Sermon*.
126 Claydon, 'Sermon Culture', 225.
127 Midgley, 'Henley'.
128 For biographical information see Kenyon, *Revolution Principles*, 74–7; 91–4; 112; 126; 133; 166; 189.
129 Sacheverell, *Character of a Low-Church-Man*.
130 Sacheverell, *New Association*.
131 Kemp, 'End of Censorship', 66.
132 Cowan, 'Chapter 1. Introduction', 1.
133 Kemp, 'End of Censorship', 47–8. See also Holmes, 'Sacheverell Riots'.
134 Kemp, 'End of Censorship', 66.
135 Holmes, 'Sacheverell Riots', 68.
136 Knights, 'Introduction', 11.
137 Hunt, 'Sacheverell, Henry'; Cowan, 'Doctor Sacheverell'.
138 Anon., *Dr. Sacheverell's Picture*; Knights, 'Introduction', 10.
139 Holmes, 'Sacheverell Riots'; Knights, 'Introduction', 2.
140 Knights, 'Introduction', 1.
141 Oates, *Jacobitism*, 4. See also Blacow, *Letter to William King*.
142 Caudle, 'Preaching in Parliament', 251–2.
143 Pittock, 'The Jacobite Diaspora', 123.
144 Midgley, 'Henley', 357.
145 Taylor, 'Hoadly', 347.
146 Starkie, *Church of England*, i.
147 Taylor, 'Hoadly', 345.
148 Claydon, *Europe*, 345.
149 Starkie, *Church of England*, i.
150 Haydon, 'Sherlock'; Taylor, 'Hoadly', 341–2; 345.
151 Taylor, 'Hoadly', 342.
152 Haydon, 'Sherlock'.
153 Ibid., 323.
154 Ibid., 324.
155 Ibid.
156 Starkie, *Church of England*, 19.
157 Pincus, *1688: The First Modern Revolution*, 813.
158 Bradley, *Religion*, 2.
159 Claydon, 'Sermon Culture'.

160 An early vindication of the political conduct of Anglican clergymen can be found in the various issues of the Tory periodical *The Examiner*, which was first printed in 1710: 'To Hate or Revile the *Clergy*, out of pretended Zeal for the *State*, is senseless Malice and Ingratitude; because they always assisted us in Times of public Danger, and have been often highly Instrumental in the Deliverance of their Country. To Hate them on account of their Revenue, favours strongly of Oppression; and whether we consider their *Tenure* by the *Law*, or by the *Gospel*, we bid fair for the Overthrow of *Property*, by weakning [sic] the clearest and strongest Title that any *British Subject* can plead to his Possessions.' Anon., 'Ego Primum', fol. 1.

161 Ihalainen, *Discourse on Political Pluralism*.

162 One of the clergymen who served as British government minister in modern times is Stephen Green, Baron Green of Hurstpierpoint, who was a Church of England priest as well as Conservative Minister of State for Trade and Investment from 2011 to 2013.

163 Miller, 'William Wake', 7.

164 Wake, *The State of the Church and the Clergy of England*, 6.

165 Ibid., 4.

166 Ibid., 541.

167 Ibid., 7.

168 Ibid., 8.

169 Jansenist thought stressed the corruption of human nature by original sin. Accordingly, true freedom was only considered possible through Christ's redemption, and good deeds required the percursory presence of divine grace. For William Wake's occupation with Gallican thought see Miller, 'William Wake'.

170 Williams, 'Translating the Jansenist Controversy'.

171 Blanchard, 'Thomas Palmer, Jansenism and England'.

172 Francis Plowden was born at Shropshire in 1749 and initially trained to become a Jesuit. Later he married and initially 'practiced as a conveyancer, the only department of the legal profession open to Catholics under the Penal Laws'. After the 1791 Relief Act, he was called to the Bar and received an honorary degree from the University of Oxford for his book *Jura Anglorum. Church and State* appeared in 1795. In 1803, however, his 'Historical Review of the state of Ireland' displeased the government, and his 1811 work 'Ireland since the Union' led to prosecution for libel. He spent the rest of his life in Paris.

173 Plowden, *Church and State*, 2.

174 Ibid., 4.

175 Ibid., 3.

176 Kramnick, *Republicanism*, 291.

177 Thompson, *Making of the English Working Class*, 350. See also ibid., 391.

178 Kramnick, *Republicanism*, ix.

179 Annet, *Judging for Ourselves*.

180 Henley, *Victorious Stroke for Old England*, 54.

181 Ibid., 20.

182 Ibid., 16.

183 Ibid., 17.

184 Ibid., 19.

185 Ibid., 54.

186 Ibid., 6. This opinion has been confirmed by modern historiography: Schaich, 'Public Sphere', 133.

187 Jefferson, 'Kentucky Resolutions', sec. 3; Kentucky General Assembly, *Resolutions*, vol. 30, sec. 3.

188 Hole, *Pulpits*, 41–3.
189 The sermon by the Rev. Gad Hitchcock, a pastor in Pembroke, Massachusetts Bay Colony, which marked the anniversary of the Election of His Majesty's Council for the province on 25 May 1774 is a fine example. This sermon paraphrased the Bible quote 'When the righteous are in authority, the people rejoice: but when the wicked beareth rule, the people mourn.' Hitchcock, *Sermon*, 5. Hitchcock did not address specific policy but 'point[ed] out some of the qualification of rulers' necessary to 'the public security and welfare': ibid., 7.
190 Hitchcock, *Sermon*, 23.
191 Ibid., 17; 40.
192 Ibid., 16.
193 Ibid., 29.
194 An anonymous pamphlet written in defence of Surrey rioter John Hartland, who was hanged for gathering forty men in a violent scuffle, featured the commentary to an anti-rioting sermon delivered by a local clergyman and daringly compared John Hartland to Jesus, who patiently took other people's sins upon himself: Anon., *John Hartland*, 12. John Wilkes's supporters also resorted to a similar rhetoric: Anon., *Britannia's Intercession*.
195 Bradley, *Religion*, 1.
196 Miller, 'Freethinking', 616–17.
197 Hole, *Pulpits*, 51.
198 After 1760, 'religion was rarely invoked in purely secular debates': ibid., 11–12.
199 Johnston, *National Thanksgivings*, 292.
200 Stevenson, *Popular Disturbances*, 137.
201 Anti-Catholicism as a unifying factor in British colonial history has been discussed by Clark, *The Language of Liberty*.
202 Field, 'Counting Religion in England and Wales', 711.
203 Anon., 'Etwas von Irlands jetziger politischen Lage', 227.
204 Field, 'Counting Religion in England and Wales', 713.
205 Simes, 'Ireland', 129; 131.
206 Jackson, *Ireland*, 9.
207 Maxwell, *Armagh*, 14–15.
208 Simes, 'Ireland', 128–9.
209 Byrne, *Memoires*, 35.
210 Ibid., 31–2; Anon., *Father Murphy*; Kennedy, *Father Murphy*; Furlong, *Fr. John Murphy*; Anon., *Trial at Large*; Gurney, *Trial of James O'Coigly*.
211 Troy, *To the Rev. Roman Catholic Clergy*.
212 Emmet's speech from the Dock, quoted according to Byrne, *Memoires*, 159–60.
213 Thompson, *Making of the English Working Class*, 429.
214 Kidd, 'Rehabilitation', 72–3.
215 For the commemorative culture that developed around the Gunpowder Plot see Anon., *Solemn Mock-Procession*, 1. For the history of English Catholicism between 1688 and 1745 see Glickman, *English Catholic Community*.
216 Papal declarations on the separation of ecclesiastical and temporal authority date back to the fifth century AD: Denzinger, *Kompendium der Glaubensbekenntnisse*, 159; 170; 335; 703.
217 Bilson, *Trve Difference*, fol. 6 r; Morton, *Exact Account*. More moderate writers claimed that differences in religion did not necessarily divide the nation: Parsons, *Treatise*; Broughton, *Iust and Moderate Answer*.
218 Suger, *Preservation of Judah*.

219 Szechi, *1715*, 209–11.
220 Ibid., 249–50.
221 Arbuthnot, *Sermon*, 4.
222 Ibid.
223 Hay, *Memorial to the Public*, 5.
224 Hay, *Memorial to the Public*.
225 Ibid., 1.
226 Ibid.
227 Ibid., 2.
228 Ibid., 3.
229 James Madison, 'Vices of the Political System of the United States', April 1787, in: Blaisdell, *United States Constitution*, 28–9.
230 Hay, *Memorial to the Public*, 4.
231 Ibid., 5.
232 Gurney, *Trial of George Gordon*, 36.
233 Ibid.
234 A dilettante in law and politics [pseud., attributed to Allan Ramsay], *Observations*, 27.
235 Stevenson, *Popular Disturbances*, 137.
236 Priestley, 'Appeal', 369.
237 Ibid., 437.
238 Ibid.
239 Ibid., 370.
240 Rosewell, *Unreasonableness of the Present Riotous and Tumultuous Proceedings*.
241 Edes, Edes Jr., and Edes, '[Birmingham, July 19]', fol. 2.
242 Stanley, 'Broomhall Riots'.
243 The riot in general was also linked with the enclosure of common land.
244 Stevenson, *Artisans and Democrats*.
245 Bradley, *Religion*, 3.
246 Kramnick, *Republicanism*, 290. A contemporary defence of Unitarianism and above all the Birmingham congregation was written by a group of Unitarian ministers: Edwards, *Letters to the British Nation*, 5.
247 Kramnick, *Republicanism*, ix.
248 Brodrick, *Political History*, 3. The act was repealed in 2001. In an 1834 debate on a repeal, MPs demanded that a future condition for the return of clergy ought to be that there was no conflict of interests and that readmission would prevent undue discrimination on religious grounds. The Parliament of the UK, 'Clergy in Parliament'. To this day, the role of clergymen in politics remains an issue of parliamentary reform. The Electoral Reform Society is critical of retaining bishops in the House of Lords.
249 Cappon, 'Introduction', xlvii.
250 Ibid.
251 The role of American preachers as judges, political authors and even violent rebellion leaders was described by Korn, *Geschichte der Kriege*, I, 77; ibid., vol. III, 89; ibid., vol. V, 4–6.
252 Kennedy, 'Faith and the Founders', 617.
253 Ibid.
254 Ibid., 618.
255 Roberts, 'Political Biography', 619.
256 Korn, *Geschichte der Kriege*, vol. III, 76–7.

257 'Hancock, Warren and S. Adams had established the custom of haranguing the people from their churches, who, bigoted beyond the most inflamed Romans, thought that their seditious orations derived a degree of sanctity from the Pulpit whence they were usually delivered.' Charles Stuart to Lord Bute, Boston, 24 July 1775, in: Bute and Stuart, *A Prime Minister and His Son*, 66.
258 Ibid., 70.
259 Bentham, *De Tumultibus Americanis*, 21.
260 Korn, *Geschichte der Kriege*, vol. IV, 3.
261 Hale, *Evolution of British Historiography*, 151.
262 A layman [pseud.], *The Church an Engine of the State*, 33.
263 Paine, *Common Sense*.
264 Schwartz, 'George Washington', 22.
265 Ibbetson, *Public Virtue*.
266 The southern states of nineteenth-century America embraced church affiliation as a strong counterpart to politics framed by the Washington establishment: A citizen of London [pseud.], *Revolution No Rebellion*.
267 Bullock, *Revolutionary Brotherhood*.
268 Scottish lodges in Paris and Tory-Masonic networks in Scandinavia were an important Jacobite resource in Europe: Schuchard, *Emanuel Swedenborg*, 3–7.
269 Ruderman, *Jewish Enlightenment*, 156; Stollberg-Rilinger, *Europa*, 317.
270 O'Shaughnessy, 'Rip'ning Buds in Freedom's Field', 543.
271 Gillray, *Anecdote Maçonnique*.
272 'Jews and Judaizing Christians are now Scheeming [sic] to buy up all our Continental Notes at two or three shillings in a Pound, in order to oblige us to pay them at twenty shillings a Pound.' John Adams to Thomas Jefferson, from Grosvenor Square, 6 June 1786, published in Cappon, *Adams-Jefferson Letters*, 134.
273 Field, 'Counting Religion in England and Wales', 715.
274 The Jew Bill sought to permit the naturalization of a small and wealthy segment of England's Jewish population via private Act of Parliament.
275 Anon., 'Ego Primum', fol. 1.
276 Rabin, 'Jew Bill', 157.
277 Browne, *Jewish and Popish Zeal*; Coningesby, *Jewish Naturalization*; McLynn, *Unpopular Front*.
278 In addition to Browne, also see Anon., *The Case of Mr. Francis Francia, the Reputed Jew*.
279 The integration of Catholics into the British army has been outlined by Weinbrot, 'Gordon Riots', 618.
280 Seume, 'Schreiben', 380.
281 Kemp, 'End of Censorship', 47.
282 Caudle, 'Preaching in Parliament', 239.
283 Hardwick, 'Anglican Church Expansion', 375.
284 Wallace, *Scottish Presbyterianism and Settler Colonial Politics*.
285 Koke, 'Communication in an Anglican Empire'.
286 'The period 1680 to 1760 can be depicted as an era of both religious renaissance and reassertion of the English state church, rather than decline.' Rhoden, 'The Pre-Revolutionary Colonial Church', 10. 'The reality was that the colonial sphere was fact becoming a pluralistic domain in which Anglicanism was but one among many officially-recognised Christian denominations. […] But all was lost. The agenda of the SPG was swept up in and reinvigorated, nay transformed, by the general tenor of Anglican renewal following the resurgence of spirituality and identity within

the English Church during the 1830s, including its perceived responsibilities with regard to the wider British Empire.' Bremner, 'The Corporatisation', paras 12-13. A resurgence of Anglican imperialism after the American crisis has also been discussed by Strong, *Anglicanism*; Strong, 'The Resurgence of Colonial Anglicanism'.
287 Bremner, 'The Corporatisation', résumés.
288 Strong, 'The Resurgence of Colonial Anglicanism', 196.
289 In the mid-nineteenth century, some Anglophone Christians even adopted the concept of 'civil disobedience', which Unitarian author Henry David Thoreau had forcefully promoted in the United States: Thoreau, 'Civil Disobedience (1849)'.
290 Norman, *Church and Society*, 15.
291 Ibid., 21.
292 Ibid.
293 Brent, *Liberal Anglican Politics*, 184.

Chapter 5

1 There were considerations to involve army officers more directly in domestic affairs and the administration of justice, for example in suggested improvements concerning the Riot Act: A dilettante in law and politics [pseud., attributed to Allan Ramsay], *Observations*, 28. Also see Stollberg-Rilinger, *Europa*; Schaich, 'Public Sphere'.
2 'But whatever it is call'd, that Government is certainly and necessarily a Military Government, where the Army is the strongest Power in the Country: And it is eternally true, that a Free Parliament and a Standing Army, are Things absolutely incompatible, and can never subsist together.' Anon., '[Military Government]', 2.
3 McCormack, 'Supporting the Civil Power', 29.
4 'Police reformers of the 1780s saw "supporting the civil power" in terms of bolstering the civil, precisely so that the military would not be required: this was partly because of their concern about "standing armies", but also because of their regard for the citizen soldier, who was *of* the civil rather than external to it.' Ibid., 38. Simes, 'Ireland'.
5 'The militia epitomized the ideal of the "citizen soldier", which was hugely influential in the eighteenth century: its importance in revolutionary America and France has long been recognized, but military historians of Britain are increasingly emphasizing its own indigenous "amateur military tradition".' McCormack, 'Supporting the Civil Power', 29.
6 [5 Magistrates], 'SP 36/138/1/100-101', 100.
7 Smith, 'Hexham Riot'.
8 Barget, 'Conflicts'.
9 UK National Archives, SP 35/27/15.
10 Hawarth, 'SP 36/80/3/15: Information of Abraham Hawarth of Manchester [Lancashire]', fol. 15.
11 Some documents relating to the event have been transcribed and digitally published by Reynolds, 'Primary Documents'.
12 US National Park Service, 'North Bridge Questions'.
13 Biggs, *Military History of Europe*. For the importance of 'military endeavour' in English culture from the Tudors to William of Orange see Smith, 'Idea of a Protestant Monarchy', 95.

14 Hillary, *Oliver Cromwell*; Gentles, *Oliver Cromwell*; Gaunt, *English Civil War*.
15 Throughout the seventeenth century, European noblemen had acted as 'entrepreneurs of war' and supported each other's military careers: Asch, *Der europäische Adel*, 17. Asch has even pointed out that the seventeenth-century rise of duelling and the active engagement of noblemen in princely armies contributed to a reduction of noble violence in general: ibid., 30. In England, the disciplined structure of the regular forces also domesticated internal conflict and integrated both social elites and lower classes into an expanding empire.
16 The new image of nobility in the eighteenth century is described by Smith, *Nobility Reimagined*, 116.
17 Smith, *Georgian Monarchy*, 104–5.
18 Pincus, *1688*, 255.
19 Saunders Webb quoted by Pincus, 'Lord Churchill's Coup', 813.
20 Robethon and Kreienberg, 'Cal. Br. 24, 1713', fol. 80.
21 Ibid., fol. 99.
22 Ibid., fol. 50.
23 Bodin, *Six livres*, 751–4; 756; 762–3.
24 Christa Hämmerle explains the educational idea of military service ('Schule des Volkes') in her essay on multinational recruiting in the Habsburg monarchy from 1866 to the First World War: Hämmerle, 'K. (U.) K. Armee', 175.
25 Smith, 'Idea of a Protestant Monarchy', 96.
26 Franklin, 'Plain Truth', 168. For the medieval Anglo-Norman definition of the Latin term '*natio*' see Hindley, *Magna Carta*, 97–8.
27 'Ab Mitte des 18. Jahrhunderts versuchte ein zweiter Modernisierungsschub, ausgehend von technischen Truppen wie Artillerie und Pionieren, für Offiziere eine professionelle Kriegsschulausbildung mit anschließendem Leistungsaufstieg durchzusetzn, trotz Abschaffung der Kompagniewirtschaft mit begrenztem Erfolg. Er wurde aber eine Professionalisierung, Bürokratisierung und Verstaatlichung eingeleitet, auf der die Revolution nur aufzubauen brauchte.' Reinhard, *Geschichte der Staatsgewalt*, 356.
28 Franklin, 'Plain Truth', 168–9.
29 Anon., *Loyal Associatiors For King and Country in the Year of Our Lord MDCCXLV*.
30 Wilson, *Sense of the People*, 173.
31 Bolingbroke, *Letters*, 59–60.
32 In Renaissance and Baroque philosophy, soldiers and especially armed peasants had often been denounced as cruel and difficult to control: see descriptions of 'le furieux soldat' and 'le Guerrier sanguinaire' in Bodin, *Six livres*, 755.] Sixteenth- and seventeenth-century objections against ruthless noble soldiers are recounted by Asch, *Der europäische Adel*, 19.
33 McCormack, 'Citizen Soldiers?'
34 Howe, *Teucro Duce Nil Desperandom*.
35 Wilhelmy, *Soldiers for Sale*, 17, cover text.
36 The most famous recruiting advertisement in patriot history was a poster printed for patriot navy general John Paul Jones in 1777: Lorenz, *John Paul Jones*.
37 Robinson, 'T 1/463', fol. 1.
38 Ibid.
39 Trumbull, *Copy of a Letter*, fol. 1.
40 Robinson, 'T 1/463', fol. 1. Also see Hume, *Popular Media*, 10–11.
41 Green, *To the People of America*, fol. 1.

42 Richardson, *Historical Magazine*, III, 2:9.
43 Green, *To the People of America*.
44 Sons of Liberty, *True Sons of Liberty*, fol. 1.
45 Ibid.
46 Bernard, *Papers of Francis Bernard*, 2007, 1:13.
47 Leonhard, 'Nationalisierung', 83.
48 Beaupré, 'Comptes Rendus', 663.
49 Heath, *Riot in Broad Street*.
50 Johnstone, *Memoirs*, 80.
51 Lengel, *This Glorious Struggle*, 184–5.
52 Hume, *Popular Media*, 10–11.
53 Journalism is always shaped by 'what it is responding to': ibid., 86.
54 Barget, 'Rebelle malgré lui'.
55 One important example on the eve of the English civil war was the mutiny of Hull against Captain Edward, who was wounded by some of his soldiers and eventually died of his injuries: T., *An Uprore in the North, at Hvll, about a Moneth Since*. Only a year later, mutiny occurred in a pro-parliamentary Portsmouth regiment, and here, too, a captain was slain by his men. Anon., *Uprore at Portsmouth*.
56 Anon., *Uprore at Portsmouth*.
57 Brandes, 'Ueber die Justiz- und Gerichtsverfassung Englands', col. 1444.
58 Nagy, *Rebellion in the Ranks*.
59 Barget, 'Rebelle malgré lui'.
60 Anon., 'Gosport, Sep. 2', 3.
61 Knouff, *Soldiers' Revolution*.
62 Nagy, *Rebellion in the Ranks*, xv.
63 Thomas, *John Paul Jones*; Sherburne, *Life and Character*; Urquhart, *John Paul Jones*; Lorenz, *John Paul Jones*.
64 Nagy, *Rebellion in the Ranks*, 29. Also see Wildes, *Anthony Wayne*; Gaff, *Bayonets in the Wilderness*.
65 Bilson, *Trve Difference*, fol. 5 r.
66 Nagy, *Rebellion in the Ranks*, 77.
67 Warner, *John the Painter*, 2004. For the history of nineteenth-century terrorism see Frank, 'Plots on London', 51–2; 54.
68 Korn, *Geschichte der Kriege*, vol. 8, 15; Wallice, *Trial at Large*; Anon., *Remarkable History and Transactions*; Smith, *Assassination*; Wolcot, *Liberty's Last Squeak*.
69 Dillinger, 'Organized Arson', 102–3.
70 Frank and Gruber, *Literature*.
71 Warner, *John the Painter*, 2004; York, *Burning the Dockyard*; Warner, *John the Painter*, 2005; Sharpe, 'John the Painter'.
72 Anon., *Life of James Aitken*.
73 Anon., *John the Painter's Ghost*. The fictitious *Short Account of the Motives Which Determined the Man Called John The Painter* illustrates the propagandistic potential of rebel biographies and alleged last dying speeches: Williams, *Short Account*.
74 Williams, *Short Account*, 5.
75 Ibid., 10.
76 Dillinger, 'Organized Arson', 101.
77 Ibid.
78 Ibid., 116.
79 'A Mordbrenner [arsonist] aimed at harming the whole community. His victim was not an individual, his victim was society.' Ibid., 115.

80 Ibid., 118.
81 Nagy, *Rebellion in the Ranks*, 295. Lower Canada, Court of Oyer and Terminer, *Trial of David McLane*. Frank, 'Plots on London', 51.
82 Referring to a psychiatrist's analysis of the conspiratorial narrative triggered by the late 1960s campus revolts, Davis believes that 'paranoid moments' are 'sometimes reasonable and may also serve important social functions.' For example, collective fear of conspiracy could deflect attention from the even more worrying recollection 'that no one was in control.' Davis, 'Introduction', xiv.
83 Ibid.; Hofstadter, 'Paranoid Style', 2.
84 Davis, 'Introduction', xiv.
85 Ibid., xv.
86 Williams, *Short Account*, 11.
87 Ibid., 15.
88 Reinhard, *Geschichte der Staatsgewalt*, 356–8.
89 Marschke, 'Princes' Power', 51.
90 Monod, 'Rebellion and Savagery', 137. Bute and Stuart, *A Prime Minister and His Son*, 64.
91 Barget, 'Concepts of Leadership'.
92 'Copy of a Letter from the Commissioners of the Customs at Boston, to the Lords Commissioners of his Majesty's Treasury. [...] The Inconveniencies we are exposed to we bear with Chearfulness [sic], and beg Leave to assure Your Lordships, that no Difficulties shall abate our Zeal in the Service; but it is impossible for us to set Foot in Boston, until there are two or three Regiments in the Town, to restore and support Government.' Memorial of the Commissioners of the Customs in North-America, 11 July 1768, published in: Bernard, Gage and Hood, *Letters to the Ministry*, 106.
93 Boston, 29 July 1768, in: Gage and Bernard, *Letters*, 118.
94 Boston, 29 July 1768, in: ibid., 119.
95 Ibid., 76.
96 Flavell, 'Government Interception of Letters', 414.
97 United States Army, *The Trial of Major John Andre*.
98 Barget, 'John André'. Holt, *Memoirs*, 1:145; 296–7.
99 Goldar, 'The Unfortunate Death of Major Andre'; Millis, *Spy*, 3; Harris, *Public Lives*, 64.
100 Holt, *Memoirs*, 1:ix.
101 Miller and Schwartz, 'Icon', 531–4; Barget, 'Concepts of Leadership'.
102 The ideal that the risks of war were shared between officers and common soldiers is, for instance, conveyed in a song allegedly 'composed by the British soldiers after Bunker Hill' in June 1775 and printed by loyalist Margaret Draper: Howe, *A Song Composed by the British Soldiers*.
103 Private letter by Alexander Hamilton to Henry Laurens, September 1780, published in: United States Army, *The Trial of Major John Andre*, 57. A positive image of British and American generals alike was also transported by German Catholic writer Christoph Heinrich Korn in his extensive history of the American Revolution: Korn, *Geschichte der Kriege*, vol. X, 60.
104 Anon., 'The Arts'.
105 'It was the general opinion of the House, as well as the gentlemen, that no act of that House could be legal, which was agreed to whilst the House was beset with soldiers and a mob.' Edes, Edes Jr., and Edes, 'House of Commons, June 6', fol. 2.
106 Ibid.
107 Luhmann, *Politik der Gesellschaft*, 57.

108 Ibid., 58.
109 'Ist der Wille, den Krieg zu verhindern, so stark, daß er den Krieg selbst nicht mehr scheut, so ist er eben ein politisches Motiv geworden, d.h. er bejaht, wenn auch nur als extreme Eventualität, den Krieg und sogar den Sinn des Krieges.' Münkler, *Politisches Denken*, 46.
110 This is a problem of communication, not a moral dilemma: Griesse, 'Aufstandsprävention', 178; 202.
111 'Soldiers, like what is said of fire and water, are excellent servants, but bad masters; for which reason I wish to see their duty in quelling riots, both authorised and limited by the supreme legislative power, and to have as little left to their own discretion as the nature of things will permit.' A dilettante in law and politics [pseud., attributed to Allan Ramsay], *Observations*, 29.
112 Royer, *English Execution Narrative*.
113 Brandes, 'Ueber die Justiz- und Gerichtsverfassung Englands', col. 1467. Smith, *Assassination*, 25; 75.
114 Brandes, 'Ueber die Justiz- und Gerichtsverfassung Englands', cols. 1459–60.
115 Ibid., cols. 1466–7.
116 Smith-Rosenberg, *This Violent Empire*, 62–3.
117 Anon., *Bloody Massacre*; Ashe, *Sermon*; Dodd, *St Bartholomew's Eve Massacre*; Downes, *Sermon*; Kingdon, *Myths*; Dwyer and Ryan, *Theatres of Violence*; Jones, 'A Sea of Blood?'
118 In 1768, an army unit violently dissolved a rally of John Wilkes's supporters. Wilkes exploited this incident in his attacks on the government and denied that the soldiers had only done their duty. The subsequent investigations and public debates are recorded in Owen Ruffhead's correspondence: Ruffhead, 'MS Hyde 77 (8.196.2)'. The Bristol Bridge Riot of 1793, which had begun as a mass protest against tolls and saw eleven protestors killed and forty-five injured, was another highly controversial armed abatement of citizens' protest: Magistrates' Court of Bristol, *Whereas Great Numbers of Persons*; Harrison, '"To Raise and Dare Resentment"'; Manson, *Riot!*
119 Thompson, *Making of the English Working Class*, 455.
120 Provincial Congress, *Rules and Regulations*.
121 Ibid. Burke, 'Concord Museum'.
122 Bute and Stuart, *A Prime Minister and His Son*, 195.
123 Ramsay, *Objections*, 35.
124 Nancy Curtin according to Jackson, *Ireland*, 7.
125 McDowell, 'Protestant Nation'.
126 Hauswedell, 'Geheimgesellschaften', 214. Barker, 'England', 118. 'The Volunteers set a precedent for using the threat of armed force to influence politics.' Simes, 'Ireland'. The formation into a military body was mainly inspired by the government establishment of the yeomanry, the Militia Act of 1793 and the Indemnity and Insurrection Acts of 1796, which sanctioned brutality against oppositional Irishmen: Ó Muirí, 'Dean Warburton's Reports', 647.
127 McDowell, 'Protestant Nation', 241–3.
128 An Orangeman [pseud.], *Orange Vindicated*, 8.
129 Bartlett, *Ireland*, 190. Similar arguments have been put forth by Hauswedell, 'Geheimgesellschaften'.
130 Byrne, *Memoires*, 12.
131 Ibid., 13.
132 Gurney, *Trial of George Gordon*, 52.

133 'The prisoner at the bar stands before you a member of one of the most considerable families in this country. At the time when this conduct is imputed to him, he was a member of the legislature; he stood in a situation which he was not likely to better by throwing the country into convulsions. A person that stood in the situation he stood in, could not make his prospect better than in seeing the affairs of the country conducted under legal government; and if he thought any inroads had been made upon those laws which the wisdom of our ancestors had enacted, it was his business to bring about the repeal of those laws, to redress those grievances, by proper legal means, and not by causing a revolt in this country. [...] The noble prisoner being, as I have said, a man standing in a situation who had every thing to expect so long as law prevailed; but nothing to expect when anarchy was substituted in the place of law.' Ibid., 3.
134 Ibid., 4.
135 An engraving of the pikes found in the homes of Downie and others were added to the printed court protocols. Witness Margaret White had misidentified one of the pike-tops as a large 'dividing knife' when she first saw it in Downie's dining room: Anon., *Trials of Robert Watt and David Downie*, fig. 1 [not paged].
136 Ibid., 50.
137 Ibid., 31; 41.
138 Ibid., figs 31; 41. P. 83-4. See also Anon., *Remarkable History and Transactions*; Anon., *Trial of David Downie*.
139 Lemaitre, *High Treason!!*, 57.
140 Morris, 'The Pop-Gun Plot', 47.
141 Ibid.
142 Knight, *Pursuit of Victory*, 558.
143 Kater, 'Bürger-Kriege', 27.
144 Voigt, 'Abschied vom Staat', 16. Traub, 'Michels Erwachen', 20.
145 Traub, 'Michels Erwachen', 20.
146 Leonhard, 'Nationalisierung'.
147 Traub and Pieper, 'Die Nation war das große Banner', 29. Rolin, *Ursprung des Staates*, 192-9.
148 Smith, *Assassination*, 72.

Chapter 6

1 Luhmann, *Politik der Gesellschaft*, 274.
2 Donald, *Age of Caricature*, 109.
3 DeNardo, *Power in Numbers*.
4 Receptions and critiques of Habermas's theories in more recent English historiography (including authors such as Nancy Fraser, Michael Warren, Hardold Mah, Alan Downie and Brian Cowan) have been summarized and discussed in Robertson, 'Habermas'.
5 Among his works translated into English is a collection of essays: Habermas, *Communication*.
6 Franklin, 'On Government. No. I', 349.
7 Ogborn, 'Power of Speech', 121-2.
8 Clifton, *The Last Popular Rebellion*.

9   Barget, 'Table of Riot and Rebellion Vocabulary: Word Count and Classification'.
10 See discussion of food riots and other economically motivated unrest in Chapter 6.
11 Rudé, 'London "Mob"', 7.
12 Royer, *English Execution Narrative*. A symbiosis of monarchy and popular consent became even more relevant after the Restoration of the British monarchy in 1660: Claydon, *Europe*, 221.
13 Although politically conservative, Charles Stuart acknowledged that the simple folk were well able to distinguish 'between anarchy and regular mild government'. Bute and Stuart, *A Prime Minister and His Son*, 82–5. Rejection of the common people's 'fickle humour' sometimes combined with the acknowledgement that nobody could deceive the 'inquisitive mind of the reflecting people.' Anon., *Cries of the Public*, 26. The Rev. Gad Hitchcock, preacher to the House of Representatives of the Province of Massachusetts Bay, expressed his conviction that the people, in general, had an ability 'to be judges of the good or ill effects of administration'.
14 Luhmann, *Politik der Gesellschaft*, 276–7.
15 Würgler, *Medien*, 132.
16 Government reactions to a riot in Edinburgh in 1774: Miller, 'SP 54/47/217'.
17 'Öffentliche Meinung ist nicht nur bestätigendes Publikum, sondern wird 'Träger der Kritik der alten Ordnung der Stände und ihrer Klientelverhältnisse, der Sekten und Faktionen und der Festlegung des sozialen Status durch Geburt.' Luhmann, *Politik der Gesellschaft*, 278.
18 The influence of public opinion on late seventeenth-century politics and the impact of a general perception that James VII/II was 'guilty of subverting the traditional constitution, as most of his subjects understood it', has been outlined by Harris, *Revolution*, 484. The most famous reactionary rebel of the late seventeenth century had been Irishman Edmund Everard, who was imprisoned in the Tower in 1679 because he had intended to 'have poysoned [sic] the Duke of Monmouth', who posed a great threat to the accession of James Stuart and the Catholic cause in Britain: Anon., *Depositions and Examinations*; Walsh, *True Narrative and Manifest*. Criminal acts committed by pro-government agents remained a challenge in the eighteenth century. Incidents of loyalist rioting against (alleged) Jacobites, American patriots or supporters of the French Revolution had to be punished despite the authorities' sympathy for the rioters' motivations.
19 Miller, *Popery and Politics in England*.
20 Neuhoff, *Memoirs of Corsica*.
21 This development was rooted in the dialectic nature of Enlightenment liberalism: Smith-Rosenberg, *This Violent Empire*.
22 Barget, 'Hired mobs'.
23 Fitts, 'Newcastle's Mob', 41.
24 Anon., *Memoranda of Evidence*. Fitts, 'Newcastle's Mob', 41. Above all, elections permitted an unusual mingling of the different social strata and created a pacifying illusion of equality: Donald, *Age of Caricature*, 109. The British Newspaper Archive lists 112 entries for election riots between 1700 and 1749 and 2028 election riot reports between 1750 and 1799.
25 Newcastle successfully controlled voting in Parliament but also availed himself of extra-parliamentary instruments of power: Fitts, 'Newcastle's Mob', 41.
26 [Wyes], 'Wyes's Letter Verbatim, London, March 5, 1724', 3679.
27 Barget, 'Hired mobs'.

28 The growing appreciation of the individual in later seventeenth-century descriptions of the body politic has been analysed by Griesse, 'Revolten als Krankheiten', 30. In contrast to the territorial states of central Europe, governments in post-civil war England did not establish a tight control of information and interpretation but traded greater freedom of the press for restricted participation: Griesse, 'Aufstandsprävention', 207.
29 Wharton, *Select and Authentick Pieces*, 54.
30 Systematic appeals to public opinion date back to the mid-seventeenth century: Schaich, 'Public Sphere', 134.
31 Bolingbroke, *Letters*, 120–1.
32 Political Looking-Glass [pseud.], 'For the Morning Post'.
33 Ibid.
34 See Franklin, 'On Government. No. I', 13.
35 This expression was predominant in seventeenth-century debates on popular protest and used as a derogatory term by royalists in the English Civil War: Covel, *Declaration*. For an early eighteenth-century reference see Defoe, *Seasonable Expostulation*.
36 Defoe, *Vox Populi, Vox Dei*; Anon., *Ex Ore Tuo Te Judico*. Details of the court trial of John Matthews are given in Howell, Cobbett, and Jardine, *Complete Collection of State Trials*, cols. 1333–4.
37 Kidd, 'Rehabilitation', 64.
38 Hale, *Evolution of British Historiography*, 147.
39 Ibid., 150.
40 Rockingham [pseud.], *A Few Words*, 6.
41 Ibid.
42 F.A. D.D. [attributed to Francis Atterbury], *Voice of the People*.
43 Defoe's collected accounts of local Jacobite revolts in 1715 lamented that Tory counsellor Mr Ayres had directed 'himself rather to the Mob than Sherrifs' and used 'many other popular Arguments to inrage [sic] and inflame them, whilst several of their Agents below bellow'd out Liberty and Property, and cry'd one and all, let's drive the Constables out of the Hall, that all the Freemen may take their last Farewel [sic] of their long enjoy'd Privileges [...].' Defoe, *Account of the Riots*, 25.
44 Political Looking-Glass [pseud.], 'For the Morning Post'.
45 Burke, 'Some Seventeenth-Century Anatomists of Revolution', 27.
46 Ibid.
47 Political Looking-Glass [pseud.], 'For the Morning Post'.
48 Paracelsianism comprises early modern medical theories and procedures inspired by the teachings of Philippus Aureolus Theophrastus Bombastus von Hohenheim (1493/94–1541, known as Paracelsus). In his teachings, Paracelsus proposed a chemical view of the human body whose health depended on a balance of fluids. For the influence of Paracelsianism on political theory, see Harris, *Foreign Bodies*; Griesse, 'Revolten als Krankheiten', 6–7.
49 William Bisset, *The Modern Fanatick. With a Large and True Account of the Life, Actions, Endowments, &c. of the Famous Dr. Sa———l*. London: s.n. 1710, S. 2.
50 Manley, *True Relation*, S. 10.
51 Skerret, *Subjects Duty*. Skerret, *National Blessings*.
52 Philipps, 'Reflections', 1.
53 Parliament of Great Britain, *Act*, 1746.

54 This view is found in letters exchanged between British officers and government officials in 1746, but also in contemporary genealogies of the Stuart family whose rise and fall is often compared to the decline of the House of Bourbon in France: Maclean, *Bonnie Prince Charlie*, 281. Boyse, *Impartial History*.
55 Johnson, *Journey to the Western Islands*. Home, *History*. Claydon, *Europe*, 360-1.
56 Cosgrove, 'The Gaelic Resurgence', 169.
57 Hume, *Essays and Treatises*, IV:117-18.
58 Maxwell, *Armagh*.
59 Hume, *Essays and Treatises*, IV:117-18. In truth, resurging conflicts in the prosperous county of Armagh resulted from the fact that Protestants had 'obtained the best lowland agricultural holdings while Catholics were forced to retreat to the less desirable uplands'. Miller, 'Origins of the Orange Order', 583.
60 Philipps, 'Reflections', 1.
61 Browne, '[Two Days]', 1.
62 Johnstone, *Memoirs*, 171-3. In the vindication of his conduct in the course of the '98 rising, Protestant United Irishmen Miles Byrne also commented that it was 'impossible to remain neutral'. Byrne, *Memoires*, 6.
63 Miller and Schwartz, 'Icon', 534.
64 Ritter, 'David Humes "Idee einer vollkommenen Republik"', 168.
65 Horn, 'Leib des Volkes', 238-42.
66 'Popular governments have not been framed without the wisest reasons. It seemed highly fitting that the conduct of magistrates, created by and for the good of the whole, should be made *liable to the inspection and animadversion* of the whole. Besides, there could not be a more potent counterpoise to the designs of ambitious men than a multitude that hated and feared ambition. Moreover, the power they possessed, though great collectively, yet, being distributed among a vast number, the share of each individual was too inconsiderable to lay him under any temptations of turning it to a wrong use.' Franklin, 'On Government. No. I', 11.
67 Ben-Atar, 'Pride', 98.
68 Paine, *Common Sense*.
69 Although the Stuarts wished to rule over all British dominions, Scottish Jacobitism defended local values and structures. The French-language Jacobite poem *The Conqueror of Scotland* offers some interesting insights into anti-English sentiments of the time: Anon., *Conquérant d'Écosse*, 13.
70 Stanwood, 'Rumours and Rebellions', 190-1.
71 Ben-Atar, 'Pride', 99.
72 Griesse, *Frühneuzeitliche Revolten*, 1.
73 Anon., *Cries of the Public*, 27.
74 Ibid., 42-4.
75 Rockingham [pseud.], *A Few Words*, 8-9.
76 Ibid., 22.
77 Old Hubert [pseud., attributed to James Parkinson], *Address*.
78 Ibid., 6.
79 Ibid., 16.
80 Greene, 'Empire', 216.
81 Goldsmith, 'Mandeville, Bernard (1670-1733)', 403.
82 Hume, *Political Discourses*, 35.
83 Anon., *Trials of Robert Watt and David Downie*, 87-8.
84 Traub and Pieper, 'Die Nation war das große Banner', 31.

Notes

85 Hobhouse, *Three Letters*.
86 Anon., *Hired Rabble*; Barget, 'Hired mobs'.
87 Wildvogel, *Dissertationem Politico-Iuridicam De Tumultibus*, 12.
88 Ibid.
89 Dalrymple, *Appeal of Reason*, 32. Five decades earlier, similar criticism had been uttered by Manley, *True Relation*, 9.
90 Dalrymple, *Appeal of Reason*, 32.
91 Ibid., 34.
92 Burke, 'Some Seventeenth-Century Anatomists of Revolution', 30.
93 Crawford, *Lives and Characters*; Boyse, *Impartial History*; Querno, *American Times*.
94 Burke, 'Some Seventeenth-Century Anatomists of Revolution', 32; 35. Solidarity between the classes could, for example, be witnessed in the many letters written by Elizabeth Charlotte, Duchess of Orléans, to her German relatives in the late seventeenth and early eighteenth centuries. Her concern for peace and the people's interest, however, was not inspired by republican or democratic ideals, but by an aristocratic sense of duty: Lalloué, *Princesse Palatine*.
95 Bohstedt, *Politics of Provisions*, 1–20.
96 Donald, *Age of Caricature*, 118.
97 Anon., *Cries of the Public*, 25.
98 Stevenson, *Popular Disturbances*, 114. Archer, *Social Unrest*, 28–9.
99 Morris, *Sex*, 33.
100 Anon., *Cries of the Public*, 42–50.
101 Rawlinson, *Inquiry*; Colquhoun, *Suggestions*.
102 Jackson, *Ireland*, 8.
103 Edes, Edes Jr., and Edes, '[Extract of a Letter]', fol. 3.
104 The oppositional *Boston Gazette* had reported the hardships of English farmers as early as 1734. A 1760 article elaborated on 'agriculture as the most solid foundation on which to build the wealth' and encouraged agricultural reform: Edes and Gill, '[To the Printers]', fol. 4.
105 The riots on the opening of Parliament in 1795 were fuelled by increased taxation and bad harvests. Accordingly, the protestors facing King George III on his way to Parliament in October 1795 demanded 'bread', 'peace' and 'no Pitt': Parliament of Great Britain, *Warning Voice*.
106 Late eighteenth-century and early nineteenth-century elites feared social reform: Thompson, *The Making of the English Working Class*, 472. Anon., *Faithful Account*.
107 More et al., *The Carpenter*.
108 A recent comparative contribution on queens' experiences of political change and the public image of queenship is Harris, *Queenship and Revolution in Early Modern Europe*.
109 Women were, for instance, involved in the so-called Thomas Bean riot. Furthermore, the Newgate Calendars covered 'the most notorious criminals of both sexes', including those sentenced for political crimes: Court of the Old Bailey, 'John Love, Thomas Bean, George Purchase, Richard Price, William Price'; Anon., *Newgate Calendar*, 1774.
110 Smith, *Grossly Material Things*; Nevitt, *Women and the Pamphlet Culture of Revolutionary England, 1640–1660*.
111 Vietto, *Women and Authorship in Revolutionary America*.
112 Crompton, 'Draper'.
113 Harris, 'Moral Economy', 2.

114 Ibid.
115 Anon., *Tryal of Thomas Collet*.
116 Hammond and Hammond, *The Village Labourer*, 121.
117 'Repräsentation [war] im Mittelalter und darüber hinaus Darstellung und Vertretung von sozialen (also nicht dinghaft sichtbaren) Einheiten wie Ständen, Körperschaften, Stiftungen, Städten, Kirchen, Innungen usw. In ihrem Sein, ihren Interessen und ihren wohlbegründeten Rechten als Teile eines Ganzen oder, was auf dasselbe hinauslief, Darstellungen dieses Ganzen "in corpore et membris". [...] Die Koordination lief nicht in erster Linie über Entscheidungsprozeduren und Abstimmungsregeln oder über Kompromisse. Sie lag vor allem in den Darstellungsbedingungen. Praktisches Ziel des Repräsentationsvorganges war Einigung und Rechtsfindung, nicht Rechtsherstellung. Unter dem Druck der neuen Anforderungen an Komplexität und Variabilität wandelt sich der Repräsentationsgedanke. Er verliert seinen festlichen Charakter und wird zur Arbeit besonders qualifizierter Kräfte an der Vorbereitung von Entscheidungen.' Luhmann, *Politische Soziologie*, 92.
118 Stevenson, *Popular Disturbances*, 9–11.
119 Hogarth, *Election Entertainment*.
120 Kesselring, 'Politics of the Excluded', 649. Andreas Würgler, too, has stressed that ritualized protest helped to avoid constant brutal conflict once revolt had been determined as a substantial crime in the late fifteenth and early sixteenth centuries: Würgler, *Unruhen*; Würgler, 'Modernisierungspotential'; Nubola and Würgler, *Bittschriften*. Kriminalisierung: Härter and de Graaf, 'Vom Majestätsverbrechen zum Terrorismus', 2012; Schmitt, *Kriminalität und Gesellschaft*.
121 Anon., *Letter*, 1771, 53.
122 Phillips, 'Popular Politics', 599.
123 Ibid., 604–6; Weinbrot, 'Gordon Riots', 616.
124 Bennett, *Civil Wars*, 272–3. The importance of petitioning by women and MP-lobbying on 'behalf of their constituencies, boroughs and corporations' in the seventeenth-century Parliaments are described by Kyle and Peacey, 'Under Cover of so Much Coming and Going', 21–3; Dean, 'Public Space', 169.
125 Boddie, *Seventeenth Century Isle of Wight County*, 155.
126 Zaret, *Origins*, 229.
127 Ibid., 221.
128 Snowden, 'By the Dutch Mails', 2.
129 'The late King of Prussia, the most arbitrary monarch in Europe, never received a petition or complaint from the meanest of his subjects, to which he did not reply within a few days; and no minister under him dared to keep back from his perusal a single letter.' Smith, *Assassination*, 36.
130 Barnard and Millar, *Complete History*.
131 Luhmann, *Politik der Gesellschaft*, 280–1.
132 Massachusetts Historical Society, *Collections*, 8; 19–20.
133 Records relating to John Adams, especially MA 206: 268-269, MA 164:64, MA 207: 418, listed in ibid., 9; 11.
134 Humphrey, *Sacrifice to Slavery*.
135 Weinbrot, 'Gordon Riots', 616.
136 Anon., *News from Galloway*.
137 'The signatures of thousands of Englishmen on petitions to the Crown and Parliament are unmistakable evidence of political participation, at least at a very

rudimentary level; but a signature alone does not necessarily indicate political awareness. Certainly historians have disagreed over the meaning of petition signing. [...] Samuel Johnson disparaged the petitioning process, noting that after the presentation of a petition at a public meeting, "those who are sober enough to write add their names and the rest would sign if they could."' Phillips, 'Popular Politics', 616.
138 Bernard, Gage, and Hood, *Letters to the Ministry*, 42.
139 Bernard, *Papers of Francis Bernard*, 2007, 1:12.
140 Barrell, *Imagining the King's Death*, 142.
141 'Some days before this meeting, a few copies of a printed handbill of an inflammatory nature had been found in a public-house in the town, and of this, great use was made to inflame the minds of the people against the Dissenters, to whom, though without any evidence whatsoever, it was confidently ascribed. The thing itself did not deserve any notice, and paragraphs of as seditious a nature frequently appear in the public newspapers and others publications, and (as would, no doubt, have been the case with this) are neglected and forgotten. But the magistrate of Birmingham, and other known enemies to the Dissenters, were loud in their exclamations against it, though perhaps fabricated for the use that was made of it; and a copy officiously sent to the secretaries of state, who ordered a strict inquiry [sic] to be made after the author, printer, or distributor; and in consequence of this, a reward of a hundred pounds was offered for the discovery of any of them.' Priestley, 'Appeal', 375. Hay, *Memorial to the Public*, 16. Ibid.
142 Gurney, *Trial of George Gordon*, 40.
143 Lord Mountstuart to his brother Charles Stuart, Hill Street, 14 June, 1780, published in Bute and Stuart, *A Prime Minister and His Son*, 193.
144 Cunningham, *A New and Complete Law-Dictionary*, II:45.
145 Gurney, *Trial of George Gordon*.
146 Ibid., 23.
147 Ibid., 29.
148 Ibid., 34.
149 Ibid., 21.
150 Ibid., 22.
151 Ibid.
152 Ibid., 23.
153 Alexander Frazer stated in his cross-examination before the Attorney General: 'I returned about one from the fields, and as soon as I got to the end of Parliament Street, (before I got home) the riot was begun. Several carriages were stopped, and some of them were pulling the people out of their carriages, and were writing upon the carriages, *No Popery*.' Ibid.
154 Ibid., 59.
155 Ibid., 9.
156 Ibid.
157 Barnard and Millar, *Complete History*.
158 Ibid., 695.
159 Ibid., 689.
160 Burgh, 'HO 42/34/42'.
161 Ibid.
162 A Native, and Member of the House of Burgesses [Thomas Jefferson], *Summary View*, 5–6.
163 Edes, Edes Jr., and Edes, 'House of Commons, June 6', 2.

164 Dalrymple, *Appeal of Reason*, 32.
165 Thompson, *Making of the English Working Class*, 418.
166 Piguenet [Piguenit], *Essay*, 3.
167 Koselleck, 'Revolution: Rebellion, Aufruhr, Bürgerkrieg', 705. Burke, 'Some Seventeenth-Century Anatomists of Revolution', 31.
168 Piguenet [Piguenit], *Essay*, 29.
169 Priestley, 'Appeal', 383.
170 Ibid.
171 'Let no man write my epitaph, for as no man who knows my motives dares now vindicate them, let not prejudice or ignorance asperse them. Let them rest in obscurity and peace; my memory be left in oblivion and my tomb remain uninscribed, until other times and other men can do justice to my character. [...] When my country takes her place among the nations of the earth, THEN and NOT TILL THEN let my epitaph be written. I have done.' Emmet's speech from the Dock, quoted according to Byrne, *Memoires*, 162.
172 Herzog, 'Revolution'.
173 Society of the Friends of the People, *Minutes of the Proceedings*, 7–8. See also Barrell, *Imagining the King's Death*, 147.
174 'North of the Trent we find the illegal tradition.' Thompson, *Making of the English Working Class*, 471.
175 Miles Byrne mentions that the United Irishmen 'soon organised parochial and baronial meetings and named delegates to correspond with the county members.' Byrne, *Memoires*, 12–13.
176 Harris, *London Crowds*, 7.
177 Abigail had accompanied her husband John as American ambassador to London in 1785. She shared her experiences in a letter to Thomas Jefferson: 'Forgiveness of injuries is no part of their Character, [...] and scarcely a day passes without a Boxing match.' Cappon, *Adams-Jefferson Letters*, 80.
178 Sir Philip, a member of the House of Commons, had not supported the Protestant Association but gave witness of the procession and riots in court. He testified that 'there was a vast number of people upon the road, and many coming back from the fields (St. George's fields outside Westminster), for the great body of them had marched away to the city; but I met vast numbers returning to the fields, and many were going from the fields, and there were great numbers in the fields. [...] I asked them what was the occasion of their assembling? There was a great number of different parties, for I rode close by the side of the foot-path. [...] I found a vast number of people in going from Westminster up to the other part of the town, and a great number of people when I came down to the lobby. [...] Those I saw in the lobby in the afternoon, neither from their appearance nor behaviour seemed the same sort of people I had seen in St. George's Fields.' Gurney, *Trial of George Gordon*, 24.
179 Harrison, '"To Raise and Dare Resentment"'.
180 Barrell, *Imagining the King's Death*, 553.
181 Henley, *Victorious Stroke for Old England*, 54.
182 He added in regard to public opinion on the Seven Years War and peace negotiation in 1761 that 'the people in general of this nation form a very just opinion of the ministers who conduct the public affairs: they judge by a sign, which, in these cases, with a few exceptions, seldom deceives; and that is, success.' Anon., *Letter to His Grace the Duke of N*********, 27.
183 A dilettante in law and politics [pseud., attributed to Allan Ramsay], *Observations*; Gillam, *Remarks on the Riot Act*.

184 Rogers, 'Popular Protest', 75–6; Stevenson, *Popular Disturbances*, 6–7.
185 A dilettante in law and politics [pseud., attributed to Allan Ramsay], *Observations*, 11.
186 Ibid., 6.
187 Ibid., 3–9.
188 Ibid., 7.
189 Dalton, *The Country Justice*, 425.
190 A dilettante in law and politics [pseud., attributed to Allan Ramsay], *Observations*, 14.
191 In 1776, magistrates in London burnt the radical republican weekly *The Crisis*: Wilson, *Sense of the People*, 243. See also York, 'George III, Tyrant', 434.
192 'In every village of the kingdom the author and his works shall be burnt in effigy: the poor man's friend shall be loaded with the curses of the misled cottager; and it shall be accounted worse than blasphemy to say, that kings are made for the people, not the people for kings. [...] The pulpits and the balladsingers are again employed; every engine is set on foot to destroy the characters of the chiefs'. Smith, *Assassination*, 2–3.
193 Shagan, *Popular Politics*, 14.
194 In the Borough of Gosport and the parish of Alverstoke, 450 people affirmed their 'loyalty [...] to the monarch, the country and the legal system' and promised '(1) to cooperate with others to preserve their liberty, property and constitution against republicans and levellers, (2) to discover and punish those involved in seditious publications, and to discourage seditious thought, (3) to pass on anything they hear which might be seditious to the Justices of the Peace, (4) to assist the magistrates in putting down any riots or illegal assemblies, so to restore the public peace, (5) that they pledge themselves and all they have to the preservation of the King and the constitution'. Curry, 'HO 42/37/195'.
195 Anon., *Bloody Massacre*.
196 Association for Preserving Constitutional Order, Liberty, and Property, *Committee of Association, for Preserving Constitutional Order*; Association for Preserving Liberty and Property against Republicans and Levellers, *Proceedings*; Association for Preserving Liberty and Property against Republicans and Levellers, *Publications*.
197 Mitchell, 'Association Movement', 56.
198 Teeling's *Personal Narrative of the Irish Rebellion* (1798), quoted in: Holt, *Memoirs*, 1:307–8. See also Wolcot, *Liberty's Last Squeak*; Byrne, *Memoires*, 180–1.
199 Smith, *Assassination*, 3.
200 Teeling's Personal *Narrative of the Irish Rebellion*: Holt, *Memoirs*, 1:307. Charles Hamilton was the younger brother of Irish rebel Bartholomew Teeling, who was court-martialled in 1798.
201 Richter, 'Role of Mob Riot', 25.
202 Ramsay, *Objections*, 35.
203 Phillips, 'Popular Politics', 624.
204 Ibid.

Conclusion

1 This ties in with T. K. Rabb's observation that the result of the political crises across mid-seventeenth-century Europe had not been one particular form of government, but rather a regional consolidation of how central authority was shared and exercised: Rabb, *Struggle for Stability*, 68.

2   Pittock et al., 'Riots, Rebellions & Revolutions'.
3   Parliament and Lord Lieutenant of Ireland, *Act to Prevent Tumultuous Risings*; A lover and strenuous supporter of the constitution [pseud.], *Constitution*. For a modern historiographical perception of constitutional government in the British tradition see Hindley, *Magna Carta*, xi.
4   Anon., *Observations*; Anon., *Letter*, 1748.
5   Parliament of Great Britain, 'Act for Preventing Tumults and Riotous Assemblies'.
6   Parliament of Great Britain, *Act*, 1748.
7   See reflections upon the early modern territorial state: Luhmann, *Politik der Gesellschaft*, 199.
8   Rolin, *Ursprung des Staates*, 103.
9   The importance of studying contemporary history was famously stressed by Lord Bolingbroke and confirmed by many other eighteenth-century writers: Barlow, *General History*, i.
10 Allen, *New and Improved History of England*.
11 'The capital use of any chart of this kind is, that it is a most excellent mechanical help to the knowledge of history, impressing the imagination indelibly with a just image of the rise, progress, extent, duration, and contemporary state of all the considerable empires that have ever existed in the world. [...] For, when we are contemplating what was doing in any one part of the world, we cannot help wishing to know what was carrying on in other parts, at the same time: and by no other means can this knowledge be gained so completely, and in so short a time.' Priestley, *Description of a New Chart*, 12; 14.
12 A dilettante in law and politics [pseud., attributed to Allan Ramsay], *Observations*, 3.
13 Priestley, *Description of a New Chart*, 18–19.
14 Ibid., 11.
15 Ibid., 18.
16 Ibid., 19.
17 Writing about the Gordon Riots of 1780 to his father in Scotland, Lieutenant-General Sir Charles Stuart explained why he would have to stay in the battered city of London: 'The times are so interesting that it is necessary for one of us to be at the fountain head of evil.' Bute and Stuart, *A Prime Minister and His Son*, 182–4.
18 Letter to James Madison, Paris, 20 December 1787; Jefferson, *Writings*, 1:332.
19 Ibid.
20 Ibid., 1:318.
21 Ibid., 1:319.
22 Anon., *Abstract*; Defoe, *Account of the Riots*.
23 Friend to Both Countries [pseud.], *America Vindicated*.
24 Priestley, 'Appeal', 353.
25 The autonomy and specialization of political institutions eventually permitted society as a whole to make political claims without 'tending to overawe or to abridge that independency in which the happy Constitution of these realms has placed all the members of its legislative body'. A dilettante in law and politics [pseud., attributed to Allan Ramsay], *Observations*, 20. Ibid., 4.
26 According to Niklas Luhmann's 'constitutional sociology', the idea of constitutionalism gives the law the ability to solve inherent paradoxes of the political and vice versa. For differences between 'classical liberal constitutional sociology' and the function of constitutions in Luhmann's systems theory: Schmidt, 'Verfassungssoziologie', 121.

27 'Laws which are made to be universally binding ought to be universally intelligible.' A dilettante in law and politics [pseud., attributed to Allan Ramsay], *Observations*, 3.
28 In their study on modern terrorism, the German Catholic Bishops' Conference lamented that 'solidarity' is often confined to social issues and hardly ever extents to our 'culture of constitutionality' ('Kultur der Rechtsstaatlichkeit'): Sekretariat der Deutschen Bischofskonferenz, *Terrorismus*, 94:43.
29 This compromise corresponds to Karl-Heinz Fezer's defence of 'normative legal positivism': Fezer, *Recht ist Recht ist Recht*, 19.
30 Thiel, 'Opposition verfassen', 120.
31 Ibid., 121.
32 Koselleck, 'Revolution: Rebellion, Aufruhr, Bürgerkrieg', 686.
33 Ibid., 693.
34 Ibid.
35 The high number of people burnt at the stake – rather than hanged, drawn and quartered – during the reigns of Henry VIII, Mary, Edward VI, Elizabeth I and even James I resulted in many glorifying stories of Protestant as well as Catholic martyrdom.
36 Parliament of Great Britain, *Act*, 1748; Parliament of Great Britain, *Act*, 1745.
37 Barlow, *Gunpowder-Treason*; Edwards, *Gunpowder Plot*.
38 The Parliament of the United Kingdom, '1532–1603'.
39 Charles II, *Act*, 1664, 1.
40 Ibid., 2.
41 Rebels and religious minorities 'offended God in contemning [sic] her Majesties Godly and lawful Government and Authority, by absenting [themselves] from Church, and from hearing Divine Service, contrary to the Godly Laws and Statutes of this Realm, and in using and frequenting disordered and unlawful Conventicles and Assemblies, under pretence and colour of exercise of Religion.' Ibid. See similar terminology in royalist pamphlets published during the English Civil War, such as Browne, *Parliaments Lamentation*.
42 Charles II, *Act*, 1664, 2.
43 Ibid., 8.
44 Ibid., 11.
45 Charles II, *Act*, 1670, 13.
46 Smith, *Innocency and Conscientiousness*. Anon., *Declaration*. Charles II, *Act*, 1664, 17.
47 Charles II, *Act*, 1664, 3.
48 Ibid., 17.
49 Ibid.
50 Burgh, *Britain's Remembrancer*.
51 Early-nineteenth-century Western authors such as Paine and Wieland have described the barbaric climax of the French Revolution as a singular catastrophe at odds with the true tradition of republicanism: Koselleck, 'Revolution: Rebellion, Aufruhr, Bürgerkrieg', 737.
52 Ibid., 719.
53 Cohen, *Revolution in Science*, 359.
54 Burke, 'Some Seventeenth-Century Anatomists of Revolution', 25; Koselleck, 'Revolution: Rebellion, Aufruhr, Bürgerkrieg', 720; 726; Benigno, *Mirrors of Revolution*, 192.
55 A Friend to the Church and Constitution [pseud.], *The Loyal: Or, Revolutionary Tory*. According to Koselleck, the French adjective 'révolutionnaire' was not used

before 1789 and stressed new organizational and ideological elements: Koselleck, 'Revolution: Rebellion, Aufruhr, Bürgerkrieg', 732.
56 Defoe, *Account of the Riots*, 2.
57 Koselleck, 'Revolution: Rebellion, Aufruhr, Bürgerkrieg', 701.
58 Griesse, 'Revolten als Krankheiten', 20.
59 Wildvogel, *Dissertationem Politico-Iuridicam De Tumultibus*, 6.
60 Ibid., 7.
61 Ibid., 9.
62 Ibid., 11.
63 Bolton, *Core Redivivus*.
64 Anon., 'Ego Primum', fol. 1. Drewe, *Church of England's Late Conflict*. Hickes, *Spirit*. Anon., *Revolution Politicks*. Anon., *A Memorial for the 30th of January*.
65 Political Looking-Glass [pseud.], 'For the Morning Post'.
66 Gurney, *Trial of George Gordon*, 32.
67 Ibid.
68 Ibid., 41.
69 Barrell, *Imagining the King's Death*, 40.
70 Sekretariat der Deutschen Bischofskonferenz, *Terrorismus*, 94:52.
71 Jefferson, 'Kentucky Resolutions', sec. 2.
72 Barrell, *Imagining the King's Death*, 551.
73 Ibid., 240.
74 Keen, 'The Spirit of Despotism', E121.
75 Brandes, 'Ueber die Justiz- und Gerichtsverfassung Englands', cols. 1453–4.
76 'Our constitution is brought, or almost brought, to such a point, a point of perfection I think it, that no king who is not, in the true meaning of the word, a patriot, can govern Britain with ease, security, honour, dignity, or indeed with sufficient power and strength.' Bolingbroke, *Letters*, 99. '[I will] lastly shew by what excellent steps our excellent constitution has attain'd to its present Perfection and wherein that Perfection consists.' Dobbs, *Thanksgiving-Sermon*, 22–3.
77 Steinmetz, 'Neue Wege', 39.
78 Ogborn, 'Power of Speech', 114.
79 Hahn, 'Besprechungen', 88.
80 Thiel, 'Opposition verfassen', 121.
81 Härter and de Graaf, 'Vom Majestätsverbrechen zum Terrorismus', 2012, 14–15; Krischer, 'Aufruhr als Hochverrat?', 381.
82 The theory 'that the North American colonies were "England's political laboratories"' was initially established by Webb but has been refuted by Pincus, 'Lord Churchill's Coup', 813.
83 Ogborn, 'Power of Speech', 111.
84 Ibid., 115.
85 Patrick Griffin, quoted by Ward, 'American Leviathan', 187.
86 The 'frontier ideology' was particularly relevant in the Whiskey Rebellion between 1791 and 1794, which was one of the United States' first major uprisings against taxation: ibid., 188.
87 This threat was impersonated by Thomas Jefferson, whom contemporary caricatures depicted as an enemy to the moderating powers of the President and Congress: Humphrey, *Sacrifice to Slavery*.
88 Massachusetts Historical Society, *Collections*, 6–7. Jefferson criticized John Adam's *Act concerning Aliens* passed in 1798: Jefferson, 'Kentucky Resolutions', sec. 4.

Notes

89 Thompson, *Making of the English Working Class*, 429.
90 Anon., *Dreadful Riot*; Thompson, *Making of the English Working Class*, 831.
91 Modern democracies are similar yet different: Kopp, *Parlamente*, 283.
92 Ibid. Also Thompson's considerations on the flourishing 'constitutionalist agitation' in the early nineteenth century: Thompson, *Making of the English Working Class*, 671.
93 Kopp, *Parlamente*, 281–2.
94 'Der Staat existiert – und ist dennoch eine Fiktion, ja mehr noch: Er muss gleichsam jederzeit von seinen Angehörigen (und auch von den anderen) fingiert werden, um in seiner Existenz Bestand zu haben.' Albrecht Koschorke, Der fiktive Staat, Vorwort, 10.
95 Wefer, *Kontingenz und Dissens*, 151.
96 Luhmann, *Politik der Gesellschaft*, 433.
97 Münkler, *Politisches Denken*, 55.
98 Maier, 'Introduction', 5.

Bibliography

[5 Magistrates]. 'SP 36/138/1/100-101: Magistrates for the Parts of Holland and the Borough of Boston [Lincolnshire] Giving an Account of Information from Joseph Robertson, Surveyor General for the Works of Sewers within the Great Commons of Wildmore and West Fens, of the Riot in the Parish of Sibsey Near Boston'. [Lincolnshire], 2 November 1757. The National Archives, Kew. https://discovery.nationalarchives.gov.uk/details/r/C17046597.

A citizen of London [pseud.]. *The Revolution No Rebellion: Or, Serious Reflections Offered to the Reverend Mr. Benjamin Hoadly, Occasion'd by His Considerations on the Bishop of Exeter's Sermon, Preach'd before Her Majesty, March the 8th, 1708*. London: Jonah Bowyer et al., 1709.

A dilettante in law and politics [pseud., attributed to Allan Ramsay]. *Observations upon the Riot Act, with an Attempt towards the Amendment of It*. London: T. Cadell, 1781.

A Friend to the Church and Constitution [pseud.]. *The Loyal: Or, Revolutionary Tory: Being Some Reflections on the Principles and Conduct of the Tories; Shewing Them True Friends to the Present Establishment, Some of the Capital Pillars of the Constitution, and Worthy of Royal Trust and Confidence*. London: J. Wilford, 1733.

A layman [pseud.]. *The Church an Engine of the State: A Sermon, Not Preached on the Late General Fast*. London: J. Almon/J. Bew, 1778.

A lover and strenuous supporter of the constitution [pseud.]. *The Constitution, or a Full Answer to Mr. Edmund Burke's Anti-Constitutional Plan of Reform. Addressed to the Honourable the Speaker of the House of Commons*. London: W. Nicoll, 1781.

A lover of social order [attr. to Robert John Thornton]. *The Politician's Creed: Or, Political Extracts*. Vol. 1. London: Robinsons/T. Cox/Dilly/Murray & Highley/Richardson/White/Becket & Edwards/Hookham & Carpenter/H.D. Symonds, 1799.

A Native, and Member of the House of Burgesses [Thomas Jefferson]. *A Summary View of the Rights of British America, Set Forth in Some Resolutions Intended for the Inspection of the Present Delegates of the People of Virginia, Now in Convention*. 2nd ed. Williamsburg, VA/London: Clementina Rind/G. Kearsley, 1776.

A society of gentlemen [pseud.]. *The Patriot: Or, Political, Moral and Philosophical Repository, Consisting of Original Pieces, and Selections from Writers of Merit*. Vol. 2. 14 vols. London: G. G. J. and J. Robinson, 1792.

Abbot, Hull. *The Duty of God's People to Pray for the Peace of Jerusalem: And Especially for the Preservation and Continuance of Their Own Privileges Both Civil and Religious, When in Danger at Home or from Abroad. A Sermon on Occasion of the Rebellion in Scotland Rais'd in Favour of a Popish Pretender; with Design to Overthrow Our Present Happy Establishment, and to Introduce Popery and Arbitrary Power into Our Nations, from Which, by a Series of Wonders, in the Good Providence of God, They Have Been Often Delivered, Preach'd at Charlestown in New-England, Jan. 12. 1745*. Boston, MA: Rogers & Fowle, 1746.

Abbott, Susannah. 'Clerical Responses to the Jacobite Rebellion in 1715'. *Historical Research* 76, no. 193 (2003): 332–46.

Abercromby, Patrick [alleged author]. *The Advantages of the Act of Security, Compar'd with These of the Intended Union: Founded on the Revolution-Principles Publish'd by Mr. Daniel De Foe.* Edinburgh: s.n., 1706.

Adams, John. 'Thoughts on Government: Applicable to the Present State of the American Colonies'. In *The American Republic: Primary Sources*, edited by Bruce P. Frohnen, 196–9. Indianapolis: Liberty Fund, 2002.

Adamson, J. S. A. 'Eminent Victorians: S. R. Gardiner and the Liberal as Hero'. *The Historical Journal* 33, no. 3 (September 1990): 641–57. doi:10.1017/S0018246X00013571.

Allen, Charles. *A New and Improved History of England, from the Invasion of Julius Cæsar: To the End of the Thirty-Seventh Year of the Reign of King George the Third.* 2nd ed. London: J. Johnson, 1798.

Almon, John. 'This Day Are Published, Price One Shilling Each, The Parliamentary Register'. *Morning Post and Daily Advertiser* 907 (2 January 1776): [not paged].

[American colonists]. 'CO 5/40: Intercepted Letters to and from American Colonists'. North America, 1782 1770. Colonial Office, Commonwealth and Foreign and Commonwealth Offices. The National Archive of the UK, Kew.

An Orangeman [pseud.]. *Orange Vindicated, in a Reply to Theobald M'kenna, Esq. with Observations on the New and Further Claims of the Catholics, as Affecting the Constitution and the Protestant Establishment.* 6th ed. Dublin: by the author, 1799.

Anne, Queen of Great Britain. *By the Queen, a Proclamation, for the Due Observance of an Act Made in the Last Session of Parliament, Intituled, An Act to Prevent All Traiterous Correspondence with Her Majesties Enemies.* London: Charles Bill, and the executrix of Thomas Newcomb, 1705.

Annet, Peter. *Judging for Ourselves; or, Freethinking, the Great Duty of Religion: Displayed in Two Lectures, Delivered at Plaisterers' Hall.* London: T.G. Ballard, 1797.

Anon. *A Bloody Massacre Plotted by the Papists Intended First against the City of London and Consequently against the Whole Land: Discovered by the Care of Alderman Towes, and Some Other Godly and Well Affected Citizens: With a Relation of the Great Uproar Munday Last: First Occassioned by Some Words betweene the Late Bishop of Lincolne, Now Archbishop of Yorke, and Some London-Apprentices, and Secondly by Lunsford and His Company: And the Bloody Skirmish at Westminster Abbey on Tuesday Night: With the Combustion Then in Thhe City and Shutting of the City Gates: With the Noble Courage and Valour Exprest by Sir Richard Wiseman at the Same Time.* London: M.R., 1641.

Anon. *A Compendious View of the Late Tumults & Troubles in This Kingdom, by Way of Annals for Seven Years.* s.l.: s.n., 1685.

Anon. *A Complete History of James Maclean: The Gentleman Highwayman, Who Was Executed at Tyburn, on Wednesday, October 3, 1750, for a Robbery on the Highway. Containing The Particulars of His Life, from His Birth to His Death.* London: Charles Corbett, 1750.

Anon. *A Declaration from the People of God, Called Quakers: Against All Seditious Conventicles, and Dangerous Practises of Any Who under Colour of Pretence or Tender Conscience, Have, or May Contrive Insurrections; the Said People Being Cleer from All Such Things, in the Sight of God, Angels and Men.* London: s.n., 1670.

Anon. *A Full Report of All the Proceedings on the Trial of the Rev. William Jackson at the Bar of His Majesty's Court of King's Bench, Ireland, on an Indictment for High Treason.* London: G.G./J. Robinson/J. Debrett, 1795.

Anon. *A Letter to a Noble Lord; Containing Some Remarks on the Nature and Tendency of Two Acts Past Last Session of Last Parliament: Namely, An Act for Vesting in His*

Majestie the Estates of Certain Traytors, &c. and An Act for Taking Away and Abolishing the Heritable Jurisdictions in [...] Scotland [...] And for Restoring Such Jurisdictions to the Crown, &c. London: Sam. Paterson, 1748.

Anon. *A Letter to Charles Grey, Esq., on His Parliamentary Conduct Respecting His Royal Highness the Prince of Wales. In Which Are Some Remarks on 'A Letter to the Prince of Wales, on a Second Application to Parliament,' and Likewise on the 'Observations'*. London: B. Crosby, 1795.

Anon. *A Letter to His Grace the Duke of N********: On the Present Crisis in the Affairs of Great Britain; Containing Reflections on a Late Great Resignation, Together with a Letter from a Right Hon. Person to ****** in the City*. London: R. Griffiths, 1761.

Anon. *A Letter to the Earl of Bute*. London: printed for the author, and sold by J. Almon in Piccadilly, 1771.

Anon. *A Memorial for the 30th of January: Or, Fanatick Loyalty. Being a Specimen of the Behaviour of the Sectaries towards the Royal Martyr King Charles the First, and Other Sovereigns*. London: A. Bettesworth, 1716.

Anon. *A Proposal for Redressing the Grievances of the Nation: Under the Following Heads, Viz. the National Debt, Taxes, Excise Laws, Penal Laws, Army, Navy, Riot Act, Septennial Act, Placemen, Corruption, &c. &c.: In a Method of Reasoning Entirely New*. London: M. Cooper, 1740.

Anon. *A Seasonable Memorial in Some Historical Notes upon the Liberties of the Presse and Pulpit*. s.l.: s.n., 1680.

Anon. *Agreeable Contrast between the Formidable John of Grant and Don Carlos of Southern Extraction*. Scotland: Engraving, 1749. http://digital.nls.uk/75240854.

Anon. *An Abstract of Some Few of Those Barbarous, Cruell Massacres and Murthers of the Protestants and English in Some Parts of Ireland, Committed since the 23 of October 1641: Collected Out of the Examinations Taken upon Oath by Persons of Trust in the Beginning of the Rebellion, by Vertue of Severall Commissions under the Great Seal of Ireland*. London: Robert Ibbitson, 1652.

Anon. *An Address to the Freeholders of the County of Oxford on the Subject of the Present Election*. London: J. Bouquett, 1753.

Anon. *An Uprore at Portsmouth: Being an Advertizement to All Captaines and Other, That Are Halting Betweene Two Opinions. Shewing How Captain Wiles, Who Was Sent Forth for the Defence of the Kingdome Did Tyrannize over His Souldiers, and How Hee Did Revolt to His Majestie. And Also How His Soulders Gave Him His Due Reward in Slaying Him for His Treacherous Heart. Whereunto Is Added, the Parliaments Determination and Resolution for the Defence of the Kingdome*. London: Richard Balden, 1642.

Anon. 'Aufruhr in Birmingham. Aufrührerisches Billet. Schreiben des Doctor Priestley an seine ehemaligen Mitbürger zu Birmingham'. *Historisch-politisches Magazin, nebst litterarischen Nachrichten* 10 (1791): 149–56.

Anon. *Britannia's Intercession for the Happy Deliverance of John Wilkes, Esq. from Persecution and Imprisonment: To Which Is Added, a Political and Constitutional Sermon*. 9th corrected and Enlarged ed. London: S. Woodgate, 1768.

Anon. *Caricature Anticipations and Enlargements: Occasioned by a Late Pious Proclamation; Also by Two Celebrated Speeches in Parliament Relative to a Repeal of the Test Act; the One by Lord North, the Other by the Chancellor of the Exchequer. With Explanatory Notes, Suitable Illustrations, Anecdotes, &c*. London: G. Kearsley, 1787.

Anon. *Critical Remarks on Dr. Nowel's Sermon, Preached on January 30, 1772, before the House of Commons: To Which Is Annexed, the Sermon Complete*. London: T. Evans, 1772.

Anon. *Dr. Sacheverell's Picture Drawn to the Life: Or, a True Character of a High-Flyer. Of Use to All Those Who Admire Originals*. London: J. Baker, 1710.

Anon. *Dreadful Riot at Musselburgh Races, Which Took Place on Thursday Last, the 31st July, 1823. Betwixt a Vast Multitude of Irishmen Who Were Attending the Races, and the Bakers of Edinburgh and Leith, Assisted by the Coaliers of Musselburgh, and after a Most Bloody Affray, in Which Several Were Killed and Many Wounded, the Irishmen Were Obliged to Fly from the Field of Battle*. Glasgow: John Muir, 1823.

Anon. 'Dublin'. *Saunders's News-Letter, and Daily Advertiser* 9189 (13 September 1786): 1–2.

Anon. 'Dublin, March 14'. *Kentish Weekly Post or Canterbury Journal*, 27 March 1731, 2.

Anon. 'Ego Primum Habe Auctores Ac Magistros Religionum Calendarum Majores Cicero de Harus'. Edited by William King and Robert Harley. *The Examiner* 5, no. 16 (22 January 1713): [not paged].

Anon. *English Liberty Established, or a Mirrour [sic] for Posterity: John Wilkes/to the Gentlemen, Clergy, and Freedholders of the County of Middlesex*. Britain: engraving and letterpress, 1768. http://www.britishmuseum.org/research/collection_online/collection_object_details.aspx?objectId=1549331&partId=1&searchText=John+Wilkes&page=1.

Anon. 'Etwas von Irlands jetziger politischen Lage'. *Historisch-politisches Magazin, nebst litterarischen Nachrichten* 11 (1792): 221–31.

Anon. *Ex Ore Tuo Te Judico. Vox Populi, Vox Dei*. s.l.: s.n., 1719.

Anon. 'Extract from Addresses to The King, on the Repeal of the American Stamp Act'. *The Scots Magazine*, 1 August 1766, 37.

Anon. *Father Murphy. Or The Wexford Men of '98*. Dublin: s.n., 1860.

Anon. 'Gosport, Sep. 2'. *Newcastle Courant*, 3 September 1748, 3.

Anon. 'High Treason. Mr. Thomas Hardy's Trial'. Edited by John Heriot. *True Briton* 573 (29 October 1794): 1–3.

Anon. 'High Treason. Old Bailey, Nov. 21. The King v. J. H. Tooke on a Charge of High Treason [Constitutional Societies]'. *The Times*, 22 November 1794, 1–3.

Anon. *John Hartland, Tried at Kingstown, March 23, 1796, for a Riot, in St. George's-Fields, Southwark: With the Chief Part of the Condemned Sermon, Brief and Remarks on the Trial*. London: printed, and sold by the booksellers in town and country, 1796.

Anon. *John the Painter's Ghost: How He Appeared on the Night of His Execution to Lord Temple, Etc. [A Poem, Relating to the American War]*. London: J. Williams, 1777.

Anon. *Le Conquérant d'Écosse [i.e. Prince Charles Edward], poème*. Édimbourg [Paris]: s.n., 1745.

Anon. 'London'. *Derby Mercury*, 11 May 1732, 3.

Anon. 'London, March 23'. *Bath and Bristol Chronicle* IX, no. 441 (30 March 1769): 1.

Anon. *Loyal Associatiors for King and Country in the Year of Our Lord MDCCXLV*. [Scotland]: engraving, 1745. http://digital.nls.uk/75241601.

Anon. *Magna Charta, Opposed to Assumed Privilege: Being a Complete View of the Late Interesting Disputes between the House of Commons and the Magistrates of London; Containing an Account of the Whole Transactions from the First Arresting of the Two Printers, to the Enlargement of the Two Illustrious Patriots (B. Crosby, Lord Mayor, and R. Oliver, Alderman of London) from the Tower, May 8, 1771*. London: G. Kearsly, 1771.

Anon. *Massacre of the French King! View of La Guillotine; or the Modern Beheading Machine, at Paris. By Which the Unfortunate Louis XVI [...] Suffered on the Scaffold, January 21st, 1793*. Engraving and Letterpress. London: Minerva Office, for William Lane, 1793. https://www.loc.gov/item/2007680140/.

Anon. *Memoranda of Evidence by Several Witnesses of the Riot at Flint during the Declaration of the Poll*. London: s.n., 1734.

Anon. '[Military Government]'. *British Journal* 4 (13 October 1722): [not paged].

Anon. 'Miscellanea'. *Review of the State of the British Nation* 123 (1707): [not paged].

Anon. *News from Galloway, or, The Poor Man's Plea against His Landlord*. Edinburgh: s.n., 1724.

Anon. 'Nube Cavâ Speculantur Amicti'. Edited by William King and Robert Harley. *The Examiner* IV, no. 5 (29 May–1 June 1713): 1–2.

Anon. *Observations upon a Bill, Entituled [sic], An Act for Taking Away, and Abolishing the Heritable Jurisdictions in That Part of Great Britain Called Scotland: And for Restoring Such Jurisdictions to the Crown [...] and for Rendering the Union More Complete; Obs. I. That the Abolishing Heritable Jurisdictions [...] Will Tend to Dissolve It [...] II. That No Equivalent or Satisfaction in Money Can Be Assessed [...] III. That the Regulations Touching Sheriff and Steward-Deputes [...] Are Attended with Inconveniences. IV. That to Raise and Discuss Suspensions before the Circuit Court Is [...] against the Treaty of Union. V. That an Attempt to Introduce Conformity Betwixt Our Circuit Courts [...] and the Assizes or Commissions of Nisi Prius in England Is [...] against Our Constitution. VI. That the Tendency of This Bill Is to Undermine the British Constitution, and Advance the Jacobite Interest [...]* Edinburgh: s.n., 1747.

Anon. *Revolution Politicks: Being a Compleat Collection of All the Reports, Lyes, and Stories, Which Were the Fore-Runners of the Great Revolution in 1688; Commencing from the Death of King Charles II. and from Thence Regularly Continued to the Settlement of the Prince and Princess of Orange upon the Throne. Wherein the Several Views and Designs of All Parties Are Exposed; and Divers Jesuitical and Fanatical Intrigues Are Detected, and Set in True Light*. London: s.n., 1733.

Anon. *Salus Populi Suprema Lex: In Which Is Considered the Rights of the People, to Assemble and Prepare Petitions to the King and Either Houses of Parliament; and the Authority of the Crown, and All Officers Appointed by That Authority, as Well as the King's Liege Subjects, to Suppress Affrays, Tumults, and Unlawful Assemblies, Riots, Insurrections, and Rebellions, and to Repel Invasion by Enemies; and Also How Far the Military, Regular Forces, Militia and Yeomanry Are Bound on Such Occasions to Obey and Assist the Civil Magistrates and Sheriffs, as Being Part of the Power of the Country*. Dublin: Richard Milliken/Graisberry and Campbell, 1819.

Anon. *Satirical Print/Print/Book-Illustration*. Britain: etching and engraving, 158 mm × 108 mm, 1771. https://www.britishmuseum.org/collection/object/P_1868-0808-9950.

Anon. 'St. James's, March 22'. *Bath and Bristol Chronicle* IX, no. 441 (30 March 1769): 1.

Anon. *The Agreable [sic] Contrast*. Scotland: engraving, 1746. http://digital.nls.uk/75241520.

Anon. *The Agreable [sic] Contrast between the British Hero, and the Italian Fugitive*. Britain: etching and engraving, 95 mm × 275 mm, 1746. https://www.britishmuseum.org/collection/object/P_1868-0808-3793.

Anon. 'The Arts'. Edited by John Heriot. *True Briton*, 30 January 1799, [not paged].

Anon. *The Case of Mr. Francis Francia, the Reputed Jew. Who Was Acquitted of High-Treason, at the Sessions-House in the Old Baily, on Tuesday, Jan. 22. 1716. Together with the Learned Arguments for and against Him, by the Council for the King and the Prisoner: As Also the Substance of the Several Intercepted Letters, between Him and His Correspondents in France; In Particular That, at the Sight of Which, Mr. Harvey of Combe, Is Said to Have Stab'd Himself. Likewise a True Copy of Another Written in Justification of His Behaviour to Mr. Cowper, One of the Council for the King, on That*

Memorable Occasion: With the Names of the Jury That Brought Him in, Not Guilty. London: John Gouldins, 1716.

Anon. *The Coalition: Or, an Historical Memorial of the Negotiation for Peace, between His High Mightiness of C—-m—-t [Claremont, i.e. the Duke of Newcastle] and His Sublime Excellency of H—y—s [Hayes, i.e. William Pitt]. With the Vouchers. Published by Authority of One of the Contracting Powers.* London: J. Hinxman, 1762.

Anon. *The Cries of the Public. In a Letter to the Duke of Newcastle.* London: Register-Office in St. James's Country Market, 1758.

Anon. *The Depositions and Examinations of Mr. Edmund Everard (Who Was Four Years Close Prisoner in the Tower of London) Concerning the Horrid Popish Plot against the Life of His Sacred Majesty, the Government, and the Protestant Religion: With the Names of Several Persons in England, Ireland, France, and Elsewhere Concerned in the Conspiracy.* London: Dorman Newman, 1679.

Anon. *The Following Is a Copy of an Infamous Thing Handed about Here Yesterday, and Now Reprinted to Satisfy the Curiosity of the Public.* Cambridge, MA: s.n., 1775.

Anon. *The Grand Coalition Medal, Struck in Base Metal Gilt.* Britain: etching, 256 mm × 219 mm, 1784. https://www.britishmuseum.org/collection/object/P_1868-0808-5289.

Anon. *The Hired Rabble, or, the Character of a No-Church Mob: A Satyr, Occasionally Written on the Bishop of Rochester's Going to Be Tryed at Westminster.* London: s.n., 1722.

Anon. *The Life of James Aitken: Commonly Called John the Painter, an Incendiary, Who Was Tried at the Castle of Winchester, on Thursday the 7th Day of March, 1777, and Convicted of Setting Fire to His Majesty's Dock-Yard, at Portsmouth, [...] The Whole Faithfully Taken down from the Convict's Own Mouth.* 2nd ed. London: J. Wilkes/S. Crowder/G. Robinson/R. Baldwin/T. Evans, 1777.

Anon. *The New Coalition.* Britain: etching, 214 mm × 170 mm, 1784. https://www.britishmuseum.org/collection/object/P_1851-0901-220.

Anon. *The Newgate Calendar, or, Malefactors Bloody Register.* London: J. Cooke, 1773.

Anon. *The Newgate Calendar: Or, Malefactors Bloody Register. Containing Genuine and Circumstantial Narratives of the Lives and Transactions, Various Exploits and Dying Speeches of the Most Notorious Criminals of Both Sexes, Who Suffered Death, [...] in Great Britain and Ireland, from the Year 1700, to the Present Time.* London: J. Cooke, 1774.

Anon. *The Politician's Dictionary: Or, a Summary of Political Knowledge: Containing Remarks on the Interests, Connections, Forces, Revenues, Wealth, Credit, Debts, Taxes, Commerce, and Manufactures of the Different States of Europe. Alphabetically Digested for the Use of Those Who Would Wish to Understand Whatever Occurs in the Science of Politics.* Vol. 2. London: George Allen, 1775.

Anon. *The Prerogative of Primogeniture: Shewing, That the Right of Succession to an Hereditary Crown, Depends Not upon Grace, Religion, &c., but Onely upon Birth-Right and Primogeniture; and That the Chief Cause of All, or Most, Rebellions in Christendom, Is a Fanatical Belief, That, Temporal Dominion Is Founded in Grace. By David Jenner, B.D. Prebendary of Sarum, and Rector of Great Warley in Essex.* s.l.: s.n., 1685.

Anon. *The Remarkable History and Transactions of Robert Watt: (Who Declared Himself a Spy Employed by Government) and David Downie, Both Members of the British Convention, Who Were Tried, Cast, and Condemned at Edinburgh, for High Treason!* London: J. Evans, 1794.

Anon. *The Royall Merlin; or, Great Brittains Loyal Observator: Foretelling, the Time and Continuation of This Present Government, under a Protector and a Parliament; Then under a Parliament and Protector; and Afterwards by Another Magistrate, Whose Royal Stile and Dignity Will Cause England to Rejoyce and Sing: Denoting Also, the Time and Year of*

These Great Changes and Revolutions; the Transcendent Actions, That Will Accrue unto His Highness, and a Prophesie Thereupon; the Revolt of Some Eminent Officers and Commanders; the New Rising of the Scots; the Ambiguous Debates, and Warlike Proceedings of Christian Princes, for Restoring the Oppressed to Their Rights; the Appearing of Three West or South-West Armies; and the Event, Atchievment, and Success of the English Naval and Land-Forces. With the Time Prefixed, for Discarding of the Egyptian Angel, and the Taking off of Taxes: From Which Future Impositions, Good Lord Deliver Us*. London: George Horton, 1654.

Anon. *The Solemn Mock-Procession: Or, the Tryal & Execution of the Pope and His Ministers, on the 17. of Nov. at Temple-Bar, Etc*. London: Nath. Ponder, etc, 1680.

Anon. *The Trial at Large o [sic] Arthur O'Connor, Esq. John Binns, John Allen, Jeremiah Leary, and James Coigley, for High Treason, before Judge Buller, &c. under a Special Commission, at Maidstone, in the County of Kent. Taken in Short Hand*. 2nd ed. London: James Ridgway, 1798.

Anon. *The Tryal of Thomas Collet [Colley], at the Assizes at Hertford, on Tuesday the 30th of July, 1751, Before the Right Hon. Sir William Lee, Knt. Lord Chief Justice of the Court of King's-Bench, For the Cruel and Inhuman MURDER of Ruth Osborne, Wife of John Osborne, of Tring, in Hertfordshire, by Ducking Her in Marlston-Mere, in the Said Parish of Tring, under Supposition of Her Being a WITCH; 'till She Was Suffocated with Mud and Water*. 3 (corrected). London: T. Brown, 1751.

Anon. *Trial of David Downie, for High Treason, before the Court, under the Special Commission of Oyer and Terminer, Held at Edinburgh. Taken in Short Hand by Mr Blanchard Revised by the Counsel on Both Sides, and Published with Permission of the Court*. Edinburgh: William Brown, 1795.

Anon. 'Trials for High Treason (The Fourth Day)'. *Oracle and Public Advertiser* 18839 (31 October 1794): [not paged].

Anon. 'Trials for High Treason (The Third Day)'. *Oracle and Public Advertiser* 18838 (30 October 1794): [not paged].

Anon. *Trials of Robert Watt and David Downie for High Treason, Before the Court of Oyer and Terminer, Held at Edinburgh, Aug. 14.15. 22. 27. - Sept. 3. 5. 6. 1794. With an Engraving of the Pikes Found in the Possession of Robert Watt and Others*. Edinburgh: Manners and Miller, 1794.

Anon. *Two Essays: I. On Lay-Preaching. II. On the Ministerial Character. (From the Preacher's Manual) Intended to Justify Lay-Preaching; and, at the Same Time to Shew, That This Does Not Supercede the Necessity of a Regular Ministry*. London: G. Auld, for Williams and Son, 1812.

Anon. *Views of the Ruins of the Principal Houses Destroyed during the Riots at Birmingham, 1791. Vues Des Ruines Des Principaux Batiments Qui Ont Souffert Dans Les Emeutes de Birmingham, 1791*. London/Birmingham: J. Johnson, 1792.

Anon. *Virtual Representation*. Britain: etching, 215 mm × 304 mm, 1775. https://www.britishmuseum.org/collection/object/P_1868-0808-4531.

Anon. [attributed to Charles Lucas]. *The Abuse of Standing Parliaments, and the Great Advantage of Frequent Elections, in a Letter to a Noble Lord*. London: s.n., 1750.

Anon. [attributed to George Washington]. 'Copy of a Letter from General Washington to Congress. Camp, near Penibacker's Mill, Oct. 5'. *Derby Mercury*, 12 December 1777, [not paged].

Applin, John. 'SP 41/5/44: Information of John Applin, Stockingmaker of Glastonbury'. Glastonbury, 26 July 1716. The National Archives, Kew.

Arbuthnot, John. *A Sermon Preach'd to the People at the Mercat-Cross of Edinburgh on the Subject of the Union in 1706, While the Act for Uniting, the Two Kingdoms Was*

Depending before the Parliament There. With a Preface by the Editor, Setting Forth the Advantages Which Have, in Fact, Accrued to the Kingdom of Scotland by Its Union with England. London: J. Roberts, 1745.

Archer, John E. *Social Unrest and Popular Protest in England, 1780–1840.* Cambridge: Cambridge University Press, 2000.

Armstrong, Karen. *Fields of Blood: Religion and the History of Violence.* London: Vintage Books, 2015.

Arnold, Benedict. *By Brigadier-General Arnold, a Proclamation: To the Officers and Soldiers of the Continental Army Who Have the Real Interest of Their Country at Heart, and Who Are Determined to Be No Longer the Tools and Dupes of Congress, or of France.* Edited by Army of Great Britain. New York: James Rivington, 1780.

Asch, Ronald G. *Der europäische Adel im Ancien Regime: von der Krise der ständischen Monarchien bis zur Revolution (ca. 1600–1789).* Edited by Internationaler Osnabrücker Kongress zur Kulturgeschichte der Frühen Neuzeit. Cologne: Böhlau, 2001.

Asch, Ronald G. 'Staatsbildung und adlige Führungsschichen in der Frühen Neuzeit. Auf dem Weg zur Auflösung der ständischen Identität des Adels?' *Geschichte und Gesellschaft* 33, no. 3: Adel in der Neuzeit (2007): 375–97.

Asch, Ronald G., and Adolf M. Birke. *Princes, Patronage, and the Nobility: The Court at the Beginning of the Modern Age, c. 1450–1650.* London: German Historical Institute London, 1991.

Asch, Ronald G., and Heinz Duchhardt. *Der Absolutismus – ein Mythos?: Strukturwandel monarchischer Herrschaft in West- und Mitteleuropa (ca. 1550–1700).* Cologne: Böhlau, 1996.

Asche, Matthias. 'Bellizität, Staat und Migration im Alten Reich'. In *Handbuch Staat und Migration in Deutschland seit dem 17. Jahrhundert,* 2015.

Ashe, St. George. *A Sermon Preached to the Protestants of Ireland, Now in London: At the Parish-Church of St. Clement Dane. October 23, 1712. Being The Day Appointed by Act of Parliament in Ireland, for an Anniversary Thanksgiving for the Deliverance of the Protestants of That Kingdom, from the Bloody Massacre Begun by the Irish Papists, on the 23rd of October, 1641.* 2nd ed. London: Samuel Buckley, 1712.

Ashworth, William J. Review of *Riotous Assemblies: Popular Protest in Hanoverian England,* by Adrian Randall. *Social History* 32, no. 4 (2007): 469–70.

Association for Preserving Constitutional Order, Liberty, and Property, ed. *The Committee of Association, for Preserving Constitutional Order, Liberty and Property, Having Made Enquiry into the Unfortunate Disturbance Which Took Place on Tuesday Evening, Think It Necessary to Thank Mr. Martin Marshall, and His Son, for Their Exertions, in Endeavouring to Suppress All Riot and Confusion.* Manchester: James Harrop, 1792.

Association for Preserving Liberty and Property against Republicans and Levellers. *Proceedings of the Association for Preserving Liberty and Property Against Republicans and Levellers.* London: John Debrett/Hookham/Carpenter, 1793.

Association for Preserving Liberty and Property against Republicans and Levellers, ed. *Publications Printed by Order of the Society for Preserving Liberty and Property against Republicans and Levellers: At the Crown and Anchor, in the Strand. Part the First. To Which Are Prefixed the Proceedings of the Society.* London: J. Downes/Hookham and Carpenter/J. Debrett/J. Sewell, 1793.

Astell, Mary. *An Impartial Enquiry into the Causes of Rebellion and Civil War in This Kingdom: In an Examination of Dr Kennetts Sermon Jan 31 1703 and Vindication of the Royal Martyr.* s.l.: s.n., 1703.

Astell, Mary. *An Impartial Enquiry into the Causes of Rebellion and Civil War in This Kingdom: In an Examination of Dr. Kennett's Sermon, Jan. 31. 1703/4*. London: printed by E. P. for R. Wilkin, 1704.

Aston, Nigel, and Clarissa Campbell Orr. *An Enlightenment Statesman in Whig Britain: Lord Shelburne in Context, 1737–1805*. Woodbridge: Boydell & Brewer, 2011.

Baer, Friederike. 'Christian Friedrich Daniel Schubart's Deutsche Chronik and the War of American Independence, 1774–1777'. *Journal for Eighteenth-Century Studies* 38, no. 3 (2015): 443–58.

Bailyn, Bernard. *Pamphlets of the American Revolution 1750–1765*. Cambridge, MA: Belknap Press of Harvard University Press, 1965.

Barget, Monika. 'Automatically Downloading Bibliographic Information (RIS Format) from WorldCat'. Screen cast. *Digital History*, 6 December 2020. https://www.youtube.com/watch?v=3DEF3Nh1XkQ.

Barget, Monika. 'British and Colonial Media Production'. Github Pages. *Conflict in the Eighteenth-Century British Empire – Data and Visualisations*, 2022. https://monikabarget.github.io/Revolts/overviews.html.

Barget, Monika. 'Chronological Table of (Alleged/Planned) Unrest'. Github Pages. *Conflict in the Eighteenth-Century British Empire – Data and Visualisations*, 2022. https://monikabarget.github.io/Revolts/event-table.html.

Barget, Monika. 'Concepts of Leadership in Early Portraits of American Revolutionaries'. In *Political Violence in Early Modern Imagery*, edited by Malte Griesse, Monika Barget, and David de Boer, 54, 263–88. Brill's Studies on Art, Art History, and Intellectual History. Leiden: Brill, 2021. https://brill.com/view/title/60088.

Barget, Monika. 'Conflicts in the Eighteenth-Century British Empire – Data and Visualisations'. Github Pages. *Conflict in the Eighteenth-Century British Empire – Data and Visualisations*, 2022. https://monikabarget.github.io/Revolts/.

Barget, Monika. 'Digital History Repository'. 2019. Reprint, Mainz: Institut für Europäische Geschichte, 2020. https://github.com/MonikaBarget/DigitalHistory.

Barget, Monika. '"Hired mobs" – öffentliche Meinung und gesteuerte Menge im frühneuzeitlichen Großbritannien'. In *Jenseits der Ordnung? Zur Mächtigkeit der Vielen in der Frühen Neuzeit*, edited by Rudolf Schlögl and Jan Marco Sawilla, 45–74. Berlin: Neofelis, 2019.

Barget, Monika. 'Interactive Map of Uprisings'. Github Pages. *Conflict in the Eighteenth-Century British Empire – Data and Visualisations*, 2022. https://monikabarget.github.io/Revolts/event-map.html.

Barget, Monika. 'John Andre, Benedict Arnold and Concepts of Heroism in the American Revolution'. Academic blog. *Revolts as Communication*, 9 December 2020. https://revolt.hypotheses.org/1240.

Barget, Monika. 'Power and Identity'. In *Cultural History of Color: Enlightenment, 1650–1800*, edited by Carole Biggam and Kirsten Wolf, 1st ed., 4, 59–72. The Cultural History Series. London/New York: Bloomsbury Academic, 2021.

Barget, Monika. '"Rebelle malgré lui" – récits de réconciliation et de réintégration dans les biographies politiques britanniques du XVIIIe siècle'. Edited by Stéphane Haffemayer. *Histoire et Civilisation du Livre. Revue Internationale* XIV (2018): 247–68.

Barget, Monika. 'Sermons and Religious Periodicals'. Github Pages. *Conflict in the Eighteenth-Century British Empire*, 2022. https://monikabarget.github.io/Revolts/sermons.html.

Barget, Monika. 'Stadt, Land und suburbaner Raum als Orte des Widerstands: Das britische Empire im 18. Jahrhundert'. *Zeitschrift für Agrargeschichte und Agrarsoziologie*

2/2017: Ländliche Akteure zwischen Protest und Revolution (18. bis 21. Jahrhundert) (2017): 35–54.
Barget, Monika. 'Table of Riot and Rebellion Vocabulary: Word Count and Classification'. *GitHub: MonikaBarget/Revolts*, 2020. https://github.com/MonikaBarget/Revolts.
Barget, Monika. '"The Hatred Which They Bear towards Their Kings" – Hanoverian Perceptions of the Glorious Revolution'. In *Writing Rebellion in Early Modern Diplomacy*, 2023 edited by Malte Griesse, Monika Barget, and David de Boer, 118–37. Politics and Culture in Europe, 1650–1750. London/Abingdon: Routledge. https://www.routledge.com/Rebellion-and-Diplomacy-in-Early-Modern-Europe/Barget-Boer-Griesse/p/book/9781032170572.
Barget, Monika. 'Zwischen Ökonomie und Ideologie – der englische Buchmarkt des 18. Jahrhunderts'. Academic blog. *Hypotheses – Das Portal der deutschsprachigen Community von Hypotheses*, August 2014. www.revolt.hypotheses.org/656.
Barker, Hannah. 'England, 1760–1815'. In *Press, Politics and the Public Sphere in Europe and North America, 1760–1820*, edited by Hannah Barker and Simon Burrows, 93–112. Cambridge: Cambridge University Press, 2002.
Barlow, Frederick. *The Complete English Dictionary: Or, General Repository of the English Language. Containing a Copious Explanation of All the Words in the English Language; Together with Their Different Significations*. Vol. 2. London/Cambridge/Oxford/York/Dublin: T. Evans/F. Blyth/Mr. Jackson/Fletcher and Hodson/Wilson/Etherington, 1772.
Barlow, Percival. *The General History of Europe: And Entertaining Traveller. Comprising an Historical and Geographical Account of All the Empires, Kingdoms, &c. in Europe, Viz. Great-Britain, Ireland, Germany, Turkey, Russia, Sweden, France, Spain, Portugal, Poland, Bohemia, Prussia, Italy, Denmark, Hungary, Sardinia, Tuscany, Norway, Venice, United Provinces, Switzerland, Austria, Genoa, Geneva, Piedmont, Montserrat, Milan, Parma, Modena, and Tartary in Europe, from Their First Establishment to the End of the Present Year; Including a Circumstantial Relation of the Origin, Progress, and Present State of Every Kingdom.* London: W. and J. Stratford, 1791.
Barlow, Thomas. *The Gunpowder Treason: With a Discourse of the Manner of Its Discovery; and a Perfect Relation of the Proceedings against the Conspirators; Wherein Is Contained Their Trials and Condemnations, Also the Confessions of Guido Fawkes and Thomas Winter; Likewise King James's Speech to Both Houses of Parliament, Including a Preface Touching the Conspiracy. Now Reprinted: A Preface Touching That Horrid Conspiracy, by the Right Reverend Father in God Thomas, Lord Bishop of Lincoln, and by Way of Appendix, Several Papers or Letters of Sir Everard Digby*. 2nd ed. London: Tho. Newcomb and H. Hills, 1679.
Barnard, Edward, and George Henry Millar. *The New, Comprehensive and Complete History of England: From the Earliest Period of Authentic Information, to the Middle of the Year, MDCCLXXXIII [...] from the Remotest Period of Time, to the Present Very Important Crisis*. London: Alex. Hogg, 1783.
Barrell, John. *Imagining the King's Death: Figurative Treason, Fantasies of Regicide, 1793–1796*. Oxford: Oxford University Press, 2000.
Bartlett, Thomas. *Ireland: A History*. Cambridge: Cambridge University Press, 2010.
Baumgart, Peter. 'Absolutismus ein Mythos? Aufgeklärter Absolutismus ein Widerspruch? Reflexionen zu einem kontroversen Thema gegenwärtiger Frühneuzeitforschung'. *Zeitschrift für historische Forschung* 27, no. 4 (2000): 573–89.
Bawn, K. P. *Social Protest, Popular Disturbances and Public Order in Dorset, 1790–1838*. Reading: University of Reading, 1984.

Bean, Charles. *The Folly and Wickedness of the Late Rebellion Considered: In a Thanksgiving-Sermon Preach'd at Barham in the County of Kent, June 7. 1716.* London: R. Burleigh, 1716.

Bean, Thomas. *The Last Speech and Confession of Thomas Bean, One of Those Executed for the Late Riot in Salisbury-Court at London.* 2nd ed. Edinburgh: s.n., 1716.

Beaupré, Nicolas. 'Comptes Rendus: Benjamin Ziemann (Dir.) Perspektiven der Historischen Friedensforschung (…)/Christian Jansen (Dir.) Der Bürger als Soldat. Die Militarisierung Europäischer Gesellschaften im Langen 19. Jahrhundert: Ein Internationaler Vergleich (…)'. *Annales. Histoire, Sciences Sociales, 59e Année* 3 (2004): 661–4.

Beckett, G. *King William III, in Roman Costume; beneath His Feet, a Manacled Monk and Two Bound Catholic Priests [Print Celebrating the Glorious Revolution].* 1689. Mezzotint, 33.8 cm (trimmed) × 24.9 cm (trimmed). Prints and Drawings. British Museum London.

Beer, Barrett L. *Rebellion and Riot: Popular Disorder in England during the Reign of Edward VI.* Kent, OH: Kent State University Press, 2005.

Ben-Atar, Doron S. 'Pride, Ambition and Resentment: The American Revolution Revisited'. In *Oxford History of the British Empire*, edited by P. J. Marshall. Vol. 2: The eighteenth century. Oxford/New York: Oxford University Press, 1998.

Benigno, Francesco. *Mirrors of Revolution: Conflict and Political Identity in Early Modern Europe.* Late Medieval and Early Modern Studies 16. Turnhout: Brepols, 2010.

Bennet, Benjamin. *A Memorial of the Reformation, (Chiefly in England) and of Britain's Deliverances from Popery and Arbitrary-Power: Since That Time, to the Year, 1716. Wherein Is Contained, Some Account of the Apostacy of the Church in Its Rise and Progress, till Popery Was Established in the World. The State of the Reformation under King Henry VIII. Edward VI. and Queen Elizabeth: With the Principles and Endeavours of Those That Have from Time to Time Stood for a Further Reformation; as a Short History of Nonconformity. A Particular Relation of All the Plots and Conspiracies of Papists and Others against the Reformation, and Civil Liberties of the Land. Some Short Memoirs of the Civil War in K. Charles the First's Time; and a Distinct Answer to the Question, Who Cut Off the King's Head.* London: S. Cruttenden and T. Cox, at the Bible and Three Crowns in Cheapside, near Mercer's Chappel, J. McEuen in Edinburgh, and R. Akenhead in New-Castle upon Tyne, 1717.

Bennett, Gareth V. *The Tory Crisis in Church and State: 1688–1730; the Career of Francis Atterbury, Bishop of Rochester.* Oxford: Clarendon Press, 1975.

Bennett, Martyn. *The Civil Wars in Britain and Ireland. 1638–1651.* Oxford/Cambridge, MA: Blackwell Publishers, 1997.

Bentham, Edward. *De tumultibus americanis deque eorum concitatoribus meditatio senilis.* Oxonii [Oxford]: J. Fletcher/D. Prince/B. White, 1776.

Berlin-Brandenburgische Akademie der Wissenschaften and Akademie der Wissenschaften zu Göttingen, eds. 'Leibniz: Sämtliche Schriften und Briefe, Reihe I. Allgemeiner, politischer und historischer Briefwechsel. Transkriptionen Januar–Dezember 1714, Akademie-Ausgabe Leibniz-Edition'. Subject to modification before final publication. Hanover: Leibniz-Archiv/Leibniz-Forschungsstelle, 2 February 2010. http://www.gwlb.de/Leibniz/Leibnizarchiv/Veroeffentlichungen/Transkriptionen.htm.

Bernard, Francis. *The Papers of Francis Bernard: Governor of Colonial Massachusetts, 1760–69.* Edited by Colin Nicolson. Vol. 1. 3 vols. Boston, MA: Colonial Society of Massachusetts, 2007.

Bernard, Francis. *The Papers of Francis Bernard: Governor of Colonial Massachusetts, 1760–69.* Edited by Colin Nicolson. Vol. 2. 3 vols. Boston, MA: The Colonial Society of Massachusetts, 2012.

Bernard, Francis, Thomas Gage, and Samuel Hood. *Letters to the Ministry from Governor Bernard, General Gage, and Commodore Hood. And Also Memorials to the Lords of the Treasury, from the Commissioners of the Customs. With Sundry Letters and Papers Annexed to the Said Memorials.* Boston, MA: Edes and Gill, 1769.

Bexon, Scipion-Jérôme. *Parallèle du code pénal d'Angleterre avec les lois pénales françaises, et considérations sur les moyens de rendre celles-ci plus utiles.* Vol. 1. Paris: Fauvelle et Sagnier, 1799. https://gallica.bnf.fr/ark:/12148/bpt6k57394139.

Bickham the Younger, George. *The [Cha]Mpion; or Even[Ing] Adver[Tiser] by Capt Hercules Vinegar, of Pall-Mall.* England: etching and engraving, 292 mm × 362 mm, 1740. https://www.britishmuseum.org/collection/object/P_1868-0808-3629.

Biggs, William. *The Military History of Europe, &c. from the Commencement of the War with Spain in 1739, to the Treaty of Aix-La-Chapelle in 1748: Containing All the Transactions of That War Both by Sea and Land: Also Comprehending a Concise and Impartial History of the Rebellion in Scotland.* London: R. Baldwin, 1755.

Bilson, Thomas. *A Discourse upon the Questions in Debate between the King and Parliament. With Certaine Observations Collected Out of The Difference between Christian Subjection and Unchristian Rebellion.* s.l.: s.n., 1642.

Bilson, Thomas. *Certain Observations Collected Out of a Treatise Called 'The Difference between Christian Subjection and Unchristian Rebellion'.* London: s.n., 1642.

Bilson, Thomas. *Certain Observations Collected Out of a Treatise Called 'The Difference between Christian Subjection and Unchristian Rebellion'.* London: s.n., 1750.

Bilson, Thomas. *The Trve Difference betweene Christian Svbiection and Vnchristian Rebellion: Wherein the Princes Lawful Power to Command for Truth, and Indepriueable Right to Beare the Sword, Are Defended against the Popes Censures and the Iesuites Sophismes, Vttered in Their Apologie and Defence of English Catholikes: With a Demonstration That the Things Reformed in the Church of England by the Lawes of This Realme Are Truly Catholike, notwithstanding the Vaine Shew Made to the Contrarie in Their Late Rhemish Testament.* London: Iohn Iackson and Edmund Bollifant, 1586.

Black, Antony. 'Althusius (Althaus), Johannes (d. 1638)'. In *The Blackwell Encyclopaedia of Political Thought*, edited by David W. Miller, Janet Coleman, William Connolly, and Alan Ryan, 8th ed., 8–9. Oxford/Malden: Blackwell, 1998.

Black, Eugene Charlton. 'The Tumultuous Petitioners: The Protestant Association in Scotland, 1778–1780'. *The Review of Politics* 25, no. 2 (1963): 183–211.

Black, Jeremy. Review of *The Eagle and the Crown: Americans and the British Monarchy.* New Haven: Yale University Press. 2008, by Frank Prochaska. *The American Historical Review* 114, no. 2 (April 2009): 434–434.

Black, Jeremy. *The English Press 1621–1861.* Stroud: Sutton Publishing Limited, 2001.

Black, William B. *The Glasgow Malt Tax Riots.* Lenzie: William B. Black, 2008.

Blacow, Richard, Canon of Windsor. *A Letter to William King [...] Containing a Particular Account of the Treasonable Riot at Oxford [...] 1747.* London: s.n., 1755.

Blaisdell, Bob, ed. *The United States Constitution. The Full Text with Supplementary Materials.* Dover Thrift Editions. Mineoly, New York: Dover Publications, 2009.

Blakemore, Steven. *Literature, Intertextuality, and the American Revolution: From Common Sense to 'Rip Van Winkle'.* Madison, NJ: Fairleigh Dickinson University Press, 2012.

Blanchard, Shaun. 'Thomas Palmer, Jansenism and England: Moral Rigorism across the Confessions'. *The Journal of Religion* 99, no. 2 (April 2019): 256–7. doi:10.1086/701874.

Blanchard, William. *The Proceedings at Large on the Trial of George Gordon: Esq; Commonly Called Lord George Gordon, for High Treason, in the Court of King's Bench,*

Westminster; [...] on Monday and Tuesday, February the 5th and 6th, 1781. Carefully Compiled from the Short-Hand Writing of Mr William Blanchard, and Revised by the Several Counsel Concerned. London: M. Harrison/Mr Blanchard/Mr Baldwin/ Mr Robson, 1781.

Blauert, Andreas, and Gerd Schwerhoff, eds. Kriminalitätsgeschichte: Beiträge zur Sozial- und Kulturgeschichte der Vormoderne. Vol. 1. Konflikte und Kultur. Konstanz: Universitätsverlag Konstanz, 2000.

Blickle, Peter. 'The Criminalization of Peasant Resistance in the Holy Roman Empire: Toward a History of the Emergence of High Treason in Germany'. Journal of Modem History 58 (supplement) (December 1986): 88–97.

Blount, Thomas. Nomo-Lexicon: A Law-Dictionary: Interpreting Such Difficult and Obscure Words and Terms, as Are Found Either in Our Common or Statute, Ancient or Modern Lawes. With Charters, Ancient Deeds, and Manuscripts, wherein the Words Are Used: And Etymologies, Where They Properly Occur. London: Tho. Newcomb, for John Martin and Henry Herringman, 1670.

Boddie, John Bennett. Seventeenth Century Isle of Wight County, Virginia: A History of the County of Isle of Wight, Virginia, during the Seventeenth Century, Including Abstracts of the County Records. 3rd ed. Chicago: Genealogical Publishing, 1973.

Bodin, Jean. Les six livres de la République. Edited by Gérard Mairet. Classiques des sciences sociales, 4413; Classiques des sciences sociales; Auteurs classiques; Livre de poche, 4619. Chicoutimi: Bibliothèque Paul-Émile Boulet de l'Université du Québec à Chicoutimi, 2001.

Bohstedt, John. The Politics of Provisions: Food Riots, Moral Economy, and Market Transition in England, c. 1550–1850. Farnham: Ashgate Publishing, 2010.

Bohun, Edmund. An Address to the Freemen and Freeholders of the Nation: In Three Parts. Together with Reflections on a Pamphlet, Stiled A Just and Modest Vindication of the Proceedings of the Two Last Parliaments: Or, A Defence of His Majesties Late Declaration. London: G. Wells, 1683.

Bolingbroke, Henry St. John. Letters on the Spirit of Patriotism: On the Idea of a Patriot King: And on the State of Parties, at the Accession of King George the First. London: A. Millar, 1749.

Bolingbroke, Henry St. John, Viscount. Bolingbroke's Political Writings: The Conservative Enlightenment. Edited by Bernard Cottret. Houndmills: Macmillan, 1997.

Bollan, William. The Freedom of Speech and Writing upon Public Affairs, Considered (...) Particularly of Late with Respect to the Colonies: And a Brief State of Their Origin and Political Nature, Collected from Various Acts of Princes and Parliaments. London: S. Barker, 1766.

Bollan, William. The Petition of Mr. Bollan, Agent for the Council of the Province of Massachusetts Bay, to The King in Council, Dated January 26, 1774. London: J. Almon, 1774.

Bolton, William. Core Redivivus: In a Sermon Preached at Christ-Church Tabernacle in London upon Sunday, September 9, 1683, Being a Day of Publick Thanksgiving for the Deliverance of His Sacred Majesties Person and Government from the Late Treasonable Rebellion and Fanatick Conspiracy. London: James Norris, 1684.

Borus, György. 'Political Parties in the Years before and after the Glorious Revolution'. Hungarian Journal of English and American Studies 13, 1/2: The Long Eighteenth Century (2007): 121–30.

Boyse, Samuel. An Impartial History of the Late Rebellion in 1745: From Authentic Memoirs; Particularly, the Journal of a General Officer, and Other Original Papers, yet Unpublished. With the Characters of the Persons Principally Concerned. To Which Is

Prefixed, by Way of Introduction, a Compendious Account of the Royal House of Stuart, from Its Original to the Present Time. By S. Boyse, M.A. Reading: D. Henry, 1748.

Braddick, Michael J., and Phil Withington. *Popular Culture and Political Agency in Early Modern England and Ireland. Essays in Honour of John Walter.* Woodbridge: Boydell & Brewer, 2017.

Bradley, James E. *Religion, Revolution, and English Radicalism. Nonconformity in Eighteenth-Century Politics and Society.* Cambridge/New York: Cambridge University Press, 1990.

Bragge, B. '[Country-m. Well, Master, Are Not You and I Much Oblig'd to the High-Flying Faction?]'. *Observator* 14 (1709): [not paged].

Brandes, Ernst. 'Ueber die Justiz- und Gerichtsverfassung Englands, vom Geheimen Canzleisecretair Brandes (Fortsetzung und Schluss)'. *Hannoverisches Magazin* 91/92 (November 1785): 1441–56; 1457–72.

Bremner, G. A. 'The Corporatisation of Global Anglicanism'. *ABE Journal. Architecture beyond Europe*, no. 2 (2 September 2012). doi:10.4000/abe.357.

Brent, Richard. *Liberal Anglican Politics: Whiggery, Religion, and Reform, 1830–1841.* Oxford: Clarendon Press, 1987.

British Library. 'Truth and Treason! Or a Narrative of the Royal Procession to the House of Peers, October the 29th, 1795'. *Catalogues & Collections.* The British Library, 4 July 2020. https://www.bl.uk/collection-items/truth-and-treason-or-a-narrative-of-the-royal-procession-to-the-house-of-peers-october-the-29th-1795.

Brodrick, George C. *The Political History of England.* Frankfurt: Outlook Verlag, 2020.

Broughton, Richard. *A Iust and Moderate Answer to a Most Iniurious, and Slaunderous Pamphlet, Intituled, An Exact Discouery of Romish Doctrine in Case of Conspiracie and Rebellion: Wherein the Innocency of Catholike Religion Is Proued, and Euery Obiection Returned vpon the Protestant Accuser, and His Owne Profession.* England: English secret press, 1606.

Brown, Keith M. 'The Scottish Nobility and the British Multiple Monarchy'. In *Der Europäische Adel Im Ancien Regime*, edited by Ronald G. Asch and Keith M. Brown, 363–84. Cologne: Böhlau, 2001.

Browne, J. *The Parliaments Lamentation. For the Distractions of the Kingdome. First, Wherein Is Declared Their Great Sorrow for the Kings Absence. Secondly, That the Church Is so Full of Disturbances and Distractions, Caused by Evill Affected Persons, Which under the Pretence of Religion, Commit All Sorts of Outrages, and by Their Tumultuary Practices Destroy Both the Peace of the Church and Kingdome. Thirdly, That Neverthelesse Though the Parliament Have Declared against Such Tumults, Which Causes His Majesty to Declare Them the Abettors and Maintainers of the Said Tumults and Distractions. Ordered That This Be Forthwith Printed.* London: T. Fawcet, 1642.

Browne, Jonas, ed. '[Two Days after the Publishing of My First Paper about the Revolution]'. *The Reconciler* 14/15 (29 May 1713): 2–4.

Browne, Simon. *Jewish and Popish Zeal Describ'd and Compar'd. A Sermon Preach'd at Portsmouth, Nov. 5. 1715. Wherein the Inconsistency of Popery with True Religion Is Manifested, and the Chief Pretences for the Present Rebellion in Britain Are Consider'd and Expos'd.* London: John Clark, 1715.

Broxap, Henry. *A Biography of Thomas Deacon, the Manchester Non-Juror. With a Portrait.* Publications of the University of Manchester. Historical Series. Manchester: Manchester University Press, 1911.

Bruce, Archibald. *Reflections on Freedom of Writing: And the Impropriety of Attempting to Suppress It by Penal Laws; Occasioned by a Late Proclamation against Seditious*

Publications, and the Measures Consequent upon It; Viewed Chiefly in the Aspect They Bear to Religious Liberty, and Ecclesiastical Reform. Edinburgh/Glasgow: W. Berry/J. Guthrie/Brash and Reid/J. Duncan and Son, 1794.

Bryan, Edward. Review of *From Jacobite to Conservative. Reaction and Orthodoxy in Britain c. 1760–1832*, by James J. Sack. *Teaching History*, no. 74 (1994): 42.

Buckley, F. H. *The Once and Future King. The Rise of Crown Government in America*. New York/London: Encounter Books, 2014.

Bullock, Steven C. *Revolutionary Brotherhood: Freemasonry and the Transformation of the American Social Order, 1730–1840*. Chapel Hill/London: University of North Carolina Press, 1996.

Burgh, James. *Britain's Remembrancer: Or, The Danger Not Over: Being Some Thoughts on the Proper Improvement of the Present Juncture. The Character of This Age and Nation. A Brief View, from History, of the Effects of the Vices Which Now Prevail in Britain [...] Some Hints, Shewing What Is in the Power of the Several Ranks of People, and of Every Individual in Britain, to Do toward Securing the State from All Its Enemies*. 2nd ed. Edinburgh: Thomas Lumisden and John Robertson, 1746.

Burgh, William. 'HO 42/34/42: Letter from William Burgh of York Dissociating the Writer and a Majority of the Householders of York from a Petition to the House of Commons Purporting to Represent the View of the Corporation of York and Praying for a Speedy Peace'. Petition. York, 14 February 1795. Home Office: Domestic Correspondence, George III. The National Archives of the UK, Kew.

Burke, Margaret R. 'Concord Museum'. Museum website, 3 November 2015. http://www.concordmuseum.org/.

Burke, Peter. 'Some Seventeenth-Century Anatomists of Revolution'. *Storia Della Storiografia* 22 (1992): 23–35.

Burkhardt, Johannes. *Deutsche Geschichte in der frühen Neuzeit*. Beck'sche Reihe 2462. Munich: Beck, 2009.

Burkhardt, Johannes. *Die Friedlosigkeit der frühen Neuzeit: Grundlegung einer Theorie der Bellizität Europas*. Berlin: Duncker & Humblot, 1997.

Burn, John, and Richard Burn. *A New Law Dictionary: Intended for General Use, as Well as for Gentlemen of the Profession. By Richard Burn, LL. D. Late Chancellor of the Diocese of Carlisle. And Continued to the Present Time by John Burn, Esq. His Son, One of His Majesty's Justices of the Peace for the Counties of Westmorland and Cumberland*. Vol. 2. 2 vols. London: A. Strahan and W. Woodfall/T. Cadell, 1792.

Burnet, Gilbert. *Engelland, wie stehts um deine Freyheit?/oder eigentliche Nachricht von dem itzigen Staat in Engelland, wie nemlich derselbe bey Regierung dieses Königes vom vorigen weit unterschieden, allen Politicis und curieusen Gemüthern zu sonderbaren Nutzen in engeländischer Sprache beschrieben*. London [i.e. Cologne]: s.n., 1689.

Busshoff, Heinrich. *Das Politische der Politik: Politik als Mechanismus zur Politisierung des Politischen*. 1st ed. Baden-Baden: Nomos, 2005.

Bute, John Stuart, Earl of, and Charles Stuart. *A Prime Minister and His Son, from the Correspondence of the 3rd Earl of Bute and of Lt.-General Sir Charles Stuart*. Edited by Violet Stuart Wortley and Rennell Rod. London: John Murray, 1925.

Byrne, Miles. *Memoires: With Ballads of 1798, and Robert Emmet's Speech from the Dock*. Edited by P. Boyne. For use in schools. Dublin: Fallon, 1946.

Campbell Orr, Clarissa. 'The Late Hanoverian Court and the Christian Enlightenment'. In *Monarchy and Religion. The Transformation of Royal Culture in Eighteenth-Century Europe*, 317–44. Studies of the German Historical Institute London. Oxford: Oxford University Press, 2007.

Caple, Jeremy N. 'Popular Protest and Public Order in Eighteenth-Century England: A Study of the Food Riots of 1756-57'. M.A. thesis, Queen's University, 1978.

Cappon, Lester J. 'Introduction: "Prospect of an Immortality in the Memories of All the Worthy"'. In *The Adams-Jefferson Letters. The Complete Correspondence between Thomas Jefferson and Abigail and John Adams*, edited by Lester J. Cappon, Reprint of the 1959 original ed., xxxi–xlix. Published for the Omohundro Institute of Early American History and Culture at Williamsburg, Virginia. Chapel Hill/London: University of North Carolina Press, 1987.

Cappon, Lester J., ed. *The Adams-Jefferson Letters. The Complete Correspondence between Thomas Jefferson and Abigail and John Adams.* Reprint of the original 1959 ed. Chapel Hill/London: University of North Carolina Press, 1987.

Castells, Manuel. *Communication Power*. 1st ed. Oxford: Oxford University Press, 2009.

Caudle, James. 'Preaching in Parliament: Patronage, Publicity and Politics in Britain, 1701–1760'. In *The English Sermon Revised. Religion, Literature and History 1600–1750*, edited by Lori Anne Ferrell and Peter McCullough, 235–64. Politics, Culture & Society in Early Modern Britain. Manchester: Manchester University Press, 2000.

Caudle, James J. 'Nowell, Thomas, (1730?–1801), Church of England Clergyman and Religious Controversialist'. In *Oxford Dictionary of National Biography*, 41, 239–40. Oxford: Oxford University Press, 1999.

Charles II, King of England and Scotland. *An Act to Prevent and Suppress Seditious Conventicles*. London: printed by John Bill and Christopher Barker, printers to the Kings most excellent Majesty, 1664.

Charles II, King of England and Scotland. *An Act to Prevent and Suppress Seditious Conventicles*. London: the assigns of John Bill and Christopher Barker, 1670.

Charles, W. *A Boxing Match, or Another Bloody Nose for John Bull*. United States: etching with watercolour, 25 cm × 34.8 cm, 1813. https://www.loc.gov/item/2002708982/.

Cheney, David M. 'Bishop George Hay'. *Catholic-Hierarchy*, 2021. http://www.catholic-hierarchy.org/bishop/bhay.html.

Chrimes, S. B. 'The Constitutional Ideas of Dr John Cowell'. *The English Historical Review* LXIV, no. CCLIII (1 October 1949): 461–87. doi:10.1093/ehr/LXIV.CCLIII.461.

Christie, I. R. 'Crosby, Brass (1725–93), of Chelsfield, Kent'. Government-owned website. *History of Parliament Online*, 8 February 2016. http://www.historyofparliamentonline.org/volume/1754-1790/member/crosby-brass-1725-93.

Church of England, ed. *An Homelie against Disobedience and Wylfull Rebellion*. London: Richard Iugge and Iohn Cawood, 1570.

Church of England. *[[II. 21.] An Homilie against Disobedience and Wylfull Rebellion. (A Thankisgeving for the Suppression of the Last Rebellion.) B.L.]*. 2nd ed. London: Richard Jugge and John Cawood, 1573.

Claffey, Hugh Joseph. 'Thanksgivings in the Reign of Queen Anne: An Investigation of Accountable Opinion'. PhD thesis, Trinity College Dublin, 2018. http://www.tara.tcd.ie/bitstream/handle/2262/83756/Thanksgivings%20of%20Queen%20Anne.pdf?sequence=2&isAllowed=y.

Clark, J. C. D. 'England's Ancien Regime as a Confessional State'. *Albion: A Quarterly Journal Concerned with British Studies* 21, no. 3 (1989): 450–74. doi:10.2307/4050089.

Clark, J. C. D. *Revolution and Rebellion – State and Society in England in the Seventeenth and Eighteenth Centuries*. Cambridge: Cambridge University Press, 1986.

Clark, J. C. D. *The Language of Liberty 1660–1832: Political Discourse and Social Dynamics in the Anglo-American World, 1660–1832*. Cambridge: Cambridge University Press, 1993. doi:10.1017/CBO9780511622076.

Clark, J. C. D. 'The Re-Enchantment of the World? Religion and Monarchy in Eighteenth-Century Europe'. In *Monarchy and Religion. The Transformation of Royal Culture in Eighteenth-Century Europe*, 41–78. Studies of the German Historical Institute, London. Oxford: Oxford University Press, 2007.

Claydon, Tony. *Europe and the Making of England, 1660–1760*. Cambridge: Cambridge University Press, 2007.

Claydon, Tony. 'The Revolution in Foreign Policy, 1688–1713'. In *The Final Crisis of the Stuart Monarchy. The Revolutions of 1688–91 in Their British, Atlantic and European Contexts*, 219–42. Studies in Early Modern Cultural, Political and Social History. Woodbridge: Boydell & Brewer, 2013.

Claydon, Tony. 'The Sermon Culture of the Glorious Revolution. Williamite Preaching and Jacobite Anti-Preaching 1685–1702'. In *The Oxford Handbook of the Early Modern Sermons*, edited by Hugh Adlington, Peter McCullough, and Emma Rhatigan, 480–94. Oxford/New York: Oxford University Press, 2011.

Clifton, Robin. *The Last Popular Rebellion: The Western Rising of 1685*. London: Maurice Temple Smith, 1984.

Cohen, I. Bernard. *Revolution in Science*. Cambridge, MA: Belknap Press of Harvard University Press, 1985.

Coles, Elisha. *An English Dictionary Explaining the Difficult Terms That Are Used in Divinity, Husbandry, Physick, Philosophy, Law, Navigation, Mathematicks, and Other Arts and Sciences Containing Many Thousands of Hard Words, and Proper Names of Places, More Than Are in Any Other English Dictionary or Expositor*. London: Peter Parker, 1692.

Colquhoun, Patrick. *Suggestions Offered to the Consideration of the Public, and in Particular to the More Opulent Classes of the Community, for the Purpose of Reducing the Consumption of Bread Corn, and Relieving at the Same Time the Labouring People, by the Substitution of Other Cheap, Wholesome and Nourishing Food, and Especially by Means of Soup Establishments*. England: s.n., 1799.

Combe, William. *The Royal Interview: A Fragment. By the Author of A Letter from a Country Gentleman to a Member of Parliament*. 3rd ed. London: Logographic Press/J. Walter, 1789.

[Committee]. 'HO 42/22/113: Copy of a Letter to Gideon Fournier, [Magistrate of the Public Office], Union Hall [Southwark], from the Committee [for Burning the Duke of Brunswick in Effigy], Enclosing a Copy of the Proclamation Issued at Kennington Common', 6 November 1792. The National Archives, Kew. https://discovery.nationalarchives.gov.uk/details/r/C10750763.

Coningesby, George. *The Jewish Naturalization Considered with Respect to the Voice of the People, Its Own Self-Inconsistency, and the Disingenuity of Its Advocates*. s.l.: s.n., 1753.

Cooper [purporting to be the will of Reverend John Ellison], William. *The Will of a Certain Northern Vicar. [...] To Which Is Annex'd, a Codicil, Etc.* 2 (with corrections). London: for the Author, 1765.

Copeland, David. 'America, 1750–1820'. In *Press, Politics and the Public Sphere in Europe and North America, 1760–1820*, 140–58. Cambridge: Cambridge University Press, 2002.

Cosgrove, Art. 'The Gaelic Resurgence and the Geraldine Supremacy (ca. 1400–1534)'. In *The Course of Irish History*, edited by Theo W. Moody and F. X. Martin, 8th revised ed., 158–73. Cork: Mercier Press, 1994.

Cotti-Lowell, Alison. 'The "Fatal Mark": Citizenship and The Stamp Act in Revolutionary Anglo-America'. Conference talk presented at the British Society of

Eighteenth-Century Studies, 44th Annual Conference, Panel 17: American Revolution, Lecture Theatre 1, St. Hugh's College, Oxford, 7 January 2015.
Court of King's Bench. 'TS 11/177/765: Rex versus John Almon, Bookseller. Publishing Libel Entitled 'Junius's Letter to the King' in The London Museum of Politics Miscellanies and Literature'. Court record. London, 1770. Treasury Solicitor and HM Procurator General, Papers. The National Archives of the UK, Kew.
Court of King's Bench. 'TS 11/660: Rex versus Ann WEST for Publishing a Libel on the North Hants Militia in The Westminster Journal and London Political Miscellany, Saturday 12 Dec 1795'. Court record. London, 1796. Treasury Solicitor. The National Archives of the UK, Kew.
Court of the Old Bailey. 'John Love, Thomas Bean, George Purchase, Richard Price, William Price, Damage to Property, 6th September 1716 (T17160906-2)'. Digital archive hosted by The University of Sheffield, Humanities Research Institute. *The Proceedings of the OLD BAILEY – London's Central Criminal Court, 1674–1913*, 7 November 2015. http://www.oldbaileyonline.org/print.jsp?div=t17160906-2.
Covel, William. *A Declaration unto the Parliament, Council of State and Army, Shewing Impartially the Cases of the Peoples Tumults, Madness and Confusions: As Also Eleven Particulars Which Will Perfectly Cure Their Distempers, with What Persons and Calling Are Usefull Therein: Also Shewing the Benefit Which Comes by a Common Wealth Rightly Constituted in Nine Particulars and Answering Six Objections/Humbly Offered to Consideration by William Covel*. London: s.n, 1649.
Cowan, Brian, ed. 'Chapter 1. Introduction: Reading the Trial of Dr Sacheverell'. *Parliamentary History* 31: Special Issue (15 October 2012): 1–34. doi:10.1111/j.1750-0206.2012.00289.x.
Cowan, Brian. 'Doctor Sacheverell and the Politics of Celebrity in Post-Revolutionary Britain'. In *Intimacy and Celebrity in Eighteenth-Century Literary Culture: Public Interiors*, edited by Victoria Joule and Emrys D. Jones, 111–37. Public Interiors. London: Palgrave Macmillan, 2018. doi:10.1007/978-3-319-76902-8_6.
Cowan, Brian. 'Mr. Spectator and the Coffeehouse Public Sphere'. *Eighteenth-Century Studies*, Critical Networks, 37, no. 3 (2004): 345–66.
Cowell, John. *A Law Dictionary, or, the Interpreter of Words and Terms Used either in the Common or Statute Laws; of That Part of Great Britain, Call'd England, and in Tenures and Jocular Customs*. Edited by White Kennett. 6th ed. London: D. Browne/R. Sare/S. Battersby/J. Walthoe/J. Nicholson, J. Sprint/G. Conyers/T. Ballard/Edw. Place, 1708.
Cox, Gary W. 'Was the Glorious Revolution a Constitutional Watershed?' *The Journal of Economic History* 71, no. 3 (September 2012): 567–600.
Crawford, George. *The Lives and Characters, of the Officers of the Crown and State in Scotland, from the Beginning of the Reign of King David I. to the Union of the Two Kingdoms: Collected from Original Charters, Chartularies, Authentick Records, and the Most Approved Histories. To Which Is Added, an Appendix, Containing Several Original Papers Relating to the Lives, and Referring to Them. By George Crawfurd, Esq*; London: Thomas Woodman, at Camden's Head, in New Round Court, in the Strand, 1736.
Crompton, Samuel Willard. 'Margaret Green Draper (Fl. 1750–1807)'. In *American National Biography*, 6, 882–3. New York/Oxford: Oxford University Press, 1999.
Cruickshanks, Eveline. *Religion and Royal Succession: The Rage of Party*. London: Royal Stuart Society, 1997.
Cruikshank, Isaac. *Seditation, Levelling and Plundering; or, the Pretended Friends of the People in Council*. London: satirical print, 400 mm × 350 mm, 1792. https://www.britishmuseum.org/collection/object/P_1868-0808-6238.

Cunningham, Timothy. *A New and Complete Law-Dictionary: Or, General Abridgment of the Law: On a More Extensive Plan Than Any Law-Dictionary Hitherto Published: Containing Not Only the Explanation of the Terms, but Also the Law Itself, Both with Regard to Theory and Practice: Very Useful to Barristers, Justices of the Peace, Attornies, Solicitors, &c.* Vol. II. London: Law printers to the King's Most Excellent Majesty, 1765.

Curry, Thomas. 'HO 42/37/195: Copy of Resolutions, Printed by J. Stead of Gosport [Hampshire] from a Meeting Chaired by Thomas Curry, Magistrate, and Signed by over 450 People'. Gosport, Alverstoke, 1795. Home Office: Domestic Correspondence, George III. The National Archives of the UK, Kew.

Dahlgren, Peter. 'The Internet, Public Spheres, and Political Communication: Dispersion and Deliberation'. *Political Communication* 22, no. 2 (1 April 2005): 147–62. doi:10.1080/10584600590933160.

Dalrymple, John. *The Appeal of Reason to the People of England, on the Present State of Parties in the Nation.* London: T. Becket, 1763.

Dalton, Michael. *The Country Justice: Containing the Practice, Duty and Power of the Justices of the Peace, as Well in as out of Their Sessions.* London: In the Savoy: printed by Henry Lintot (assignee of Edw. Sayer, Esq;) and sold by S. Birt, at the Bible and Ball in Ave-Mary-Lane; D. Browne, at the Black Swan without Temple-Bar; and J. Shuckburgh, at the Sun next the Inner Temple-Gate in Fleetstreet, 1742.

Davies, Kenneth Gordon, ed. *Documents of the American Revolution, 1770–1783.* Colonial Office Series. Shannon: Irish University Press, 1972.

Davis, David Brion. 'Introduction'. In *The Fear of Conspiracy: Images of Un-American Subversion from the Revolution to the Present*, edited by David Brion Davis, xiii–xxiv. Ithaca, NY/London: Cornell University Press, 1971.

Davis, David Brion, and Steven Mintz. *The Boisterous Sea of Liberty: A Documentary History of America from Discovery through the Civil War.* Oxford University Press, 1998.

Davis, Mark. 'The Online Anti-Public Sphere'. *European Journal of Cultural Studies* 24, no. 1 (1 February 2021): 143–59. doi:10.1177/1367549420902799.

Davis, Richard W. Review of *English Society, 1688–1832: Ideology, Social Structure, and Political Practice during the Ancien Regime*, by J. C. D. Clark. *The American Historical Review* 92, no. 2 (1987): 412–13.

Dean, David. 'Public Space, Private Affairs: Committees, Petitions and Lobbies in the Early Modern English Parliament'. In *Parliament at Work. Parliamentary Committees, Political Power and Public Access in Early Modern England*, 169–78. Woodbridge: Boydell & Brewer, 2002.

Defoe, Daniel. *A Seasonable Expostulation with, and Friendly Reproof unto James Butler: Who, by the Men of This World, Is Still'd Duke of O-d, Relating to the Tumults of the People. By the Same Friend That Wrote to Thomas Bradbury, the Dealer in Many Words, and Henry Sacheverell, the High-Priest of St. Andrew's Holbourn.* 2nd ed. Dublin: Thomas Humes, 1715.

Defoe, Daniel. *An Account of the Riots, Tumults, and Other Treasonable Practices; since His Majesty's Accession to the Throne: With Some Remarks, Shewing the Necessity of Strengthening the Laws against Riots; Humbly Offered to the Consideration of the Parliament.* London: J. Baker, 1715.

Defoe, Daniel. *The Advantages of Scotland by an Incorporate Union with England, Compar'd with These [sic] of a Coalition with the Dutch, or League with France. In Answer to a Pamphlet, Call'd, The Advantages of the Act of Security, &c. To Which Is Added, a Postscript in Answer to the Letter Concerning the Consequence of an Incorporating Union.* Edinburgh: s.n., 1706.

Defoe, Daniel. *Vox Populi, Vox Dei: Being True Maxims of Government*. London: T. Harrison, 1709.
DeNardo, James. *Power in Numbers: The Political Strategy of Protest and Rebellion*. Princeton, NJ: Princeton University Press, 1985.
Dent, William. *Revolution Anniversary or, Patriotic Incantations*. London: etching, 248 mm × 348 mm, 1791. http://www.britishmuseum.org/research/collection_online/collection_object_details.aspx?assetId=148574001&objectId=1634906&partId=1.
Denzinger, Heinrich. *Kompendium der Glaubensbekenntnisse und der kirchlichen Lehrentscheidungen. Verbessert, erweitert, ins Deutsche übertragen und unter Mitarbeit von Helmut Hoping herausgegeben von Peter Hünermann*. 40th ed. Freiburg im Breisgau/Basel/Rome/Vienna: Herder, 2005.
Department of Justice Canada. 'The French Revolution and the Organization of Justice – Introduction'. *Department of Justice Canada*, 6 August 2017. http://www.justice.gc.ca/eng/rp-pr/csj-sjc/ilp-pji/rev1/index.html.
Dickinson, H. T. *British Pamphlets on the American Revolution, 1763–1785*. London: Pickering & Chatto, 2008.
Dickinson, H. T. 'How Revolutionary Was the "Glorious Revolution" of 1688?' *Journal for Eighteenth-Century Studies* 11, no. 2 (1988): 125–42.
Dillinger, Johannes. 'Organized Arson as a Political Crime. The Construction of a «Terrorist» Menace in the Early Modern Period'. *Crime, Histoire & Sociétés/ Crime, History & Societies* 10, no. 2 (2006): 101–22.
Dillon, Patrick. *The Last Revolution: 1688 and the Creation of the Modern World*. London: Pimlico, 2007.
Dobbs, Richard [falsely attributed to 'Arthur' in the British Library Catalogue]. *A Thanksgiving Sermon, Preach'd October the 9th, 1746: For the Happy Suppression of the Late Unnatural Rebellion*. Belfast: James Magee, 1746.
Dodd, Daniel. *The St Bartholomew's Eve Massacre: Men, Women and Children Are Thrown out of Windows or Slaughtered with Swords and Pikes on the Streets of Paris in 1572*. Engraving after D. Dodd, 1765, 1765.
Dodsley, Robert. *The Art of Preaching; in Imitation of Horace's Art of Poetry*. London: s.n., 1735.
Donald, Diana. *The Age of Caricature: Satirical Prints in the Reign of George III*. New Haven, CT: Paul Mellon Centre for Studies in British Art by Yale University Press, 1996.
Downes, Henry. *A Sermon Preach'd in Christ's-Church, Dublin, on Friday October 23rd. 1719: Being the Anniversary Commemoration of the Happy Deliverance from the Irish Rebellion and Massacre in 1641. Before His Grace Charles Duke of Bolton, Lord Lieutenant of Ireland, and the Lords Spiritual and Temporal in Parliament Assembled*. Dublin: J. Carson/J. Pepyat, 1719.
Downes, Paul. *Democracy, Revolution, and Monarchism in Early American Literature*. Cambridge: Cambridge University Press, 2009.
Drewe, Patrick. *The Church of Englands Late Conflict with, and Triumph over the Spirit of Fanaticism: Wherein Is Shown, That Dr. Sacheverells Method of Treating Fanaticks Was Apostolical. That the Distemper of Lucifer Is the Original of Dissention. That Toleration Is Unlawful in the Judgment of Dissenters Themselves*. London: J. Morphew, 1710.
Duff, Gordon E. *A Century of the English Book Trade*. 2nd ed. Folcroft, PA: Folcroft Library Editions, 1972.
Dunton, John. 'Observator. 1. On the Jacobites Objections from Religion and Our Laws against the Resisting of King James 2. Arguments from the Commission Granted by

God to Kings; That the Resisting of King James Was No Resisting of the Ordinance of God 3. Reasons Why We Ought to Submit to the Decisions of the Parliament in That Case'. *Pegasus Being an History of the Most Remarkable Events* 28 (1696): 1–2.

Dunton, John, ed. 'Quest. I. Whether the Gunpowder-Treason Was Only, as Some Tell Us, a Plot of Cecil's Making – and What's the Reason Why the Word FACTION, Etc. Charged upon the Papists, in the Common-Prayer-Book, Made in King James the First's Time, after the Discovery of the Plot, Shou'd Be Left out in Our Divine Service for That Day, for above These Twenty Years Last Past; and Those Words Being Not Repeal'd, Why Are They Not Read Still?' *Athenian Gazette or Casuistical Mercury* 19 (29 November 1691): [not paged].

Dupont, John. *The Peculiar Happiness and Excellency of the British Nation Consider'd and Explain'd: A Sermon Preach'd at Aysgarth, October 9, 1746. Being the Day Appointed by Authority for the Celebration of a General Thanksgiving to Almighty God, for the Success of His Majesty's Arms under His Royal Highness the Duke of Cumberland; and for the Entire Supression of the Late Wicked and Most Unnatural Rebellion in Scotland*. York/London: J. Hildyard/Mess. Knapton/Mess. Longman and Shewell/M. Cooper, 1747.

Dwyer, Philip G., and Lyndall Ryan. *Theatres of Violence: Massacre, Mass Killing, and Atrocity throughout History*. New York: Berghahn Books, 2012.

Earle, Peter. *Monmouth's Rebels: The Road to Sedgemoor, 1685*. London: Weidenfeld & Nicolson, 1977.

Edes, Benjamin, Benjamin Edes Jr., and Peter Edes. '[Birmingham, July 19]'. *The Boston Gazette* 1931 (1791): [not paged].

Edes, Benjamin, Benjamin Edes Jr., and Peter Edes. 'Extract of a Letter from Newcastle, May 29'. *The Boston Gazette* 1623 (1785): [not paged].

Edes, Benjamin, Benjamin Edes Jr., and Peter Edes. 'House of Commons, June 6'. *The Boston Gazette* 1359 (1780): 2.

Edes, Benjamin, and John Gill, eds. '[To the Printers]'. *The Boston Gazette* 1245 (1760): [not paged].

Edwards, Francis. *The Gunpowder Plot: A Lecture Delivered on 10 November, 1972*. Ilford: The Royal Stuart Society, 1972.

Edwards, John, ed. *Letters to the British Nation, and to the Inhabitants of Every Other Country Who May Have Heard of the Late Shameful Outrages Committed in This Part of the Kingdom, Parts 1–4. Occasioned by the Appearance of a Pamphelet, Intitled 'A Reply to the Rev. Dr. Priestley's Appeal to the Public, on the Subject of the Riots in Birmingham,' Being the Joint Production of the Principal Clergy of That Place and of Its Vicinity.* 2nd ed. London/Birmingham: s.n., 1791.

Elliot, Gilbert. 'MS Hyde 77 (5. 420): Gilbert Elliot, Earl of Minto, to Mr. Leslie, at Mr. Spottiswoode's, London (England)'. Autograph letter, signed. Berwick, 15 September 1786. Houghton Library, Harvard University, Cambridge, MA.

[Ernest Augustus, Duke of Brunswick-Calenberg and Elector of Hanover]. 'Cal. Br. 24, 1700: Die Maßregeln gegen den englischen Prätendenten und wegen der englischen Sukzession'. Diplomatic relations, severely damaged by mildew, restored in 1970. London, 1700–1715. Außenstelle Pattensen. Niedersächsisches Landesarchiv Hannover.

Erskine-Hill, Howard. 'Preface: Eveline Cruickshanks, an Appreciation'. In *Loyalty and Identity. Jacobites at Home and Abroad*, edited by Paul Monod, Murray Pittock, and Daniel Szechi, xi–xiii. Studies in Modern History. Basingstoke: Palgrave Macmillan, 2010.

Étienne, Bruno. 'Fin du politique ou fin de la politique ?' *La pensee de midi* Hors série, no. 4 (2009): 96–104. https://www.cairn.info/revue-la-pensee-de-midi-2009-4-page-96.htm.

Evans, Eric J. *William Pitt the Younger*. London/New York: Routledge/Taylor & Francis e-Library, 1999.
F.A. D.D. [attributed to Francis Atterbury]. *The Voice of the People, No Voice of God: Or, the Mistaken Arguments of a Fiery Zealot, in a Late Pamphlet [Attributed to Daniel Defoe or Lord Somers] Entitl'd Vox Populi, Vox Dei, since Publish'd under the Title of The Judgement of Whole Kingdoms and Nations, &c. Fully Confuted*. London: s.n., 1710.
Falk, Barbara J. 'Making Sense of Political Trials: Causes and Categories'. *Munk Centre for International Studies Occasional Paper Series*, 1 January 2008. https://www.academia.edu/34000206/Making_Sense_of_Political_Trials_Causes_and_Categories.
Falk, Barbara J. 'Political Trials'. Academic talk presented at the History Department Colloquium, Maastricht University, 2022.
Fechner, Fabian. 'Satirical Rebels? Irritating Anticipations in European Visualizations of Black American Insurgents around 1800'. *Revolts and Political Violence in Early Modern Imagery*, 29 October 2021, 289–313. doi:10.1163/9789004461949_014.
Fezer, Karl-Heinz. '*Recht ist Recht ist Recht ist Recht*': die Auslegung der Welt – Normativer Rechtsrealismus. Konstanz: Universitätsverlag Konstanz, 2015.
Field, Clive D. 'Counting Religion in England and Wales: The Long Eighteenth Century, c. 1680–c. 1840'. *The Journal of Ecclesiastical History* 63, no. 4 (2012): 693–720. doi:10.1017/S0022046911002533.
Fielding, Henry. *The Coffee-House Politician; or, the Justice Caught in His Own Trap. A Comedy. As It Is Acted at the Theatre Royal in Lincoln's Inn-Fields*. London: J. Watts, 1730.
Fischer, Ernst. 'Buchmarkt'. Text. *EGO – Europäische Geschichte Online*, 3 December 2010. http://ieg-ego.eu/de/threads/hintergruende/buchmarkt.
Fisher, David R. 'Vyse, Richard (1746–1825)'. *History of Parliament Online*, 1986. http://www.historyofparliamentonline.org/volume/1790-1820/member/vyse-richard-1746-1825.
Fitts, James L. 'Newcastle's Mob'. *Albion: A Quarterly Journal Concerned with British Studies* 5, no. 1 (1973): 41–9.
Flavell, Julie M. 'Government Interception of Letters from America and the Quest for Colonial Opinion in 1775'. *The William and Mary Quarterly* 58, no. 2 (April 2001): 403–30.
Flinders, Matthew. *Defending Politics: Why Democracy Matters in the 21st Century*. Oxford: Oxford University Press, 2012.
Flümann, Claudia. *Freiheit und Tyrannei: Zu einem begrifflichen Grundmuster der Englischen Revolution des 17. Jahrhunderts*. Vol. 39. Arbeitskreis Deutsche England-Forschung. Berlin: Philo, 1999.
Föcking, Marc, and Claudia Schindler. *Der Krieg hat kein Loch: Friedenssehnsucht und Kriegsapologie in der Frühen Neuzeit*. Heidelberg: Universitätsverlag Winter GmbH, 2014.
Fordyce, David, and Robert Dodsley. *Theodorus: A Dialogue Concerning the Art of Preaching*. Oxford: R. Dodsley in Pall-Mall, 1700.
Fordyce, James, and Hugh Mitchell. *The Preacher's Manual, Containing the Art of Preaching, in Imitation of Horace's Art of Poetry, by Dr. Fordyce. The Popular Preacher, or, Twenty Rules for the Man Who Would Be a Popular Preacher*. Edinburgh: D. Webster and Son, 1820.
Formisano, Ronald P. 'State Development in the Early Republic: Substance and Structure, 1780–1840'. In *Contesting Democracy. Substance & Structure in American Political History 1775–2000*, edited by Byron E. Shafer and Anthony J. Badger, 7–36. Kansas: University Press of Kansas, 2001.

Frank, Michael C. 'Plots on London'. In *Literature and Terrorism: Comparative Perspectives*, edited by Michael C. Frank and Eva Gruber, 41–65. Studies in Comparative Literature 66. Amsterdam: Rodopi, 2012.

Frank, Michael C., and Eva Gruber, eds. *Literature and Terrorism. Comparative Perspectives*. Studies in Comparative Literature 66. Amsterdam/New York: Editions Rodopi B.V., 2012.

Franklin, Benjamin. 'On Government. No. I, from the Pennsylvania Gazette, April I, 1736'. In *The Works of Benjamin Franklin in Twelve Volumes. Including the Private as Well as the Official and Scientific Correspondence Together with The Unmutilated and Correct Version of the Autobiography*, reprinted ed., II, 10–14. New York/London: The Knickerbocker Press, 1904.

Franklin, Benjamin. 'On Government. No. II, from the Pennsylvania Gazette, April 8, 1736'. In *The Works of Benjamin Franklin in Twelve Volumes. Including the Private as Well as the Official and Scientific Correspondence Together with The Unmutilated and Correct Version of the Autobiography*, Repr., II, 14–17. New York/London: The Knickerbocker Press, 1904.

Franklin, Benjamin. 'Plain Truth; or Serious Considerations on the Present State of the City of Philadelphia and the Province of Pennsylvania, by a Tradesman of Philadelphia'. In *The Works of Benjamin Franklin in Twelve Volumes. Including the Private as Well as the Official and Scientific Correspondence Together with The Unmutilated and Correct Version of the Autobiography*, Repr., II, 150–70. New York /London: The Knickerbocker Press, 1904.

Fraser, James. *A Genuine Narrative of the Life, Behaviour, and Conduct, of Simon, Lord Fraser, of Lovat: From His Birth at Beaufort near Inverness, in 1667, to His Execution on Tower-Hill, on Thursday, April 9, 1747. Containing a Vast Variety of Actions in the Different Scenes of Life in Which His Lordship Was Engag'd; His Artful Management in Procuring a Pass from the Duke of Queensberry, to Go into the Highlands to Execute a Commission from the Court of France, to Stir Up a Rebellion, and the Double Part He Acted till He Had Done His Business, and Got Safe Back to France*. London: B. Cole, 1747.

Friend to Both Countries [pseud.]. *America Vindicated from the High Charge of Ingratitude and Rebellion: With a Plan of Legislation, Proposed to the Consideration of Both Houses for Establishing a Permanent and Solid Foundation, for a Just Constitutional Union, between Great Britain and Her Colonies*. Devizes/London: T. Burrough/Ridley/Stuart, 1775.

Furlong, Nicholas. *Fr. John Murphy of Boolavogue: 1753–1798*. Reprint of 1991 ed. Kellystown, Drinagh: Distillery Press, 2007.

Garcia-Gibson, Francisco. 'Undemocratic Climate Protests'. *Journal of Applied Philosophy* 39, no. 1 (1 February 2022): 162–79. doi:10.1111/japp.12548.

Gaff, Alan D. *Bayonets in the Wilderness: Anthony Wayne's Legion in the Old Northwest*. Norman: University of Oklahoma Press, 2008.

Gage, Thomas. *By His Excellency the Honourable Thomas Gage, Esq; A Proclamation: Whereas the Infatuated Multitudes, Who Have Long Suffered Themselves to Be Conducted by Certain Well Known Incendiaries and Traitors [...] Have at Length Proceeded to Avowed Rebellion [...] Given at Boston, This Twelfth Day of June*. Boston: Margaret Draper, 1775.

Gage, Thomas. *By His Excellency the Honourable Thomas Gage, General and Commander in Chief of All His Majesty's Forces in North America, &c. &c. &c: Whereas, Complaints Have at Times Been Made by the Country People, of Not Obtaining the Payments Due to Them for the Transportation of Troops, Provisions, Military Stores, &c*. New York: s.n, 1769.

Gage, Thomas, and Francis Bernard. *Letters to the Right Honourable the Earl of Hillsborough, from Governor Bernard, General Gage, and the Honourable His Majesty's Council for the Province of Massachusetts-Bay. With an Appendix, Containing Divers Proceedings Referred to in the Said Letters*. Boston, MA/London: Edes and Gill/J. Almon, 1769.

Garnham, Neal. 'Riot Acts, Popular Protest, and Protestant Mentalities in Eighteenth-Century Ireland'. *The Historical Journal* 49, no. 2 (2006): 403–23.

Gaunt, Peter. *English Civil War: A Military History*. London: I.B. Tauris, 2014.

Gentles, Ian. *Oliver Cromwell: God's Warrior and the English Revolution*. 1st ed. British History in Perspective. Basingstoke: Palgrave Macmillan, 2011.

Gerard, Alexander. *Liberty the Cloke of Maliciousness: Both in the American Rebellion, and in the Manners of the Times. A Sermon Preached at Old Aberdeen, February 26, 1778, Being the Fast-Day Appointed by Proclamation, on Account of the Rebellion in America*. Aberdeen/London/Edinburgh: J. Chalmers & Co./Alexander Thomson/T. Cadell/W. Creech, 1778.

German Chancellery in London. 'Hann. 92, 59: Deutsche Kanzlei in London. Gratulationen an Georg I zur Thronfolge in Großbritannien'. Correspondence. London et al., 1714. Außenstelle Pattensen. Niedersächsisches Landesarchiv Hannover.

Gestrich, Andreas. 'The Early-Modern State and the Rise of the Public Sphere. A Systems-Theory Approach'. In *Beyond the Public Sphere. Opinions, Publics, Spaces in Early Modern Europe*, edited by Massimo Rospocher, 27, 31–52. Annali Dll'Istituto Storico Italo-Germanico in Trento/Jahrbuch Des Italienisch-Deutschen Historischen Instituts in Trient. Bologna/Berlin: Società editrice il Mulino/Duncker & Humblot, 2012.

Gillam, Samuel. *Remarks on the Riot Act, with an Application to Certain Recent and Alarming Facts*. London: G. Kearsley, 1768.

Gillray, James. *A Birmingham Toast, as given on the 14th of July, by the Revolution Society*. England: hand-coloured etching, 275 mm × 500 mm, 1791. https://www.britishmuseum.org/collection/object/P_1851-0901-538.

Gillray, James. *Anecdote Maçonnique. A Masonic Anecdote*. England: hand-coloured etching, 500 mm × 505 mm, 1786. https://www.britishmuseum.org/collection/object/P_1868-0808-5578.

Gillray, James. *Anti-Saccharites, -or- John Bull and His Family Leaving off the Use of Sugar*. London: hand-coloured etching, 313 mm × 397 mm, printed by H. Humphrey, 1792. https://www.britishmuseum.org/collection/object/P_1851-0901-592.

Gillray, James. *The Tree of Liberty Must Be Planted Immediately!* England: hand-coloured etching, 355 mm × 251 mm, 1797. https://www.britishmuseum.org/collection/object/P_1868-0808-6594.

Gilmour, Ian. *Riot, Risings and Revolution: Governance and Violence in Eighteenth-Century England*. London: Pimlico, 1993.

Glickman, Gabriel. *The English Catholic Community, 1688–1745: Politics, Culture and Ideology*. Woodbridge: Boydell Press, 2009.

Godsey, Jr, William D. *Nobles and Nation in Central Europe: Free Imperial Knights in the Age of Revolution, 1750–1850*. Cambridge: Cambridge University Press, 2004.

Goldar, John. 'The Unfortunate Death of Major Andre (Adjutant General to the English Army) at Head Quarters in New York, Octr. 2, 1780, Who Was Found within the American Lines in the Character of a Spy'. In *The New, Comprehensive and Complete History of England: From the Earliest Period of Authentic Information to the Middle of the Year, MDCCLXXXIII*, edited by Edward Barnard and John Millar. London: A. Hogg, 1783.

Goldsmith, M. M. 'Mandeville, Bernard (1670-1733)'. In *Oxford Dictionary of National Biography. In Association with The British Academy. From the Earliest Times to the Year 2000*, 36, 398-403. Oxford: Oxford University Press, 2004.

Gordon, Alan. 'Introduction: The New Cultural History and Urban History: Intersections'. *Urban History Review/Revue d'histoire Urbaine* 33, no. 1 (2004): 3-7.

Gotthard, Axel. *Das Alte Reich: 1495-1806*. Darmstadt: Wissenschaftliche Buchgesellschaft, 2003.

Gould, Philip. *Writing the Rebellion: Loyalists and the Literature of Politics in British America*. Oxford: Oxford University Press, 2013.

Graves, Michael A. R. *The Parliaments of Early Modern Europe, 1400-1700*. New York: Longman, 2001.

Green, B., ed. 'London, October 4/London, October 15'. *Boston News-Letter* 624 (2 April 1716): 2.

Green, B., ed. 'There Having Lately Been Great Endeavours Used by a Sort of People Fomerly Unknown to This and the Other Provinces of New-England to Debauch the Minds of Unheeding Youth, as to Their Religion, by Divers Printed Pamphlets, and Their Loyalty by More Private Practices, It Seems Not Unseasonable to Publish from the Political State of Sept. Last Two of the Celebrated BRITISH CATO's Lucubrations, Being as Follows'. *Boston News Letter* 1050 (12 March 1724): 1-4.

Green, Timothy, ed. *To the People of America: Stop Him! Stop Him! Stop Him! One Hundred Pounds Lawful Money Reward! A Wolf in Sheep's Clothing! A Traitor! Whereas Isaac Wilkins, of the Province of New-York, Has Made His Escape from the Place of His Former Residence, after Having Betrayed the Confidence of His Constituents, and Villanously Consented, That They [...] Should Become Abject Slaves, to the Mercenary and Tyrannical Parliament of Great-Britain*. New London, CT: Timothy Green, 1775.

Greene, Jack P. 'Empire and Identity from the Glorious Revolution to the American Revolution'. In *The Eighteenth Century*, edited by P. J. Marshall, 208-30. The Oxford History of the British Empire, II. Oxford: Oxford University Press, 1998.

Greene, Jack P. *The Constitutional Origins of the American Revolution*. Cambridge: Cambridge University Press, 2010.

Greenstein, Fred I. 'Presidential Difference in the Early Republic: The Highly Disparate Leadership Styles of Washington, Adams, and Jefferson'. *Presidential Studies Quarterly* 36, no. 3 (2006): 373-90.

Gregory, Jeremy, and John Stevenson. *The Routledge Companion to Britain in the Eighteenth Century*. Abingdon: Routledge, 2007.

Greig, Martin. 'Burnet, Gilbert (1643-1715), Bishop of Salisbury and Historian'. In *Oxford Dictionary of National Biography. In Association with The British Academy. From the Earliest Times to the Year 2000*, 8, 908-23. Oxford: Oxford University Press, 2004.

Griesse, Malte. 'Aufstandsprävention in der Frühen Neuzeit: Länderübergreifende Wahrnehmungen von Revolten und Verrechtlichungsprozesse'. In *Revolten und politische Verbrechen vom 12.-19. Jahrhundert. Reaktionen der Rechtssysteme und juristisch-politische Diskurse/Rivolte e crimini politici tra XII e XIX secolo: Reazioni del sistema giuridico e discorso giuridico-politico*, edited by Angela de Benedictis and Karl Härter, 173-209. Studien zur europäischen Rechtsgeschichte. Frankfurt: Klostermann, 2013.

Griesse, Malte, ed. *Early-Modern Revolts in Their Transnational Representation*. Bielefeld: transcript, 2013.

Griesse, Malte. *Frühneuzeitliche Revolten als Kommunikationsereignisse. Konzeption der Nachwuchsgruppe*. Konstanz: Universität Konstanz, 2013.

Griesse, Malte. 'Revolten als Krankheiten im politischen Körper: England als paracelsischer Sonderweg in der frühneuzeitlichenKörpermetaphorik?' In *Körpermetaphern in der politischen Semantik der Vormoderne*, edited by Hiram Kümper, 1-32, [in print].

Grimm, Dieter. 'Der Staat in der kontinentaleuropäischen Tradition'. In *Abschied vom Staat - Rückkehr zum Staat?*, edited by Rüdiger Voigt, 27-50. Baden-Baden: Nomos, 1993.

Guidi, [Giuseppe]. 'Hann. 92, 2221: Abbé Guidi nach London'. Diplomatic relations. Hanover et al., 1700-1800. Außenstelle Pattensen. Niedersächsisches Landesarchiv Hannover.

Gurney, Joseph, ed. *The Trial of George Gordon: Esquire, Commonly Called Lord George Gordon. For High Treason, at the Bar of the Court of King's Bench, on Monday, February 5th, 1781. The Second Part. Taken in Short-Hand*. 2nd ed. London: G. Kearsly/M. Gurney, 1781.

Gurney, Joseph. *The Trial of James O'Coigly, Otherwise Called James Quigley, Otherwise Called James John Fivey; Arthur O'Connor, Esq., John Binns, John Allen, and Jeremiah Leary for High Treason, under a Special Commission, at Maidstone, in Kent, on Monday the Twenty-First, and Tuesday the Twenty-Second Days of May, 1798*. Edited by Special Commission of Oyer and Terminer. London: M. Gurney, 1798.

Habermas, Jürgen. *Communication and the Evolution of Society*. Translated by Thomas McCarthy. Oxford: Alexander Street Press, 1991.

Hahn, Peter-Michael. 'Besprechungen: C. Sozialgeschichte: Ronald G. Asch: Europäischer Adel in der Frühen Neuzeit. Eine Einführung (UTB 3086). Böhlau/Cologne/ Weimar/Vienna 2008, 383 S., 17,90 EUR.' *VSWG: Vierteljahrschrift für Sozial- und Writschaftsgeschichte* 96, no. 1 (2009): 88-9.

Hale, John Rigby. *The Evolution of British Historiography. From Bacon to Namier. [An Anthology]*. London: Meridian Books, 1967.

Halloran, Brian M. 'Hay, George (1729-1811), Vicar Apostolic of the Lowland District'. In *Dictionary of National Biography*, 25, 1000-2. Oxford: Oxford University Press, 2004.

Hämmerle, Christa. 'Die K. (u.) K. Armee als "Schule des Volkes"? Zur Geschichte der Allgemeinen Wehrpflicht in der multinationalen Habsburgermonarchie (1866-1914/18)'. In *Der Bürger als Soldat: Die Militarisierung europäischer Gesellschaften im langen 19. Jahrhundert: ein internationaler Vergleich*, edited by Christian Jansen, 175-213. Essen: Ruhr Klartext-Verlag, 2004.

Hammond, J. L. (John Lawrence), and Barbara (Bradby) Hammond. *The Village Labourer 1760-1832, a Study in the Government of England before the Reform Bill*. London, New York [etc.]: Longman's, Green, and Co., 1912. http://archive.org/details/villagelabourer00hammiala.

Hardwick, Joseph. 'Anglican Church Expansion and the Recruitment of Colonial Clergy for New South Wales and the Cape Colony, c. 1790-1850'. *The Journal of Imperial and Commonwealth History* 37, no. 3 (1 September 2009): 361-81. doi:10.1080/03086530903157565.

Harris, Carolyn. *Queenship and Revolution in Early Modern Europe: Henrietta Maria and Marie Antoinette*. New York: Palgrave Macmillan, 2016.

Harris, Christopher. *Public Lives, Private Virtues: Images of American Revolutionary War Heroes, 1782-1832*. New York/London: Garland, 2000.

Harris, Jonathan Gil. *Foreign Bodies and the Body Politic: Discourses of Social Pathology in Early Modern England*. Vol. 25. Cambridge Studies in Renaissance Literature and Culture. Cambridge: Cambridge University Press, 1998.

Harris, Mark Cameron. 'The Moral Economy of the 1719–20 Calico Riots'. PhD thesis, University of Alberta, 2015.
Harris, Sean. 'The Massacre of St George's Fields and the Petition of William Allen'. *UK Parliament – Petitions Committee*, 31 October 2016. https://committees.parliament.uk/committee/326/petitions-committee/news/99182/the-massacre-of-st-georges-fields-and-the-petition-of-william-allen/.
Harris, Tim. *London Crowds in the Reign of Charles II: Propaganda and Politics from the Restoration until the Exclusion Crisis*. Cambridge: Cambridge University Press, 1987.
Harris, Tim. Review of *Governed by Opinion*, by Dagmar Freist. *Albion: A Quarterly Journal Concerned with British Studies* 30, no. 3 (1998): 494–6. doi:10.2307/4053309.
Harris, Tim. *Revolution: The Great Crisis of the British Monarchy, 1685–1720*. London: Allen Lane, 2006.
Harrison, Mark. '"To Raise and Dare Resentment": The Bristol Bridge Riot of 1793 Re-Examined'. *The Historical Journal* 26, no. 3 (1983): 557–85.
Härter, Karl, and Beatrice de Graaf. 'Vom Majestätsverbrechen zum Terrorismus. Politische Kriminalität, Recht, Justiz und Polizei zwischen Früher Neuzeit und 20. Jahrhundert'. In *Vom Majestätsverbrechen zum Terrorismus. Politische Kriminalität, Recht, Justiz und Polizei zwischen Früher Neuzeit und 20. Jahrhundert*, edited by Beatrice de Graaf and Karl Härter, 1–22. Studien zur europäischen Rechtsgeschichte. Veröffentlichungen des Max-Planck-Institus für europäische Rechtsgeschichte 268. Frankfurt: Klostermann, 2012.
Hartley, Cody. 'John Singleton Copley: Portrait of H. R. H. the Prince of Wales at a Review, Attended by Lord Heathfield, General Turner, Col. Bloomfield, and Baron Eben; Col. Quinton in the Distance (1809)'. *Museum of Fine Arts, Boston*, 7 November 2014. http://www.mfa.org/collections/object/portrait-of-h-r-h-the-prince-of-wales-at-a-review-attended-by-lord-heathfield-general-turner-col-bloomfield-and-baron-eben-col-quinton-in-the-distance-32175.
Hatton, Ragnhild Marie. *George I, Elector and King*. London: Thames and Hudson, 1978.
Hauswedell, Christa. 'Geheimgesellschaften gegen LAW AND ORDER. Radikalisierung und Militarisierung nationaler, sozialer und konfessioneller Gegensätze in Irland im 19. Jahrhundert'. In *Der Bürger als Soldat: Die Militarisierung europäischer Gesellschaften im langen 19. Jahrhundert: ein internationaler Vergleich*, 214–29. Essen: Ruhr Klartext-Verlag, 2004.
Hawarth, Abraham. 'SP 36/80/3/15: Information of Abraham Hawarth of Manchester [Lancashire]'. Manchester, 18 January 1746. SP 36/80/3/15. The National Archives, Kew. https://discovery.nationalarchives.gov.uk/details/r/C15669418.
Hawkins, Jonathan. 'Imperial '45: The Jacobite Rebellion in Transatlantic Context'. *The Journal of Imperial and Commonwealth History* 24, no. 1 (January 1996): 24–47.
Hay, George. *A Memorial to the Public: In Behalf of the Roman Catholics of Edinburgh and Glasgow; Containing, an Account of the Late Riot against Them on the Second and Following Days of February, 1779*. 2nd ed. London: J. P. Coghlan, 1779.
Haydon, Colin. 'Sherlock, Thomas, Bishop of London'. *Oxford Dictionary of National Biography*, 2004. https://doi.org/10.1093/odnb/9780192683120.013.25380.
Haywood, Ian. *The Revolution in Popular Literature. Print, Politics and the People, 1790–1860*. Cambridge/New York/Melbourne/Madrid/Cape Town: Cambridge University Press, 2004.
Heath, James. *The Riot in Broad Street, on the Seventh of June 1780/To the Gentlemen of the London Light Horse Volunteers and Military Foot Association, This Memorial of Their Patriotic Conduct, Is Inscribed by Their Obliged Servants, John and Josiah Boydell*. London: John & Josiah Boydell, 1790.

Hellmann, Kai-Uwe, and Karsten Fischer. 'Einleitung: Niklas Luhmanns politische Theorie in der politikwissenschaftlichen Diskussion'. In *Das System der Politik. Niklas Luhmanns Politische Theorie*, 9–18. Wiesbaden: Westdeutscher Verlag, 2003.

Helmers, Helmer. 'Public Diplomacy in Early Modern Europe: Towards a New History of News'. *Media History* 22, no. 3–4 (2016): 401–20.

Henley, John. *The Victorious Stroke for Old England: All Preachers Make All Hearers One Man against Her Enemies, and Down Jericho: Explain'd and Enforc'd in Several Remarkable Discourses, Occasion'd by a Case, Interesting Every Man in Britain, of a Preacher in London*. 5th ed. London: Primate Reason, Esq, 1748.

Henshall, Nicholas. 'Power and Politics in Old Regime France & The Ancien Regime'. *History Today Book Reviews*. Accessed 9 August 2017. http://www.historytoday.com/nicholas-henshall/power-and-politics-old-regime-france-ancien-regime.

Herzog, Martin. 'Revolution in Großbritannien: Wir Sind Das Volk!' *DIE ZEIT*, No. 20/2014, 27 July 2014. http://www.zeit.de/2014/29/franzoesische-revolution-john-thelwall.

Hessayon, Ariel, and David Finnegan, eds. *Varieties of Seventeenth- and Early Eighteenth-Century English Radicalism in Context*. Farnham: Ashgate, 2011.

Hickes, George. *The Spirit of Fanaticism: Exemplify'd in the Tryals of Mr. James Mitchel (a Presbyterian Minister, Who Was Hang'd at Edinburgh, for an Attempt Made upon the Archbishop of St. Andrews.) And Major Thomas Weir (a Gifted Brother at the Knack of Extempore Prayer) Who Was Burnt between Edinburgh and Leith April the 11th, 1670. for Adultery, Beastiality with a Mare and a Cow, and Incest with His Own Sister, Who Was Likewise Hang'd the Next Day after Him*. London: E. Curll, 1710.

Hillary, Anthony Aylmer. *Oliver Cromwell and the Challenge to the Monarchy*. Commonwealth and International Library. History Division. Oxford: Pergamon, 1969.

Hindley, Geoffrey. *Magna Carta. The Origins of Liberty, from Runnymede to Washington*. First paperback edition of 2008 hard cover. A Brief History Of. Edinburgh: Constable & Robinson Ltd, 2015.

Hitchcock, Gad. *A Sermon Preached before His Excellency Thomas Gage, Esq; Governor : The Honorable His Majesty's Council, and the Honorable House of Representatives, of the Province of the Massachusetts-Bay in New-England, May 25th, 1774. Being the Anniversary of the Election of His Majesty's Council for Said Province*. Boston, MA: Edes and Gill, 1774.

Hobhouse, Benjamin. *Three Letters [Addressed to 'the Several Patriotic Societies in London and Its Neighbourhood' and to the Editor of the Morning Chronicle, Occasioned by the 'Prevailing Disposition to Riot and Insurrection']*. London: s.n., 1792.

Hofstadter, Richard. 'Chapter One: Party and Opposition in the Eighteenth Century'. In *Chapter One. Party and Opposition in the Eighteenth Century*, 1–39. Berkeley: University of California Press, 2020. doi:10.1525/9780520341609-002.

Hofstadter, Richard. 'The Paranoid Style in American Politics'. In *The Fear of Conspiracy: Images of Un-American Subversion from the Revolution to the Present*, edited by David Brion Davis, 2–8. Ithaca, NY/London: Cornell University Press, 1979.

Hogarth, William. *An Election Entertainment Plate I/Four Prints of an Election*. London: etching and engraving, 415 mm × 543 mm, 1755. https://www.britishmuseum.org/collection/object/P_1850-0810-523.

Hogg, Alexander, ed. *The Malefactor's Register: Or, the New Newgate and Tyburn Calendar. Containing the Authentic Lives, Trials, Accounts of Executions, and Dying Speeches, of the Most Notorious Violators of the Laws of Their Country; [...] from the Year 1700, to Lady-Day 1780 [...] Embellished with a Most Elegant and Superb Set of Copper Plates*. London: Alexander Hogg, 1781.

Hole, Robert. *Pulpits, Politics and Public Order in England, 1760–1832.* Cambridge: Cambridge University Press, 1989.

Holmes, Geoffrey. 'The Sacheverell Riots: The Crowd and the Church in Early Eighteenth-Century London'. *Past & Present* 72, no. 1 (1976): 55–85.

Holt, Joseph. *Memoirs of Joseph Holt: General of the Irish Rebels, in 1798.* Edited by Thomas Crofton Croker. Vol. 1. London: H. Colburn, 1838.

Home, John. *The History of the Rebellion in the Year 1745.* London: A. Strahan/T. Cadell, Jun./W. Davies, 1802.

Hoppit, Julian. *Land of Liberty?: England 1689–1727.* Oxford: Clarendon Press, 2000.

Horn, Eva. 'Der nackte Leib des Volkes: Volkskörper, Gesetz und Leben in Georg Büchners Danton's Tod'. In *Bilder und Gemeinschaften*, edited by Beate Fricke, Markus Klammer, and Stefan Neuner, 237–70. Munich: Fink, 2011.

Horsmanden, Daniel. *The New-York Conspiracy, or, A History of the Negro Plot: With the Journal of the Proceedings against the Conspirators at New-York in the Years 1741–2.* History of the Negro Plot. New York: Southwick & Pelsue, 1810.

Howe, John. *A Song Composed by the British Soldiers, after the Battle at Bunker-Hill, on the 17th Day of June, 1775.* Edited by Margaret Draper. Boston, MA: Draper's printing-office, 1775.

Howe, William. *Teucro Duce Nil Desperandom. First Battalion of Pennsylvania Loyalists, Commanded by His Excellency Sir William Howe, K.B.* Philadelphia: James Humphreys, 1777.

Howell, Thomas Jones, William Cobbett, and David Jardine, eds. *A Complete Collection of State Trials and Proceedings for High Treason and Other Crimes and Misdemeanors: From the Earliest Period to the Year 1783: With Notes and Other Illustrations.* London: Longman/Hurst/Rees/Orme/Browne, 1812.

Hume, David. *Essays and Treatises: On Several Subjects.* 2nd ed. Vol. IV. Edinburgh: A. Kincaid, and A. Donaldson, 1753.

Hume, David. *Political Discourses.* 2nd ed. Edinburgh: R: Fleming, for A. Kincaid and A. Donaldson, 1752.

Hume, Janice. *Popular Media and the American Revolution: Shaping Collective Memory.* New York: Routledge, 2014.

Humphrey, George. *A Sacrifice to Slavery, Dedicated without Permission to the Puppet Player in Downing Street (Description).* Hand-coloured etching, 1787. The British Museum, London. https://www.britishmuseum.org/collection/object/P_1868-0808-5601.

Humphrey, William. *A Coalition between the Fox & the Badger, or the Honey Moon of Their Happy Union (1784).* Etching, 1783. The British Museum, London. https://www.britishmuseum.org/collection/object/P_1868-0808-4937.

Hunt, Lynn, ed. *The New Cultural History. Studies on the History of Society and Culture.* Berkeley/Los Angeles/London: University of California Press, 1989.

Hunt, William, ed. 'Sacheverell, Henry'. In *Dictionary of National Biography*, 50, [not paged]. London: Smith, Elder & Co., 1885–1900. https://en.wikisource.org/wiki/Dictionary_of_National_Biography,_1885-1900/Sacheverell,_Henry.

Hutchinson, Thomas. 'Hutchinson to the Gentlemen of the House of Representatives'. Manuscript letter. Boston, MA, 9 June 1773. Massachusetts State Archives Collection, Colonial Period, 1622–1788, Speeches and messages, 1766–1774. Massachusetts State Archives, Boston, MA.

Ibbetson, James. *Public Virtue, the Great Cause of the Happiness and Prosperity of Any People,* 1746.

Iggers, Georg G. *Geschichtswissenschaft im 20. Jahrhundert. Ein kritischer Überblick im internationalen Zusammenhang.* Göttingen: Vandenhoeck & Ruprecht, 2007.
Ihalainen, Pasi. *The Discourse on Political Pluralism in Early Eighteenth-Century England: A Conceptual Study with Special Reference to Terminology of Religious Origin.* Vol. 36. Bibliotheca Historica. Helsinki: Suomen Historiallinen Seura, 1999.
Ingoldsby, William. *The Doctrine of the Church of England [...] against Disobedience and Wilfull Rebellion.* London: G.I., 1642.
Jackson, Alvin. *Ireland 1798-1998: War, Peace and Beyond.* 2nd ed. Chichester: Wiley-Blackwell, 2010.
Jackson, Clare. 'Jonathan Swift's Peace of Utrecht'. In *Performances of Peace: Utrecht 1713*, edited by Renger E. de Bruin, Cornelis van der Haven, Lotte Jensen, and David Onnekink, 142-58. Leiden: Brill, 2015.
Jacob, Giles. *A New Law-Dictionary: Containing the Interpretation and Definition of Words and Terms Used in the Law, and Also the Whole Law and Practice Thereof, under All the Heads and Titles of the Same, Together with Such Informations Relating Thereto as Explain the History and Antiquity of the Law, and Our Manners, Customs, and Original Government, Collected and Abstracted from All Dictionaries, Abridgments, Institutes, Reports, Year-Books, Charters, Registers, Chronicles, and Histories, Published to This Time.* Edited by Sir John Holt. 7th ed. London: H. Lintot, for R. Ware, 1756.
Jefferson, Thomas. 'Kentucky Resolutions of 1798 and 1799 [The Original Draft Prepared by Thomas Jefferson]', Kindle ed. s.l.: The Perfect Library, originally published in 1799.
Jefferson, Thomas. *Memoir, Correspondence, And Miscellanies, From the Papers of Thomas Jefferson.* Edited by Thomas Jefferson Randolph. Vol. 1. 3 vols. The Writings of Thomas Jefferson. Charlottesville, VA: F. Carr & Co., 1829.
Jefferson, Thomas. *The Writings of Thomas Jefferson: Being His Autobiography, Correspondence, Reports, Messages, Addresses, and Other Writings, Official and Private.* Edited by H. A. Washington. Repr. Vol. 1. 9 vols. Cambridge Library Collection. Cambridge/New York: Cambridge University Press, 2011.
Johnson, Samuel. *A Journey to the Western Islands of Scotland.* 2nd ed. London: William Strahan and Thomas Cadell, 1775.
Johnston, Warren. *National Thanksgivings and Ideas of Britain, 1689-1816.* Woodbridge/Rochester, NY: Boydell & Brewer, 2020.
Johnstone, James. *Memoirs of the Rebellion in 1745 and 1746.* London: Longman, Hurst, Rees, Orme, Brown, 1820.
Jones, Clyve. '1720-23 and All That: A Reply to Eveline Cruickshanks'. *Albion: A Quarterly Journal Concerned with British Studies* 26, no. 1 (1994): 41-53. doi:10.2307/4052098.
Jones, Inga. 'A Sea of Blood? Massacres during the Wars of the Three Kingdoms'. In *Theatres of Violence. Massacre, Mass Killing and Atrocity throughout History*, edited by Philip G. Dwyer and Lyndall Ryan, 63-80. Studies on War and Genocide 11. New York/Oxford: Berghahn Books, 2012.
Jordanova, Ludmilla J. *The Look of the Past: Visual and Material Evidence in Historical Practice.* Cambridge: Cambridge University Press, 2012.
Kater, Thomas. 'Bürger-Krieger: Immanuel Kant, Adam Smith und Adam Ferguson über Militär und Gesellschaft'. In *Der Bürger als Soldat: Die Militarisierung europäischer Gesellschaften im langen 19. Jahrhundert: ein internationaler Vergleich*, edited by Christian Jansen, 27-46. Essen: Ruhr Klartext-Verlag, 2004.
Keen, Paul. Review of *The Spirit of Despotism: Invasions of Privacy in the 1790s*, by John Barrell. *Modern Philology* 107, no. 4 (2010): E121-25.

Kemp, Geoff. 'The "End of Censorship" and the Politics of Toleration, from Locke to Sacheverell'. *Parliamentary History* 31, no. 1 (2012): 47–68.
Kennedy, Patrick. *Father Murphy: Patriot Priest of Boolavogue*. Dublin: Veritas Publications, 1988.
Kennedy, Rick. Review of *Faith and the Founders of the American Republic*, by Daniel L. Dreisbach and Mark David Hall. *Journal for Eighteenth-Century Studies* 38, no. 4 (December 2015): 617–18.
Kentucky General Assembly. *Resolutions Adopted by the Kentucky General Assembly*. Edited by Princeton University Library. Vol. 30. The Papers of Thomas Jefferson. Princeton, NJ: Princeton University Press, 1798. https://jeffersonpapers.princeton.edu/selected-documents/resolutions-adopted-kentucky-general-assembly.
Kenyon, J. P. *Revolution Principles: The Politics of Party 1689–1720*. Cambridge: Cambridge University Press, 1990.
Kenyon, Lady Mary. 'DDKE/Acc. 7840 HMC/1393A: Mary, Lady Kenyon, to Lord Kenyon'. Letter. London, 16 July 1795. DDKE/acc. 7840 HMC/1393A. Lancashire Archives. https://discovery.nationalarchives.gov.uk/details/r/64e7b05b-cc3f-4267-8b54-5e6c89a5a256.
Kesselring, K. J. Review of *The Politics of the Excluded, c. 1500–1850*, by Tim Harris. *Albion: A Quarterly Journal Concerned with British Studies* 34, no. 4 (December 2002): 649–50.
Kidd, Colin. 'The Rehabilitation of Scottish Jacobitism'. *The Scottish Historical Review* LXXVII/1, no. 203 (1998): 58–76.
Kingdon, Robert M. *Myths about the St. Bartholomew's Day Massacres, 1572–1576*. Cambridge, MA: Harvard University Press, 1988.
Kléber Monod, Paul, Murray G. H. Pittock, and Daniel Szechi. 'Introduction: Loyalty and Identity'. In *Loyalty and Identity. Jacobites at Home and Abroad*. Studies in Modern History. Basingstoke: Palgrave Macmillan, 2010.
Kluxen, Kurt. Review of *Voters, Patrons, and Parties. The Unreformed Electoral System of Hanoverian England, 1734–1832*, by Frank O'Gorman. *Historische Zeitschrift* 253, no. 2 (1991): 465–6.
Knight, Roger. *The Pursuit of Victory. The Life and Achievement of Horatio Nelson*. 2nd ed. London/New York: Penguin Books, 2006.
Knights, Mark. 'Introduction: The View from 1710'. *Parliamentary History* 31, no. 1 (2012): 1–15.
Knouff, Gregory T. *The Soldiers' Revolution: Pennsylvanians in Arms and the Forging of Early American Identity*. University Park, PA: Pennsylvania State University Press, 2004.
Koke, Andrew M. 'Communication in an Anglican Empire: Edmund Gibson and His Commissaries, 1723–1748'. *Anglican and Episcopal History* 84, no. 2 (2015): 166–202.
Kopp, Hans W. *Parlamente: Geschichte, Größe, Grenzen*. Frankfurt: Fischer Bücherei, 1966.
Korn, Christoph Heinrich. *Geschichte der Kriege in und ausser Europa*. 9 vols. Nürnberg: Gabriel Nikolaus Raspe, 1777.
Koselleck, Reinhart. 'Revolution: Rebellion, Aufruhr, Bürgerkrieg'. In *Geschichtliche Grundbegriffe*, edited by Otto Brunner, Werner Conze, and Reinhart Koselleck, Band 5, 653–788. Stuttgart: Klett-Cotta, 2004.
Kovarik, Bill. *Revolutions in Communication: Media History from Gutenberg to the Digital Age*. 2nd ed. New York/London: Bloomsbury, 2015.
Kramnick, Isaac. *Republicanism and Bourgeois Radicalism: Political Ideology in Late Eighteenth-Century England and America*. Ithaca, NY/London: Cornell University Press, 1990.

Krischer, André. 'Aufruhr als Hochverrat? Drei Londoner Riots vor Gericht (1668, 1710, 1780)'. In *Revolten und politische Verbrechen zwischen dem 12. und 19. Jahrhundert*, edited by Angela De Benedictis and Karl Härter, 381–414. Studien zur europäischen Rechtsgeschichte 285. Frankfurt: Klostermann, 2013.

Krischer, André. 'Noble Honour and the Force of Law – Trial by Peers, Aristocracy and Criminal Law in England from the Sixteenth to the Eighteenth Century'. In *What Makes the Nobility Noble? Comparative Perspectives from the Sixteenth to the Twentieth Century*, edited by Jörn Leonhard and Christian Wieland, 2, 67–89. Schriftenreihe Der FRIAS School of History. Göttingen: Vandenhoeck & Ruprecht, 2011.

Kulkarni, Parashar, and Steven Pfaff. 'The "Glorious" Revolution's Inglorious Religious Commitment: Why Parliamentary Rule Failed to Secure Religious Liberty'. *Social Science History* (July 2022): 1–26. doi:10.1017/ssh.2022.15.

Kyle, Chris R., and Jason Peacey. '"Under Cover of so Much Coming and Going": Public Access to Parliament and the Political Process in Early Modern England'. In *Parliament at Work. Parliamentary Committees, Political Power and Public Access in Early Modern England*, edited by Jason Peacey and Chris R. Kyle, 1–24. Woodbridge: Boydell & Brewer, 2002.

Lake, Peter. '"To Lye upon a Stationers Stall, like a Piece of Coarse Flesh in a Shambles": The Sermon, Print and the English Civil War'. In *The English Sermon Revised. Religion, Literature and History 1600–1750*, edited by Lori Anne Ferrell and Peter McCullough, 188–207. Politics, Culture & Society in Early Modern Britain. Manchester: Manchester University Press, 2000.

Lalloué, Christiane, ed. *Princesse Palatine. Une Princesse allemande à la cour de Louis XIV (1672 à 1712)*. Paris: Union Générale d'Éditions, 1962.

Lambe, Charles. *When God Is on Our Side: A Thanksgiving-Sermon for the Suppression of the Late Unnatural Rebellion, Preach'd on Sunday, June the 10th, The Suppos'd Birth-Day of the Pretender, at St. Katherine Cree-Church and All-Hallows-Barkin. In Which Are Consider'd, The Sad Consequences, If the Rebellion Had Succeeded; and the Happy Consequences That It Did Not*. London: Bernard Lintot/J. Roberts, 1716.

Lambert, Ralph. *A Sermon Preach'd in Christ's-Church, Dublin, on Wednesday October, 23rd, 1717. Being the Anniversary Commemoration of the Happy Deliverance from the Irish Rebellion and Massacre in 1641. Before His Grace Charles Duke of Bolton, Lord Lieutenant of Ireland, and the Lords Spiritual and Temporal in Parliament Assembled*. Dublin: Fairbrother, 1717.

Lamont, Michèle, and Laurent Thévenot. 'Conclusion: Exploring the French and American Polity'. In *Rethinking Comparative Cultural Sociology: Repertoires of Evaluation in France and the United States*, edited by Michèle Lamont and Laurent Thévenot, 307–27. Cambridge: Cambridge University Press, 2000.

Lauritsen, John. '"This Isn't Who We Are": Minnesota Lawmakers Tweet from Inside U.S. Capitol as Mob Storms Building', 6 January 2021. https://minnesota.cbslocal.com/2021/01/06/minnesota-lawmakers-tweet-from-inside-u-s-capitol-as-mob-storms-building/.

Laveaux, Jean-Charles. *Discours sur les vices de la constitution anglaise, prononcé par J.-Ch. Laveaux dans la séance [de la Société des Jacobins] du 1er pluviôse an II de la République française*. Paris: s.n., 1794. https://gallica.bnf.fr/ark:/12148/bpt6k6258547p.

Lawson, George. *Politica Sacra & Civilis: Or, a Modell of Civil and Ecclesiasticall Government: Wherein, besides the Positive Doctrine Concerning State and Church in General, Are Debated the Principall Controversies of the Times. Concerning the Constitution of the State and Church of England, Tending to Righteousness, Truth and*

Peace. Vol. 1. London: for John Starkey at the Miter, neer the middle-Temple Gate in Fleetstreet, 1660.

Layman [pseud]. *The Layman's Sermon. Occasioned by the Present Rebellion Which Was (or Ought to Have Been) Preach'd at St. Paul's Cross, on the 1st of October, 1745*. Dublin: A. Reilly, for John Smith, 1745.

Lemaitre, Paul Thomas. *High Treason!! Narrative of the Arrest, Examinations before the Privy Council, and Imprisonment of P.T. Lemaitre: Accused of Being a Party in the Pop-Gun Plot, or, a Pretended Plot to Kill the King! In Which Is Introduced the Correspondence with the Privy Council, &c*. 2nd ed. London: J. Smith, 1795.

Lengel, Edward G., ed. *This Glorious Struggle: George Washington's Revolutionary War Letters*. Charlottesville: University of Virginia Press, 2010.

Leonhard, Jörn. 'Die Nationalisierung des Krieges und der Bellizismus der Nation: Die Diskussion um Volks- und Nationalkriege in Deutschland, Großbritannien und den Vereinigten Staaten seiten den 1860er Jahren'. In *Der Bürger als Soldat: Die Militarisierung europäischer Gesellschaften im langen 19. Jahrhundert: ein internationaler Vergleich*, edited by Christian Jansen, 83–108. Essen: Ruhr Klartext-Verlag, 2004.

List and Index Society and Public Record Office London, eds. *State Papers Domestic. George I (SP 35). Index to Lists Parts I to IV. 1714–1727*. London: Swift Printers, 1981.

Loewenstein, David. *Representing Revolution in Milton and His Contemporaries: Religion, Politics, and Polemics in Radical Puritanism*. Cambridge: Cambridge University Press, 2001.

Lorenz, Lincoln. *John Paul Jones: Fighter for Freedom and Glory*. New York: Naval Institute Press, 2014.

Lottes, Günter. 'Das englische Vorbild war kein Königsweg. Kommentar zu den Referaten von Hermann Wellenreuther und Ernst Schubert'. In *Britain and Germany Compared: Nationality, Society and Nobility in the Eighteenth Century*, 13, 231–9. Göttinger Gespräche zur Geschichtswissenschaft. Göttingen: Wallstein, 2001.

Lower Canada, Court of Oyer and Terminer. *The Trial of David McLane for High Treason: At the City of Quebec, in the Province of Lower-Canada. On Friday, the Seventh Day of July, A.D. 1797. Taken in Short-Hand, at the Trial*. Quebec: W. Vondenvelden, 1797.

Luhmann, Niklas. *Die Politik der Gesellschaft*. Edited by André Kieserling. 2nd ed. Darmstadt: Wissenschaftliche Buchgesellschaft, 2002.

Luhmann, Niklas. *Politische Soziologie*. Edited by André Kieserling. Berlin: Suhrkamp, 2010.

Maclean, Fitzroy. *Bonnie Prince Charlie*. Reprint. Edinburgh: Canongate, 1995.

Macpherson, John. 'MS Hyde 77 (8. 170. 2): Sir John Macpherson, to Unidentified Recipient'. Autograph draft letter fragment. Essex Court, Temple [London, England], not dated. Houghton Library, Harvard University, Cambridge, MA.

Macpherson, John. 'MS Hyde 77 (8. 170. 3): Sir John Macpherson, to Unidentified Recipient, Concerning the Need for National Unity'. Autograph draft letter fragment, signed, no place. Essex Court, Temple [London, England], not before 1795. Houghton Library, Harvard University, Cambridge, MA.

Macquoid, Gilbert Samuel. *Jacobite Songs and Ballads*. Historical Collection from the British Library. London: The British Library, 2013.

Magistrates' Court of Bristol. *Whereas Great Numbers of Persons Did Last Night and This Day Assemble Themselves Together near Bristol-Bridge, to the Disturbance of the Public Peace*. Bristol: s.n., 1793.

Maier, Charles S. 'Introduction'. In *Changing Boundaries of the Political. Essays on the Evolving Balance between the State and Society, Public and Private in Europe*, edited by Charles S. Maier, 1–26. Cambridge: Cambridge University Press, 1987.

Manley, Mary Delariviere. *A True Relation of the Several Facts and Circumstances of the Intended Riot and Tumult on Queen Elizabeth's Birth-Day: Gathered from Authentick Accounts: And Published for the Information of All True Lovers of Our Constitution in Church and State.* 2nd ed. London/Edinburgh: John Morphew/James Watson, 1712.

Manson, Michael. *Riot!: The Bristol Bridge Massacre of 1793*. 2nd ed. Bristol: Bristol Books CIC/Central Books Ltd, 2012.

Mar, James, Earl of. 'SP 54/10/32B: Mar: Order Prohibiting Anyone from Obeying Argyll's Call for Volunteers; Forbidding Ministers to Acknowledge the Elector of Brunswick as King and Ordering That Those Who Do Should Be Seized and Their Churches Closed'. Order. Scotland, 1 November 1715. State Papers Scotland, Secretaries of State: State Papers Scotland Series II. The National Archives of the UK, Kew.

Marschke, Benjamin. 'Princes' Power, Aristocratic Norms, and Personal Eccentricities: Le Caractère Bizarre of Frederick William I of Prussia (1713–1740)'. In *The Holy Roman Empire, Reconsidered*, edited by Jason P. Coy and David W. Sabean, 49–70. Spektrum: Publications of the German Studies Association 1. New York: Berghahn Books, 2010.

Marschke, Benjamin. '"Von dem am Königl. Preußischen Hofe abgeschafften Ceremoniel": Monarchical Representation and Court Ceremony in Frederick William I's Prussia'. In *Orthodoxies and Diversity in Early Modern Germany*, edited by Randolph C. Head and Daniel Christensen. Boston, MA: Brill, 2007.

Marshall, Geoffrey. 'Rule of Law'. In *The Blackwell Encyclopaedia of Political Thought*, edited by David W. Miller, Janet Coleman, William Connolly, and Alan Ryan, 8th ed., 458–9. Oxford/Malden: Blackwell, 1998.

Marshall, Nathaniel. *The Use and Importance of a Preaching Ministry: Considered in a Sermon Preach'd in the Church of St. Laurence Jewry, upon Opening the Tuesday Lecture There, October 10, 1727*. London: William and John Innys, 1727.

Martin, F. X. 'The Normans: Arrival and Settlement (1169–c. 1300)'. In *The Course of Irish History*, edited by Theo W. Moody and F. X. Martin, 8th revised ed., 123–43. Cork: Mercier Press, 1994.

Mary II, Queen of England, Scotland and Ireland. *Recht des Congressus zur Wahl und der Princessin Marien Stuardin zur Cron von Engelland, ausgeführt wider das Schreiben des gewesenen Königs Jacobi des andern an die Lords in geheimen Raht [in notes appended to it], und Gegen-Fragen auff die dabey angefügte funffzehn Fragen: sampt angehangter Verantwortung des Parlaments wegen ihres hierin gefasten Schlusses.* London: s.n., 1689.

Maseres, Francis. *The Moderate Reformer: Or, a Proposal to Correct Some Abuses in the Present Establishment of the Church of England, in a Manner That Would Tend to Make It More Useful to the Advancement of Religion, and Increase the Respect and Attachment of the People to Its Clergy.* London: G. Stafford/J. Debrett/J. Johnson, 1791.

Massachusetts Historical Society, ed. *Collections of the Massachusetts Archives: John Adams*. Revised ed. Boston, MA: The Massachusetts Archives, 2002.

Massie, Joseph. *No Ruinous and Riot-Breeding Taxes*. London: s.n., 1782.

Maxwell, Ian. *Armagh: History & Guide*. Dublin: Nonsuch Publishing, 2009.

Mc Inerney, Timothy. 'The Better Sort: Nobility and Human Variety in Eighteenth-Century Great Britain'. *Journal for Eighteenth-Century Studies* 38, no. 1 (March 2015): 47–63. doi:https://onlinelibrary.wiley.com/doi/10.1111/1754-0208.12138.

McCormack, Matthew. 'Citizen Soldiers? The Identity of the English Militiamen, 1757-1815'. Conference talk presented at the British Society of Eighteenth-Century Studies, 44th Annual Conference, Panel 6: Taking arms: Political Identities, Ho Tim Room, St. Hugh's College, Oxford, 8 January 2015.

McCormack, Matthew. *Embodying the Militia in Georgian England*. Oxford: Oxford University Press, 2015.

McCormack, Matthew. 'Supporting the Civil Power: Citizen Soldiers and the Gordon Riots'. *The London Journal* 37, no. 1 (2012): 27-41.

McDowell, Robert Brendan. 'The Protestant Nation (1775-1800)'. In *The Course of Irish History*, edited by Theo W. Moody and F. X. Martin, 8th revised ed., 232-47. Cork: Mercier Press, 1994.

McKelvey, James Lee. *George III and Lord Bute: The Leicester House Years*. Durham, NC: Duke University Press, 1973.

McLynn, Frank. *Unpopular Front: Jews, Radicals and Americans in the Jacobite World-View*. Huntingdon: Royal Stuart Society, 1988.

Meiners, Christoph, and Ludwig Timotheus Spittler, eds. 'II. Summarische Entwicklung der Entstehung-Geschichte des Englischen Parlaments'. *Göttingisches Historisches Magazin* (1789): 613-53.

Melleuish, Greg. 'Of "Rage of Party" and the Coming of Civility'. *M/C Journal* 22, no. 1 (2019). doi:10.5204/mcj.1492.

Midgley, Graham. 'Henley, John [known as Orator Henley] (1692-1756)'. In *Oxford Dictionary of National Biography*, edited by H. C. G. Matthew and B. Harrison, 26, 355-7. Oxford: Oxford University Press, 2004.

Milbourne, Luke. *Sedition and Rebellion in the State, the Natural Product of Separation from the Church: A Sermon Preach'd, January 30, 1717/18. at St. Ethelburga's [...] By Luke Milbourne, [...]* London: E. Sawbridge/A. Bettesworth, 1718.

Milbourne, Luke. *The Originals of Rebellion, or, The Ends of Separation: A Sermon Preached on the Thirtieth of January, 1682 in the Parish-Church of Great Yarmovth*. London: J. Wallis for Walter Kettilby, 1683.

Miller, David W. 'The Origins of the Orange Order in County Armagh'. In *Armagh: History & Society: Interdisciplinary Essays on the History of an Irish County*, edited by Art J. Hughes and William Nolan, 583-607. Interdisciplinary Essays on the History of an Irish County. Dublin: Geography Publications, 2001.

Miller, Eugene F., and Barry Schwartz. 'The Icon of the American Republic: A Study in Political Symbolism'. *Review of Politics* 47, no. 4 (1985): 516-43.

Miller, John. *Popery and Politics in England*. Cambridge: Cambridge University Press, 1973.

Miller, John. 'The Rage of Party, 1700-1714', 29 March 2007. doi:10.1093/acprof:o so/9780199288397.003.0013.

Miller, Peter N. '"Freethinking" and "Freedom of Thought" in Eighteenth-Century Britain'. *The Historical Journal* 36, no. 3 (1993): 599-617.

Miller, Thomas (Lord Glenlee). 'SP 54/47/217: Lord Justice Clerk Miller, Reporting That a Catholic Chapel Was Burned during a Riot in Edinburgh'. Edinburgh, 4 February 1779. State Papers Scotland, Secretaries of State: State Papers Scotland Series II. The National Archives of the UK, Kew.

Miller, Victoria C. 'William Wake and the Reunion of Christians'. *Anglican and Episcopal History* 62, no. 1 (1993): 7-35.

Millis, Wade. *A Spy under the Common Law of War*. Addison, MI: Courier Printing House, 1925.

Millstone, Noah. 'The Politic History of Early Stuart Parliaments'. In *Writing the History of Parliament in Tudor and Early Stuart England*, edited by Paul Cavill and Alexandra Gajda, 172–93. Manchester: Manchester University Press, 2018. doi:10.7228/manchester/9780719099588.003.0008.

Mitchell, Austin. 'The Association Movement of 1792–3'. *The Historical Journal* 4, no. 1 (1961): 56–77.

Mitchell, Leslie. 'Charles James Fox'. *Oxford Dictionary of National Biography*, 28 December 2015. https://doi.org/10.1093/ref:odnb/10024.

Monod, Paul. Review of *Rebellion and Savagery: The Jacobite Rising of 1745 and the British Empire*, by Geoffrey Plank. *The International History Review* 29, no. 1 (2007): 136–8.

Monod, Paul. 'The Jacobite Press and English Censorship, 1689–95'. In *The Stuart Court in Exile and the Jacobites*. Cambridge: Cambridge University Press, 1995.

Montesquieu, Charles de Secondat, Baron de. 'Montesquieu: L'Esprit des Lois. Livre I'. In *Montesquieu, Jean-Jacques Rousseau: Discours et écrits*, 9–21. Les grands combats de la liberté. Courtry (Seine et Marne): Les éditions de l'Épervier, 2010.

More, Hannah, Samuel Hazard, R. White, and John Marshall. *The Carpenter, or, The Danger of Evil Company; The Gin-Shop, or, A Peep into a Prison; The Riot, or, Half a Loaf Is Better than No Bread: In a Dialogue between Jack Anvil and Tom Hod; Patient Joe, or, The Newcastle Collier. The Execution of Wild Robert: Being a Warning to All Parents. A New Christmas Carol, Called The Merry Chirstmas [sic] and Happy New Year*. London/Bath: J. Marshall/R. White/S. Hazard, 1795.

Moréri, Louis, Jeremy 1650–1726. Collier, Jean 1657–1736. Le Clerc, Robert 1645–1703. White, Thomas Newborough, Elizabeth fl. 1699–1711 Harris, and Assigns of Luke Meredith. *The Great Historical, Geographical, Genealogical and Poetical Dictionary; Being a Curious Miscellany of Sacred and Prophane History [...]*. 2nd ed. London: Henry Rhodes/Thomas Newborough/the assigns of L. Meredith/Elizabeth Harris, 1701.

Morris, A. D. 'The Pop-Gun Plot'. In *James Parkinson: His Life and Times*, edited by A. D. Morris and F. Clifford Rose, 38–53. History of Neuroscience. Boston, MA/Basel/Berlin: Birkhäuser, 1989. doi:10.1007/978-1-4615-9824-4_4.

Morris, Marilyn. *Sex, Money & Personal Character in Eighteenth-Century British Politics*. New Haven, CT: Yale University Press, 2014.

Morris, Mary, and William Morris. *Dictionary of Word and Phrase Origins*. New York, Hagerstown, San Francisco: Harper & Row, 1977.

Morton, Thomas. *An Exact Account of Romish Doctrine in the Case of Conspiracy and Rebellion: By Pregnant Observations Collected Out of the Express Dogmatical Principles of Popish Priests and Jesuites. Written and Printed Immediately after the Discovery of the Gunpowder Treason. And Now upon the Discovery of the Present Popish Plot*. Reprint. London: John Starkey, 1679.

Mossom, Robert. *The King on His Throne, or, a Discourse Maintaining the Dignity of a King, the Duty of a Subject, and the Unlawfulnesse of Rebellion: Delivered in Two Sermons Preached in the Cathedrall Church in York*. York: s.n., 1643.

[Multiple witnesses]. 'MS 3069/Acc1926-021/328833: Walsall. Brief of Evidence against Thomas James and Several Other Persons Concerned in the Riot at Walsall'. Walsall, 29 May 1750. Birmingham: Archives, Heritage and Photography Service. https://discovery.nationalarchives.gov.uk/details/r/2faa3286-3831-4a8f-aca8-8abc2f72b43d.

[Multiple witnesses]. 'U908/L19/6: Allegations on Behalf of the Defendants Sherrard and Perry 7th Dec. 1743'. 2 documents, 1743. Kent History and Library Centre. https://discovery.nationalarchives.gov.uk/details/r/f034a1b2-1a31-4f62-978a-b8fa8b3a6af3.

Münkler, Herfried, ed. *Politisches Denken im 20. Jahrhundert. Ein Lesebuch*, 4th paperback ed. Munich: Piper, 2002.

N. D. *A Letter Intercepted Printed for the Use and Benefit of the Ingenuous Reader: In Which the Two Different Forms of Monarchy and Popular Government, Are Briefly Controverted. The Common-Wealth Party Are Advised Not to Buy This*. London: s.n., 1660.

Nagy, John A. *Rebellion in the Ranks: Mutinies of the American Revolution*. Yardley, PA: Westholme Publishing, 2008.

Neill, Debra R. 'The Disestablishment of Religion in Virginia: Dissenters, Individual Rights, and the Separation of Church and State'. *Virginia Magazine of History and Biography* 127, no. 1 (2019): 2–41.

Neubauer, Hans-Joachim. *Fama: Eine Geschichte Des Gerüchts*. Aktualisierte Neuausgabe. Berlin: Matthes & Seitz, 2009.

Neuhoff, Frédéric de [also known as Frederick Colonel]. *Memoirs of Corsica: Containing the Natural and Political History of That Important Island; Also an Account of Its Products, [...] Situation, and Strength. [...] Together with a Variety of [...] Particulars [...] Hitherto Unknown*. London: S. Hooper and J. Almon, 1768.

Nevitt, Marcus. *Women and the Pamphlet Culture of Revolutionary England, 1640–1660*. London: Taylor & Francis, 2017.

Norman, Edward. *Church and Society in England 1770–1970: A Historical Study*. Oxford: Clarendon, 1976.

Novak, Maximillian E. 'From Pilloried Libeller to Government Propagandist'. In *Daniel Defoe: Master of Fictions: His Life and Works*, edited by Maximillian E. Novak, 189–212. Oxford University Press, 2003. doi:10.1093/acprof:o so/9780199261543.003.0021.

Nubola, Cecilia, and Andreas Würgler, eds. *Bittschriften Und Gravamina: Politik, Verwaltung Und Justiz in Europa (14. –18. Jahrhundert)*. Vol. 19. Schriften des Italienisch-Deutschen Historischen Instituts in Trient. Berlin: Duncker & Humblot, 2005.

Ó Muirí, Réamonn. 'Dean Warburton's Reports on the United Irishmen in County Armagh'. In *Armagh: History & Society: Interdisciplinary Essays on the History of an Irish County*, edited by Art J. Hughes and William Nolan, 639–712. Interdisciplinary Essays on the History of an Irish County. Dublin: Geography Publications, 2001.

Oakley, Francis. *The Conciliarist Tradition: Constitutionalism in the Catholic Church, 1300–1870*. Oxford: Oxford University Press, 2003.

Oates, Jonathan. *Jacobitism in Eighteenth Century English Schools and Colleges*. Salisbury: Royal Stuart Society, 2007.

Offe, Claus. 'Challenging the Boundaries of Institutional Politics: Social Movements since the 1960s'. In *Changing Boundaries of the Political. Essays on the Evolving Balance between the State and Society, Public and Private in Europe*, edited by Charles S. Maier, 63–106. Cambridge: Cambridge University Press, 1987.

Ogborn, Miles. 'The Power of Speech: Orality, Oaths and Evidence in the British Atlantic World, 1650–1800'. *Transactions of the Institute of British Geographers* 36, no. 1 (January 2011): 109–25.

Old Hubert [pseud., attributed to James Parkinson]. *An Address to the Hon. Edmund Burke from the Swinish Multitude*. London: J. Ridgway, 1793.

Oldmixon, John. *The False Steps of the Ministry after the Revolution, Shewing That the Lenity and Moderation of That Government Was the Occasion of All the Factions Which Have since Endanger'd the Constitution: With Some Reflections on the License of the Pulpit and Press. In a Letter to My Lord—*. London: J. Roberts, 1714.

Orléans, Charlotte-Elisabeth, Duchess of. *Liselotte von der Pfalz in ihren Harling-Briefen: Sämtliche Briefe der Elisabeth Charlotte, duchesse d'Orléans, and die Oberhofmeisterin Anna Katharina von Harling, geb. von Offeln, und deren Gemahl Christian Friedrich von Harling, Geheimrat und Oberstallmeister, zu Hannover.* Edited by Hannelore Helfer and Malte-Ludolf Babin. Hanover: Hahn, 2007.

O'Shaughnessy, David. "'Rip'ning Buds in Freedom's Field": Staging Irish Improvement in the 1780s'. *Journal for Eighteenth-Century Studies* 38, no. 4 (2015): 541–54.

Paine, Thomas. *Common Sense.* Digital ed. Chicago: The University of Chicago Press, originally published in 1776. http://press-pubs.uchicago.edu/founders/documents/v1ch4s4.html.

Palier, Bruno, and Yves Surel. 'Le politique dans les politiques'. *Espace Temps* 76, no. 1 (2001): 52–67. doi:10.3406/espat.2001.4164.

Parker, Henry. *The Manifold Miseries of Civill Vvarre and Discord in a Kingdome: By the Examples of Germany, France, Ireland, and Other Places: Vvith Some Memorable Examples of Gods Iusitice in Punishing the Authors and Causes of Rebellion and Treason.* London: George Lindsey, 1642.

Parliament and Lord Lieutenant of Ireland. *An Act to Prevent Tumultuous Risings and Assemblies, and for the More Effectual Punishment of Persons Guilty of Outrage, Riot, and Illegal Combination, and of Administering and Taking Unlawful, Oaths [27 Geo. III. Cap. XV.].* Dublin: G. Grierson, 1792.

Parliament of Great Britain. *A Warning Voice to the People of England, on the True Nature and Effect of the Two Bills Now before Parliament [i.e. the 'Bill for the Safety of His Majesty's Person,' and the 'Bill for Preventing Seditious Meetings,' Read 6 and 12 Nov. 1795 Respectively].* London: Richard White, 1795.

Parliament of Great Britain. 'An Act for Preventing Tumults and Riotous Assemblies, and for the More Speedy and Effectual Punishing the Rioters'. In *Anno Regni Georgi I Regis Magnae Britanniae, Franciae, & Hiberniae, Primo. At the Parliament Begun and Holden at Westminster, the Seventeenth Day of March, Anno Dom. 1714. Lord George, by the Grace of God, of Great Britain, France, and Ireland, King, Defender of the Faith, &c. Being the First Session of This Present Parliament,* 243–8. London: John Baskett/Thomas Newcomb/Henry Hills, 1715.

Parliament of Great Britain. *An Act for the More Easy and Speedy Trial of Such Persons as Have Levied, or Shall Levy War against His Majesty; and for the Better Ascertaining the Qualifications of Jurors in Trials for High Treason, or Misprision of Treason, in That Part of Great Britain Called Scotland.* London: Thomas Baskett and the assigns of Robert Baskett, 1745.

Parliament of Great Britain. *An Act for the More Effectual Disarming the Highlands in Scotland; and for More Effectually Securing the Peace of the Said Highlands; and for Restraining the Use of the Highland Dress; and for the Further Indemnifying Such Persons as Have Acted in Defence of His Majesty's Person and Government, during the Unnatural Rebellion; and for Indemnifying the Judges and Other Officers of the Court of Judiciary in Scotland, for Not Performing the Northern Circuit in May, One Thousand Seven Hundred and Forty Six; and for Obliging the Masters and Teachers of Private Schools in Scotland, and Chaplains, Tutors and Governors of Children or Youth, to Take the Oaths to His Majesty, His Heirs, and Successors, and to Register the Same.* London: Thomas Baskett and the assigns of Robert Baskett, 1746.

Parliament of Great Britain. *An Act for the More Effectual Trial and Punishment of High Treason and Misprision of High Treason, in the Highlands of Scotland; and for Abrogating the Practice of Taking Down the Evidence in Writing in Certain Criminal Prosecutions; and for Making Some Further Regulations Relating to Sheriffs Depute and*

Stewarts Depute, and Their Substitutes; and for Other Purposes Therein Mentioned. London: Thomas Baskett and the assigns of Robert Baskett, 1748.

Parsons, Robert. *A Treatise Tending to Mitigation Tovvardes Catholicke-Subiectes in England: VVherin Is Declared, That It Is Not Impossible for Subiects of Different Religion, (Especially Catholickes and Protestantes) to Liue Togeather in Dutifull Obedience and Subiection, Vnder the Gouernment of His Maiesty of Great Britany. Against the Seditious Wrytings of Thomas Morton Minister, & Some Others to the Contrary. Whose Two False and Slaunderous Groundes, Pretended to Be Dravvne from Catholicke Doctrine & Practice, Concerning Rebellion and Equivocation, Are Ouerthrowne, and Cast vpon Himselfe.* Edited by François Bellet. Saint-Omer: F. Bellet, 1607.

Peltonen, Markku. *Classical Humanism and Republicanism in English Political Thought 1570–1640.* Cambridge: Cambridge University Press, 1996.

Pettegree, Andrew. *The Invention of News: How the World Came to Know About Itself*, New Haven, CT/London: Yale University Press, 2014.

Philalethes [pseud.]. '[Untitled]'. *View of the Times, Their Principles and Practices* 13 (22 November 1707): 3–4.

Philipps, John. 'Reflections upon the Advice from England'. Edited by Randal Taylor. *Present State of Europe or the Historical and Political Monthly Mercury* 2 (1 May 1691): 1–3.

Phillips, Edward. *The Nevv Vvorld of Vvords. Or a General English Dictionary Containing the Proper Significations, and Etymologies of All Words Derived from Other Languages.* London: W. R. for Robert Harford, 1678.

Phillips, John A. 'Popular Politics in Unreformed England'. *Journal of Modern History* 52 (December 1980): 599–625.

Philocles [pseudonym]. *A Letter to a Noble Lord, in Answer to a Letter to a Member of Parliament, for Bringing in a Bill to Revise, Amend, or Repeal Certain [...] Statutes [...] Called The Ten Commandments. Shewing That It Is Not, yet, a Proper Time to Repeal Those Statutes.* London: s.n., 1739.

Pickard, Victor. Review of *Book review: Manuel Castells, Communication Power. Oxford: Oxford University Press, 2009*, by Manuel Castells. *Global Media and Communication* 7, no. 54 (2011): 54–6.

Pickering, Paul A., and Michael T. Davis. *Unrespectable Radicals?: Popular Politics in the Age of Reform.* Aldershot: Ashgate Publishing, Ltd, 2008.

Pierce, Helen. *Unseemly Pictures: Graphic Satire and Politics in Early Modern England.* Edited by Paul Mellon Centre for Studies in British Art. New Haven, CT: Yale University Press, 2008.

Piers, Henry. *Religion and Liberty Rescued from Superstition and Slavery, Great Subjects of Thanksgiving a Sermon Preached in the Parish-Church of Bexley, in Kent, on the 9th of October, MDCCXLVI. The Day Appointed [...] for a General Thanksgiving for the Suppression of the Rebellion.* Bristol/Bath/London: F. Farley, and sold by J. Wilson, 1746.

Piguenet [Piguenit], C. D. *An Essay on the Art of News-Paper Defamation, in a Letter to Mr. William Griffin, Printer and Publisher of the Morning Post, a Master of That Art.* London: printed for the author, 1775.

Pincus, Steve. Review of *Lord Churchill's Coup: The Anglo-American Empire and the Glorious Revolution Reconsidered*, by Stephen Saunders Webb. *The American Historical Review* 102, no. 3 (1997): 812–14.

Pincus, Steven C. A. *1688: The First Modern Revolution.* The Lewis Walpole Series in Eighteenth-Century Culture and History. New Haven, CT: Yale University Press, 2009.

Pincus, Steven C. A. *1688: The First Modern Revolution*. New Haven, CT: Yale University Press, 2011.
Pitt, William. 'SP 63/416/3317: Rt Hon William Pitt to Duke of Bedford. Draft Letter Expressing Opinions of HM's Servants on the Riot Outside the Houses of Parliament'. Whitehall, 20 December 1759. The National Archives, Kew.
Pittock, Murray. Review of *Jacobite Prisoners of the 1715 Rebellion: Preventing and Punishing Insurrection in Early Hanoverian Britain*, by Margaret Sankey. *The Scottish Historical Review* 87, no. 223 (2008): 162–3.
Pittock, Murray, Adriana Craciun, Emma Macloed, and Paddy Bullard. 'Riots, Rebellions & Revolutions. 44th Annual Conference of the British Society of Eighteenth-Century Studies. Closing Discussion'. Closing discussion presented at the Thursday Celebration Drinks and Closing Discussion, Maplethorpe Hall, St. Hugh's College, Oxford, 8 January 2015.
Pittock, Murray G. H. *Religious Politics under Charles I and James II*. Huntingdon: Royal Stuart Society, 1991.
Pittock, Murray G. H. 'The Jacobite Diaspora'. In *Jacobitism*, edited by Murray G. H. Pittock, 123–37. British History in Perspective. London: Macmillan Education UK, 1998. doi:10.1007/978-1-349-26908-2_6.
Plowden, Francis. *Church and State*. London: printed for G. G. and J. Robinson, Paternoster-Row, 1795.
Political Looking-Glass [pseud.]. 'For the Morning Post. To Sir George Warren'. *The Morning Post, and Daily Advertiser* 907 (22 September 1775): [not paged].
Priestley, Joseph. *A Description of a New Chart of History, Containing a View of the Principal Revolutions of Empire That Have Taken Place in the World*. J. Johnson, 1777.
Priestley, Joseph. 'An Appeal to the Public, on the Subject of the Riots in Birmingham [1792]'. In *The Theological and Miscellaneous Works of Joseph Priestley, LL.D. F.R.S. &c with Notes, by the Editor*, edited by John Towill Rutt, XIX: Containing Defences of Unitarianism for 1788 and 1789; A Letter to the Right Hon. William Pitt; Familiar Letters to the Inhabitants of Birmingham; and An Appeal to the Public on the Riots in Birmingham, 345–434. New York: Kraus Reprint, 1972.
Prochaska, Frank K. *Royal Bounty: The Making of a Welfare Monarchy*. New Haven, CT: Yale University Press, 1995.
Provincial Congress. *Rules and Regulations for the Massachusetts Army*. Boston, MA: Benjamin Edes, 1775.
Querno, Camillo. *The American Times: A Satire: In Three Parts. In Which Are Delineated the Characters of the Leaders of the American Rebellion*. London: William Richardson, 1780.
Quinault, Roland Edwin, and John Stevenson. *Popular Protest and Public Order. Six Studies in British History, 1790-1920*. London: George Allen & Unwin, 1974.
Rabb, Theodore K. *The Struggle for Stability in Early Modern Europe*. New York: Oxford University Press, 1975.
Rabin, Dana. 'The Jew Bill of 1753: Masculinity, Virility, and the Nation'. *Eighteenth-Century Studies* 39, no. 2 (2006): 157–71.
Ramsay, James. *Objections to the Abolition of the Slave Trade, with Answers. To Which Are Prefixed, Strictures on a Late Publication, Intitled [sic], 'Considerations on the Emancipation of Negroes, and the Abolition of the Slave Trade, by a West India Planter'*. London: J. Phillips, 1788.
Rancière, Jacques. 'Onze Thèses Sur La Politique'. *Filozofski Vestnik* XVIII, no. 2 (1997): 91–106.

Randall, Adrian. *Riotous Assemblies: Popular Protest in Hanoverian England*. Oxford: Oxford University Press, 2016.

Randall, David. 'Epistolary Rhetoric, the Newspaper, and the Public Sphere'. *Past & Present* 198 (2008): 3–32.

Rawlinson, Christopher. *An Inquiry into the Management of the Poor: And Our Usual Polity Respecting the Common People; with Reasons Why They Have Not Hitherto Been Attended with Success, and Such Alterations Offered to the Consideration of the Legislature, as May Probably Introduce a More General Spirit of Industry and Order, and Greatly Lessen the Publick Expence [sic]*. London: Benjamin White, 1767.

Raymond, Joad. 'The Newspaper, Public Opinion, and the Public Sphere in the Seventeenth Century'. *Prose Studies* 21, no. 2 (1998): 109–36.

Reinhard, Wolfgang. *Geschichte der Staatsgewalt: Eine vergleichende Verfassungsgeschichte Europas von den Anfängen bis zur Gegenwart*. Munich: C. H. Beck, 1999.

Representative of a cyder-county [pseud.]. *An Address to Such of the Electors of Great-Britain, as Are Not Makers of Cyder and Perry*. London: W. Nicoll, 1763.

Revere, Paul. *Four Coffins of Men Killed in the Boston Massacre*. Boston, MA: engraving and letterpress, printed by Edes and Gill, 1770. https://www.loc.gov/item/2004672647/.

Reynolds, Bart. 'Primary Documents Relating to the Seizure of Powder at Williamsburg, VA, April 21, 1775'. Private history website. *RevWar'75*, 20 October 2021. http://www.revwar75.com/battles/primarydocs/williamsburg.htm.

Rhoden, Nancy L. 'The Pre-Revolutionary Colonial Church of England'. In *Revolutionary Anglicanism: The Colonial Church of England Clergy during the American Revolution*, edited by Nancy L. Rhoden, 10–36. London: Palgrave Macmillan, 1999. doi:10.1057/9780230512924_2.

Richardson, Benjamin C., ed. *The Historical Magazine, and Notes and Queries Concerning the Antiquities, History, and Biography of America*. Vol. III, 2. New York: Henry B. Dawson, 1868.

Richter, Donald. 'The Role of Mob Riot in Victorian Elections, 1865–1885'. *Victorian Studies* 15, no. 1 (1971): 19–28.

Ridley, Joseph. *The Hexham Chronicle, or, Materials for a Modern History of Hexham: A Hundred Years Ago, or, The Hexham Riot*. Hexham: William Cooke, 1861.

Riotte, Torsten. 'Vom "Staatsfeind" zum Oppositionsführer: wie sich Opposition historisch wandelte'. *Forschung Frankfurt: Wissenschaftsmagazin der Goethe-Universität* 29, no. 3 (2011): 32–6. http://publikationen.ub.uni-frankfurt.de/frontdoor/index/index/docId/24378.

Ritter, Gerhard A. 'David Humes "Idee einer vollkommenen Republik" und ihr Einfluß auf die amerikanische Verfassung'. In *Ein solches Jahrhundert vergißt sich nicht mehr. Lieblingstexte aus dem 18. Jahrhundert*, 168–9. Munich: C. H. Beck, 2000.

Robert, Fellowes. 'HO 42/36/85: Letter from Robert Fellowes of Shotisham [Shotesham, Norfolk]'. Shotesham, 19 October 1795. The National Archives, Kew. https://discovery.nationalarchives.gov.uk/details/r/C12762349.

Roberts, Clayton. Review of *The Politics of Religion in Restoration England by Tim Harris; Paul Seaward; Mark Goldie*, by Tim Harris, Paul Seaward, and Mark Goldie. *Albion: A Quarterly Journal Concerned with British Studies* 23, no. 3 (1991): 547–8.

Roberts, Matthew. Review of *A Political Biography of Thomas Paine*, by William Arthur Speck. *Journal for Eighteenth-Century Studies* 38, no. 4 (December 2015): 618–19.

Robertson, Randy. 'Habermas and the English Public Sphere Reconsidered'. *Journal of Interdisciplinary History of Ideas* 9, no. 17 (12 August 2020): [not paged].

Robethon, Jean de, and C. F. Kreienberg. 'Cal. Br. 24: Zeitungen aus London 1714–1715'. Diplomatic relations. London, October 1714. Außenstelle Pattensen. Niedersächsisches Landesarchiv Hanover.

Robethon, Jean de, and C. F. Kreienberg. 'Cal. Br. 24, 1713: Zeitungen Robethons resp. Kreienbergs aus London'. Diplomatic relations. London, 1714–1716. Außenstelle Pattensen. Niedersächsisches Landesarchiv Hanover.

Robinson, John. 'T 1/463: Commissioner Robinson, Regarding His Proposed Visit to England, and the Southern Colonies and Enclosing Copy of a Notice from Rhode Island Addressed to the Sons and Daughters of Liberty Urging Seizure of the Customs Money Due to Be Taken to England in Lieu of Money Owed to the Colony by Treasury'. Diplomatic correspondence. Massachusetts, 22 February 1768. Treasury Board Papers and In-Letters. The National Archives of the UK, Kew.

Rockingham [pseud.]. *A Few Words Addressed to the Right Honourable Charles James Fox on the Sacred Duty of Insurrection*. London: G. Cawthorn, 1796.

Rogal, Samuel J. 'Religious Periodicals in England during the Restoration and Eighteenth Century'. *The Journal of the Rutgers University Libraries* 35, no. 1 (1971). doi:10.14713/jrul.v35i1.1522.

Rogers, Nicholas. 'Popular Protest in Early Hanoverian London'. *Past & Present* 79 (1978): 70–100.

Rolin, Jan. *Der Ursprung des Staates. Die naturrechtlich-rechtsphilosophische Legitimation von Staat und Staatsgewalt im Deutschland des 18. und 19. Jahrhunderts*. Grundlagen der Rechtswissenschaft 4. Tübingen: Mohr Siebeck, 2005.

Romaniello, Matthew P., and Charles Lipp. 'The Spaces of Nobility'. In *Contested Spaces of Nobility in Early Modern Europe*, 1–10. Farnham/ Burlington, VT: Ashgate, 2011.

Rose, Colin. *A Renaissance of Violence: Homicide in Early Modern Italy*. Cambridge/New York: Cambridge University Press, 2019. https://doi.org/10.1017/9781108627948.

Rosewell, Samuel. *The Unreasonableness of the Present Riotous and Tumultuous Proceedings: As They Are Directed against His Majesty King George; and His Faithful Subjects, the Protestant Dissenters*. London: M. Lawrence, 1715.

Rospocher, Massimo. 'Beyond the Public Sphere: A Historiographical Transition'. In *Beyond the Public Sphere. Opinions, Publics, Spaces in Early Modern Europe*, edited by Massimo Rospocher, 27, 9–30. Annali Dll'Istituto Storico Italo-Germanico in Trento/Jahrbuch des Italienisch-Deutschen Historischen Instituts in Trient. Bologna/Berlin: Società editrice il Mulino/Duncker & Humblot, 2012.

Royer, Katherine. *The English Execution Narrative, 1200–1700*. London: Pickering & Chatto, 2014.

Rozdilsky, Jack L. 'Thought the U.S. Capitol Attack Couldn't Happen? Think Again: The Insurrection Threat Isn't over'. *The Conversation*, 7 January 2021. http://theconversation.com/thought-the-u-s-capitol-attack-couldnt-happen-think-again-the-insurrection-threat-isnt-over-152810.

Rudé, George. 'The London "Mob" of the Eighteenth Century'. *The Historical Journal* 2, no. 1 (1959): 1–18.

Ruderman, David B. *Jewish Enlightenment in an English Key: Anglo-Jewry's Construction of Modern Jewish Thought*. Princeton, NJ: Princeton University Press, 2000.

Ruff, Julius Ralph. *Violence in Early Modern Europe: 1500–1800*. New Approaches to European History 22. Cambridge: Cambridge University Press, 2001.

Ruffhead, Owen. 'MS Hyde 77 (8. 196.2): Owen Ruffhead to William Strahan'. Autograph letter, signed. Essex Court, Temple [London, England], 21 July 1768. Houghton Library, Harvard University, Cambridge, MA.

Ryan, Alan. 'Freedom'. In *The Blackwell Encyclopaedia of Political Thought*, edited by David W. Miller, Janet Coleman, William Connolly, and Alan Ryan, 8th ed., 163–6. Oxford/Malden: Blackwell, 1998.

Ryrie, Alec. 'Tudor Brexit: From Ecclesia Anglicana to Anglicanism'. *Studies: An Irish Quarterly Review* 106, no. 424 (2017): 425–30.

Sacheverell, Henry. *The Character of a Low-Church-Man: Drawn in Answer to The True Character of a Church-Man: Shewing the False Pretences to That Name*. London: s.n., 1702.

Sacheverell, Henry. *The New Association of Those Called, Moderate-Church-Men, with the Modern-Whigs and Fanaticks, to under-Mine and Blow-Up the Present Church and Government, Occasion'd, by a Late Pamphlet [by J. Dennis] Entituled [sic], The Danger of Priest-Craft, &c., with a Suppl., by a True-Church-Man*. 3rd corrected ed. London: s.n., 1702.

Sack, James J. *From Jacobite to Conservative: Reaction and Orthodoxy in Britain, c. 1760 to 1832*. New York: Cambridge University Press, 1993.

Schaich, Michael. 'Monarchy and Religion (Introduction)'. In *Monarchy and Religion. The Transformation of Royal Culture in Eighteenth-Century Europe*, 1–40. Studies of the German Historical Institute London. Oxford: Oxford University Press, 2007.

Schaich, Michael. 'The Public Sphere'. In *A Companion to Eighteenth-Century Europe*, edited by Peter H. Wilson, 125–40. Malden, MA/Oxford: Blackwell Publishing Ltd, 2008.

Schlögl, Rudolf. *Anwesende und Abwesende. Grundriss für eine Gesellschaftsgeschichte der Frühen Neuzeit*, 2014.

Schlögl, Rudolf. 'Politik beobachten. Öffentlichkeit und Medien in der Frühen Neuzeit'. *Zeitschrift für Historische Forschung* 35, no. 4 (2008): 581–616.

Schlögl, Rudolf. 'Revolutionsmedien – Medienrevolutionen. Was Historiker daran interessiert'. In *Revolutionsmedien – Medienrevolutionen*, edited by Sven Grampp, Kay Kirchmann, Marcus Sandl, Eva Wiebel, and Rudolf Schlögl, 19–24. Konstanz: UVK Verlagsgesellschaft mbH, 2008.

Schmidt, Rainer. 'Verfassungssoziologie als Kulturwissenschaft: Zur Spannung von rechtlichen und sozialen Normen'. In *Verfassungsidee und Verfassungspolitik*, edited by Marcus Llanque and Daniel Schulz, 117–36. Berlin: De Gruyter Oldenbourg, 2015.

Schmitt, Sigrid. *Kriminalität und Gesellschaft in Spätmittelalter und Neuzeit*. Stuttgart: Steiner, 2005.

Schmohl, Johann Christian, ed. *Über Nordamerika und Demokratie: ein Brief aus England*. Koppenhagen [Königsberg]: s.n., 1781.

Schnapp, Jeffrey T., and Matthew Tiews. 'Introduction: A Book of Crowds'. In *Crowds*, edited by Jeffrey T. Schnapp and Matthew Tiews, ix–xvi. Standford, CA: Stanford University Press, 2006.

Schuchard, Marsha Keith. *Emanuel Swedenborg, Secret Agent on Earth and in Heaven: Jacobites, Jews, and Freemasons in Early Modern Sweden*. Leiden/Boston, MA: Brill, 2012.

Schwartz, Barry. 'George Washington and the Whig Conception of Heroic Leadership'. Edited by American Sociological Association. *American Sociological Review* 48, no. 1 (1983): 18–33.

Schweizer, Karl Wolfgang. 'Stuart, John, Third Earl of Bute (1713–1792)'. In *Oxford Dictionary of National Biography. In Association with The British Academy. From the Earliest Times to the Year 2000*, 53, 173–8. Oxford: Oxford University Press, 2004.

Schwerhoff, Gerd. Review of *B. Stollberg-Rilinger, Kulturgeschichte des Politischen; Asch, Ronald G.; Freist, Dagmar, Staatsbildung als kultureller Prozess and Brakensiek, Stefan;*

Wunder, Heide, Ergebene Diener ihrer Herren?: Herrschaftsvermittlung im alten Europa and Stollberg-Rilinger, Barbara, Was heißt Kulturgeschichte des Politischen?, by Barbara Stollberg-Rilinger, Ronald G. Asch, Stefan Brakensiek, Dagmar Freist, and Heide Wunder. H-Soz-u-Kult, H-Review, October 2006. https://www.h-net.org/reviews/showrev.php?id=19828.

Scot, James. 'SP 54/15/59: James Scot, Reporting the Attack on Him by a Mob in Dundee during His Journey Home'. Dundee, 5 August 1725. SP 54/15/59. The National Archives, Kew.

Sekretariat der Deutschen Bischofskonferenz. *Terrorismus als ethische Herausforderung. Menschenwürde und Menschenrechte.* Vol. 94. Die deutschen Bischöfe. Bonn: DBK, 2011.

Seume, Johann Gottfried. 'Schreiben aus Amerika nach Deutschland'. *Neue Litteratur und Völkerkunde (1787–1791)* 3, no. 2 (1789): 362–81.

Shagan, Ethan H. *Popular Politics and the English Reformation.* Cambridge: Cambridge University Press, 2003.

Shagan, Ethan H. *The Rule of Moderation: Violence, Religion and the Politics of Restraint in Early Modern England.* Cambridge: Cambridge University Press, 2011.

Sharpe, J. 'John the Painter: The First Modern Terrorist'. *The Journal of Forensic Psychiatry & Psychology* 18, no. 2 (2007): 278–81.

Sherburne, John Henry. *The Life and Character of John Paul Jones, a Captain in the United States Navy: During the Revolutionary War.* 2nd ed. Ann Arbor, MI: University Microfilms International, 1976.

Shuger, Debora. 'Absolutist Theology. The Sermons of John Donne'. In *The English Sermon Revised. Religion, Literature and History 1600–1750*, edited by Lori Anne Ferrell and Peter McCullough, 115–35. Politics, Culture & Society in Early Modern Britain. Manchester: Manchester University Press, 2000.

Siebenhüner, Kim, and Kaspar von Greyerz. 'Einleitung'. In *Religion und Gewalt in der Frühen Neuzeit. Konflikte, Rituale, Deutungen*, edited by Kaspar von Greyerz and Kim Siebenhüner, 215, 9–25. Veröffentlichungen des Max-Planck-Instituts für Geschichte. Göttingen: Vandenhoeck & Ruprecht, 2006. https://boris.unibe.ch/66215/.

Sikora, Michael. *Der Adel in der Frühen Neuzeit.* Geschichte kompakt. Darmstadt: Wissenschaftliche Buchgesellschaft, 2009.

Simes, Douglas. 'Ireland, 1760–1820'. In *Press, Politics and the Public Sphere in Europe and North America, 1760–1820*, 113–39. Cambridge: Cambridge University Press, 2002.

Skerret, Ralph. *National Blessings Proper Motives to National Piety: A Sermon Preach'd before the Right Honourable the Lord Mayor, the Aldermen, and the Citizens of London, in the Cathedral Church of St. Paul, on Thursday the 7th of June, 1716. Being the Day of Publick Thanksgiving for the Blessing of God upon His Majesty's Counsels and Arms in Suppressing the Late Unnatural Rebellion.* London: Eman. Matthews/E. Symon, 1716.

Skerret, Ralph. *The Subjects Duty to the Higher Powers: Set Forth in a Sermon Preach'd before the Right Honourable the Lord Mayor, the Aldermen, and the Citizens of London, in the Cathedral Church of St. Paul, on Munday [sic] the 30th of January, 1715, Being the Day of the Martyrdom of King Charles I.* London: J. Phillips/E. Symon/J. Roberts, 1716.

Skinner, Quentin. *Hobbes and Republican Liberty.* Cambridge: Cambridge University Press, 2008.

Skinner, Stephen. *A New English Dictionary Shewing the Etymological Derivation of the English Tongue, in Two Parts. Part I. Explaining All the Common English Words, and Shewing Their Derivation from the Proper Fountains. Part II. An Etymological Explication of the Proper Names of Men, Women, Rivers, Counties, Cities, Towns,*

Villages, &c. Which Were Formerly Used by the English-Saxons, or Are Now Common amongst Us. A Work of Great Use to the English Reader, Who Is Curious to Know the Original of His Mother Tongue. Early English Books, 1641–1700/1955:08. London: E. H. and W. H./Timothy Childe, 1691.

Skjönsberg, Max. 'Party in Eighteenth-Century Politics'. Government-owned website. *The History of Parliament*, 23 February 2021. https://thehistoryofparliament.wordpress.com/2021/02/23/party-in-eighteenth-century-politics/.

Skjönsberg, Max. *The Persistence of Party: Ideas of Harmonious Discord in Eighteenth-Century Britain*. Ideas in Context. Cambridge: Cambridge University Press, 2021. doi:10.1017/9781108894500.

Skuncke, Marie-Christine, Robert Darnton, Jean Sgard, John Brewer, and Carla Hesse. 'Media and Political Culture in the Eighteenth Century'. *Kungl. Vitterhetsakademien. Kungl. Vitterhets Historie Och Antikvitets Akademien*, 24 March 2017. http://vitterhetsakad.bokorder.se/en-US/article/127/media-and-political-culture-in-the-eighteenth.

Slaughter, Thomas P. *The Whiskey Rebellion: Frontier Epilogue to the American Revolution*. New York: Oxford University Press, 1988.

Small, Stephen. *Political Thought in Ireland 1776–1798. Republicanism, Patriotism, and Radicalism*. Oxford: Clarendon Press/Oxford University Press, 2002.

Smith, D. W. 'The Hexham Riot'. This article was first published in the NDFHS Journal, Vol. 5, Number 2, January 1980. *Northumberland & Durham Family History Society*, April 2009. http://ndfhs.org/Articles/HexhamRiot.html.

Smith, Hannah. *Georgian Monarchy. Politics and Culture, 1714–1760*. Cambridge Studies in Early Modern British History. Cambridge: Cambridge University Press, 2006.

Smith, Hannah. 'The Idea of a Protestant Monarchy in Britain 1714–1760'. *Past & Present* 185 (November 2004): 91–118.

Smith, Helen. *Grossly Material Things: Women and Book Production in Early Modern England*. Oxford: Oxford University Press, 2012.

Smith, Jay M. *Nobility Reimagined: The Patriotic Nation in Eighteenth-Century France*. Ithaca, NY: Cornell University Press, 2005.

Smith, John, ed. *Assassination of the King! The Conspirators Exposed; or, an Account of the Apprehension, Treatment in Prison, and Repeated Examination before the Privy Council of John Smith and George Higgins, on a Charge of High Treason*. London: John Smith, 1795.

Smith, William. *The Innocency and Conscientiousness of the Quakers: Asserted and Cleared from the Evil Surmises, False Aspersions, and Unrighteous Suggestions of Judge Keeling, Expressed in His Speech [...] at the Sessions-House in the Old Baily [...] for the Tryal of Some of the Said People by the Late Act Made to Prevent and Suppress Seditious Conventicles: Wherein Also Is Shewed That This Law Doth Not Concern Them [...] They Being No Seditious Sectaries*. London: s.n., 1664.

Smith-Rosenberg, Carroll. *This Violent Empire: The Birth of an American National Identity*. Chapel Hill, NC: Omohundro Institute of Early American History and Culture/University of North Carolina Press, 2003.

Smuts, Malcolm. 'Introduction: The Historiographical Legacies of David Underdown'. *History Compass* 11, no. 5 (2013): 331–40.

Snowden, Thomas. 'By the Dutch Mails That Arriv'd on Tuesday Night, and One That Came Yesterday, We Have the Following Advices'. *The Flying Post, or, The Post Master* 508 (12 August 1698): 1–2.

Society of the Friends of the People. *The Minutes of the Proceedings of the General Convention of the Delegates, from the Societies of the Friends of the People throughout*

Scotland. At Their Several Sittings in Edinburgh, on the Eleventh, Twelfth, and Thirteenth of December, 1792. Edinburgh: J. Robertson, 1793.

Sons of Liberty. *The True Sons of Liberty and Supporters of the Non-Importation Agreement, Are Determined to Resent Any the Least Insult or Menace Offer'd to Any One or More of the Several Committees Appointed by the Body at Faneuil-Hall, and Chastise Any One or More of Them as They Deserve and Will Also Support the Printers in Any Thing the Committees Shall Desire Them to Print.* Boston, MA: s.n, 1768.

Sowerby, Scott Andrew. 'James II's Revolution: The Politics of Religious Toleration in England 1685-1689'. PhD thesis, Harvard University, 2006. Copac.

Sowerby, Scott Andrew. *Making Toleration: The Repealers and the Glorious Revolution*. Cambridge, MA: Harvard University Press, 2013.

Speck, William Arthur. 'The Current State of Sacheverell Scholarship'. *Parliamentary History* 31, no. 1 (February 2012): 16-27.

Spencer, Benjamin, William Hicks, and William Villers. 'HO 42/35/36: Letter from [Dr Benjamin Spencer], William Hicks and William Villers, Magistrates at the Public Office, Birmingham [Warwickshire]'. Letter. Birmingham, 23 June 1795. HO 42/35/16. The National Archives, Kew. https://discovery.nationalarchives.gov.uk/details/r/C12281905.

Stanhope, Philip Dormer [4th Earl of Chesterfield], and Thomas [Duke of Newcastle] Pelham-Holles. *Private Correspondence of Chesterfield and Newcastle, 1744-46, [...] with an Introduction and Notes*. Edited by Richard Lodge. Camden, Third Series, 44. London: Royal Historical Society, 1930.

Stanley, Laura. 'The Broomhall Riots of 1791'. Educational website owned by the city council. *Our Broomhall: Past and Present Stories from a Vibrant Urban Community in Sheffield*, 21 January 2016. http://www.ourbroomhall.org.uk/content/explore/topics/politics/the-broom-hall-riots.

Stanwood, Owen. 'Rumours and Rebellions in the English Atlantic World, 1688-9'. In *The Final Crisis of the Stuart Monarchy. The Revolutions of 1688-91 in Their British, Atlantic and European Contexts*, edited by Tim Harris and Stephen Taylor, 189-242. Studies in Early Modern Cultural, Political and Social History. Woodbridge: Boydell & Brewer, 2013.

Starkie, Andrew. *The Church of England and the Bangorian Controversy, 1716-1721*. Woodbridge: Boydell & Brewer, 2007.

Steinmetz, Willibald. 'Neue Wege einer historischen Semantik des Politischen'. In *'Politik' : Situationen eines Wortgebrauchs im Europa der Neuzeit*, 9-40. Frankfurt: Campus, 2007.

Steinmetz, Willibald, and Heinz-Gerhard Haupt. 'The Political as Communicative Space in History. The Bielefeld Approach'. In *Writing Political History Today*, edited by Heinz-Gerhard Haupt, Willibald Steinmetz, and Ingrid Gilcher-Holtey, 11-33. Frankfurt/New York: Campus, 2013.

Steinmetz, Willibald, Claus Kröger, and Rebecca Moltmann, eds. *Abschlussbericht des SFB 584 'Das Politische als Kommunikationsraum in der Geschichte', 3. Förderphase (2008-2012)*. Bielefeld: Universität Bielefeld, 2013.

Stevenson, John. *Artisans and Democrats: Sheffield and the French Revolution, 1789-97*. London: Historical Association, 1989.

Stevenson, John. *Popular Disturbances in England 1700-1832*. E-Book. Abingdon: Routledge, 2014.

Stollberg-Rilinger, Barbara. *Europa im Jahrhundert der Aufklärung*. Stuttgart: Reclam, 2000.

Stollberg-Rilinger, Barbara. *Rituale*. Frankfurt: Campus, 2013.

Stollberg-Rilinger, Barbara. 'Symbolische Kommunikation in der Vormoderne: Begriffe – Thesen – Forschungsperspektiven'. *Zeitschrift für historische Forschung* 31, no. 4 (2004): 489–527.

Strong, Rowan. *Anglicanism and the British Empire c. 1700–1850*. Oxford: Oxford University Press, 2007.

Strong, Rowan. 'The Resurgence of Colonial Anglicanism: The Colonial Bishoprics Fund, 1840–1'. *Studies in Church History* 44 (2008): 196–213. doi:10.1017/ S0424208400003594.

Sturtevant, S. T., and Anquetil Matthew Henderson. *The Preacher's Manual: Lects. on Preaching*. Revised with an introductory essay by A. M. Henderson, 4th ed. London: s.n., 1866.

Suger, Zachary. *The Preservation of Judah from the Insults and Invasion of the Idolatrous Assyrians. A Sermon Preach'd at York, on Sunday, the 29th Day of Sept. 1745. On Occasion of the Present Rebellion in Scotland, and Intended Invasion by the French*. York: John Hildyard; and sold by J. and P. Knapton in Ludgate-Street; T. Longman and T. Shewell, in Pater-Noster-Row; and A. Dod, in the Strand, 1745.

Swift, Jonathan. *The Works of Jonathan Swift, Containing Additional Letters, Tracts, and Poems, with Notes, and a Life of the Author, by W. Scott*. Vol. 3. Edinburgh/London: Archibald Constable & Co., 1824.

Szechi, Daniel. *1715: The Great Jacobite Rebellion*. New Haven, CT/London: Yale University Press, 2006.

Szechi, Daniel. 'A Blueprint for Tyranny? Sir Edward Hales and the Catholic Jacobite Response to the Revolution of 1688'. *The English Historical Review* 116, no. 466 (2001): 342–67.

Szechi, Daniel. 'Professor Daniel Szechi (Subject Areas)'. *The University of Manchester: School of History, Arts and Cultures*, 2013. http://www.arts.manchester.ac.uk/ subjectareas/history/academicstaff/danielszechi/.

Szechi, Daniel. Review of *Riot, Risings, and Revolution: Governance and Violence in Eighteenth-Century England*, by Ian Gilmour. *The Journal of Modern History* 67, no. 3 (1995): 703–5.

Szechi, Daniel. *The Jacobites*. Manchester: Manchester University Press, 1994.

T., H. [pseud.]. *An Uprore in the North, at Hvll, about a Moneth Since*. London, 1641.

Taylor, David Francis. 'Coalition Dances. Georgian Caricature's Choreographies of Power'. *Music in Art. International Journal for Music Iconography*, Research Center for Music Iconography 36, no. 1/2 (2011): 117–30.

Taylor, Stephen. 'Hoadly, Benjamin (1676–1761), Bishop of Winchester'. In *Oxford Dictionary of National Biography*, 27, Hickeringill-Hooper, 340–8. Oxford: Oxford University Press, 2004.

Taylor, Stephen. 'The Clergy at the Courts of George I and George II'. In *Monarchy and Religion. The Transformation of Royal Culture in Eighteenth-Century Europe*, edited by Michael Schaich, 129–52. Studies of the German Historical Institute London. Oxford: Oxford University Press, 2007.

Tenax [pseud.]. 'To the Author of the DAILY COURANT. The Conclusion of Fog of the 13th of October Refuted'. Edited by Samuel Buckley. *Daily Courant* 5544 (12 January 1734): 1–2.

The History of Parliament Trust. 'Parliaments 1715–1754'. Educational website owned by The History of Parliament Trust, maintained by the Historical Research Institute. *The History of Parliament. British Political, Local and Social History*, 2013. http:// www.historyofparliamentonline.org/research/parliaments/parliaments-1715-1754.

The History of Parliament Trust. 'Parliaments 1754–1790: Wilkes, America and Reform'. Educational website owned by The History of Parliament Trust, maintained by the

Historical Research Institute. *The History of Parliament. British Political, Local and Social History*, 2013. http://www.historyofparliamentonline.org/research/parliaments/parliaments-1754-1790.

The Parliament of the United Kingdom. '1532–1603'. Government-owned website. *Living Heritage*, 12 April 2015. http://www.parliament.uk/about/living-heritage/evolutionofparliament/parliamentaryauthority/the-gunpowder-plot-of-1605/keydates/1532-1603/.

The Parliament of the United Kingdom. 'The Clergy In Parliament' on Thursday 8 May 1834'. Government-owned website. *UK Parliament.* Accessed 5 December 2021. https://hansard.parliament.uk//Commons/1834-05-08/debates/f9504d04-7c26-418a-833a-c61a020cdffa/TheClergyInParliament.

The People [pseud.]. *Whereas It Has Been Reported That a Permit Will Be Given by the Custom-House for Landing the Tea Now on Board a Vessel Laying in This Harbour, Commanded by Capt. Hall: This Is to Remind the Publick, That It Was Solemnly.* Boston, MA: s.n., 1773.

Thévenot, Laurent. *L'action au pluriel. Sociologie des régimes d'engagement.* Textes à l'appui. Politique et sociétés. Paris: Éditions la Découverte, 2006.

Thiel, Thorsten. 'Opposition verfassen. Demokratie, Republikanismus und die Etablierung von Gegenmacht'. In *Verfassungsidee und Verfassungspolitik*, edited by Marcus Llanque and Daniel Schulz, 271–92. Berlin: De Gruyter Oldenbourg, 2015.

Thomas, Evan. *John Paul Jones: Sailor, Hero, Father of the American Navy.* New York: Simon & Schuster, 2007.

Thompson, Andrew C. 'Charles Watson-Wentworth, 2nd Marquess of Rockingham'. Educational website owned by the UK Government. *History of Government Blog*, 25 February 2015. https://history.blog.gov.uk/2015/02/25/charles-watson-wentworth-2nd-marquess-of-rockingham/.

Thompson, Andrew C. 'George I and George II. The New Monarchs'. In *Als die Royals aus Hannover kamen. The Hanoverians on Britain's Throne 1714–1837*, edited by Katja Lembke, 46–67. Hanover: Niedersächsisches Landesmuseum Hanover, 2014.

Thompson, Andrew C. 'The Hanoverian Succession in Britain and European Politics, c. 1700–1720'. *Oxford Dictionary of National Biography*, 3 July 2014. https://doi.org/10.1093/ref:odnb/106970.

Thompson, Edward Palmer. *The Making of the English Working Class.* London: V. Gollancz, 1963.

Thoreau, Henry David. 'Civil Disobedience (1849)'. In *Civil Disobedience and Other Essays*, edited by Philip Smith, 1–18. Dover Thrift Editions. New York: Dover Publications, 1993.

Thorne, R. G. 'Fox, Hon. Charles James (1749–1806), of St. Anne's Hill, Chertsey, Surr.' Educational website owned by The History of Parliament Trust, maintained by the Historical Research Institute. *The History of Parliament. British Political, Local and Social History*, 2015. http://historyofparliamentonline.org/.

Thyrêt, Isolde. *Between God and Tsar: Religious Symbolism and the Royal Women of Muscovite Russia.* DeKalb: Northern Illinois University Press, 2001.

Towers, Joseph. *A Letter to the Rev. Dr. Nowell, Principal of St. Mary Hall, King's Professor of Modern History, and Public Orator in the University of Oxford: Occasioned by His Very Extraordinary Sermon Preached before the House of Commons on the Thirtieth of January, 1772.* London: Joseph Towers, 1772.

Traub, Rainer. 'Michels Erwachen. Wie Deutsche im "Vormärz" beginnen, aufzumucken'. *Der Spiegel Geschichte: Die Revolution von 1848. Als Deutschland die Freiheit entdeckte*, no. 3 (2014): 16–23.

Traub, Rainer, and Dietmar Pieper. '"Die Nation war das große Banner" – der Historiker Deiter Hein über ein umwälzendes Jahr'. *Der Spiegel Geschichte: Die Revolution von 1848. Als Deutschland die Freiheit entdeckte*, no. 3 (2014): 24–31.
Troy, John Thomas. *To the Rev. Roman Catholic Clergy, of the Archdiocess of Dublin*. Dublin: s.n., 1803.
Trumbull, John. *A New Proclamation!* Hartford: Ebenezer Watson, 1775.
Trumbull, Jonathan. *Copy of a Letter to His Excellency Gen. Gage*. Boston, MA: s.n., 1775.
Tutchin, John. '[Country-m. Master, Here's a Letter to You from a Gentleman, Proposing a Method to Prevent Abuses in Electing Members to Parliament]'. *Observator* 87 (1707): [not paged].
United States Army, ed. *The Trial of Major John Andre: With an Appendix, Containing Sundry Interesting Letters Interchanged on the Occasion*. Palmer, MA: Ezekiel Terry, for James Warner, Wilbraham, 1810.
Urquhart, James. *John Paul Jones, America's Greatest Seaman: Nithdale's Greatest Son, 1776–1976: A Bicentennial Salute and Souvenir from Great Britain*. Dumfries: J. Urquhart, 1982.
US National Park Service. 'North Bridge Questions – Minute Man National Historical Park'. Government-owned website. *Lexington and Concord*, 10 October 2015. http://www.nps.gov/mima/north-bridge-questions.htm.
Valliere, Paul. *Conciliarism: A History of Decision-Making in the Church*. Cambridge/New York: Cambridge University Press, 2012.
Vietto, Angela. *Women and Authorship in Revolutionary America*. Aldershot/Burlington, VT: Routledge, 2017.
Villani, Stefano. 'Seventeenth Century Italy and English Radical Movements'. In *Varieties of Seventeenth- and Early Eighteenth-Century English Radicalism in Context*, edited by Ariel Hessayon and David Finnegan, 145–59. Farnham: Ashgate, 2011.
Visscher, Christian de. 'Autorités politiques et haute administration: une dichotomie repensée par la NGP ?' *Revue internationale de politique comparee* 11, no. 2 (2004): 205–24.
Voigt, Rüdiger. 'Abschied vom Staat – Rückkehr zum Staat?' In *Abschied vom Staat – Rückkehr zum Staat?*, 9–26. Baden-Baden: Nomos, 1993.
Vyse, William. 'MS Hyde 77 (3. 148): William Vyse to Mr. Barker of Lichfield (England)'. Autograph letter, signed. Birmingham, 21 November 1753. Houghton Library, Harvard University, Cambridge, MA.
Wake, William. *The State of the Church and Clergy of England, in Their Councils, Synods, Convocations, Conventions*. London: for R. Sare, at Gray's-Inn-Gate in Holborn, 1703.
Waldstreicher, David. 'The Nationalization and Racialization of American Politics'. In *Contesting Democracy. Substance & Structure in American Political History 1775–2000*, edited by Byron E. Shafer and Anthony J. Badger, 37–64. Kansas: University Press of Kansas, 2001.
Wallace, Valerie. *Scottish Presbyterianism and Settler Colonial Politics: Empire of Dissent*. Cambridge Imperial and Post-Colonial Studies (CIPCSS). London: Palgrave Macmillan, 2018.
Wallice, James. *The Trial at Large of Francis Henry de La Motte, for High Treason, at the Sessions House in the Old Bailey, on Saturday the Fourteenth of July, 1781*. London: Davis, 1781.
Walsh, Robert. *A True Narrative and Manifest, Set Forth by Sir Robert Walsh Knight and Batt: Which He Is Ready All Manner of Ways to Justify, as Relating unto Plots, Designs, Troubles and Insurrections, Which Were Intended to Have Been Set a Foot, towards the*

Subversion of His Most Excellent Majesties Laws and Government, Not by a Private Information, or Other, but before Any Court of Justice, Discipline; Either in the Civil, Common, or Marshal Law, and to Reply, or Disanul the Printed Paper, in Part of Edmund Everard an Irish Man, Who Was so Long Prisoner in the Tower. And to Make out Why He Was so Detained, Nothing Relating to the Plot, but Was for His Intent, to Have Poysoned the Duke of Monmouth, as Shall More Amply Be Made out in This Manifest. London: for the author, 1679.

Walter, John. *Understanding Popular Violence in the English Revolution: The Colchester Plunderers*. Cambridge: Cambridge University Press, 1999.

Walzer, Michael. *The Revolution of the Saints: A Study in the Origins of Radical Politics*. Cambridge, MA: Harvard University Press, 1965.

Ward, Edward, and John Dunton. *The Whigs Unmask'd: Being the Secret History of the Calf's-Head-Club. Shewing the Rise and Progress of That Infamous Society since the Grand Rebellion*. 8th ed. London: J. Morphew, 1713.

Ward, Matthew C. Review of *American Leviathan: Empire, Nation, and Revolutionary Frontier*, by Patrick Griffin. *The Journal of American History* 95, no. 1 (2008): 187–8.

Ward, Sir Adolphus William. *The Electress Sophia and the Hanoverian Succession*. London: Goupil & Co., 1903.

Warner, Jessica. *John the Painter: Terrorist of the American Revolution*. New York: Four Walls Eight Windows, 2004.

Warner, Jessica. *John the Painter: Terrorist of the American Revolution: A Brief Account of His Short Life*. London: Profile Books, 2005.

Watson, George, ed. *The New Cambridge Bibliography of English Literature*. Vol. 2, 1600–800. Cambridge: Cambridge University Press, 1971.

Wefer, Matthias. *Kontingenz und Dissens. Postheroische Perspektiven des politischen Systems*. Studien zur Politischen Gesellschaft. Wiesbaden: VS Verlag für Sozialwissenschaften, 2004.

Weinbrot, Howard D. Review of *The Gordon Riots Redivivus*, by Ian Haywood and John Seed. *Huntington Library Quarterly* 75, no. 4 (2012): 615–20.

Welch, Ellen R. 'State Truths, Private Letters, and Images of Public Opinion in the Ancien Régime: Sévigné on Trials'. *French Studies: A Quarterly Review* 67, no. 2 (April 2013): 1–14.

Wellenreuther, Hermann. 'The Political Role of the Nobility in Eighteenth-Century England'. In *Britain and Germany Compared: Nationality, Society and Nobility in the Eighteenth Century*, 13, 99–140. Göttinger Gespräche Zur Geschichtswissenschaft. Göttingen: Wallstein, 2001.

Welsh, Frank. *The Four Nations: A History of the United Kingdom*. New Haven, CT/London: Yale University Press, 2002.

Wharton, Philip. *Select and Authentick Pieces Written by the Late Duke of Wharton. Viz. I. His Speech on [...] the Bill to Inflict [...] Penalties on Francis Lord Bishop of Rochester. II. His Single Protest on That Occasion; with the Previous Protest of the Other Lords. III. His Letter to the Bishop in the Tower. IV. His Letter in Mist's Journal, Aug. 24. 1728. V. His Reasons for Leaving His Native Country, and Espousing the Cause of [...] King James III. VI. A Letter from Wolfe the Printer to Sir R.W.* Boulogne: J. Wolfe, 1731.

Whitehead, J. 'SP 89/59/12: Consul J. Whitehead to [E. Weston ?]'. Oporto, 23 January 1764. SP 89/59/12. The National Archives, Kew. https://discovery.nationalarchives.gov.uk/details/r/C6846653.

Wildes, Harry Emerson. *Anthony Wayne, Trouble Shooter of the American Revolution*. New York: Harcourt, Brace & Co, 1941.

Wildvogel, Christian. *Dissertationem Politico-Iuridicam De Tumultibus = Vulgo von Auflauff, Aufruhr*. Jena: Johann Adolf Müller, 1714.

Wilhelmy, Jean-Pierre. *Soldiers for Sale: German 'Mercenaries' with the British in Canada during the American Revolution (1776-83)*. Montréal: Baraka Books, 2011.

Wilkes, John. *Letters, from the Year 1774 to the Year 1796, Addresses to His Daughter, the Late Miss Wilkes: With a Collection of His Miscellaneous Poems, to Which Is Prefixed a Memoir of the Life of Mr. Wilkes*. Edited by Sir William Rough. London: Longman, Hurst, Rees, and Orme, 1804.

Wilkes, John. *The Voluntary Exile; or, the English Poet's Sermon in Verse, Written upon Divers Important Subjects, before He Embarked for France, and Dedicated a La Coterie, or the Society of English Patriots. Part the First. With Variety of Notes, Religious, Historical, and Political*. Edited by Dr. Free [pseud.?]. London: for the family of the author/J. Almon in Piccadilly/J. Warcus, 1765.

Williams, Charles. *The New Minister – or as It Should Be*. Britain: hand-coloured etching, 346 mm × 340 mm, printed by Walker, 1806. https://www.britishmuseum.org/collection/object/P_1868-0808-7425.

Williams, John, ed. *A Short Account of the Motives Which Determined the Man, Called John The Painter; and a Justification of His Conduct; Written by Himself, and Sent to His FRIEND, Mr. A. TOMKINS, with a Request to Publish It after His Execution*. London: s.n., 1777.

Williams, Mark R. F. 'Translating the Jansenist Controversy in Britain and Ireland'. *English Historical Review* 134, no. 566 (28 February 2019): 59–91. doi:10.1093/ehr/cey397.

Wilson, Kathleen. *The Sense of the People: Politics, Culture and Imperialism in England, 1715-1785*. Cambridge: Cambridge University Press, 1995.

Winkler, Karl Tilman. *Handwerk und Markt: Druckerhandwerk, Vertriebswesen und Tagesschrifttum in London 1695-1750*. Stuttgart: Franz Steiner Verlag, 1993.

Winkler, Karl Tilman. *Wörterkrieg: politische Debattenkultur in England, 1689-1750*. Stuttgart: Franz Steiner Verlag, 1998.

Winstanley, D. A. *Lord Chatham and the Whig Opposition*. Cambridge: Cambridge University Press, 2011.

Wolcot, John, ed. *Liberty's Last Squeak; Containing an Elegiac Ballad, an Ode to an Informer [&c.] by Peter Pindar, Esq*. London: s.n., 1795.

Wolff, Francis. 'La politique divise, le politique rassemble'. *Le Monde.fr*. 11 February 2015, digital ed. https://www.lemonde.fr/idees/article/2015/02/11/la-politique-divise-le-politique-rassemble_4574280_3232.html.

Wood, Andy. *Riot, Rebellion and Popular Politics in Early Modern England*. Social History in Perspective. Basingstoke: Palgrave, 2002.

Würgler, Andreas. 'Das Modernisierungspotential von Unruhen im 18. Jahrhundert: Ein Beitrag zur Entstehung der politischen Öffentlichkeit in Deutschland und der Schweiz'. *Geschichte und Gesellschaft* 21 (1995): 195–217.

Würgler, Andreas. 'Fama und Rumor: Gerücht, Aufruhr und Presse im Ancien Régime'. *Werkstatt Geschichte* 15 (1996): 20–32.

Würgler, Andreas. *Medien in der frühen Neuzeit (Enzyklopädie deutscher Geschichte, Band 85)*. 1st ed. Munich: Oldenbourg Wissenschaftsverlag, 2009.

Würgler, Andreas. 'Rezension von: Das Mediensystem im Alten Reich der Frühen Neuzeit (1600-1750)'. *sehepunkte. Rezensionsjournal für die Geschichtswissenschaft* 11, no. 2 (2011): [not paged].

Würgler, Andreas. *Unruhen und Öffentlichkeit: Städtische und ländliche Protestbewegungen im 18. Jahrhundert*. Vol. 1. Frühneuzeit-Forschungen. Tübingen: Bibliotheca Acad., 1995.
[Wyes]. 'Wyes's Letter Verbatim, London, March 5, 1724'. *Caledonian Mercury*, 12 March 1724, 3678–9.
Yates, Nigel. *Eighteenth Century Britain: Religion and Politics 1714–1815*. Harlow: Routledge, 2007.
York, Neil. 'George III, Tyrant: The Crisis as Critic of Empire, 1775–1776'. *History* 94, no. 316 (2009): 434–60.
York, Neil Longley. *Burning the Dockyard: John the Painter and the American Revolution*. Portsmouth: Portsmouth City Council, 2001.
Zagorin, Perez. *Rebels and Rulers, 1500–1660*. Vol. I. Cambridge: Cambridge University Press, 1982.
Zaret, David. *Origins of Democratic Culture. Printing, Petitions, and the Public Sphere in Early-Modern England*. Princeton, NJ: Princeton University Press, 2000.

Index

This index lists people, places and concepts in alphabetical order. Most events covered in this book, such as riots occurring in a particular town or region, can be found by looking up the related place name.

Abercromby, Patrick 49, 61
abolitionism 16, 53, 71, 86, 89, 103
absolutism 38, 49, 56
abuses 14, 16, 43, 45, 97, 99, 110
Adams, Abigail 102
Adams, John 15, 51, 57, 74, 102, 111
Adams, Samuel 37
admonitions 75, 84
Africa 98, 111
agrarian, also see *rural* 65, 89, 91
agriculture 34, 97
Aitken, James [John the Painter] 7, 86
alcohol 31, 53, 89, 103
alien [foreign] 3–5, 7, 15, 17, 29, 39, 44, 47, 62, 64, 69, 71–72, 76, 88, 90–91, 95, 107, 110–111
alliances 48, 59, 67, 73, 87–88, 97, 111
Almon, John 15, 17, 56
Althusius, Johannes [Althaus] 29
American Revolution 7, 13, 15, 28, 32, 37, 40, 48, 60, 63, 75, 80, 87, 97, 99, 107
amnesty 36–37
anarchy 52, 63, 85, 95
André, John 87
Anglicanism [Church of England] 23–24, 28, 31, 41, 44, 47, 50, 59–65, 67–72, 74–77, 89, 91, 94, 96, 105, 107–109
Anne, Queen of England and Scotland (Great Britain since 1707) and Ireland 17, 28, 35, 44, 46, 61, 68, 76
aristocracy 1, 4, 9, 15, 24, 27, 29, 31–32, 39–40, 67, 81, 97
Armagh 57, 72, 95
armies 7, 18, 29, 34, 41, 50, 63, 75–76, 79–85, 87–90, 102

arms [weapons] 1, 3, 7, 24, 29, 38, 41–42, 50, 53, 57–58, 72, 75, 79–81, 85–86, 88–90, 95–96, 100, 102–103, 107, 109–110
arson, also see *incendiaries* 7, 85–86
Asia 7
assassination 28, 38, 86, 90
assault 41, 91, 93
assemblies 9, 13, 15, 28, 35, 44, 51, 53, 57, 63–64, 66, 70, 91, 99, 102
associations 17, 19, 23–24, 38, 52, 57–58, 62, 71, 73, 77, 99–100, 103
attacks 7, 17, 27–28, 37, 39, 41, 46, 50, 53, 58, 68, 72–74, 81–82, 84–86, 90, 96, 98, 100, 109
Atterbury, Francis, Lord Bishop of Rochester 18, 45, 47
attorneys 38, 57, 99, 110
Augusta of Saxe-Gotha-Altenburg, Dowager Princess of Wales 40–41
autonomy 2, 13, 52, 60, 70

Bacon, Nathaniel 98
Bangorian Controversy 44, 68–69
battles 14, 31, 36, 38, 41, 69, 75, 80–81, 84–85, 89, 93, 95
Bean, Thomas 31, 45
beheading 111
Belfast 67–68
Bentham, Edward 15, 20, 75
Bernard, Francis 13–16, 53, 99
Bexon, Scipion Jérôme 4
Bible 12, 38, 40, 63, 67, 71, 75
Birmingham 18–19, 46, 56, 58, 74, 99, 101
birthdays (royal) 98
blood 8, 28, 33, 36, 39–40, 55, 63, 89, 103, 105, 107, 109

Index

Bodin, Jean 11, 81
Bohun, Edmund 31
Bollan, William 16
Bonaparte, Napoleon 1
bonfires 29
borders 1, 14, 24, 36, 87, 95
Boston 7, 15, 61, 74–75, 79, 87, 89, 99
bourgeoisie 13, 40–41, 86
Brandenburg-Ansbach, Caroline of 62
Brandshagen, Elisabeth 44
bravery 41, 81, 85
bread 17, 59, 97
bribery 32, 56
Bridgwater 79
Bristol 7, 34, 85
Britain 1–9, 11–20, 22–25, 27–77, 79–112
British Convention 38, 90
Britishness 24, 73
Broomhall 74
Broomhead 57
brutality 70, 87
buildings [as places of unrest] 24, 36, 50, 55, 63–64, 67, 94, 97, 101
Bunker Hill 75
Burgh, William 11, 20, 100
Burke, Edmund 31, 46, 74, 96
burning 8, 16, 29, 32, 68, 74, 100
business, also see *economy* 13, 30, 34, 37, 44, 55, 70, 82, 84, 95, 102
Bute, John Stuart, Lord 40–41, 55

Calico Riots 7
calumny 60, 67
Calvinism 51, 69–70, 75
Camden 55
camouflage 73
Canada 37, 76
captives [prisoners] 11, 17, 23, 50, 85, 87–88
Caribbean 9, 111
caricatures 28, 37, 55, 99
casualties 102
Catholic Relief 7–8, 50, 52, 56, 63
Catholicism 5, 7–8, 15, 19, 50, 52, 56, 59–65, 67, 70, 72–77, 89, 91, 93, 95, 99–100, 108
censorship 15–16, 57, 76, 102
ceremonies [rituals] 2, 12, 32, 34, 45, 57, 61, 68–70, 75, 80, 93

Charles I, King of England, Scotland, and Ireland 29, 44, 63, 67, 108–109
Charles II, King of England, Scotland, and Ireland 44, 108–109
Chartists 58
children 53, 82, 88, 97, 100, 110
Christianity 3, 33, 40, 42, 60, 63–65, 67–71, 73, 75–77, 96, 109
citizens [citizenship] 4–6, 8, 13, 15–17, 20, 33, 37–38, 40–41, 52–53, 55–57, 60, 64, 73, 75, 79, 81–82, 85–86, 88–91, 93–94, 96–97, 99–103, 107, 109–110
civilians 30–31, 62, 79, 86, 101
civilization 11, 56, 88, 94, 96, 98
Clarendon Code 108
clashes 32, 46, 72, 93
class 2–3, 5, 7, 21–22, 29, 31, 33, 40, 45, 47–48, 53, 57, 60, 63, 68, 76, 79, 81–82, 85, 92–93, 97–98, 100–103
clergy 15, 38, 52, 59–65, 68–74, 76, 89, 94, 97, 99, 102, 108
Clinton, (Sir) Henry 84–85
clothes [costumes, attires] 5, 8, 13, 18, 22–23, 28, 34–35, 53, 55–56, 62–65, 74, 81–82, 85, 87, 91, 96–100, 109, 112
clubs 22, 54–55, 57, 62–63, 94, 110
coalitions 48, 67
cockades, also see *clothes* 53, 57, 100
coffeehouses 22, 55, 91, 101
Colley (Collet), Thomas 41, 45
colonies [colonialism] 1, 3–4, 7, 13–15, 24, 27–28, 32, 37, 50–51, 53, 57, 63–64, 71, 75–76, 81–82, 85–87, 95–98, 100, 107, 111
colour 12, 81, 85
commemoration 29, 32, 89, 98, 110
commerce 14, 18, 22, 56, 93, 96, 98
committees 53–54, 57, 82–83, 99
Commons, House of 28–30, 43–46, 53, 74, 81, 96, 100
Commonwealth of England 29, 33, 52
compensations 8, 12, 85, 93
conciliarism 62, 70
Concord 75, 80
Confederation, Articles of 51
conformity 22, 62, 65, 67, 73, 108
Congregationalism 62
congregations 75, 98
conscience 70, 85, 108

conscriptions 79, 92
conservatism 6, 32–33, 39–41, 48, 50, 55–58, 64, 71–72, 74, 84, 89, 94, 97, 107
conspiracy [plots] 3, 17–18, 23, 28–29, 38, 47, 57, 72–74, 76, 85–86, 90, 95, 97, 100, 103, 107–110
Constitutional Convention 52
consumers 40, 92
Continental Congress 15, 110
contractual theory 25, 29, 32, 51, 68, 106
controversialism 67, 69
conventicles 108–109
conversion 62, 69, 76
conviction 34, 38, 73, 86–87, 90, 107–108, 110
Cooper, Anthony Ashley, 3rd Earl of Shaftesbury 95
cooperation 5–6, 17, 20, 50, 55, 58, 62, 81, 86, 94
corn, also see *food* 18, 53, 97
coronations 93
corruption 34, 37, 39, 47, 55–56, 98, 101
Corsica 93
costs 22, 30, 45, 52, 76, 87, 89, 93
cotton, also see *silk* 7, 53, 98
councils 39, 51, 107
counterfeiting, also see *forgery* 14
courtiers 29, 40, 56, 87
courts of law 4, 15–16, 18, 23–24, 32–33, 39, 42, 60, 86, 100, 105, 108, 111
crafts 13, 23, 63
credibility 14, 17, 99
crime 4, 16–18, 24, 37, 55, 86, 102, 110
Cromwell, Oliver 3, 29, 40, 63, 80
Cromwellian Protectorate 3, 29
crop [harvest] 34, 109
Crosfield, Robert Thomas, also see *London Corresponding Society* 38, 90
crowds [masses] 2, 6–8, 13, 18, 21, 29, 53, 56–57, 63, 68, 74, 79–81, 88, 90–91, 93–94, 96–98, 100–102
cruelty 37, 41, 96
Culloden, battle of 36, 63, 95
Cumberland, Duke of 37
cypher 17–18

Dalrymple, John 96
damage 3, 31, 46, 88, 93, 102

death 7, 22, 30, 34, 37–38, 40, 48, 54, 65, 67, 85–88, 101, 106, 110
debt 34, 44, 53
decency 99, 101
decision-making 23–24, 41, 44, 51, 60
declarations 23, 35–36, 100, 108
de-escalation 43, 102
defamation 16, 60
Defenders (Ireland) 72, 89
Defoe, Daniel 94
democracy 4–5, 22, 40, 64, 74
denunciations 103
deserters 84
despotism 37, 40, 52, 62, 106
Diamond, Battle of the 89
diplomacy 14, 33, 61, 81
disaffection 28–29, 38
discipline 56–57, 69, 84, 88–89, 97–98, 101
disguise, also see *clothes* 62, 65, 109
disorders 45, 65, 68, 87, 94
dissent 4–5, 11, 29, 31, 56, 59–64, 67–72, 74–76, 94, 108, 110
disturbances 8, 18–19, 65, 72, 102–103
divinity 32–33, 62, 68, 75, 106
doctrine 61–63, 67, 69, 71, 88
Downie, David, also see *British Convention* 38, 90
Dublin 43, 50, 65, 72, 89, 101
Dundass, Ralph, Lieutenant 50
Dundee 46
Dunmore 80
Durham 79
Dutch Republic 8
duty 20–21, 29–30, 33, 49, 58, 64–65, 68–71, 75, 86, 100

East India Company 34
economy, also see *business* 2–3, 21, 24, 28, 33–34, 40, 49, 52–53, 56, 59–60, 63, 80, 91–93, 96–97, 105–106, 110
Edinburgh 8, 15, 36, 49–50, 67, 73, 90, 98, 101
education 20–22, 29, 34, 72, 77, 81, 97, 101, 110–111
egalitarianism 42, 80, 83
elections, also see *voters* 6–8, 19, 24–25, 33, 38, 43, 45–46, 48, 50–51, 53–56, 58, 63–64, 66–67, 79, 81–82, 92–94, 98–99, 103–105, 107

Index

elites 1, 18–22, 24, 29, 33, 39–40, 45, 48, 57, 72, 81, 92–94, 97, 111
Elizabeth Charlotte, Duchess of Orléans 14
Elizabeth I, Queen of England and Ireland 67, 108
Emmet, Robert 72, 101
Emperor, Holy Roman 29, 81
empowerment 22, 90, 94
Enlightenment 1, 7, 11–12, 14, 27, 33, 39–41, 51, 90–91, 93–94, 106, 112
entrepreneurs 7, 17, 55, 68, 98
episcopacy [bishops] 18, 30, 45, 47, 61, 65, 69–70, 72, 76
equality 25, 75, 80, 111
Erskine, Thomas, 1st Baron Erskine 50, 100
escape 7, 37, 41
espionage [spies] 24, 76, 84, 87, 90, 103
ethnicity 3, 13, 24, 76, 82, 95, 103, 106, 110–111
exclusion 4, 9, 46, 70, 105, 110
executive 34, 39, 44, 47, 57, 105, 111
exile 47, 73, 101
exploitation 9, 34, 40, 68–69, 93, 103

faction, also see *parties* 3, 5, 14, 28, 32–34, 38, 40, 44–49, 51–52, 54–55, 61, 63, 67–68, 70, 72, 94, 100, 102, 109
faith, also see *religion* 31, 59, 61, 65, 72–75, 89, 91
fanaticism 65, 75, 85, 109
farmers 40, 52, 93, 97, 109
Fawkes, Guy 29
felony 90
festivities [celebrations] 8, 29, 32, 37, 45, 56–57, 67, 74, 85
finances 16, 33–34, 52, 56–57, 76, 82, 96, 111
fire 29, 37, 55, 74, 85–86, 90, 101
flags [banners] 34, 57, 85, 100
food, also see *crops* 2, 7, 53, 91–93, 97–98
forgery, also see *counterfeiting* 14–15
Fortescue, (Sir) John 21
Fox, Charles James 48, 56, 99
Fox, Henry 48
France 2–5, 7–8, 13–15, 17, 21, 28–29, 32, 36, 38, 40–42, 51, 53, 55–56, 61–64, 70, 72, 74–77, 81, 83, 85, 87–88, 90, 93, 96–97, 101, 107, 109, 111

Franklin, Benjamin 28, 52, 69, 91
fraud 14, 100, 103
freeholders 41, 51
Freemasons 63, 76
freemen 21, 33, 51, 56
French Revolution 17, 28–29, 56, 64, 70, 74, 83, 90, 96, 109, 111
Friends of the People 38, 101

Gage, Thomas 37, 87
Galway 45
gangs 50, 55
gender 14, 40, 60, 98
gentry 15, 40–41, 56, 102
George I, King of Britain and Ireland 14, 17, 28, 32–34, 36–41, 44, 46, 48, 53, 55, 61–62, 69, 81, 86, 90, 96, 103
George II, King of Britain and Ireland 17, 28, 32, 37–38, 40–41, 48, 53, 55, 62, 81, 86, 90, 96, 103
George III, King of Britain and Ireland 17, 28, 32, 38, 41, 48, 53, 55, 86, 90, 96, 103
Georgia 9, 17
gibbets 39
Glasgow 8, 15, 73
Glorious Revolution 5, 7, 14, 23, 25, 27, 29–31, 39, 43–44, 59, 64, 68, 81, 93, 105, 109
God 11, 60–61, 67–68, 71, 75, 94, 106, 108–109
Gordon, George, Lord 19, 50, 52, 60, 73, 83, 89–90, 99–101
Gosport 84
gossip [rumours] 12, 14–15, 50, 56, 76
governance 24, 31, 34, 41, 62, 71, 112
governors 13–16, 28, 37, 39, 53, 71, 75, 80–81, 87, 99
Grattan, Henry 89
greed 40, 67, 74, 87, 94, 97, 100, 102, 109
grievances 13, 34–35, 52–53, 70, 91–92, 97–98, 109
guards 24, 47, 50–52, 55
Guildhall 94
Gunpowder Plot 3, 29, 72, 80, 107, 110

Haiti 9, 39
Hamilton, Alexander 52
Hamilton, Walter (Lord Provost) 50
Hancock, John 37

hand-bills 18, 56
hand-writing 18–19
Hanover (dynasty) 3, 8, 31, 33–34, 36–37, 44–45, 47–49, 56, 61–62, 67, 69, 73, 109
Hardy, Thomas, also see *London Corresponding Society* 56
Hay, George (Vicar Apostolic) 15, 50, 73
heaven 14, 67–68, 94
hegemony 59, 93
Henley, John 71
Henry St John, 1st Viscount Bolingbroke 33, 47, 81, 94
Henry VIII, King of England 3, 6, 60–61, 70
heresy 60–61, 107
heroism 39, 41, 81, 84–88
Hertfordshire 98
Hesse-Kassel, Landgraviate of 41, 62, 76, 85
Hexham 63–64, 79–80
hierarchy 1, 13, 24, 37, 52, 61, 63, 75, 77, 84, 86–87, 90, 110
Higgins, George 38, 90
Highlanders 13, 95
Highlands 18, 69, 95, 105, 111
Hillsborough, Earl of 15
Hitchcock, Gad 71
Hoadly, Benjamin 69
Hobbes, Thomas 11, 51, 95
Holt, Joseph 87
Holy Roman Empire 1–2, 5, 8, 14, 21, 29, 32, 41–42, 61, 75, 82, 87, 90–91, 93, 96, 107
Holyroodhouse, Palace of 36
honour 40, 55, 87, 89
horses 75, 102
Huguenots 36, 62
humanity 2, 11, 18, 40–42, 51, 54, 84, 87–88, 95, 101, 106, 112
Hume, David 12, 51, 58, 94
hunger 94
Hutchinson, Thomas 15

ideology 1, 5, 20, 24, 41, 43, 48, 50, 54, 60–61, 69, 111
Igbo Landing 9
imagery 39, 94, 98, 103
immorality 103

impartiality 12, 38, 44, 95, 106
impeachments 46, 57
imperialism 1
imports [importation] 7, 53, 97
impressment, also see *recruitment* 50, 79
imprisonment, also see *captives* and *prisons* 20, 22, 32, 41, 47, 63, 72, 110
incendiaries, also see *arson* 37, 85
independence 7, 41, 48, 56, 74–75, 82, 84–85, 95, 107, 111
India 7, 34, 53, 56, 76, 97, 111
Indigenous, also see *native* 7
individualism 39
indulgence 108
in-effigy 28–29
infiltration 110
informers 17, 103
infrastructures 1–2, 13, 64, 81
inhabitants 3, 35, 61, 80, 82, 95, 98, 103
injustice 49, 52, 60
institutionalisation 9, 23, 39, 44, 64, 73, 77, 90–91, 105, 112
insults 82
insurgents 2, 7, 24, 31, 37–38, 98
insurrections 2, 4, 7, 19, 50, 52, 58, 90, 105–106, 108
intellectuals 1, 44, 62, 94
interceptions 15, 20, 33
intercessions 44, 61
intermediation 20, 24, 42, 54
intimidation 82, 88
investigations 8, 17–18, 57
Ireland 2–3, 5, 13, 19, 23, 25, 43, 45, 47, 49–50, 57, 59–63, 65, 70, 72–73, 76, 87, 89, 91, 95–97, 101, 103, 111
Irish Rebellion 2, 59–60, 85, 103
Italy 14, 93, 97

Jacobinism 3, 90, 100, 103
Jacobitism 2–3, 5, 7, 11, 14–15, 18, 24, 27–28, 31, 33–34, 36–37, 39, 44–45, 47, 55–56, 59–63, 65, 67, 69–70, 72–73, 76, 80–81, 87, 93–96, 98, 103, 105, 109
James II, King of England and Ireland, King of Scotland as James VII 5, 27, 44, 49, 109
Jansenism 70
Jefferson, Thomas 22, 52, 74, 106
Jesuits 62

Jew Bill 76
John Russell, 4th Duke of Bedford 55
Johnston, Alexander 36, 65, 100
Johnstone, James 36
Judaism 76, 86
judges 3, 14, 20, 34, 40, 44, 90, 94
judicature 4, 32, 44, 54
Junius [pseudonym] 17
juries 46, 53

killing [murders] 7, 13, 32-33, 36, 38, 43, 81-82, 88, 98
King's Bench 17, 38, 99
kingship 27, 29-31, 33, 36, 38-39, 41, 62, 67
Korn, Christoph Heinrich 75

laity 1, 5, 7-8, 12-13, 17-19, 23-24, 31-32, 37, 45, 49, 57, 59-60, 63-65, 68-71, 73, 76, 80-81, 84, 89, 98, 102-103
landowners 50, 53, 97, 99
Langrishe, (Sir) Hercules 96
Laveaux, Jean-Charles 3-4
Leibniz, Gottfried Wilhelm 44
Leith 50
LeMaitre, Thomas, also see *London Corresponding Society* 90
Levellers 20, 48
Lexington, also see *Concord* 80
liability 12, 17, 24, 31, 45, 71, 99, 111
libels 12, 15-17, 32, 50, 68, 102
liberalism 5, 7, 41, 63, 74
licentiousness 32, 40, 51
Lichfield 46
Lincoln 60
Liverpool 7, 97
lobbying 54, 57, 71, 89, 101, 110
Locke, John 11, 58
London Corresponding Society 17, 23, 54, 57, 90
Lords, House of 28, 39, 43-45, 53
Loughgall 57, 89
Louis XIV, King of France 81, 87
Louis XVI, King of France 96
love 31, 40, 45, 68, 86
Lowlands, Scottish 15, 73
loyalists 15, 20, 47, 60, 71, 82, 88-89, 94, 98, 103
Lutheranism 76
luxury 34, 96

Machiavelli, Niccolò 93
Macpherson, (Sir) John 29, 48-49
Madison, James 51-52
madness 2-4, 15-16, 20, 30, 32-33, 35-38, 48-49, 51, 53, 56-57, 60-62, 64, 68, 70-71, 74, 76, 79, 84, 86-88, 94-95, 97-98, 100-102, 106-108, 110
magistrates 7, 18, 36, 65, 73, 89-90, 97, 103
majorities 8, 39, 44-45, 51, 61-62, 65, 73, 96, 100-101, 107
Malt Tax Riots 8
Manchester 5, 74, 79, 88
Mansfield, Lord 17, 73
manufacturers 18, 97
maps 6-8, 46, 60, 65, 80, 92, 106
marches 2, 36, 50, 57, 81, 99
markets 13, 17, 33-35, 39, 53, 93
marriages 40, 106
martyrdom 85
Mary II, Queen of England, Scotland, and Ireland
Massachusetts 13, 15-16, 52-53, 71, 79, 88, 99, 106, 110
massacres 7, 79, 88
Matthews, John 94
mediation 24, 42, 54, 77
men [masculinity] 1-9, 11-25, 27-77, 79-112
mercenaries 1, 53
merchants 34-35, 89
Methodism 62
Middle Ages 36, 60, 70
migration 13, 72, 111
militarization 57, 80-81, 83, 88, 90
military, also see *soldiers* 7, 9, 18, 23-24, 36, 40-41, 50, 57, 61, 73, 76-77, 79-85, 87-90, 92, 102, 106
militia 1, 6-7, 17, 63-64, 77, 79-80, 83, 88-89, 105
ministers 20, 28-30, 32, 34, 36, 38, 44, 47, 50, 53, 55, 60, 65, 71, 74, 86-87, 101, 106
minorities 5, 9, 45, 47-48, 51, 61, 72, 75-76, 95, 103, 107-108
mischiefs 100, 102, 108
miscommunication 13
misconception 55
misdemeanour 16

misprision 17–18
mobs, also see *rabble* 15, 21, 45–46, 74, 76, 89, 93–97, 100–101
mockery 8, 28–29, 32, 37, 55, 61, 65, 68
monarchy 1, 4–5, 9, 17, 21, 25, 27–42, 44, 47, 55, 59, 61, 65, 67, 69, 74–75, 81, 87, 93, 96–97, 99, 102, 107–109, 111
Monmouth, James, Duke of 22–23, 66, 92
monopolies 86, 96
monotheism 76
Montagu-Scott, Charles, 4th Duke of Buccleuch (in some sources: Buccleugh) 50
Montesquieu, Charles-Louis de Secondat, Baron de La Brède et de 11
morals 14, 17, 37, 41, 50, 59, 64, 68, 70, 77, 82, 87, 89, 91, 98, 101, 103
multitudes 18, 37, 49, 51, 90, 94, 96
Munster 65
mutinies 79, 84–86, 97

nation [nationhood, nationalism] 1, 3–4, 11–14, 17, 19–20, 22, 24–25, 27–29, 33–34, 36, 38–39, 41, 44–45, 47–65, 67, 69–72, 74, 76–77, 79, 81, 83–84, 86–87, 89–91, 93, 95–99, 101–102, 105–107, 109–111
native [populations], also see *indigenous* 29, 56, 62–63, 75–76, 88, 95
nature 4–5, 21, 35, 37, 43, 48, 51, 54–55, 58, 63, 69–70, 75–76, 95–96, 99–100, 110
navy 79, 81, 85, 102
negotiations 2, 4, 7, 11, 15, 20, 24, 31, 40, 43, 46, 72, 81, 93, 102, 105
neutrality 71–73
Newcastle 55, 63–64, 94, 97
Newcastle-under-Lyne 94
newsletters 15, 61, 65
newspapers 12–17, 19, 23, 34–35, 37, 45, 48, 52, 56–57, 61, 64, 68, 84, 94, 98
Nicholson, Margaret 41
nobility 5, 12, 39–41, 55, 70, 81, 87, 95, 105
Nonconformity 60, 62, 70, 72–73, 108
non-jurors 69
Norwich 60

oath 33, 75
obedience 17, 33, 40, 52, 58, 60–61, 63, 67, 70, 90, 108
offences 13, 17, 36, 81
offenders 83, 86, 100, 103
Old Bailey 31
opinions 5, 11, 13, 15, 20–21, 23–24, 30, 41, 47–50, 52, 54–55, 67–68, 71–74, 77, 79, 85, 90–91, 93–94, 97, 102, 107
oppression 33, 35, 51–52, 67, 75, 96
orality 12, 14, 17–18, 20, 23, 28, 37, 41, 48, 50, 59, 64–65, 68–70, 73, 77, 82, 87, 89, 91, 98, 101, 103
Orange Order 19, 57
Ottoman Empire [Turkey] 106

Paine, Thomas 74–75
pamphleteering 3, 14, 23, 31, 38, 45, 48–49, 55–56, 58, 69, 71, 75, 82, 84, 90, 94, 102
Paracelsianism 95
parades 89
paramilitarism 9, 77, 79, 88–89
pardons 8, 84–85
parishes 64–65, 67–68, 74–75, 79
Parliament, members of 48, 50–51, 54–56, 58, 65, 68, 88, 94, 100
parodies 37, 69
parties, also see *factions* 9, 19, 23, 25, 33, 43–49, 51–55, 57–60, 63, 69–71, 76, 84, 89, 92, 94, 96–98
partisanship 34, 36, 43, 47, 54, 94
patriots 15, 18, 32, 37, 48, 51, 73, 75, 86–87, 95–96, 99, 107
patronage 46, 55, 81
peace 1–2, 7–8, 24, 33, 35–36, 41, 44, 54, 57–58, 64, 70, 73, 79–80, 87, 89–90, 94–95, 100–102, 106
peasants 23, 95–97
Peep o' Day Boys
peers 33, 40, 45, 90, 99, 103
Pelham-Holles, Thomas, 1st Duke of Newcastle 94
penal laws 31, 73
penalties 4, 35, 45–46
Pennsylvania 52, 85
pensioners 53, 64

people, the 1, 3, 6-9, 11, 13, 15, 18-21, 23, 27, 29, 31, 33-34, 37-41, 45, 47, 51-53, 56, 58, 64-65, 67, 73-76, 82-83, 86-88, 90-102, 105, 109-110
periodicals 8, 12, 15, 18, 64, 69
persecution 17, 102
Peterloo 7, 88
petitioning 8, 12, 14, 17-18, 21, 24, 34-35, 53-54, 56, 63, 80, 82, 87, 90, 98-101, 111
Philadelphia 52
Philip, Duke of Wharton 18, 39, 45
philosophy 11, 22, 58, 64, 81, 91, 95, 107
physicians 61, 97
piety 72, 85
piracy 7, 17, 23, 28, 38, 86, 103, 109
Pitt, William, 1st Earl of Chatham 5, 9, 48, 53, 55, 99
pleas 21, 24, 61, 68, 73, 90, 99-101
poetry 8, 34, 64, 76, 97
poison 38, 86
polemics 31, 45, 56, 75, 109
policing 42, 79, 86
Popery [Popish plots] 21, 28, 49-50, 56, 59-60, 72, 75, 85-86, 97, 108
Pop-Gun Plot 38, 90, 103
portraits 12, 32, 51, 87-88
Portsmouth 85
prayers, also see *sermons* and *thanksgiving* 61, 71, 73, 100
preachers 65-69, 71-72, 75
prerogatives (royal) 20, 30, 35, 90
Presbyterianism 19, 49, 61-62, 67-68, 89, 91
presidency 15, 23, 42, 111
Pretender 36
prices 7, 31, 45, 53, 59, 74, 97
Priestley, Joseph 19-20, 74, 99, 101, 106
printers 13, 16-17, 23, 36, 56, 83, 85, 94, 98, 102-103
prisons, also see *captives* and *imprisonment* 7, 11, 16-17, 22-23, 32, 38, 41, 87-88, 105
privileges 16, 20, 29, 33-34, 55, 59, 70, 93
Privy-Council 3, 28, 35, 38
processions 8, 18, 34, 57, 90, 93, 100-101
proclamations 12, 14, 29-30, 35-37, 102

propaganda 15-16, 23, 25, 40, 72, 75-76, 81, 83, 98, 111
property 3-4, 30-31, 33, 46, 52, 86, 91, 93, 100, 102-103, 105, 109
prosecution 14, 18, 30, 73, 110
Prosser, Gabriel 9
Protectorate 3, 63
Protestantism 15, 31, 33, 40, 44, 52, 59, 61-62, 64-65, 67, 69-70, 72-76, 89-91, 94, 99-100, 102, 107-108
protestors 64, 100, 102, 109
protests 7, 16, 28, 45, 50, 53, 79, 88, 92-93
provinces 3, 13, 49, 87, 99
Provincial Congress 88
Prussia 29, 40-41, 87
Prussia, Frederick of 21, 40-41, 62, 87
public spheres 4-9, 12-17, 19-23, 28-43, 45-48, 50-60, 62-64, 65, 68-71, 73-76, 81-84, 86-105, 107-109, 111-112
publishing 2, 13-14, 16-17, 37, 56, 61, 64-65, 68, 72, 98
pulpits 62, 75
punishments 4, 11, 16, 18, 30, 46, 84, 86-87, 102, 105, 109
Puritanism 29, 69, 74

rabble, also see *mobs* 34, 73, 94, 96, 100
radicalism 4-5, 7, 17-20, 25, 38, 40, 45, 48, 56, 58, 62, 68-69, 71, 73-77, 82, 89-90, 95-96, 101, 103, 107, 111
rallying 8, 12, 17-18, 27-29, 31-32, 39, 51, 53, 56, 64, 67, 72, 76, 82, 86, 88, 94-95, 99-100
Ramsay, Allan 73, 102
Ramsay, James 89, 103
Rancière, Jacques 22
reconciliation 16, 20, 24, 29, 47-48, 70, 72, 84-86, 95, 108
recruitment 7, 23, 63, 75, 81-82, 89, 92
Reformation 3, 6, 25, 40, 50, 60-61, 67, 107
reformers 3, 48, 58, 89-90, 96, 102, 106-107
regicide 74
regime 22, 47, 93, 108
regular troops, also see *soldiers* 1, 4, 7, 50-51, 77, 79, 83, 88-89, 94, 106, 111
rehabilitation 95
religion, also see *faith* 1-5, 7, 9, 19-20, 23-24, 27, 29, 31, 33-34, 37, 43, 47, 50,

52, 54, 57–65, 67–77, 79, 85–86, 89, 91–92, 96, 98, 100, 107–109
remonstrances 13, 16, 98
republicanism 4, 7, 29, 32, 38, 40, 47–48, 50–52, 58, 62, 73–76, 81, 86–87, 90, 97, 102, 109, 111
resistance 2–4, 11–12, 22–23, 29, 38, 43, 48, 53, 58–60, 63, 68–69, 71–72, 76, 84, 92, 109
Restoration 3, 25, 33, 48, 60–61, 80, 98, 106, 108
revolutionaries 29, 38, 51, 81
rhetorics 4, 24, 31–32, 42, 57, 62, 67, 74–75, 79, 85, 88, 96–97
ribbands, also see *clothes* 53
Riot Act 50, 80, 102, 105
rioters 7–8, 31–32, 34–35, 38, 45, 50, 65, 74, 88, 100, 102–103
roads, also see *streets* 22, 102
Robethon, Jean de 36
Rome 3–4, 36, 49, 61, 64, 70
ropemakers 92
Roundheads 48
Rousseau, Jean-Jacques 11
royalists 3, 40, 84, 89
rural, also see *agrarian* 5, 63, 67, 92, 95
Russell, John, 4th Duke of Bedford 55

sabotage 7, 84–86
Sacheverell, Henry 50, 60, 68
sailors 85, 97
salesmen 97
sarcasm 55, 102
sashes, also see *clothes* 57
satire 12, 28, 40, 64
Schmohl, Johann Christian 40
science 1, 11, 21, 54, 63, 70, 85, 106, 108–109
Scotland 3, 5, 11, 13–15, 17–19, 27, 29–30, 36, 38, 41, 46, 49–50, 52–53, 61, 64–65, 72–73, 76, 79, 81, 88, 95–96, 99, 101, 105, 111
seaports [harbours] 2, 4–5, 7–9, 12–24, 28–29, 31–39, 41, 44–46, 48–57, 59–73, 75–76, 79–89, 92–100, 102–104, 106, 110
secrecy [secrets] 13, 15, 23, 36, 54–55, 57–58, 74, 84, 101

sectarianism 63, 72, 89, 91
sedition 15–18, 28, 32, 34, 56, 62, 68, 71, 73, 85, 96, 101–103, 107–109
Septennial Act 43–44
sermons, also see *preachers* 12, 50, 59, 65–69, 71–72
servants 31, 45, 82, 98
Seume, Johann Gottfried 76
sexuality 39–40
Sheffield 57–58, 74, 101
Shelburne, Earl of 16
sheriffs 94
Sherlock, Thomas 69
ships 2, 15–16, 21, 27–31, 33, 36–41, 43, 48, 54, 56, 62–64, 67, 69–70, 72–73, 75–77, 79–82, 84–85, 87, 89, 92–93, 101–102, 109
shipwrights 92
shooting 6–7, 85, 88
shop-owners 93, 97
shops, also see *buildings* 17, 61, 65, 69, 81
Sibsey 79
silk, also see *cotton* and *wool* 98
slavery 9, 31, 38–39, 53, 60, 67, 71–72, 89, 97, 103, 111
Smith, John 38, 53, 90, 102, 106
sociability 14, 63, 79
Society of Friends [Quakers] 62, 108
sociology 2, 21, 91
soldiers, also see *regular troops* 1, 3, 7–8, 17–18, 33–34, 36–37, 41, 50, 57, 63, 74–75, 77, 79, 81–89, 95, 100, 102
solidarity 3, 39, 41, 51, 56, 72, 84, 90, 97, 103, 107
songs 8, 12
Sophia, Electress of Hanover 49
sovereignty 29, 40, 52, 86, 106
Spain 81, 97
speakers [orators] 12, 71
speeches 12, 15, 24, 31, 49, 53–54, 67, 83, 86, 92, 94
spirituality 68–70, 75, 80
Spithead 85
St. George's Fields 7, 32, 34
Staffordshire 28, 46
statesmen 55, 95
Steinghens, Baron von 44
Steinghens, Elisabeth 44, 50

Index

sticks, also see *arms* 100
stones, also see *arms* 50, 101
streets, also see *roads* 16, 18, 22–23, 45, 50, 56, 68, 74, 94, 96, 98, 110
Stuart, (Captain/Sir) Charles 75, 84
Stuart, Charles Edward 36–37, 69
Stuarts (dynasty) 14, 31, 33, 36–37, 49, 61
subversion 2, 36, 57, 68, 85–86, 88, 96, 100
succession 3, 7, 31, 33, 67, 85, 93, 98, 102, 105–106, 108
sufferings 14, 37, 96–97
suffrage 58, 90, 110
supplies 16, 44, 80, 85
supremacy 49, 73, 96, 111

talent 41, 48–49, 56, 68, 88
taverns, also see *buildings* 23, 45, 92, 103
taxation 7–8, 16, 21, 34, 36, 44, 48, 53, 82, 90, 93, 96, 98, 102, 109, 111
Teeling, Charles Hamilton and Bartholomew 103
tenderness 41, 108
terrorism 85
testimonies, also see *witnesses* 23, 46
thanksgiving, also see *prayers* 35, 65, 67, 98
theatres, also see *buildings* 3, 88
Thelwall, John (London Corresponding Society) 23
toleration 5, 16, 32, 52, 60, 63–64, 72, 76, 87, 89, 97
Toryism 5, 14, 31, 34, 37, 43–48, 61, 68–69, 71, 82, 93–94, 109
trade 1, 7, 16, 22, 33–34, 44, 53, 62, 73, 80, 89, 91, 93, 95–97, 111
Tranent 7, 79
treason 7, 16–18, 24, 36–38, 52, 56, 73–74, 84, 88–90, 103, 105, 107, 109–111
trespassing (legal offence) 91, 93
trials (legal) 4, 7, 12, 17–18, 22, 27, 31, 38–39, 45, 50, 53, 56, 73, 86, 88–90, 99, 103, 105, 107, 110
Triennial Act 43
Troy, (Archbishop) John Thomas 72
Trumbull, Jonathan 37
trust 14, 18, 24, 39, 68, 84, 89, 103, 110
truth 17, 20, 55, 60, 68–69, 94
Tudors (dynasty) 29, 44
tumults 3, 19, 35, 94, 96, 102, 109

turncoats 24
tyranny 3–4, 29, 32, 37–38, 40, 49, 51, 53, 62, 84, 107
Tyrie, David 88

Ulster 72
uniformity 61–62, 66, 108, 110
Unitarians 20, 74, 101, 106
United States of America 15, 18, 42, 51–52, 76, 87, 93, 110–111
Upton, Thomas 38, 57
urban 1, 3, 5–6, 8, 13–14, 18–19, 21–22, 28–30, 34, 36, 41, 44–45, 50–51, 53, 55–56, 63, 65, 72, 74, 80–81, 84, 87, 91–98, 100–103
usurpation 28–29, 40, 49, 67

victims 29, 37, 57, 74, 98
violence 1–5, 7–8, 11–12, 14–15, 24, 27–29, 32–34, 38, 41–43, 45, 50, 57–60, 62–63, 65, 72–75, 81–82, 84, 86–91, 94, 98, 100–102, 106, 109, 111
Virginia 9, 80, 98
virtues 14, 33, 35, 40, 52, 57, 81, 85, 87
volunteering (military) 72, 79, 88–89
voters 43, 45, 99

Walpole, (Sir) Robert, 1st Earl of Orford 39
Walsall 28
warfare 1, 3, 12, 30, 41, 54, 81, 83, 90, 95, 98, 106, 108
warrants 50, 65, 79, 103, 110
Washington, George 18, 52, 84, 88
Watson-Wentworth, Charles, 2nd Marquess of Rockingham 47–48, 58, 94
Watt, Robert, also see British Convention 38, 90
Wayne, (General) Anthony 84–85, 95
wealth 20, 29, 33, 52–53, 60, 63, 96
weavers 7, 98
West Indies 111
Westminster 17, 76
Westphalia, Peace of 1
Wexford 72
Whiggism 2, 5, 11, 14, 20, 27–28, 31, 34, 43–44, 46–50, 61, 68–69, 93–94, 109
White Boys 65
Wildvogel, Christian 3, 96, 109

Wilkes, John 32, 34, 41, 56, 82
Wilkins, Isaac 74, 82
William III of England and Ireland, William II of Scotland 3, 16, 29, 31–32, 45–46, 48, 54, 57, 61–62, 64, 69–70, 75, 80–81, 87, 89, 94–95, 100
Williamsburg 80
witchcraft 86, 98

witnesses 12, 18, 23, 28, 50, 99–101
women [femininity] 3, 8–9, 32, 40–41, 44, 53–54, 62, 68–69, 88, 90, 96–98
wool, also see *cotton* and *silk* 98
workers 58, 92, 101–102, 111

yeomanry 89

Printed in the USA
CPSIA information can be obtained
at www.ICGtesting.com
LVHW010902250424
777897LV00042B/262